COLLABORATIVE INNOVATION IN THE PUBLIC SECTOR

Public Management and Change Series

BERYL A. RADIN, *Series Editor*

Editorial Board

Robert Agranoff
Michael Barzelay
Ann O'M. Bowman
H. George Frederickson
William Gormley
Rosemary O'Leary
Norma Riccucci
David H. Rosenbloom

Select Titles in the Series

Challenging the Performance Movement: Accountability, Complexity, and Democratic Values
Beryl A. Radin

Collaborating to Manage: A Primer for the Public Sector
Robert Agranoff

Collaborative Governance Regimes
Kirk Emerson and Tina Nabatchi

The Collaborative Public Manager: New Ideas for the Twenty-First Century
Rosemary O'Leary and Lisa Blomgren Bingham, Editors

Crowdsourcing in the Public Sector
Daren C. Brabham

The Dynamics of Performance Management: Constructing Information and Reform
Donald P. Moynihan

Federal Service and the Constitution: The Development of the Public Employment Relationship, Second Edition
David H. Rosenbloom

The Future of Public Administration around the World: The Minnowbrook Perspective
Rosemary O'Leary, David Van Slyke, and Soonhee Kim, Editors

How Information Matters: Networks and Public Policy Innovation
Kathleen Hale

Implementing Innovation: Fostering Enduring Change in Environmental and Natural Resource Governance
Toddi A. Steelman

Managing Disasters through Public-Private Partnerships
Ami J. Abou-bakr

Managing within Networks: Adding Value to Public Organizations
Robert Agranoff

Public Administration: Traditions of Inquiry and Philosophies of Knowledge
Norma M. Riccucci

Public Value and Public Administration
John M. Bryson, Barbara C. Crosby, and Laura Bloomberg, Editors

Public Values and Public Interest: Counterbalancing Economic Individualism
Barry Bozeman

Work and the Welfare State: Street-Level Organizations and Workfare Politics
Evelyn Z. Brodkin and Gregory Marston, Editors

COLLABORATIVE INNOVATION IN THE PUBLIC SECTOR

JACOB TORFING

Georgetown University Press / Washington, DC

© 2016 Georgetown University Press. All rights reserved. No part of this book may be reproduced or utilized in any form or by any means, electronic or mechanical, including photocopying and recording, or by any information storage and retrieval system, without permission in writing from the publisher.

Library of Congress Cataloging-in-Publication Data

Names: Torfing, Jacob, author.
Title: Collaborative innovation in the public sector / Jacob Torfing.
Other titles: Public management and change.
Description: Washington, DC : Georgetown University Press, 2016. | Series: Public management and change series | Includes bibliographical references and index.
Identifiers: LCCN 2016001903 (print) | LCCN 2016006087 (ebook) | ISBN 9781626163591 (hc : alk. paper) | ISBN 9781626163607 (pb : alk. paper) | ISBN 9781626163614 (eb)
Subjects: LCSH: Public administration. | Public-private sector cooperation. | Intergovernmental cooperation.
Classification: LCC JF1351 .T58 2016 (print) | LCC JF1351 (ebook) | DDC 352.3/7--dc23
LC record available at http://lccn.loc.gov/2016001903

∞ This book is printed on acid-free paper meeting the requirements of the American National Standard for Permanence in Paper for Printed Library Materials.

17 16 9 8 7 6 5 4 3 2 First printing

Printed in the United States of America

Cover design by N. Putens.

CONTENTS

ILLUSTRATIONS

FIGURES

TABLES

ACKNOWLEDGMENTS

IN WRITING THIS BOOK I have received invaluable intellectual inspiration and support from my wife and colleague, Eva Sørensen, from Roskilde University and my longtime friend and academic collaborator Chris Ansell from the University of California–Berkeley. I am also indebted to the participants in the large-scale research project on Collaborative Innovation in the Public Sector and my colleagues at the Roskilde School of Governance who have helped foster many of the ideas presented in this volume. Last but not least, I want to thank series editor Beryl Radin and the two anonymous peer reviewers who have been helpful in pointing out loose ends and areas in need of improvement.

INTRODUCTION

Collaborative Innovation in the Public Sector

WHILE GOVERNMENTS AIM to promote large-scale social and economic reforms from the top down, local administrative agencies and frontline staff members try to renew the public sector from below. Two examples related to the attempt to curb gang-related violence in large cities illustrate this bottom-up transformation process.

> *In Oakland, California, the city discovered that it often took several weeks before at-risk youths leaving the Juvenile Justice Hall reentered the public school system. During the interim, many of them became reinvolved with the gang-related activities that had brought them into the Juvenile Justice Hall in the first place. To solve this urgent problem, the city decided to establish a transit center with a manager responsible for finding the kids an appropriate school before they left the Juvenile Justice Hall and for assigning them a case manager who would help them settle in, stay in school, and avoid rejoining criminal activities. The Oakland Department of Human Services initiated the new Wrap-Around Project of the Juvenile Justice Center, but it was developed and implemented in collaboration with the Oakland Unified School District, the Alameda County Probation Department, and five different community organizations. These agencies provide the case managers who work to support the at-risk youths and prevent them from rejoining gang-related activities.*

INTRODUCTION

In the Danish capital, Copenhagen, the deprived neighborhood of Mjølnerparken has many immigrants and refugees who are poor, unemployed, and in some cases traumatized by the events they have fled. For many youngsters, who lack support from their families and Danish society, crime offers an attractive alternative to poverty, scarce opportunities, and boredom. As a result, problems with gangs of both adults and at-risk youths shooting at each other in drug-related turf wars have been on the rise. A new part-time job project aims to solve the problem by providing legitimate income, social recognition, and positive job experiences for at-risk youths in the neighborhood. The municipal Job Center, which normally deals with people older than eighteen years of age, runs the project. Staffers meet the youngsters in their local neighborhood and help them test and develop their job skills. They teach the youths about their rights and obligations as employees, instruct them in how to write a curriculum vitae and put it on the Internet, and offer them part-time jobs in the public sector. A local politician initiated the project, and a project manager at the Job Center developed the project together with a private association that promotes the integration of immigrants and refugees and with the director of the Internet-based job market called Jobindex. The youth section of the local trade union and the Youth Education Network were involved in establishing the competence-building program, and local neighborhood organizations and the municipal youth clubs were key partners in implementing the project.

These two empirical cases can be seen as timely administrative responses to important governance problems or as welfare programs aiming to deal with social risks. They can also be analyzed as the results of public policymaking, the exercise of public leadership, or the use of project organization in the public sector. This book adopts a different perspective by viewing the two cases as examples of collaborative innovation in the public sector. In both cases public innovation—defined as the development and implementation of new ideas—emerges as a result of network-based collaboration between public and private stakeholders who together possess the necessary motivation, ideas, skills, and resources to craft new public solutions that seem to outperform previous practices or to meet hitherto unfulfilled demands. In line with this interpretation of the two cases, this book endeavors to scrutinize and promote collaborative innovation as a new approach to studying and enhancing public innovation. It explores the complex and interactive processes of collaborative innovation, analyzes the drivers and barriers that may enhance or impede such processes, and reflects on the role of institutional design, public management, and governance reform for spurring collaborative innovation in the public sector.

Governments around the world are struggling hard, and often in vain, to remove policy deadlocks, change low-performing programs, reform inefficient organizations, and improve public services. They are driven by demands from citizens and private stakeholders, the proliferation of complex societal problems, and growing fiscal constraints. However, there are many barriers to policy renewal, organizational reform, and service development. Thus, governments often exhibit a psychological resistance to focusing on intractable and hard-to-solve problems and a profound shortage of new and creative ideas as social and political actors are caught in habits and ideologies. In addition, organizational silos, adversarial professional cultures, and different worldviews prevent the exchange of knowledge, expertise, and ideas. Finally, the lack of interorganizational coordination and the fear that innovations will fail and lead to public scandals tend to hamper the implementation of new and bold initiatives. In this troublesome predicament, a collaborative approach to policy, organizational, and service innovation facilitated by the construction of crosscutting governance networks seems to offer a promising and viable way forward. *Governance networks* bring together relevant and affected actors with different ideas, skills, and resources. The public and private actors' recognition of their mutual dependence in relation to the problems and challenges at hand prompts a collaborative interaction that facilitates mutual learning. Moreover, the empowered participation of public and private actors in processes of creative problem solving tends to create a joint ownership to new and bold ideas and spreads the costs of failure. Accordingly, governance networks may spur collaborative learning processes that, in turn, may lead to innovation in public policy, organizations, and services.

Although governance networks carry a huge potential for collaboration and public innovation (Powell and Grodal 2004), they are nevertheless no panacea. Governance networks are not always formed spontaneously when they are needed. They often fail to motivate and involve all the relevant and affected actors. Sometimes they might turn into mere "talk shops" or become sites of bitter and long-lasting conflicts. Moreover, if they fail to produce proper outputs and desired outcomes, holding them to account can be really difficult. Nevertheless, in the right circumstances and with the appropriate institutional design, careful public management, and supportive governance structures (Straus 2002; Ansell and Gash 2007; Metze 2010), there is a good chance that networks of relevant and affected actors will facilitate collaborative interaction and provide a potent tool to enhance public innovation.

INTRODUCTION

Collaborative forms of governance in networks and partnerships might even, at least in certain respects, provide a better vehicle for public innovation than both the traditional bureaucratic forms of organization and the new forms of quasi-markets in which public organizations and private firms compete to produce and deliver public goods and services purchased by public authorities. On the one hand, public bureaucracies have strategic leadership, stable procedures for change and adaptation, much competence and expertise that enable the development of new ideas, centralized command and coordination that facilitates implementation of new ideas, and large budgets that enable them to absorb the costs of innovation failures. On the other hand, public bureaucracies are divided into hierarchically organized, rule-governed, and compartmentalized organizations that prevent the exchange and cross-fertilization of ideas. They are manned by professionals who subscribe to a particular set of methods and who do not want to be challenged by lay people with different and allegedly "unscientific" conceptions and ideas. Likewise, the market-based provision of public services may spur the development and adoption of new ideas and technologies, but the fierce rivalry between private and public contractors in cutthroat markets often prevents the trust-based collaboration that facilitates the joint exploration of new avenues and the development of new methods and services.

As we shall see, the problems inherent to public bureaucracies and quasi-markets can be overcome with the formation of governance networks, which provide a new and underexplored tool for enhancing public innovation by facilitating collaboration across organizational and institutional borders while ensuring a commitment to the joint exploration and exploitation of new and bold ideas. The questions, therefore, become how and why collaboration can spur public innovation and how the potential impact of collaboration on the development and realization of innovative solutions in the public sector can be brought out and perhaps even accelerated through public sector reform.

By focusing on how networked collaboration can generate public innovation, this book aims to contribute to the growing research on public governance that hitherto has neglected the crucial role of interactive forms of governance for enhancing public innovation. Simultaneously, by emphasizing the role of multi-actor collaboration, the book provides a novel approach to the study of public innovation that takes us beyond the celebration of the entrepreneurial spirit of elected politicians, public managers and employees, private firms, social entrepreneurs, and lead users. Thus, the book endeavors to create an analytical and theoretical interface between governance research and public innovation studies that previously have been largely unconnected. Its key objective is to advance collaborative public innovation as a new interdisciplinary field of research that can help turn the emerging and somewhat tentative forms of collaborative innovation into a systematic practice that pervades the entire public sector.

The purpose of the book is neither to present a detailed analysis of empirical cases of collaborative innovation in the public sector nor to develop a coherent and comprehensive theory of collaborative innovation based on a few axiomatic assumptions. Already a number of empirical studies of public innovation emphasize the role of collaboration (see Roberts and King 1996; Van de Ven et al. 2008; Ansell and Torfing 2014), and what we really need are systematic, theoretical reflections on the processes and mechanisms that may or may not drive collaborative innovation in the public sector. However, as the study of collaborative innovation is still in its infancy, any attempt to develop a unified theory covering all aspects of collaborative innovation in the public sector and offering a coherent set of empirically testable hypotheses is premature. Consequently, this book aims to develop a systematic set of reflections and derive some general propositions about some of the key issues in the emerging field of collaborative public innovation. These reflections and propositions are informed by empirical examples from different parts of the world and draw on a broad range of theories that can help us understand how, why, and when networked collaboration enhances public innovation. However, the book does not aspire to provide a practical guide on how processes of collaborative innovation can be triggered and sustained by public leaders and managers. Its ultimate ambition is to lay the foundation for elaborating a cross-disciplinary theoretical framework by combining different theoretical building blocks, among which theories of governance and governance networks will be primus inter pares.

THE RISE OF GOVERNANCE AND GOVERNANCE NETWORKS

In the last two decades we have witnessed a dramatic surge in the study of governance in political science, public administration, organizational sociology, business economics, urban planning, legal studies, and international relations (Kettl 2002; Kersbergen and Waarden 2004; Chhotray and Stoker 2010; Torfing et al. 2012). The assumption underlying the governance debate in the field of public policy and administration research is that the governing of social and economic relations can no longer be assumed to be congruent with the bureaucratic forms of command and control associated with the formal institutions of government. To understand how legitimate rule and effective and efficient societal regulation are produced, we must envisage the role and functioning of a broad range of formal and informal governance mechanisms and explore their impact on the production of public policy and services. We are witnessing a profound pluralization of public governance that shifts our attention from the formal institutions of government to the less formal processes of governance.

At the most general level, *governance* refers to the *governing of society and the economy through collective action and in accordance with common goals and standards* (Torfing et al. 2012). Thus, the study of governance tends to focus more on dynamic processes of governing than on the stable institutions and structures of government. In addition, governance tends to be conceived of as a decentered governing process as it is assumed that no single actor, public or private, has the knowledge and expertise, comprehensive perspective, and political and organizational capacity to solve complex, dynamic, and diversified societal challenges (Kooiman 2003, 11).

At a more concrete level of analysis, the research on governance has branched out to include studies of the normative objectives underlying particular governance practices, the form and function of different tools of governance, and the role and impact of interactive forms of governance. In terms of the *normative objectives*, it is sometimes believed that the new focus on "good governance" may help reduce negligence and corruption and enhance the rule of law and the civic responsiveness of elected government in developing countries (IMF 1997). Governance is also supposed to facilitate a more flexible and efficient governing of local or sector-specific problems and challenges by creating spaces for "regulated self-regulation" (Sørensen and Triantafillou 2009). Finally, governance may contribute to a democratization of society by facilitating the participation of relevant and affected actors in public governance and thereby enhancing the democratic legitimacy of public policy (Warren 2009; Torfing and Triantafillou 2011).

However, the focus on governance not only permits us to achieve important normative objectives but also facilities the development of new and softer governing tools that are more informal, value based, voluntary, and dialogical than the traditional law-based ones (Salamon 2002). Examples are the increasing use of information campaigns, standardizations, benchmarking, peer review, self-evaluation, and procedures for the naming and shaming of underperforming programs, agencies, and actors.

Last but not least, the traditional modes of governance through hierarchical forms of government and market-based competition tend to be supplemented and supplanted with new interactive modes of governance such as quasi-markets based on relational contracts, public-private partnerships aiming to exploit the complementary resources of public organizations and private firms and associations, and governance networks consisting of relevant and affected actors in a particular policy field (Torfing et al. 2012). These interactive forms of governance are particularly interesting because they tend to cut across institutional and political boundaries, thus blurring the lines of demarcation between different organizations, sectors, levels, and policy areas.

Interactive governance is a *pluricentric mode of governance that brings together a diversity of public and/or private actors in more or less institutionalized arenas of negotiated interaction, which contribute to the production of public value through formulating and implementing public policy and regulation or through producing and delivering particular solutions and services.* Governance networks are a typical example of interactive governance (see Torfing and Triantafillou 2011). The important role of networks in public policymaking was discovered by Heclo (1978), who found that beneath the surface of congressional politics, public and private actors interact in a range of sector-specific "policy subsystems." Later Marsh and Rhodes (1992) developed the notion of policy networks and distinguished between the different types of policy networks in their search for an alternative to the far too exclusive, tightly knit, and corporatist iron triangles. Mayntz (1993a, 1993b) used the same notion to describe collaborative alternatives to hierarchies and markets that, for systemic reasons, were regarded as incapable of governing our complex, fragmented, and multilayered societies. In the research literature, *networks* are usually defined as *a stable set of relations and non-relations between actors who are engaged in processes of mutual interaction.* Networks might be based on kinship, affection, or functional interdependence, but in policy research the network actors are interacting because their problem-solving capacity depends on the exchange and pooling of resources, competences, and ideas (Rhodes 1997), and their interaction is supported by the development of shared norms and understandings (Hajer 2009). Therefore, the actors are held together by a substantial, rather than an affective or functional, interdependency.

Many Western countries increasingly rely on governance networks in public policymaking (Marcussen and Torfing 2007). Many will probably object to this claim by insisting that the lion's share of public regulation and public services is still provided by large-scale public bureaucracies. This may be true, especially with relation to public regulation based on the exercise of authority and the production and delivery of standardized public services. However, it does not alter the fact that the initiation, formulation, and revision of public policies, more often than not, are subject to networked negotiations between a plurality of public and private actors. Most often, the public decision makers simply cannot govern and produce public policy alone; they need to interact with key stakeholders who possess relevant information, knowledge, and resources. In addition, we should not forget that the increased reliance on voluntary regulation and the growing use of relational contracts in public quasi-markets tend to enhance negotiated interaction between public and private actors (Salamon 2002). Thus, governance networks seem to add a new layer of strategic policymaking and interactive governance on the top of the old layer of bureaucratic regulation and service production.

One of the key explanations for the proliferation of governance networks is that public governors face a large, and perhaps growing, number of complex, ill-defined, and hard-to-solve problems that are pervaded by value and goal conflicts and that involve multiple arenas, actors, and publics (Hajer 2009). Such problems can be solved either through authoritative strategies that allow formal authorities to impose a particular definition of and solution to the problem or by competitive strategies that permit the actors prevailing in competitive power struggles to get their way (Roberts 2000). However, the best strategy for solving wicked and unruly problems is to involve relevant and affected actors from the public and/or the private sector in sustained processes of collaborative interaction (Koppenjan and Klijn 2004; Weber and Khademian 2008). Networked interaction between public and private stakeholders can often help craft more effective and legitimate solutions than both formal hierarchies and competitive markets are capable of producing (Scharpf 1999). Governance networks may grow by themselves from below, but they are frequently initiated and facilitated by governments that aim to mobilize the knowledge, resources, and energies of private actors and that believe the nature and character of the problems and tasks at hand make reliance on market forces inappropriate or misguided (Torfing et al. 2012).

Since the mid-1990s, the research on governance networks has been growing steadily, and the analytical focus has gradually shifted in the course of this development (Sørensen and Torfing 2007). The first wave of governance network research was preoccupied with defining governance networks as a distinctive mode of governance, with explaining why they are formed, and with describing their roles and impact in different policy areas and at different regulatory scales (Kenis and Schneider 1991; Marsh and Rhodes 1992;

Mayntz 1993a, 1993b; Scharpf 1994; Rhodes 1997). The second wave of governance network research has further expanded the research agenda to include questions about the conditions for network governance failure, the role and impact of network management, and the contribution of governance networks to effective and democratic governing of contemporary societies (Kickert, Klijn, and Koppenjan 1997; Jessop 2002; Provan and Kenis 2005; Benz and Papadopoulos 2006).

The analysis and assessment of the outcomes of network types of governance have gained an increasing prominence in the international research community (Sørensen and Torfing 2009), but the focus has mainly been on how governance networks enhance effective and democratic governance. Researchers frequently argued that despite the high transactions costs and the low degree of institutionalization, the combination of flexibility and authority in governance networks will tend to enhance effective governance (Provan and Milward 1995; Provan and Kenis 2008). In much the same vein, others have claimed that despite the lack of transparency and accountability in governance networks, their contribution to the enhancement of empowered participation, public deliberation, and democratic legitimacy tends to have a democratizing effect on society and public governance (Klijn and Skelcher 2007; Warren 2009).

By comparison, the contribution of governance networks to public innovation has received much less attention in the recent research on governance networks. Some researchers have talked about how governance networks contribute to "improved coordination" and "conflict resolution," while others have highlighted their role in fashioning a "more responsive problem solving" based on a "broader knowledge base" and "mutual learning" (Agranoff 2007; Rhodes 1997; Koppenjan and Klijn 2004). Although some of these arguments implicitly invoke references to public innovation, there are relatively few explicit attempts in the research literature on interactive governance to analyze the contribution of governance networks to public innovation. A more explicit reference to innovation is found in the new research focusing on how governance networks, partnerships, and other forms of interactive and participatory governance can foster democratic innovation (Saward 2000; Smith 2009; Bevir and Bowman 2011), but the focus here is more on the renewal of the institutions and practices of liberal democracy than on innovation in public policy, organizational designs, and services. In sum, *governance network theory* tends to focus on the collaborative production of public value rather than on the collaborative creation of public innovation (Bommert 2010, 18).

INTRODUCTION

The scant regard for the innovative capacity of governance networks is surprising since the role of networks for producing and disseminating innovation is well established in the social sciences (Rogers 1995; Freeman 1991). The field of institutional economics has an abundance of research on how innovation can be enhanced through collaborative interaction in more or less (in)formal networks (Teece 1992; Weber 2003; Powell and Grodal 2004; Gloor 2005). By contrast, only a small number of studies take on the task of scrutinizing the role of multi-actor collaboration in enhancing policy, service, and organizational innovation in the public sector (Gray 1989; Roberts and Bradley 1991; Roberts and King 1996; Van de Ven et al. 2008). In the few studies of public innovation that explicitly adopt a network perspective, the analytical focus is most often on the implementation and dissemination of innovation through networks (Rogers 1995); few concentrate on the collaborative processes through which problems are framed and new solutions are crafted and selected (see, e.g., O'Toole 1997; Mintrom and Vergari 1998). Fortunately, the interest in the innovative capacities of collaborative forms of network governance has recently surged (Hartley 2005; Considine, Lewis, and Alexander 2009; Eggers and Singh 2009; Bommert 2010), and with the growing emphasis on the need for public innovation, there is a good chance that network-driven innovation in the public sector will gradually develop into a new and important field of research.

COLLABORATION AS A SOURCE OF PUBLIC INNOVATION

The dearth of studies focusing on collaborative innovation in the public sector is regrettable in light of the growing demand for public innovation. As we shall see, it reflects an insufficient understanding of the sources of public innovation and the innovative potential of collaboration.

Driven by the introduction of new computer technologies, the 1980s saw a growing interest in public innovation, but the focus was mostly on diffusing and adopting digital technologies rather than on developing and designing innovative solutions (Perry and Kraemer 1978; Kraemer and Perry 1979, 1980, 1989; Perry and Danziger 1980). From the early 1990s onward, the North American "reinventing government" movement deepened the interest in public innovation, which then expanded to include organizational innovation and service innovation (Osborne and Gaebler 1992). Innovation was no longer seen as technology driven; rather, it was perceived as a product of a high-powered incentivizing of the public sector in general and public managers in particular (see Ansell and Torfing 2014). The demand for public innovation was further stimulated by the competitive pressures that resulted from the move toward globalization, the growing expectations from firms and citizens, the proliferation of wicked problems that cannot be solved by standard solutions and increased funding, and the fiscal constraints following in the wake of the credit crunch (O'Toole 1997; Borins, 2001b; Eggers and Singh 2009).

As a clear and visible result of the mounting interest in public innovation, many governments in both developed and developing countries have launched, or are about to launch, national programs and initiatives to enhance innovation in public services and regulation (Hartley 2008; Ferreira, Farah, and Spink 2008; Bason 2010). International organizations such as the United Nations and the Organization for Economic Cooperation and Development (OECD) have also highlighted the need for public sector innovation and recommended the development of national strategies and initiatives for enhancing public innovation (United Nations 2009; OECD 2010). The argument for public innovation has not yet been engaged, let alone won, in the majority of OECD countries (Mulgan 2007, 13). In most governments and public service organizations, the attempts to enhance public innovation are not sufficiently institutionalized, with the result that public innovators are usually marginalized. Nevertheless, both government officials and public employees have increasingly focused on public innovation and seem eager to learn how to enhance the quantity and quality of public innovations.

Despite the growing interest in spurring innovation in the public sector, the current understanding of how it can be done is inadequate. Most protagonists of public innovation rely exclusively on the role and impact of technical inventions and scientific discoveries. Although new information technologies and scientific breakthroughs undoubtedly have triggered many innovations in the public sector, we should be careful not to exaggerate their role since they are only one of many factors driving public innovation. Moreover, we should not forget that innovation is always driven by purposeful social actors who face specific problems and who deliberately choose to exploit new opportunities and combine them with existing practices in order to craft novel and creative solutions. Hence, the development of new technologies and the circulation of new scientific knowledge cannot in themselves spark any innovations. Their ability to trigger innovation depends on the purposeful actions of social and political actors who perceive specific technological and scientific inventions as a lever for solving particular problems or for bringing about desired changes and who interact with other actors inside and outside their organization in order to design, test, and implement new and innovative solutions.

Based on this important recognition, there has been a growing interest in the entrepreneurial role of different kinds of innovation champions who are seen as the primary vehicle of public innovation (Mulgan 2007). In his now classic study, Polsby (1984) focused on the entrepreneurial role of political executives who need to advance new ideas as a part of their constitutionally prescribed routines, such as the State of the Union address in the United States, and when competing for votes in election campaigns. The advocates of New Public Management (NPM) have emphasized the innovative solutions that public managers and private contractors produce in response to competitive pressures either within the public sector or in recently created quasi-markets (Hood 1991; Osborne and Gaebler 1992). Human resource managers and some European white-collar trade unions have highlighted the importance of tapping into the ideas and resources of public employees who can draw on their professional skills and knowledge to find innovative solutions to the problems and challenges they encounter in their daily work (Kesting and Ulhøi 2010). Finally, inspired by Hippel (1988), interest has also been growing in user-driven innovation, especially in the health care sector, where public managers and employees aim to learn from or about different user groups in order to reshape public policies, services, and organizations in response to new or previously undetected needs (Røtnes and Staalesen 2009).

However, despite the important and unique contributions of all these differing innovation champions, public innovation is seldom the result of the individual efforts of singular actors (Csikszentmihalyi 1996). In most cases, public sector innovation requires collaborative interaction between a host of different public and private actors including politicians, civil servants, experts, private firms, interest organizations, community-based associations, and user groups (Borins 2001b, 312). In short, public innovation is essentially a "team sport" based on the joint efforts of different actors with different skills. Hence, I shall claim that multi-actor collaboration is the key tool for creating innovative solutions that can break policy deadlocks and improve public organizations and services. Collaborative innovation opens up the innovation process for a broad range of public and private actors. It implies that "the locus of innovation is determined by the availability of innovation assets and not by the formal boundaries of a bureaucratic organization" (Bommert 2010, 16).

To compensate for the unfortunate failure of governments, researchers, and others to understand and exploit the potential of multi-actor collaboration for enhancing public innovation, this book aims to advance collaborative innovation as a cross-disciplinary approach to studying and enhancing public innovation. Public bureaucracies might also contribute to public innovation by establishing stable procedures for exploration and exploitation (March and Olsen 1995), and the construction of quasi-markets in the public sector may sometimes enhance innovation through increased competition and user orientation (Lubienski 2009). However, a third and relatively unexplored source of public innovation is provided by network-based forms of collaboration that bring together diverse public and private actors in dense interactions that may enable trust building, facilitate transformative learning, mobilize invaluable resources, and create joint ownership over new and bold solutions (Dente, Bobbio, and Spada 2005). In the future, researchers and practitioners should join forces in trying to unleash the huge, yet underexploited, potential of collaborative interaction in networks and partnerships for fostering public innovations that can solve tough problems and meet the rising and increasingly complex demands of citizens, private stakeholders, and public employees.

THEORETICAL AND EMPIRICAL FOUNDATIONS FOR A PROBLEM-DRIVEN STUDY

This book aims to substantiate the claim that collaborative innovation is a key tool for public value production that we must learn to master so we can handle the problems and challenges facing the public sector. It takes the first steps in developing an analytical framework for studying collaborative innovation by combining theoretical and empirical insights in systematically analyzing the key aspects of the processes of collaborative innovation. Although the number of empirical studies of collaborative innovation is growing, few have attempted to reflect upon the analytical framework for studying collaborative innovation in the public sector, and virtually none discuss the theoretical concepts, propositions, and arguments in the light of comparative empirical insights. This book endeavors to compensate for these shortcomings by combining theoretical insights from different disciplines with empirical findings from different countries and by applying them in a systematic study of collaborative innovation in the public sector.

The analytical framework advanced in the book draws on central insights from innovation theory, public administration theory, public management research, discourse theory, institutional theory, theories of learning, complexity theory, and theories of collaborative network governance (see chapter 3). *Innovation theory* provides an obvious starting point because it helps us understand what innovation is and how the innovation process can open up for different actors to participate. *Public administration theory* helps us understand the shifting conditions for innovation in the public sector, and *public management research* sheds light on how collaborative innovation processes are managed. While innovation theory tends to see innovation as triggered by objectively defined problems or challenges, *discourse theory* provides an analytical tool for analyzing the discursive construction of problems, solutions, and decision-making premises and for studying how actors with diverging interests are kept together by common narratives and story lines that may create a momentum for change. Collaborative innovation is not only framed by different discourses but also conditioned by *institutional frameworks* of rules, norms, and cognitive scripts. This recognition is captured by different forms of historical and sociological institutionalism that help us understand the institutional embeddedness of collaborative innovation and the impact of institutional design on processes, outputs, and outcomes. Institutions facilitate and constrain the processes of collaborative innovation, but they do not tell us much about what actually happens in the processes that lead to innovation. Here *learning theory*, with its emphasis on motivation, creativity, and transformative learning, provides some important insights, and there has been a growing interest in collective learning processes in social systems such as workplaces. *Complexity theory* has its strength in relation to grasping the dynamic, iterative, and adaptive character of such systems. Last but not least, *theories of collaborative network governance* help us understand why and how a plethora of social and political actors interact and collaborate in complex and learning-based processes that are framed by discourses and conditioned by institutions. Governance network theory also allows us to understand how relatively self-governing governance networks can be metagoverned in order to spur collaboration, creativity, and innovation.

There is always a danger of eclecticism when drawing on theoretical insights from different disciplines. This problem can be avoided by selecting theories that argue social and political actors work on the basis of socially constructed meanings and reasons and within discursive and institutional contexts that, on the one hand, define the conditions of possibility for thinking and acting but, on the other hand, are ambiguous, polyvalent, and subjected to smaller or larger dislocations that unravel the sedimented conditions of action and lead to the construction of new ones.

Empirical cases are introduced in the book to exemplify, challenge, and nuance the theoretical informed reflections and arguments. The empirical cases of collaborative innovation are drawn from European countries such as

Britain, Germany, Italy, and Denmark, as well as from North America and the Antipodes. Some of the empirical cases come from a comparative analysis of collaborative innovation in deprived neighborhoods in Copenhagen and Oakland that was conducted in 2010–12. The analysis and discussion of the empirical cases reflect upon how specific social, political, and economic conditions facilitate or constrain collaborative innovation in these different countries.

Theoretical reflections and empirical insights are combined in an attempt to answer specific research questions, including the following:

- What is innovation? What has stimulated the increasing interest in innovation in the public sector, and what are the systematic differences between the conditions for innovation in the public and private sectors? (chapter 1)
- What drives the surging use of governance networks? What is collaboration, and how can multi-actor collaboration improve the different phases of the innovation process? What can go wrong? (chapter 2)
- What are the main contributions of the most important precursors to a theory of collaborative innovation, and how can different bodies of theory help us build a solid theoretical framework for studying processes of collaborative innovation? (chapter 3)
- What triggers and drives innovation and collaboration in the public sector, and what role does discursive framing and dramaturgical enactment play in innovation processes? (chapter 4)
- How are actors becoming involved and empowered in governance networks? What makes them collaborate, and how is their collaboration institutionalized in order to facilitate the production of innovative outputs and outcomes? (chapter 5)
- What kind of learning will produce creative and innovative solutions in collaborative settings? How can we facilitate that kind of learning? (chapter 6)
- How can networks of actors make and implement bold and creative decisions? What role do deliberation, passion, and leadership play in these decisions? (chapter 7)
- What is the role of networks in diffusing innovative solutions within and between public organizations? (chapter 8)
- What are the main drivers and barriers of collaborative innovation? How can the barriers be overcome through the exercise of public leadership and management? (chapter 9)

- How can governance reforms that aim to supplement and supplant New Public Management with governance practices associated with New Public Governance (NPG) spur collaborative innovation? (chapter 10)

The conclusion summarizes the answers to these questions by setting out a number of propositions about innovation, collaboration, and how the latter can enhance the former. The conditions for enhancing and benefitting from collaborative innovation in the public sector are also pinpointed. The main findings follow:

1. Multi-actor collaboration can strengthen each of the constitutive phases in the complex and potentially chaotic innovation cycle.
2. The engagement of relevant and affected actors in processes of collaborative innovation cannot be taken as a given; instead, it is conditioned on institutional and ideational factors as well as on the role perceptions of different actors.
3. Developing mutual, reflexive, and transformational learning is important for collaboration to foster new and innovative solutions.
4. Not only the creation and realization of innovative solutions but also their diffusion may benefit from networked collaboration.
5. Collaboration innovation is a contingent and precarious phenomenon that requires public leaders and managers to act as conveners, facilitators, and catalysts to enhance the chances of producing desirable outputs and outcomes.
6. Public governance reforms aiming to implement ideas and practices associated with New Public Governance are likely to further stimulate collaborative innovation to the benefit of citizens, private stakeholders, elected politicians, and society at large.

GOVERNANCE NETWORK THEORY AS THE MAIN ANALYTICAL VANTAGE POINT

None of the questions raised in this book can be adequately answered from a single theoretical perspective. Instead, they call for the development of a cross-disciplinary framework that combines theoretical insights from different bodies of literature. As previously emphasized, theories of collaborative network governance provide the main analytical vantage point for studying collaborative innovation in the public sector. Although the primary focus of governance network theory is on producing public value rather than creating public innovation per se, this theory persistently emphasizes the need to involve a plurality of public and private actors in formulating, implementing, and revising public policy and in producing and delivering new and better public services (Bommert 2010, 17–18). Therefore, the arguments presented in this book are elaborated on the basis of a critical engagement with different strands of governance network theory: rational choice institutionalism, normative institutionalism, interpretative governance theory, network management theory, and governmentality theory (see Sørensen and Torfing 2007). As we shall see, these different schools of thought in governance network theory all provide important insights into networked collaboration and the enhancement of public innovation, but they also suffer from different problems and weaknesses that can be compensated by combining their ideas. A brief *tour de horizon* reveals the comparative advantages of the different theories of network governance.

Rational choice institutionalism (Ostrom 1990; Scharpf 1994, 1998) perceives public policy and governance as a result of the interaction of social and political actors who pursue their interests based on a bounded rationality that permits them to make satisfactory rather than optimal choices (Simon 1991). This actor-centered view of public policy and governance is combined with an institutionalist perspective of how *institutions*—defined as *systems of rules and resource allocations*—provide opportunity and incentive structures for rational actors to overcome collective action problems, reduce the level of conflict, and facilitate nonhierarchical coordination (Ostrom 1990). The interaction between social and political actors takes place in *governance networks*, which are defined as *informal institutional structures that shape the games played by rational actors* (Scharpf 1994). Rational choice institutionalism helps us understand the role of institutions in building trust, reducing different kinds of transaction costs, and providing incentives for collaboration and innovation. It also highlights the strategic uncertainty in implementing innovative solutions in network settings and draws our attention to the importance of risk assessment and risk management so that the network actors will be willing to produce innovative solutions (O'Toole 1997).

Despite the importance of these arguments, rational choice institutionalism can be criticized for reducing actors to calculating agents and institutions to incentive structures (March and Olsen 1995). Although actors are sometimes placed in circumstances where they are expected to act on the basis of a more or less incomplete calculation of costs and benefits, which are shaped by particular institutional incentives, this calculative approach to understanding governance networks only captures a fragment of what actors are and what institutions do. Social action is often structured by habits and social norms, and institutions tend to provide normative and cognitive scripts that shape the identity and behavior of social actors.

Normative institutionalism (March and Olsen 1989, 1995) solves both of the problems inherent to rational choice institutionalism. It claims that social and political actors do not merely act according to a "logic of consequentiality" that bids them to calculate, compare, and choose between the consequences of different actions in relation to already given preferences and objectives. Indeed, most of the time, actors are rule followers who behave in accordance with institutionally embedded rules, norms, and scripts. Social and political actors are placed in institutional contexts that are dominated by a particular "logic of appropriateness," which prescribes what actors with socially constructed identities are supposed to do in a particular situation. The institutional logic of appropriate action is determined by a complex ensemble of rules, norms, values, cognitive scripts, cultural codes, and rituals (March and Olsen 1989). Thus, governance networks in this context are defined as *institutional arenas of interaction that bring together relevant and affected actors who become normatively integrated through the gradual institutionalization of common rules, norms, values, and forms of knowledge* (DiMaggio and Powell 1983; March and Olsen 1995).

Normative institutionalism urges us to appreciate the role of identity and the impact of institutional rules and cultural norms when studying exchange processes that may or may not give rise to collaborative innovation. Social identities and institutional traditions and cultures may either hamper or encourage collaboration and innovation. For example, some public administrators may see themselves as guardians of well-established norms, rules, and traditions, while others may perceive themselves as policy entrepreneurs. Such differences in role perceptions are often shaped and sustained by the institutional context of the public administrators.

Normative institutionalism also draws our attention to the existence of stable procedures for adaptation and change and offers a nonrationalistic theory of learning. Learning in collaborative arenas of public governance seldom takes the form of scientific investigations that provide hard evidence for the best solution. Rather, it involves pragmatic experimentation through which new ideas are developed, tested, and evaluated on the basis of normative criteria and institutional norms.

Despite these advantages, normative institutionalism is hampered by its weak account of the active role of agency in changing institutional structures and reforming public policy and governance. Normative institutionalism insists that actors play an active role in matching rules and norms to the particular situations in which they are applied and in interpreting the content of the often ambiguous rules and norms they face (March and Olsen 1995). However, the normative and integrative force of institutions seems to outweigh the transformative capacities of interdependent, though operationally autonomous, actors. Thus, the space for an effective agency is limited. At least the capacity of social and political actors to create new interpretations of the world is downplayed, and there is no account of using power and power struggles as a way of transforming public governance.

Interpretative governance theory (Bevir and Rhodes 2006; Bevir and Richards 2009; Bevir 2010) offers a decentered approach to public governance that focuses on "the social construction of a practice through the ability of individuals to create and act on meaning" (Bevir and Richards 2009, 3). Compared to normative institutionalism, the focus here is on the individual actors and the meanings they are constructing and acting upon rather than on what Bevir (2010) terms "reified institutions." As with rational choice institutionalism, interpretative governance theory focuses on individual actors; however, the individual actors are not calculative but act on the basis of interpretations. The actors construct interpretations of their beliefs, desires, and actions against the background of different, more or less sedimented traditions and often in response to particular dilemmas or problems. Dilemmas may arise from the clash between different traditions and discourses, and problems occur when public governance produces failures that conflict with people's beliefs. People confront the various dilemmas and problems differently because they draw on dissimilar contexts, and this results in political conflicts over the nature of the puzzles and problems and how to solve them (Bevir and Richards 2009, 7). These political conflicts are fought out and partly resolved through networked interaction. As such, governance networks in this context are defined as *emerging patterns of interaction between actors who construct and act upon particular narratives.*

Interpretative governance theory enables us to understand how public innovation is conditioned by the interweaving of narratives that frame problems as urgent and manageable and new solutions as feasible and desirable. Narratives are powerful tools for motivating actors to act on specific problems and to collaborate to find a joint solution. Interpretative governance theory also provides a bottom-up account of the formation of governance networks and portrays them as arenas of power struggles, public contestation, and pragmatic problem solving. Despite the presence of formal and informal rules of conduct, governance networks can create innovative solutions as a result of contingent combinations of dissimilar ideas and experiences that are advanced by the social and political actors.

On the downside, interpretative governance theory seems to be so busy trying to avoid reifying conceptions of aggregate social phenomena that it fails to provide a proper account of the institutional and organizational conditions for social and political action. There is no account of the role of the state, law, and bureaucracy. They are dissolved into a flux of language games and not addressed as institutional terrains with asymmetrical effects on the attempt of situated actors to articulate or advance a particular set of ideas, demands, and interests. Neither is there any account of the role of political leadership and public management in facilitating interaction and authorizing new ideas and solutions.

Network management theory is associated with the Dutch "governance club" at the Erasmus University in Rotterdam (Kooiman 1993; Kickert, Klijn, and Koppenjan 1997; Koppenjan and Klijn 2004). In sharp contrast to Bevir's interpretative governance theory, it emphasizes the institutional and managerial conditions for the complex policy interactions that bring together interdependent actors who act strategically based on uncertain perceptions of substantive issues, political interests, and the strategic importance of different policy arenas (Koppenjan and Klijn 2004). Governance networks are defined here as *interorganizational arenas for interest mediation between self-interested actors who interact because of the presence of a mutual resource dependency.* Without a joint utility function, their interaction and the emerging policy outcomes are marked by conflicts, but the actors are kept together by their interdependency and the development of shared norms, perceptions, and ideologies. The policy performance of governance networks depends on cooperation, and public network managers play a crucial role in generating improved interactions between the current members and in making changes to the existing networks in terms of the membership and institutional framework (Kickert, Klijn, and Koppenjan 1997). Network management theory thus helps us understand both the centrifugal and the centripetal forces of governance networks; such knowledge is crucial in enhancing the prospect for collaboration. The theory also pays attention to the need to manage uncertainty in complex networks and to the limits of collaborative innovation. The latter is frequently hampered by the regulative and normative framework for networked interaction that tends to be a result of old and long-forgotten compromises. Policymaking is path dependent and often ends up preserving the status quo.

The critique of network management theory is that it treats governance networks as tools for pragmatic problem solving (Torfing et al. 2012). Governance networks are institutional mechanisms that are formed and manipulated with the purpose of getting things done. Thus, the theory contains almost no reflections on the constitutive role of power in shaping identities, interactions, and the institutional frameworks of network governance.

Governmentality theory is a poststructuralist approach to the analysis of the state, governance modes, and concrete acts of government (Foucault 1991; Dean 1999; Rose 1999). It focuses on the collective and institutionally embedded ideas, perceptions, rationalities, and technologies that are articulated in a historically contingent governmentality, which shapes the way that people govern and are governed (Foucault 1991). Per this theory, concrete acts of government are conditioned and formed by hegemonic discourses that construct the subjects and objects of regulation as well as the modes and telos of public regulation (Dean 1999). Governmentality theory does not make any references to governance networks. However, power is not seen as emanating from a sovereign state but is viewed in terms of decentered networks of social and political forces that act on each other. Moreover, the way that Western societies are governed has shifted; so today the dominant governmentality tends to favor the use of power technologies that facilitate some kind of "regulated self-regulation." According to the prevailing governmentality, advanced liberal societies should be regulated neither from above through the exercise of sovereign power and the deployment of disciplinary institutions and normalizing discourses nor from below through a neoliberal reliance on allegedly self-regulating market forces. Rather, societal regulation should involve creating and monitoring self-regulatory assemblages of actors who are capable of crafting responsible and legitimate solutions through a more or less institutionalized interaction (Dean 1999).

With its emphasis on the role of regulated self-regulation, governmentality theory reveals how freedom and power are really two sides of the same coin. On the one hand, advanced liberal societies deploy *technologies of agency* to mobilize the competencies, resources, and energies of free and responsible actors through the construction of networks, partnerships, and other forms of interactive governance. On the other hand, they use *technologies of performance* to ensure that actors engaged in governance practices use their free and empowered actions in a way that conforms to the overall goals of the political and administrative system.

Governmentality theory does not focus on public innovation, but it can help us see public innovation and the construction of collaborative arenas as a part of a particular governmentality that is shaped by discursive power strategies. It also encourages us to understand the negotiated interactions between different actors in terms of decentered power struggles that are driven not merely by resource asymmetries but also by attempts to shape the institutional conditions of individual and collective action. Hence, collaborative innovation is not an innocent attempt to improve public policy, services, and organizations by developing new ideas and doing the right thing. On the contrary, it is a power-ridden practice shaped by discursive power strategies operating both at the macro level, through campaigns and institutional technologies, and at the micro level, where social and political actors struggle to define the agenda, the rules of the game, and the meaning of the past, the present, and the future.

The problem with governmentality theory is that it does not say much about why and how actors interact within relational assemblages and does not analyze the conditions for these actors to produce policies and regulations that are both continuous and discontinuous with the past. Despite its focus on concrete governmental technologies, governmentality theory remains at a fairly general and abstract level of analysis.

The five theoretical perspectives are compared in table I.1, which briefly outlines the key dimensions, strengths, and weaknesses of various approaches to the study of governance networks.

In sum, each of the five perspectives on governance networks offers something important when one analyzes the processes of collaborative innovation. Rational choice institutionalism highlights the institutional conditions for strategic action in the context of risk and uncertainty. Normative institutionalism emphasizes the role of identity, cultural norms, and pragmatic experimentation for adapting public institutions to new conditions. Interpretative governance theory draws our attention to the role of narratives and bottom-up processes of networked collaboration. Network management theory insists that governance networks must be designed and managed to function properly and claims that policy renewal is path dependent. Last but not least, governmentality theory highlights the role of discursive power strategies for shaping new forms of governance and for framing the actions

TABLE I.1. Comparison of theoretical perspectives on governance networks

	Rational choice institutionalism	Normative institutionalism	Interpretative governance theory	Network management	Governmentality theory
Conception of governance networks	Institutional structures shaping the games played by actors	Institutional arenas of interaction between social and political actors	Emerging patterns of interaction between actors who construct and act on problems	Interorganizational arenas for interest mediation between interdependent actors	Institutional forms of regulated self-regulation in assemblages of social and political actors
Social action theory	Actor-centered theory focusing on institutional conditions for rational calculations and strategic choice	Institution-centered theory focusing on the normative integration of actors and their interpretation of appropriate action	Hermeneutic theory focusing on how situated actors interpret the world and act on their interpretations	Political actors act on the basis of perceptions and interests, but their actions are conditioned by institutions	Discourse-centered theory assuming that both the capacity to act and the standards for measuring outcomes are discursively constructed
View of conflicts and power	Incentive structures and trust building may help overcome conflicts	Conflicts and power struggles are civilized by common norms and identities	Conflicting interpretations arise from clashes between discourses and traditions	Actors with diverging interests are kept together by interdependency and shared norms	Power shapes the identity of social and political actors as well as the terrain for interaction
Major strength	Highlights the role of uncertainty and risks in relation to strategic actions in networked contexts	Draws attention to how institutions may drive change through stable procedures and experimental learning	Shows that narratives drive action and networks are formed from the bottom up	Recognizes that complex networks must be designed and managed to function properly	Highlights the role of power and discourse in shaping the conditions for action
Major weakness	Reduces actors to calculating subjects	Limits the space for transformative social action	Fails to account for the institutional conditions for action	Does not reflect on the constitutive role of power in shaping identities and interaction	Fails to account for why and how actors interact in public governance

of social and political actors engaged in public governance. As discussed, the different governance network theories also engage with different kinds of problems, but together and in various combinations, they offer a strong foundation for developing a theoretical framework for analyzing collaborative innovation in the public sector.

1

DEFINING AND CONTEXTUALIZING INNOVATION IN THE PUBLIC SECTOR

THIS CHAPTER sets the stage for studying collaborative innovation in the public sector. The first step shows that we need a concept of innovation that helps us distinguish between different kinds of change, transformation, and development. The second step involves defining the concept of innovation and providing examples of different types of public innovation. The third step explains the growing interest in public innovation and justifies the need for a new public innovation agenda that both researchers and practitioners should pursue. The chapter concludes with a few cautious remarks about the role and impact of public innovation. These observations are counterbalanced by some empirical examples of the positive impact that public innovation may have on cutting costs, improving quality, and enhancing the effectiveness of public policies, organizations, and services.

WHY DO WE NEED A CONCEPT OF INNOVATION?

Since the publication of the Trilateral Commission's report in 1975, political and administrative interest in public sector reforms has grown. The report problematized the growth of public bureaucracies and the development of the modern welfare state by pointing out their structural limits. The commission claimed the public welfare systems were under severe pressure as they were caught in a bad situation characterized by the "overload of government" and "the ungovernability of society" (Crozier, Huntington, and Watanuki 1975).

Its claim was sustained by the observations that the citizens' expectations for the public sector tend to grow faster than the resources available to the public sector and that increasing societal fragmentation and individualization, which is reflected in the steady decline of public spiritedness, tend to make governing modern societies more and more difficult for public authorities. To avoid a mounting distrust in elected government among Western populations that potentially could spur the growth of totalitarian movements and cause a demise of liberal democracy, reforms of the public sector were considered strictly necessary. This bleak diagnosis of the problems in Western democracies was further perpetuated by the deep economic recession in the early 1970s that was marked by rising oil prices, stagnating economies, surging unemployment, soaring inflation, and increasingly large public deficits. The joint occurrence of a political-ideological crisis and a socioeconomic crisis produced a society-wide recognition that the public sector urgently needed reform.

Neoliberal politicians and right-wing think tanks used this window of opportunity to call for a dismantling of the modern welfare state and for an increasing reliance on private market forces (Pierson 1994). Although this political project found support in some Anglo-Saxon governments, it had limited appeal to governments on the European continent, where the neoliberal attempt to roll back the welfare state was replaced with a less radical and more nuanced reform program that was referred to as New Public Management (Hood 1991). The NPM reform movement recommended privatizing public enterprises, contracting out public services, and introducing management techniques from the private sector to help reinvigorate the remaining public sector (Osborne and Gaebler 1992).

Although the impact of the NPM reform movement on the size and form of the public sector in the Western world is mixed and varied (Pollitt and Bouckaert 2004; Klausen and Ståhlberg 1998), it has produced the new and widely accepted idea that the public sector should be capable of constantly renewing and developing itself. Along these lines, elected politicians should formulate the overall targets for developing public organizations and should create strong incentives for public managers to generate new and innovative ways of producing and delivering public goods and services. To encourage constant service improvement, public managers should be subjected to competitive pressures from customers and private contractors, and elaborate systems of performance management should monitor and assess their performance. Last but not least, the salaries and career prospects of public managers should depend on their strategic performance and their ability to innovate the public sector in the pursuit of radical efficiencies.

This new discourse on how strategic managers in the public sector should initiate and drive efficiency-enhancing reforms and innovations completely redefined the administrative agenda. It was no longer enough for public administration and public governance to be legal, rational, efficient, planned, and coordinated. Instead, the protagonists of New Public Management persistently argued that public organizations should be subject to constant and deliberate changes that optimize their operation and functioning vis-à-vis the political objectives and performance targets set by elected politicians and the social and political demands advanced by citizens in their capacity as "users," "customers," or "stakeholders."

In its most perverse forms, this discourse on perpetual reforms and restless transformation turns change into a goal in itself. Accordingly public organizations are only viewed as legitimate if they are constantly changing as a result of deliberate reform strategies. Without a proper problem diagnosis and a thorough evaluation of the effects of previous, ongoing, and proposed reforms, such changes might reduce the problem-solving capacity of the public sector, diminish the quality and impact of public services, and thus have detrimental effects on the citizens, private firms, and other beneficiaries. At the very least, this restless transformation process tends to create a stressful working environment for public managers and employees who must endure an endless number of rationalization strategies.

For these reasons the discourse on uninterrupted public reforms and transformations is clearly problematic. Nevertheless, we should not forget that the new public reform discourse creates some much-welcomed opportunities for amending and improving public policies, organizations, and services. Numerous policy deadlocks in the field of social welfare, health care, education, planning, and environmental policy cause great frustration for elected politicians, policy advisers, private stakeholders, and citizens and, thus, elicit calls for profound changes in public policy and governance. In addition, public managers and employees have many unfulfilled professional ambitions; to meet them would require both policy changes and organizational and cultural transformations. Finally, the changing needs of citizens and private firms necessitate constant adaptations in the roles, contents, repertoires, and amounts of public goods and services. These legitimate demands for change reveal the ambiguity of the discourse on perpetual public transformation and may warrant a cautious embrace.

Despite the perverse examples of "change for the sake of changing," the new discourse of public change may serve the valuable purpose of breaking policy logjams and political stalemate, permitting a knowledge-based renewal of outdated organizational procedures and practices, and meeting the changing and unfulfilled needs of citizens, private firms, and other beneficiaries. If we accept this argument, then we need to comprehend the semantics of change in order to grasp the different meanings of the many terms indicating some kind of change. We frequently talk about how public policies, organizations, and services "change," "develop," or "improve," and about how and to what extent they are subject to "transformation," "reconceptualization," or even "innovation." Although these terms are sometimes used interchangeably, they are subtly different, and "innovation" seems to be the joker in the pack as it tends to capture some crucial aspects that the other terms fail to catch.

If things "change," or "have changed," then they are no longer the same as they were before. This is a binary code: change versus remain the same. The size or depth of a change may vary considerably, and we will often want to know how and how much things have changed. When we claim that something "has developed" or "is developing," we are referring to a gradual process of more or less multidimensional change that can be measured on a quantitative or qualitative scale. The term "development" has a slightly positive connotation. Hence, we like development but resist change. Development is often preferred to the preservation of the status quo, which is associated with stalemate; moreover, the more developed something is, the better it is often assumed to be. However, a development can also go up and down or be cyclical and go back and forth, thus not producing anything new.

Sometimes we want to express a positive assessment and talk about a development as an "improvement," indicating that it has gone in a direction that we desire and applaud. This does not necessarily mean that it has been subject to qualitative changes. Improvement often means there is simply more of what we know and desire than there was before. We usually use the term "transformation" to indicate a thorough and radical change, but the term does not implicitly indicate the direction of such a profound change. That being said, a transformation undoubtedly brings about a new state of affairs, although it is not necessarily the result of a premeditated set of actions. The notion of "reconceptualization" implies that there has been an attempt to rethink particular problems, programs, and practices in order to produce new visions, ideas, and ways of doing things, but they are not necessarily implemented or put into practice.

By contrast, "innovation" seems to refer to a reconceptualization that has been implemented in practice and, as a result of some proactive effort, has produced a transformation that brings about something new and potentially valuable. Innovation is a particular form of change and a particular form of transformation that adds not only direction and newness but also the idea of a proactive effort to generate and implement new ideas. In short, innovation involves an intentional redesign of existing designs through some kind of rupture.

This brief semantic excursus seems to suggest that we need a concept of innovation when discussing the ongoing attempts to reinvigorate the public sector. We can talk about the change, development, improvement, transformation, or reconceptualization of public policies, organizations, and services, but we gain a certain conceptual precision when talking about something as being, or not being, an innovation. Innovation seems to capture the idea of a premeditated action to develop and implement new ideas in order to produce a stepwise change that is more than a "continuous improvement," which merely gives us more or less of what we already have, and less than a "radical transformation," which replaces one action system with another (Hartley 2006).

HOW TO DEFINE INNOVATION

As noted, innovation has a positive connotation. We tend to see innovation as something inherently good, and the concept of innovation invokes images of brilliant inventors, inspiring front-runners, and brave pioneers who help us do things in smarter and more ingenious ways than before. Innovation appears to create winners by rewarding the innovators with new and better ways of accomplishing particular goals and tasks and of satisfying unfulfilled needs and demands. The positive, and sometimes overly optimistic, discourse on innovation threatens to reduce innovation to an empty rhetorical device—that is, a magic concept that is better suited for official speeches and glossy government reports than for practical political attempts to transform public policies, organizations, and services (Pollitt and Hupe 2011). To avoid an unfortunate reduction of the notion of innovation to the latest fad, we need to develop a more rigorous definition that permits a precise and nuanced assessment of the promise of public innovation.

Innovation is often defined in short, catchy phrases such as "new ideas that work" (Mulgan and Albury 2003) or "new stuff that is made useful" (McKeown 2008). Although such definitions capture the gist of the concept, they lack the precision necessary for a deeper analysis. A more cumbersome but ultimately more adequate definition describes innovation as *an intended but inherently contingent process that involves the development and realization, and frequently also the spread, of new and creative ideas that challenge conventional wisdom and disrupt the established practices within a specific context.*

This definition aims to settle some of the ongoing conceptual disputes about what innovation means and how to define it, especially in relation to the public sector. First of all, the definition insists that innovation is a result of intentional but inherently contingent actions. As it has been repeatedly argued, innovation is an open-ended and rather unpredictable process that is triggered and influenced by unforeseen events and chance discoveries, and it is frequently based on processes of trial and error that produce experimental learning (Van de Ven et al. 2008). Thus, innovation can neither be programmed nor planned; instead, it requires a mental state characterized by curiosity, open-mindedness, and courage, as well as a pragmatic attitude toward accidents, contingencies, risks, and failures. Nevertheless, innovation is based on intentional actions through which different social and political actors aim to respond to problems and challenges, or to exploit new opportunities, by doing things in new ways that may outperform the existing practices. Innovation involves deliberate and practical attempts to change, or even improve, the current state of affairs in light of present and future demands. However, when multiple streams of problems, solutions, and contingent events are connected and worked on by different actors in particular contexts and unacknowledged circumstances (Kingdon 1984), the final result becomes a mixture of intended and unintended outcomes.

Second, the definition clearly stresses that innovation is not merely about developing a new and inspiring idea through a creative process based on a combination of divergent and convergent thinking. To foster a new and creative idea, and perhaps turn it into a prototype that can be tested in practice, may qualify as an invention, but an invention only becomes an innovation when it is adopted in practice, consolidated, and applied so widely and frequently that it is capable of producing some clearly discernible effects. In short, innovation involves both the exploration and exploitation of new ideas (Mulgan and Albury 2003). Dreaming up new and promising solutions that remain on the drawing board may involve creative thinking, but it is not innovation. Innovation entails putting new and creative ideas into practice and getting results.

Next, although innovation aims to bring about change, we are talking about a particular kind of second or third order of change (see Hall 1993).

Innovation is not about producing and delivering more or less of the same kind of goods, services, or solutions ("first order change"). Rather, it is about changing the form, content, and repertoire of goods, services, and organizational routines ("second order change") or transforming the underlying understanding of the problem, the policy objective, and the program theory ("third order change"). In short, innovation involves producing qualitative rather than quantitative transformation (Slappendel 1996). There is no objective way of determining or measuring the amount of qualitative change that is needed for a transformation to qualify as an innovation. Too much depends on the subjective perceptions of situated actors who may perceive the same transformation in different ways. However, as a rule of thumb, qualitative changes will tend to challenge conventional wisdom and sedimented practices because they change how we give meaning to and interpret particular problems and the ways of solving them. In other words, innovation is predicated on learning and on a willingness to reform established ideas and procedures.

In addition, the definition maintains that innovation is always relative to a specific context. While innovation brings about a new solution, it does not necessarily have to be unknown to the world. Its novel use in a particular context, field, or domain is sufficient (Zaltman, Duncan, and Holbek 1973). Even if an idea or practice has been adopted before, or can be found in another place, the subsequent adoption of a similar idea or practice in another institutional context or domain may qualify as an innovation (Hartley 2005). Thus, it is not the source of innovation but the context of its implementation and the perceptions of people in that context that determine whether something qualifies as an innovation (Roberts and King 1996, 5). Not only will the adoption of a particular idea or practice in a new context result in a qualitative transformation of that particular context, but also the very process of transferring ideas and practices to a new context tends to involve a contingent selection, combination, and modification of the ideational and practical elements of the innovation that is being transferred (Røvik 1992). Hence, when public organizations are importing a new idea or practice from other public organizations, or from the private sector, the former usually end up following the exporting organization's example but in a slightly different way and with a slightly different impact.

Finally, although innovation processes are motivated by the wish to produce new and better methods that outperform previous practices, the presented definition does not cover whether the consequences of an innovation are good or bad (Hartley 2005). Innovations might fail and might not lead to any improvement, but they are still innovations in the sense that new ideas are realized in practice and produce particular effects. We also may talk about successful innovations in terms of being perceived ex post to generate desirable results in the eyes of particular public and private stakeholders. Ideally, the outcome of public innovation should correspond with the political preferences of the elected politicians, help make life easier for the public managers and employees, create a higher degree of user satisfaction, and benefit society at large. In real life, however, politicians, public managers, street-level bureaucrats, user groups, and the general public often evaluate the outcome of public innovation differently. The different or even conflicting evaluations reflect not only the relative gains and losses of the actors but also the fact that innovation can serve different purposes. Public innovation may be directed at improving efficiency, effectiveness, quality, equity, or democracy, but there are often trade-offs between these different objectives.

Innovation is a multidimensional, complex, and potentially chaotic process (Van de Ven et al. 2008). Actors combine multiple streams of problems, solutions, and events in processes of exploration and exploitation that facilitate learning and reform and that produce context-dependent results. Different actors will evaluate these results dissimilarly, thus triggering new and ongoing innovation processes. For heuristic purposes, we can identify five constitutive phases in the innovation cycle (Eggers and Singh 2009). The five phases are modeled on the traditional stages in the policy process.

Defining problems and challenges in need of innovation often begins with acknowledging a discrepancy between the formal and informal objectives and ambitions of public policies, organizations, and services on the one hand and the present and future performance and the unexploited opportunities that may enhance performance on the other hand. To start crafting innovative solutions, the problems, challenges, and opportunities must be properly understood and defined. This step involves devising a thorough description of the problem at hand, outlining its significance, scope, conditions, and causes. When facing complex and intractable problems, providing a precise and agreed-upon definition is difficult, and the attempt to get a handle on the problem will be an ongoing learning process subject to constant reformulations. The overall expectations for the innovative solution, including the underlying goals and values, also need to be clarified to direct the process of creative problem solving. Diffuse goals will fail to mobilize committed and entrepreneurial actors, because they prevent the potential actors from seeing what they can gain from engaging in cumbersome innovation processes. Last but not least, the problems, challenges, and opportunities must be framed in such a way that they appear important and urgent enough for the social and

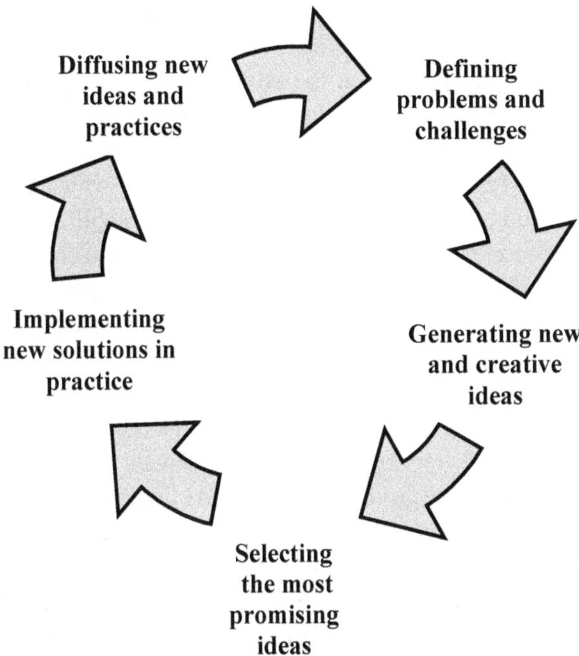

FIGURE 1.1. The innovation cycle

political actors to devote their time and energy to dealing with them and to engage in innovative processes that carry an imminent risk of failure.

Generating new and creative ideas calls for an open-minded development, combination, and revision of ideas. Developing new ideas requires learning processes that go beyond correcting errors and mistakes and that challenge our understanding of what we want and how to achieve it. Idea generation may also involve testing new ideas through prototyping and design experiments. Since new ideas tend to be disturbing and disruptive and are likely to make the social and political actors involved in innovation processes uncomfortable, developing new ideas will only begin when the social and political actors are dissatisfied with the current state of affairs and agree that it must be changed. Public and private actors can foster new and creative ideas by combining existing ideas in original ways. Moreover, they may also benefit from integrating new and emerging ideas that come from other contexts, scientific discoveries, or attempts to grasp the unknown through intuition, imagination, and the tossing of metaphors.

Selecting the most promising ideas involves decisions about which ideas are worth pursuing, testing, and bringing to fruition. Ideally, ideas should be big, bold, and transformative while, at the same time, feasible, safe, and broadly accepted among the key stakeholders. Thus, negotiation, compromise, and conflict settlement are key features of the process of idea selection. This phase is ridden with more or less subtle power struggles in which the social and political actors aim to gain support for their ideas by mobilizing their talents: their ability to argue persuasively for a particular solution (Logos); their reputation and credibility as competent, creative, and responsible innovators (ethos); and their rhetorical skills in order to arouse particular emotions (pathos).

Implementing new solutions in practice involves converting ideas into new policies, procedures, and services. Clear and robust objectives, flexible action plans, trial runs, broad support, and access to adequate resources are essential in implementing new and promising ideas and concepts. Changing existing patterns of behavior is a very difficult task that requires exercising leadership, constructing ownership, and creating incentives. Since many things can go wrong in the implementation phase, innovators must be prepared to deal with uncertainties, risks, unforeseen problems, and temporary setbacks.

Diffusing new ideas and practices requires circulating information and knowledge about new ways of doing things, either within an organization or from one organization to another (Rogers 1995). Innovation diffusion involves highlighting the gains obtained by first movers, establishing contacts with potential followers, overcoming standard objections such as "we do not need any changes" and "this is not invented here," and adapting innovative ideas and concepts to new and different circumstances. When innovative practices are diffused and put to work in new, wider, or different contexts, they will be evaluated by a new set of public and private stakeholders, and the feedback might trigger other innovation processes.

The five phases in the innovation cycle do not always follow neatly after each other in a well-ordered and linear fashion; instead, they are often repeated, rearranged, combined, and integrated in complex processes with many leaps and feedback loops. Dissatisfaction with the result of innovative service delivery, unforeseen problems with the realization of new and creative policy solutions, or a failure to create a broad consensus for a new and promising idea might send the would-be innovators back to the drawing board to rethink and adapt the innovative solutions. The efforts to adapt an innovative solution to a new context might clash with the explicit political preferences for a particular innovative solution and necessitate a dialogue between designers and political decision makers. Practical learning in the implementation phase might change the selected solution and incorporate elements from alternative solutions. Last but not least, the *evaluation* of an innovative solution might reveal that it unexpectedly solves another problem.

Nevertheless, the five phases of the innovation cycle are important building blocks in the complex, iterative, and messy processes of innovation. Innovation cannot take place without clearly defining the problems and challenges, generating and selecting new ideas, and implementing and diffusing new practices. The constitutive phases of the innovation cycle may be integrated and combined in different ways, but they are driven by different rationalities. Hence, defining problems and ideas requires knowledge gathering and discursive framing; generating ideas calls for curiosity, creative exploration, and a recombination of old and new ideas; selecting the most promising ideas involves coping with uncertainty and assessing potential gains and risks; implementing new practices entails planning, coordination, and flexibility; and diffusing new ideas and practices relies on networking and adaptation.

DIFFERENT TYPES OF PUBLIC INNOVATION

Having defined the concept of innovation and the constitutive phases of the innovation cycle, it is time to reflect on the difference between public and private innovation. The public and private sectors clearly provide different conditions, incentives, and barriers for innovation, but perhaps the most striking difference between public and private innovation has to do with the value that they create (Hartley 2006). Hence, in the private sector, firms invest in innovation to create private value that is often protected by intellectual property right laws, but in the public sector, innovation contributors relinquish ownership and control of their innovative solutions and thus make them public goods (Hippel and Krogh 2003, 212–13). In other words, whereas private innovation produces private value for specific business firms or industrial branches, public innovation creates public value (Moore 1995)—in terms of policies, services, or public infrastructures that generate political value (e.g., solutions to complex policy problems and enhancement of democracy), social value (e.g., satisfaction of social needs and enhancement of social capital, recognition, and cohesion), or economic value (e.g., generation of growth and employment and improvement of public sector finances).

Public innovation can take different forms by targeting different aspects of the public value production. Originally Schumpeter (1934) divided private sector innovations into three types: *technical innovations* that include product and process innovation, *organizational innovations* in private firms or whole industries, and *market innovations* that bring about new sources of supply of raw materials and half-fabricated goods or new ways of marketing and selling products (see also Hagedoorn 1996). The typology for innovation in the public sector looks slightly different. It makes good sense to talk about technical innovations of products and processes and about organizational innovations of the form and functioning of public institutions and their relationships to external actors. Market innovation seems to be less relevant, however, although quasi-markets, voucher schemes, and new forms of public procurement clearly represent important public sector innovations.

Nevertheless, when dealing with innovation in the public sector, we have to add other types of innovation that focus on public services or pertain to governance, policymaking, and societal discourse (see Hartley 2005). We can distinguish between the following types of public innovation accordingly:

- *Product innovation*: new products that are either used in the public sector (e.g., new instruments or pharmaceutical products used in hospitals) or delivered by public agencies to needy citizens (e.g., new technologies enabling multihandicapped people to stay in their homes)
- *Service innovation*: new forms of service (e.g., offers of subsidized job training to unemployed people instead of passive benefits) and new ways of delivering service (e.g., digital self-service or the introduction of vouchers)
- *Process innovation*: new ways of producing public goods and services (e.g., the digitalization of case management, contracting out, cooperation with voluntary organizations, or reliance on chronically ill patients to coordinate their own treatment)
- *Organizational innovation*: new ways of organizing public bureaucracies (e.g., devolution of tasks to local governments, creation of special-purpose agencies, horizontal integration of departments, separation of front-office from back-office tasks, or new forms of citizen participation)
- *Governance innovations*: new modes of governance (e.g., construction of quasi-markets, production of voluntary standards, introduction of voucher schemes, creation of user boards, participatory budgeting, formation of governance networks or enhanced use of crowdsourcing)

- *Policy innovation*: new objectives, instruments, and assessment tools (e.g., transition from welfare to workfare, free school choice, renewed emphasis on preventive health care, or removal of taxes on electric cars)
- *Discourse innovation*: new language, concepts, and rhetorical figures aiming to make sense of public problems and challenges (e.g., the discourse on sustainable development) or to change the role and image of public authorities (e.g., community policing aiming to be "smart on crime" rather than "tough on crime")

Concrete public innovations will often fall into several of these categories, and the intention to produce a particular type of innovation will often lead to unintended innovations of a different type. Thus, governance innovation might appear to be a necessary condition for advancing a certain policy innovation, and transforming the role of public authorities vis-à-vis private actors might be an unplanned outcome of service innovations.

In reality, product and service innovation are difficult to separate from each other, and the same goes for process, organizational, and governance innovation, which often tend to overlap. The lines of demarcation between discourse and policy innovation are also blurred. Consequently, we can collapse the six categories listed earlier into three general categories and talk about service innovation, organizational innovation, and policy innovation as broadly defined types of innovation.

There are other frequently used categorizations of public innovation. Thus, it is common to distinguish between radical and incremental innovations depending on whether the steps taken are large and pathbreaking or small but significant disruptions that gradually take things in a new direction. Innovations that come from above are sometimes referred to as *top-down innovations*, whereas those innovations that are initiated by lower-level managers, employees, or users are referred to as *bottom-up innovations*. Last but not least, we can distinguish *global innovations* that are adopted in all parts of the public sector from more *local innovations* that do not escape the confines of a single program or organization.

THE RECENT QUEST FOR PUBLIC INNOVATION

Innovation has always been a buzzword in the public sector, but there are several indications of a growing emphasis on and interest in public innovation both in the practical and academic worlds. Many governments and public authorities in Europe, North America, the Antipodes, and South America have commissioned white papers on how to spur public innovation and launched public innovation programs. Government innovation labs such as the Australian DesignGov, the British Nesta (formerly the National Endowment for Science Technology and the Arts), the Danish MindLab, the Dutch Kennisland, and the Mexican Laboratorio para la Ciudad are proliferating, and they bring together researchers and practitioners in joint efforts to study, create, and disseminate public innovation. Transnational networks such as Social Innovation Europe are emerging to link innovators across sectors and countries. Global private companies such as IDEO play the same role.

Meanwhile, public sector innovation awards are increasingly used to stimulate the search for next practices (Borins 1998; Ferreira, Farah, and Spink 2008), and a growing number of public innovation surveys report a rise in public innovations (Arundel and Smith 2013; Kattel et al. 2014). Websites such as the Government Innovators Network sponsored by Harvard's John F. Kennedy School of Government facilitate the discussion and circulation of new and innovative ideas and practices. New innovation journals are being formed along with a steady stream of scientific reports and books on public innovation (Borins 2008, 2014; Eggers and Singh 2009; Bason 2010; Steelman 2010; Bekkers, Edelenbos, and Steijn 2011; Valkama, Bailey, and Anttiroiko 2013; Ansell and Torfing 2014).

All of these activities are part of the new and expanding innovation discourse that was triggered by the development of new digital technologies and the emergence of the reinventing government movement. They continue to gain momentum in government offices and administrative agencies around the world. To better understand the present quest for public innovation, we have to consider the sources of the growing demand for innovation in the public sector.

First of all, the ongoing processes of globalization tend to stimulate the demand for public innovation (Bugge et al. 2010). Globalization creates new problems, such as the distribution and integration of refugees and immigrants, global terrorism, climate change mitigation, airport congestion, and disease control, that prompt the development of new and innovative public solutions. Globalization is strongly associated with mounting competitive pressures that call for government intervention in efforts to secure the conditions for continued growth and prosperity. It is discursively constructed as a competitive game that nations, regions, and localities can either win or lose depending on their innovative capacities. Innovation in strategically important economic sectors has the highest priority, but it is increasingly recognized, especially in the European context and to some extent also within the OECD (2010), that economic innovation thrives on public innovation. Public innovation can free resources that can then be used to finance public research and development (R&D) activities, which may spur innovation in the private sector. In addition, innovation in public service and regulation can provide the conditions, support, and incentives for the private sector to become more innovative. Good examples are educational reforms that stimulate learning and encourage entrepreneurialism and the development of stricter environmental demands that force private companies to innovate. Consequently, there is not only an innovation spillover from the private to the public sector, as New Public Management suggests, but also a potential spillover from public innovation to private sector innovation. In sum, public innovation appears to be essential for those nations, regions, and localities that seek to win, or aim not to fall behind in, the competitive globalization game. It provides an important precondition for attracting foreign investments and highly educated labor power.

Next, citizens and private firms and associations have high and rising expectations for the quality, availability, and effectiveness of public services, and they increasingly demand that governments should be responsive to the needs of society (Vigoda-Gadot et al. 2008). The demand for tailor-made services and flexible regulations is also on the rise, especially in the increasingly affluent middle class and among private business firms (Bowden 2005; Carter and Bélanger 2005). At the same time, public resources are limited due to a combination of structural and political factors, and many public employees find themselves struggling to meet growing demands. Given the labor-extensive character of public service provisions, the public sector cannot produce the same high level of productivity gains found in the private sector, which tends to define the general level of wage increases. The result is that the salaries of public employees become a growing fiscal burden (Baumol's Disease). In addition, no matter whether the aggregate tax level is high or low, there seems to be a strong political resistance to raising taxes in order to cater to the growing demands of citizens and private firms. Thus, the public sector is caught in a cross fire between rising demands and scarce resources, and public innovation that leads to more efficient and effective solutions seems to be the only fix.

In addition, professionals, public managers, and elected politicians have growing ambitions regarding the quality of public governance and its ability to solve social, economic, and environmental problems. Therefore, governments at different levels aim to deliver more effective, knowledge-based, responsible, flexible, targeted, efficient, and integrated forms of governance. At the same time, society is becoming increasingly difficult to govern given the growing complexity and fragmentation of social, political, and economic processes and the increasing number of wicked problems that are ill defined, are hard to solve given their conflicting demands, require specialized knowledge, involve a large number of stakeholders, and carry a high potential for disputes (Kooiman 1993; Koppenjan and Klijn 2004). The endeavor to narrow this gap between official governance ambitions and the actual performance of public policy calls for the development of new and innovative solutions.

Finally, the economic recession following in the wake of the global credit crisis of 2008 has put greater strains on public finance. The typical reaction of politicians and executive managers to the fiscal crisis was to propose "blind," across-the-board cuts that could not avoid affecting vital public expenditures for health, education, and social welfare. Sometimes overall political priorities help to steer budget allocations and safeguard vital areas from massive cuts, but given that health, education, and social welfare programs carry a great deal of weight in public budgets, decreases in these important areas are difficult to avoid without imposing massive savings in other areas that are likely to trigger a fierce resistance. The intelligent and politically attractive alternative to across-the-board cuts and politically prioritized savings is to spur public innovation, which can lead to new and smarter solutions. Expensive and poorly performing programs can sometimes be replaced with new and better ones that cost less because they are more efficient and address problems in novel and more direct ways. An example is the cleaning of public hospitals. New methods have been developed for completely cleaning hospital wards and sterilizing operation theaters. Although they cost more than the old and inefficient cleaning methods, the extra costs of improved cleaning are more than compensated by the money saved on not having to treat hospital-induced infections.

This list of factors driving the present quest for public innovation does not claim to be exhaustive. It does allow us, however, to better understand the promulgation of the discourse of innovation and its practical and institutional support.

TOWARD A NEW INNOVATION AGENDA IN THE PUBLIC SECTOR

There is a stubborn myth that red tape, institutional inertia, and political stalemate pervade the public sector and that, therefore, the demand for and the attempt to spur public innovation are futile. This misconception has been a key part of the neoliberal critique of the public sector when blaming it for not being sufficiently dynamic and innovative. However, despite the presence of a risk-averse, "zero-error" culture in some parts of the public sector, the neoliberal critique of the public sector as being inhospitable to innovation is exaggerated. In fact, the public sector has seen a great deal of innovation in the postwar period. If we compare the form and content of today's public policies and services with what was offered forty to fifty years ago, clearly the public sector has undergone a dramatic transformation resulting from a combination of incremental and radical innovations. One has only to think of the significant changes in areas such as social welfare, employment policy, crime prevention, and health care to envision and appreciate the scale of these transformations. Moreover, as pointed out by Mazzucato (2013), we should not forget that public institutions created spectacular innovations such as the Internet and the Global Positioning System (GPS).

Hence, the problem is not a general absence of innovation in the public sector but that most public innovations are one-off changes driven by more or less accidental events that do not leave public organizations with a lasting capacity to innovate (Eggers and Singh 2009, 5–6). As the analysis of 217 applications to the Ford Foundation's innovation award program in the mid-1990s shows, public innovation has many triggers: public spending cuts, sudden changes in the demand for a program, local adaptions to new national legislation, organizational initiatives taken by newly recruited executive managers who want to prove their worth, crises triggered by failures and shortcomings that become scandals when reported by the mass media or disclosed by external performance reviews, and new opportunities stemming from technological inventions (Borins 2001b, 313). Other drivers of contingent innovation are national campaigns to adopt a new best practice and local experimentation facilitated by access to time-limited, special-purpose funding.

The accidental character of public innovation demonstrates the need for a new innovation agenda that aims to turn innovation into a permanent and systematic activity that pervades the entire public sector at the local, regional, and national levels and in the different international and supranational governance arenas. Hence, public innovation should be permanent, not in the sense of invoking constant transformations but in the sense of being an integral part of the vision, goals, and practices of public organizations. In addition, public innovation should be a systematic activity that is supported by institutional and organizational procedures for exploration and exploitation and a relevant theory of change. Finally, public innovation should be pervasive as a common practice in all parts and at all levels of public organizations, preferably by constituting the core, or even the modus operandi, of public organizations.

There have been numerous attempts to advance this new public innovation agenda. Its successful realization depends on creating a strong advocacy coalition consisting of leading politicians, public managers, street-level bureaucrats, professional associations, user and interest organizations, consultancy firms, academic experts, think tanks, and the mass media. Together these actors can build a new public innovation agenda that not only aims to incorporate innovation as a central ambition for the public sector but also begins to enhance the institutional capacity for innovation. More important the social and political actors themselves can construct forums and arenas for developing and exchanging new ideas and for testing the most promising ones in practice. However, political commitment and determined action are not enough to make the public sector more innovative. As we shall see, the form and functioning of the public sector provide a number of barriers and drivers for public innovation that also play a crucial role in determining the fate of the new and emerging agenda.

FAVORABLE AND UNFAVORABLE CONDITIONS FOR PUBLIC INNOVATION

Private firms operating in cutthroat markets are forced by economic competition to innovate their products, production processes, organizational designs, and marketing techniques. If they fail to do so, they lose market share and eventually cease to exist. Consequently, private firms tend to hire skillful designers and developers, create dedicated task forces, establish large-scale R&D departments, and collaborate with other firms or public agencies to gain access to innovative ideas and practices. The private firms and the financial markets that finance their investments in innovative projects are to a large extent geared toward the creation of innovation (Baumol 2002), and the organizations' shareholders can register the immediate result of the many efforts to enhance innovation by reviewing the bottom line of the financial statements that the chief executive officers issue.

The picture is slightly different and less favorable in terms of stimulating innovation when we look at public organizations. Hence, public bureaucracies contain a number of barriers to innovation (Halvorsen et al. 2005; Røste 2005). Indeed, it is well known that the strong adherence to bureaucratic rules and procedures, the lack of competition, and the absence of economic incentives in terms of profit, patents, and bonus payments tend to stifle public innovation (Borins 2001b; Kelman 2005). Another problem is that public policies, organizations, and services are relatively complex, multifunctional, and based on (inter)national laws and statutory rights; therefore, they are difficult to alter without stirring up all kinds of political conflicts (Hartley 2005). A third problem is that the absence of venture capital and the use of income budgeting, which merely allocates public revenues to different programs and administrative units, make financing public innovation and measuring the subsequent gains difficult. Last but not least, the public sector is governed by elected politicians and executive public managers who tend to be rather risk averse because failures receive intensive and negative media coverage that may undermine, or even ruin, their political or administrative careers (Borins 2001b). Unlike private firms, there is a divided political leadership at the top of public organizations that are inclined to block innovations from below that carry a significant risk of failure.

In addition to these barriers inherent in public bureaucracy, the new audit regime introduced by the advocates of New Public Management also tends to hamper public innovation (Power 1999; Newman, Raine, and Skelcher 2001). The strict demands for documenting the performance of public agencies in relation to pre-given standards and targets are not only extremely taxing and time consuming but also penalize public agencies for innovating policies and services once the old practices are no longer performed and the new practices are not measured.

This being said, we should remember also that important and distinctive drivers of innovation are found in the public sector (Halvorsen et al. 2005; Røste 2005). The high ambitions, the strong commitment, and the professional education and competences of the public managers and employees are potent levers for public innovation. Public scrutiny of the performance of public agencies and an active and engaged feedback from users and customers contribute to keeping politicians and civil servants in public bureaucracies on their toes. Moreover, the sheer size of the public sector and thus its ability to absorb the costs of innovation failures might help to reduce risk-averse behavior. Last but not least, the recent introduction of competitive pressures, strategic management, and the focus on results tend to force public agencies to change established rules, norms, and routines. Thus, despite the caveats mentioned earlier, undoubtedly New Public Management has spurred public innovation.

Whether the drivers of public innovation outweigh the barriers is an empirical question and varies from case to case, but a conscious effort to remove the barriers and exploit the drivers will greatly improve the chances for advancing the public innovation agenda, which seems to be becoming a top priority in many Western countries. We shall return later to the question of how public governance can be transformed to enhance public innovation. At this point, suffice it to say that paradigmatic changes appear necessary for innovation to become a part of the DNA of the public sector.

THE IMPACT OF PUBLIC INNOVATION

Public innovation can have damaging effects when innovation becomes a goal in itself and things that are working well are changed simply for the sake of change and perhaps even so that public leaders and managers can build their reputations for being "dynamic," "entrepreneurial," and "capable of producing results." Another and related problem occurs when successful projects are scrapped because funding must be freed to finance new innovations. This process leads to serial innovation with no lasting impact. A third problem is that central government grants tied to the adoption of new best practices sometimes are tempting local governments to launch innovative projects that nobody really wants or that conflict with the political priorities of the local governments. Finally, innovation might be used as a smoke screen for making public spending cuts. For example, reforms that aim to reduce the costs of welfare services either by making them more selective, needs based, or means tested or by trying to shift the responsibility for service provision from public authorities to private providers or local communities may be sold as public innovations. Public innovations may help lower the costs of welfare services or create a new division of labor between service providers, but expenditure cuts should not be passed off as innovations if they do not emanate from implementing new and creative ideas that increase the productivity, efficiency, and effectiveness of public service organizations.

These cautious and skeptical remarks should not hide the fact that public innovations can reshape public policies, organizations, and services in ways that advance public values, objectives, and ambitions; improve the working conditions for public employees; and provide clear benefits to citizens, private firms, and other stakeholders. Innovation can help augment the efficiency, quality, and effectiveness of public regulation and service provisions, and it can spur democratic participation and civic engagement (Bason 2010, 46). A few examples will provide a better understanding of the potentially positive impact of public innovation and explain why we need more of it.

Let us begin with an illustration of the merits of policy innovation. The European Union encourages its member states to develop a new kind of active employment policy that aims to supplement the passive unemployment benefits with active offers of counseling, education, training, and subsidized jobs to enhance the "employability" of the unemployed. In countries observing best practices such as Denmark, the shift to the new active employment policy contributed significantly to bringing down the unemployment rate from 12 percent in 1993 to 2 percent in 2008 while keeping inflation below 2 percent (Torfing 2007). The new Danish "activation policy" that was implemented in the mid-1990s onward has supported the creation of an extremely flexible labor market. The absence of restrictions on hiring and firing labor power is counterbalanced by relatively high unemployment benefits and relatively strong incentives for benefit claimants to reenter the labor market. The unemployed only receive the unemployment benefits in a certain period, during which they are legally required to participate in public programs that aim to maintain and develop their skills, competences, and labor-market experience. Even when the fiscal crisis hit the small, open Danish economy in 2008, unemployment only rose to about 6 percent because the country's innovative employment policy combines labor-market flexibility, social security, and strong incentives to find gainful employment.

Participatory budgeting is another example of an organizational innovation in public governance. The process has radically changed the procedures for making decisions about public spending and investments in the Brazilian city of Porto Alegre. Local neighborhood assemblies are involved in determining public spending and investment priorities, and the actual allocations in the city budget have usually followed the citizens' recommendations. As a result, the citywide coverage of basic public services such as running water, sewers, and social assistance has increased. Moreover, democratic participation has empowered ordinary citizens and reduced the impact of patron-client relations on decisions about public investments (Fung 2008, 65). Today participatory budgeting has spread around the world and become a global phenomenon.

An example of both organizational innovation and policy innovation is found in the US court system. Since 1989 the diffusion and institutionalization of special drug courts at the city and county levels have brought a therapeutic element into the judicial process for nonviolent drug offenders (Hale 2011). The innovative approach to crime prevention, which blends efforts to protect public safety, provide public health services through treatment, and change the behavior of offenders, is associated with "reductions in recidivism that endure significantly beyond the duration of the individual's program participation" (Hale 2011, 84). The drug courts have also brought public interventions in the field of drug-related crime in line with shifts in public opinion, and they have moved toward offering treatment and rehabilitation for drug offenders as opposed to simply mandating their incarceration and other forms of punishment (Hale 2011, 34).

Strong private stakeholders who benefit from the maintenance of the status quo often oppose public innovation in regulatory regimes. In the field of environmental regulation, however, public innovation is in high demand and may benefit large numbers of people. A good example is found in coal mining. One of the negative externalities from coal mining in West Virginia is that it leads to acidification of the water that flows through the mines. As the outflow of acidic water in the watershed increases, the concentration of heavy metals also builds and becomes toxic to plants and animals. A public-private partnership has agreed upon and implemented a new voluntary scheme of watershed regulation that reduces acidification and uses peer pressure to deal with instances of noncompliance. People living close to the watershed appreciate greatly the innovative efforts to counter the problem and restore the local habitat (Steelman 2010, 101–37).

Service innovation tends to be more frequent, resulting in some spectacular and often-cited examples. In New York City innovative ways of funding and producing public services have resulted in a profound revitalization of public parks. In the 1990s city officials faced the huge challenge of repairing the large system of run-down, underfunded, and underutilized urban parks. The Parks and Recreation Department solved the problem by raising more than $50 million from private community organizations and wealthy individuals and by creating local citizen groups that both guided the parks' reconstruction and provided voluntary labor. During the reconstruction and development process, the department's role was transformed from that of a "park steward" to a "network manager" (Fung 2008, 59–60). The result of this innovative service production in New York is that the public utilization of its vitalized parks has increased manyfold.

Citizen engagement seems to be an important feature of many recent service innovations. The website Fix My Street, which the voluntary organization mySociety established in the United Kingdom, provides an easy way for citizens to report physical problems such as potholes and vandalism in their local community. Users can identify the exact location of the problem on a map of the local area, write a detailed description of the problem they have identified, and submit a picture that documents the problem. All reports are sent to the local city council, which can use the information in its efforts to improve the local neighborhoods (Eggers and Singh 2009, 87). Along these lines, new opportunities for civic engagement may foster better public services and provide them more quickly and efficiently than before.

Service innovation that benefits local citizens is not always a result of citizen engagement; sometimes it stems from enhanced cooperation between different agencies in the public sector. One example comes from Australia, where an integrated service for homeless youths links the service silos of housing, employment, and welfare by providing a single case manager for each participant in the program. The new joined-up, or combined, service aims to solve closely related problems such as homelessness, unemployment, and basic welfare in a coordinated and more holistic way while greatly improving services for homeless youths (Considine and Hart 2008).

A final example of service innovation is found in Danish municipalities that have developed training courses for chronically ill patients. Taught partly by experienced nurses and partly by specially trained patients with chronic diseases, patients learn how to interact and communicate with the relevant health and treatment agencies, how to live an active life despite their illness, or how to tackle chronic pain. These courses have a significant impact on the effectiveness of various forms of treatment and help prevent complications. The training courses also empower the patients and improve their quality of life.

These empirical examples highlight the benefits and achievements of different types of public innovation, but they beg the question of how public innovation is produced. What are the sources of public innovation, and how can we enhance innovation in the public sector? Chapter 2 answers these questions by emphasizing the crucial role of multi-actor collaboration.

CONCLUSION

This chapter has explored the semantics of change in the public sector in order to demonstrate the need for a concept of innovation that enables us to capture the idea of a premeditated action aiming to develop and implement new ideas to create a step change in the public sector. The chapter has defined the concept of innovation in relation to some of the conceptual disputes in innovation research and has explained the various phases of the innovation cycle and the different forms of innovation that are encountered in the public sector. Pressures from the ongoing social, political, and economic globalization; the rising expectations of what the public sector can deliver in terms of services and problem solving; the growing ambitions of professionally trained public employees; and the dire fiscal constraints in the wake of the 2008 economic crisis—all explain a current surge in interest in public innovation. These factors combine to produce a serious cross pressure between growing problems, challenges, expectations, and ambitions on the one hand and limited public resources on the other hand. What the public sector seems to have recognized is that this cross pressure can only be escaped by producing new and innovative solutions that give us more, better, and smarter solutions that cost less.

Innovation in the public sector faces both barriers and drivers, but on the whole the public sector seems to be more dynamic and innovative than its reputation. Nevertheless, there is still some way to go before the pursuit of innovation has become a permanent and systematic effort that pervades all levels and aspects of the public sector. The numbers of innovations in the public sector are increasing, but the sector still generally lacks strategic focus, innovation methods, and supportive institutional values, norms, and procedures.

2

COLLABORATIVE INTERACTION AS A SOURCE OF PUBLIC INNOVATION

THIS CHAPTER argues that multi-actor collaboration is a crucial and yet relatively unexplored source of innovation in the public sector. In the private sector, competition rather than collaboration is often considered as the key source of economic innovation (Porter 1985). Competition forces private businesses to reduce their costs by introducing new technologies, more efficient production processes, or new and cheaper raw materials, and it prompts them to increase their sales by developing new products and marketing techniques. The reward for winning the competitive innovation battle with other private enterprises might be growing profits, increasing market shares, and perhaps even developing a patent that other firms must pay to use. Failure to innovate may result in declining sales and profits. In the final instance, it might lead to bankruptcy.

However, competition is not the only source of economic innovation. Without questioning the important role of rivalry and pluralism, Teece (1992) has shown that competition can have negative, unintended consequences and that interfirm collaboration can help spur innovation in competitive environments. Competition sometimes leads to too little innovation because firms know that they are unable to effectively exclude other firms from "free riding," or using the innovative technologies or designs that are under development. Competition might also produce too much innovation when firms apply too many resources in the early stage of the race to reach the patent office first. In an unfortunate result known as "overbidding," many of the firms drop out of the industry when the patent race is over and the serious development work begins (Teece 1992, 4–5). Collaboration with other firms through strategic alliances enables firms to overcome both problems by facilitating collective agreements about how to share the costs and benefits of innovation among a group of firms with different forms of expertise.

Monopolized industries can also solve these problems, but the lack of diversity of ideas and approaches and the absence of competitive pressures are likely to reduce the innovative capacity of monopolists. By contrast, collaboration and strategic alliances enable private firms to access complementary technologies, competences, and assets on relatively favorable terms to facilitate the production and successful commercialization of their innovations and to assist them in defining the technical standards that ensure the compatibility between new innovations (Teece 1992). In addition, collaboration with public institutions and authorities enables private firms to benefit from publicly financed research at universities and other research institutions, to influence regulatory frameworks that determine the demand for new products and services, and to gain access to large public markets (Lundvall 1985). Finally, Hippel (1988) has shown that collaboration with users helps private firms to better understand their various needs and to get critical feedback on various prototypes that can thereby help ensure successful commercialization of new innovations. In sum, collaboration appears to be an important complement to competition when it comes to enhancing economic innovation. Thus, it is hardly surprising that from the late 1970s onward, R&D collaborations at both the national and international levels have been growing sharply (Powell and Grodal 2004, 57).

That business economists highlighted the role of collaboration for enhancing innovation is important because the public sector cannot exploit the innovation potential of competitive pressures in the same way that private markets can. The public sector is a large-scale bureaucracy that in most cases has a regulatory monopoly and is the sole provider of particular goods and services. NPM reforms have introduced a series of market-inspired arrangements in the public sector such as contracting out public services and offering the free choice of service providers. In most countries, however, competition in the field of public service delivery is still limited, with several constraints on the formation of quasi-markets in the public sector (Le Grand and Bartlett 1993; Mackintosh 1997). First of all, many public services in the area of education and social care do not lend themselves to contracting out because their high asset specificity makes it difficult to define what should be purchased and to compare price and quality. Second, given that the public quasi-markets are often relatively small in size, private contractors (with the military industry as a notable exception) do not consider them particularly lucrative. These factors limit the potential number of for-profit providers and thus the competition among them. Third, the transactions costs of preparing, initiating, and regulating service contracts with private firms are often considerable. Last but not least, social habits, geographical proximity, and community bonds rather than price and quality often end up determining the citizens' choice of service providers. For example, many parents with a free school choice send their children to the local school rather than sending them to a better one farther away because they know the school well, it is close by, and the other neighborhood kids go there. The limits to the recent attempts to enhance the role of market arrangements in the public sector mean that competition is unlikely to establish itself as the key driver of public innovation.

Alongside the recent effort to enhance competition, since the 1990s we have witnessed an astonishing proliferation of interorganizational collaboration through networks, partnerships, joined-up government, and the use of project organization and task forces. Sometimes the different kinds of networks are formed to overcome the institutional fragmentation caused by New Public Management (Rhodes 1997), while at other times they are established to solve ill-defined problems that cut across the boundaries of organizations, sectors, and policy domains (Koppenjan and Klijn 2004). Some scholars see the proliferation of interorganizational networks as part of the new public administration paradigm known as New Public Governance (Osborne 2009). As we shall see, the collaborative interaction between public and private actors in different kinds of networks carries a huge potential for public innovation. How public managers and other relevant stakeholders, supported by favorable initial conditions and an appropriate institutional design, can realize this potential is the key question in the new and growing literature on collaborative innovation in the public sector (Eggers and Singh 2009; Bommert 2010; Bason 2010; Steelman 2010; Bekkers, Edelenbos, and Steijn 2011; Ansell and Torfing 2014).

This chapter situates the new focus on collaborative innovation in the public sector in the context of the recent debate on public governance, interactive governance, and network governance. The first section considers and explains the surge of the governance debate and the growing interest in interactive forms of governance through partnerships and networks. The second section explores the new research on governance networks that in the last decades has moved from the initial discovery of networks, via the analysis of the forms and functions of governance networks, to assessments of the normative outcomes in terms of effective governance, democratic governance, and public innovation. The third section claims that governance networks can be seen as institutional arenas of multi-actor collaboration and discusses what collaboration actually means. Section 4 presents a set of analytical propositions that show how collaboration can enhance public innovation. The link between collaboration and public innovation is further sustained through some recent empirical results, and different strategies for organizing collaborative innovation are identified. To enhance our understanding of the scope of conditions for collaborative innovation, section 5 presents examples of when collaboration fails to foster innovation. The chapter concludes with a discussion of the relative importance of collaborative innovation vis-à-vis other methods of public innovation.

THE SURGE OF GOVERNANCE, INTERACTIVE GOVERNANCE, AND GOVERNANCE NETWORKS

Since the early 1990s, the debate on governance has been growing (Pierre 2000). With more than 100 million hits in a recent Internet search, "governance" is one of today's most frequently used social science terms. The concept of governance appeals to both researchers and practitioners as it offers a new perspective on an emerging reality in which governments seem to have lost their alleged monopoly on public policymaking and service production and the governing of society and the economy is largely a result of multilateral action involving a host of public and private actors in a large array of interactive governance arrangements.

Traditionally students of political science and public administration have focused on the formal institutions of government and described the linkages among voters, elected politicians, government officials, public managers, street-level bureaucrats, and citizens in terms of a chain of principal-agent relations. The voters delegate power to and control the elected assembly, and it, in turn, controls the government, which is in charge of the large-scale public bureaucracies that provide regulation and deliver goods and services to citizens and private firms. Although the formal institutions of government and its elaborate system of delegation, steering, and control continue to play a vital role in structuring public policy processes and service production, it has become increasingly clear that the formulation and implementation of public policy in most cases involve complex, decentered, and multilayered processes in which a large number of social and political actors interact in formal and informal arenas and across multiple levels, organizational boundaries, and policy areas. As the classical notion of *government* fails to capture this multifarious, messy, and potentially chaotic process, the notion of *governance* has emerged as a broad concept for understanding the different ways that society and the economy are steered and regulated through collective action and in accordance with common objectives (Torfing et al. 2012). Governance in the generic sense of collective steering processes can take many different forms and thus may include unicentric forms of government, multicentric forms of market steering, and pluricentric forms of interactive governance (Kersbergen and Waarden 2004).

Interactive forms of governance have received growing attention in the research literature because it is widely recognized that many problems and challenges call for multilateral action and collaborative interaction (Roberts 2000; Koppenjan and Klijn 2004). Public authorities alone cannot enhance public safety in deprived neighborhoods, generate economic growth in rural districts, fight AIDS problems in Africa, prevent obesity in children, or reduce pollution in watersheds. Solving these kinds of wicked and unruly problems and meeting pressing challenges such as confronting climate change, reducing poverty, and providing state-of-the-art health care require mobilizing and exploiting the knowledge, resources, and energies of a plurality of social and political actors through sustained interaction. Governments at different levels must collaborate with a large array of private actors to exchange and pool resources, generate new ideas, and enhance their legitimacy and operational reach.

Fortunately, and contributing to the growth of interactive forms of governance, we are witnessing an increasing empowerment of citizens, private firms, and associations that are eager to influence and contribute to public policymaking and service production. As the general level of education rises, many citizens are monitoring the performance of the public sector and are willing to help boost it because they want to improve their living conditions and their quality of life. Regarding implications for civic engagement, Putnam (2000) has warned us about the apparent collapse of social capital due to the increasing individualization that makes us "bowl alone" rather than together. However, indications are that the ego-centered 1990s are giving way to an intense search for strong communities and meaningful action that seem to encourage civic engagement (Putnam, Feldstein, and Cohen 2003). At the same time, interest organizations and civil society associations are growing and becoming increasingly professionalized and thus more capable of engaging in a permanent dialogue with public authorities in finding new and better solutions. Private firms have huge capacities, and many of them are prepared to assume greater social responsibility for their employees, the local community, and society at large. Also a proliferation of private think tanks and consultancy firms now are actively engaged in public problem solving, and many academics are politically engaged and involved in advising governments and public authorities at different levels. Thus, public agencies can work with committed and resourceful private partners to solve the problems and challenges that they face. Moreover, the development and dissemination of new information and communication technologies and social media facilitate a fast and flexible way of circulating ideas and an intense and sustained dialogue among the public and private partners.

Interactive governance can be defined as *the complex process through which social and political actors with diverging interests interact in order to formulate, promote, and achieve common objectives through the mobilization, exchange, and pooling of different ideas, rules, and resources* (Torfing et al. 2012). Interactive governance is complex, for one, because it involves many different actors who contact each other and communicate in multiple ways and with shifting intensities and frequencies. Its complexity also arises from the often great uncertainty about the substantial issues at stake in the policy process, the commitment and preferences of the actors, and the relative importance of different policy arenas (Koppenjan and Klijn 2004). Complexity is further enhanced by the presence of more or less ambiguous institutional rules, norms, and procedures that facilitate and constrain the interaction of the various actors in different and unpredictable ways. Finally, the degree of complexity is augmented by the endogenous character of information, preferences, and ground rules that are reinterpreted and transformed as a result of social and political conflicts and through processes of mutual learning (March and Olsen 1995).

The preceding definition of interactive governance captures a large array of interactive governance arrangements such as quasi-markets based on relational contracts, public-private partnerships, and governance networks (Torfing et al. 2012). We focus here on the role of governance networks; it seems to have grown at all levels of government, in all parts of the policy process, and in most policy areas (Heffen, Kickert, and Thomassen 2000; Hajer and Wagenaar 2003; Marcussen and Torfing 2007; Heinrich, Lynn, and Milward 2010). The surge of governance networks does not necessarily reduce the traditional forms of bureaucratic regulation and service provision that continue to play a vital role in the public sector. Governance networks proliferate in a plus-sum game with the traditional forms of governance and emerge where old-style bureaucracy or new forms of market governance are failing or where they are deemed to be inappropriate for solving the task or problem at hand.

A *governance network* can be defined as *a horizontal articulation of interdependent but operationally autonomous actors who interact through negotiations that take place within a relatively institutionalized framework and facilitate self-regulated policymaking in the shadow of hierarchy* (Sørensen and Torfing 2007). The driving force behind the formation of governance networks is the resource dependency of the social and political actors. This resource dependency can be more or less symmetric, but the network actors all recognize that they need something that the other actors have: knowledge, ideas, competences, authority, or money. Accordingly, the network actors exchange and/or pool their resources to solve problems and meet challenges that they are not able to handle on their own. However, the actors remain operationally autonomous as the network cannot force them to think or act in certain ways, and they are free to exit the network if they wish. The network actors thus engage in negotiations that combine elements of strategic bargaining based on well-defined interests and elements of open-ended deliberation that aim to construct both definitions of common problems and joint solutions. When they join the network, the social and political actors each have their own rules and resources, but over time they usually develop a joint set of rules, norms, values, and discourses that guide their interactions, create integration and cohesion, and help them reduce and manage uncertainty and contingency.

While stable interaction in the network tends to facilitate self-regulated policymaking and service delivery, its capacity for self-regulation is limited because network governance always takes place in the shadow of hierarchy (Scharpf 1994). Public authorities and other resourceful and legitimate actors shape the conditions for empowered self-regulation in governance networks, but they also threaten to take control if the governance network does not deliver what it is supposed to deliver. The final result of the regulated self-regulation in governance networks, in a broad sense, is the production of public value: visions, plans, scenarios, initiatives, policy solutions, standards, regulations, resource allocations, and services.

Applying the preceding definition of governance networks in empirical analysis reveals different types of governance networks that are distinguished by the main functions that they are undertaking. For example, some networks aim to facilitate cooperation through knowledge sharing. Other networks enhance coordination in order to avoid having incompatible and duplicated projects and initiatives and to create synergies that facilitate achieving overlapping objectives. Some networks may even enable collaboration by crafting joint definitions and solutions of emerging problems and formulating a common strategy for how to meet particular challenges or to exploit new opportunities. Indeed, many governance networks are struggling to combine elements of cooperation, coordination, and collaboration (Keast, Brown, and Mandell 2007).

The forms that governance networks might take also vary. Some networks are mandated from above while others grow naturally from below, driven by the recognition of interdependency and the need for interaction. Some networks are formal and relatively closed in terms of access and membership, while others are informal and relatively open. While some networks are short lived and cease to exist when the task is done, others are relatively permanent and constantly invent new tasks for themselves. In addition, governance networks might vary in terms of their composition. Some networks are formed within public organizations (intra-organizational networks), between public organizations (joined-up government), or between public and private actors (policy networks).

Last but not least, governance networks often carry different labels. They are referred to as councils, consortia, pacts, committees, commissions, strategic partnerships, planning cells, collaboratives, and think tanks. Governance networks are not always called networks, but according to the definition presented earlier, interactive forms of governance that are labeled in different ways often qualify as governance networks.

GOVERNANCE NETWORKS: DISCOVERED, ANALYZED, AND ASSESSED

In the literature on public policymaking, the notion of networks began to appear in the late 1960s and early 1970s (Kenis and Schneider 1991). Both pluralist and neo-corporatist theories of policymaking began describing the relationships between politicians, administrative agencies, and organized interests in terms of networks (Bentley 1967; Rokkan 1969; Schmitter and Lehmbruch 1979). Whereas the shortcoming of pluralist theory was its failure to understand the privileged and hierarchical role of the state and the restricted and selective access of organized interests, the limitation of neo-corporatism was its narrow focus on the tight and often personal relationships between major social, political, and administrative actors in particular policy areas. In sharp contrast to the elitist focus on small and exclusive networks, commonly referred to as "iron triangles," Heclo (1978) discovered the formation and spread of "issue networks" that consist of a large number of loosely coupled social, political, and administrative actors and that provide a new, informal policy formulation and coordination structure supplementing the formal institutions of government. Later on, public administration scholars in the United States used the notion of networks to analyze the role and impact of different kinds of implementation networks (Provan and Milward 1995; Meier and O'Toole 2001, 2003). This literature is important as it shows that networks not only facilitate interest mediation in policy formulation processes but also play a broader role in governance processes by facilitating communication and coordination.

Some European scholars have maintained the original focus on public policy formulation. For example, British scholars have primarily concentrated on the form, functioning, and impact of policy networks (Marsh and Rhodes 1992; Marsh 1998). They have also analyzed the role of networks in facilitating governance in the increasingly differentiated polities where public regulations and services are delivered by a large number of special-purpose agencies, private contractors, and civil society organizations (Rhodes 1997). Further, German, Dutch, and Danish scholars have seen networks as a new mode of governance that helps solve complex problems in modern societies (Marin and Mayntz 1991; Mayntz 1993a, 1993b; Scharpf 1994; Kickert, Klijn, and Koppenjan 1997; Kooiman 2003; Sørensen and Torfing 2007).

The study of governance networks not only has become fashionable in the field of public policymaking but also has caught on in a number of adjacent social science disciplines. The recent studies of multilevel governance aim to analyze the vertical and horizontal networks that link social and political actors in federalist and nonfederalist systems (Bache and Flinders 2004; Scharpf 2001). International relations theorists problematize the realist paradigm that tends to give nation-states a privileged role in international politics, and they have begun to explore the role of advocacy coalitions, epistemic communities, and transnational networks that bring together a host of governmental and nongovernmental actors (Haas 1992; Sabatier and Jenkins-Smith 1993; Djelic and Sahlin-Andersson 2006). Theories of collaborative planning see planning as a result of interactive forms of governance based on power sharing, relationship building, empowered participation, mobilization of local knowledge, and processes of mutual learning (Healey 1997, 2007; Booher and Innes 2010). The long-standing research on the interaction between science, technology, and society emphasizes the role of networks, partnerships, and deliberative forums in facilitating dialogue among government, industry, universities, civil society organizations, and lay actors (Callon, Lascoumes, and Barthe 2001; Banthien, Jaspers, and Renner 2003). Organizational studies are no longer analyzing organizations as closed or open systems; instead, they are focusing on the interorganizational relationships through which information and resources are exchanged (Benson 1978; Aldrich 1979; and DiMaggio and Powell 1983). Last but not least, business economists analyze how interfirm coordination is achieved in and through organic, informal governance networks (Jones, Hesterly, and Borgatti 1997). This brief overview of the new research literature demonstrates the cross-disciplinary relevance of the study of governance networks.

After the empirical discovery of governance networks that was theoretically supported by different strands of neo-institutionalist theory (Sørensen and Torfing 2007), the new research on governance networks began to explore the relationship between networks, hierarchies, and markets. It also aimed to determine the factors explaining the apparent surge and proliferation of governance networks in different countries and at multiple levels. Finally, it engaged in empirical studies of the role and impact of governance networks in different countries and policy domains and at different levels of governance. Let us briefly look at these three new elements of the governance debate.

In the early days of governance network studies, researchers commonly viewed governance networks as a hybrid of hierarchies and markets (Powell 1991; Mayntz 1993a, 1993b; Scharpf 1994). Governance networks were praised for their ability to combine the authority of public hierarchies with the flexibility of private markets. More recently governance networks have been depicted as a distinct alternative to both hierarchies and markets (Jessop 2002). Governance networks are arenas of pluricentric interaction based on varying degrees of collaboration, and they tend to involve multiple interdependent actors from the state, the market, and civil society. Therefore, governance networks are considered a new mode of governance alongside unicentric hierarchies in which one actor is authorized to make binding decisions and rule through imposition and multicentric markets with an almost infinite number of autonomous actors (Kersbergen and Waarden 2004).

As mentioned earlier, there has been a huge interest in trying to explain the recent surge in the role of governance networks for public policymaking. Some explanations refer to the functional differentiation of society and the fragmentation of the public sector caused by New Public Management, which has allegedly generated an urgent need for the formation of crosscutting governance networks (Mayntz 1993a, 1993b; Rhodes 1997). Other explanations focus on the increasing complexity of policy problems that force social and political actors to exchange different kinds of knowledge and expertise (Kickert, Klijn, and Koppenjan 1997; Agranoff 2007). Arguments about how governance networks can enhance civic participation in order to increase the input and output legitimacy of public policymaking have also been frequent (Scharpf 1999; Grote and Gbikpi 2002; Skelcher and Torfing 2010). Last but not least, a crucial factor in spurring the rise of network governance seems to be the general shift in the collective and institutionalized ways of thinking about how to govern and be governed (Dean 1999). Governmental ideas, technologies, and rationalities favoring governance through regulated self-regulation tend to supplant the traditional forms of bureaucratic steering and replace the neoliberal celebration of the merits of free and unfettered markets (Sørensen and Triantafillou 2009).

Perhaps most important, the discovery of governance networks has led to a large number of empirical studies that analyzed the role and impact of governance networks in different national contexts and policy areas and at different levels (Marsh and Rhodes 1992; Marsh 1998; Heffen, Kickert, and Thomassen 2000; Hajer and Wagenaar 2003; Agranoff 2007; Marcussen and Torfing 2007; Provan and Kenis 2008). These empirical studies identify the key participants in governance networks, analyze the structure and mode of their interaction, reflect on the role of conflicts and power struggles in the production of negotiated policy solutions and service delivery, and explore the causal links between leadership and management and between network structure and governance performance.

Since the early 2000s, the research on governance networks has gradually shifted its attention from focusing on internal dynamics and policy impact to assessing normative outcomes. Governance networks may bring together a plurality of actors in deliberative processes that influence public policies, but what is actually achieved by relying on governance networks rather than on hierarchies and markets? This question has triggered a growing interest in analyzing the contribution of governance networks to effective and democratic governance of modern societies (Provan and Milward 2001; Benz and Papadopoulos 2006; Edelenbos, Steijn, and Klijn 2010; Sørensen and Torfing 2009; Warren 2009). The mobilization and exchange of knowledge and resources, the crafting of joint solutions that go beyond the least common denominator, and a flexible and continuous adjustment of new regulations and services can help improve the efficiency and effectiveness of public policymaking. Likewise, the inclusion and empowered participation of relevant and affected actors in processes of democratic deliberation may help democratize society (Fung and Wright 2003), but crucial challenges still exist in terms of biased participation, the predominance of a few strong actors, and the lack of transparency and accountability.

Whereas business economics has been very interested in exploring the link between governance networks and economic innovation (Weber 2003; Powell and Grodal 2004; Gloor 2005), as mentioned previously, it has shown little interest in the governance network literature for how governance networks can help spur public innovation (for important exceptions, see Dente, Bobbio, and Spada 2005; Hartley 2005; Eggers and Singh 2009). The contribution of governance networks to complex problem solving and policy development has been analyzed, but few explicit attempts have been made to link governance networks with public innovation. This is surprising. It seems so obvious that the capacity of a network of different, competent, and resourceful actors to reframe problems, generate new learning, develop bold and creative ideas, and select and implement the most promising solutions through converted action will often be considerably larger than the capacities of the insulated and compartmentalized public bureaucracies and the private markets, both of which are driven by such fierce competition that the actors are forced to give priority to short-term gains.

Governance networks may facilitate collaborative processes that will spur innovation, but governance networks are precarious social and political constructs that are rife with uncertainties and conflicts and often have a low degree of institutionalization (O'Toole 1997). Thus, governance networks might fail not only to enhance effective and democratic governance but also to promote innovation in public policies, organizations, and services where the preservation of the status quo is unacceptable and new and better solutions are needed. To counter the inherent risk of failure, the research on governance networks has insisted that public authorities and other resourceful actors need to metagovern governance networks by facilitating, managing, and directing the networked interactions in respect for their capacity for self-regulation and without reverting to traditional hierarchical forms of command and control (Jessop 2002; Kooiman 2003; Sørensen and Torfing 2007, 2009; Torfing et al. 2012). As metagovernance plays a crucial role in realizing the innovative potential of governance networks, we further discuss the concept and practices of metagovernance in chapter 9.

GOVERNANCE NETWORKS AS ARENAS FOR MULTI-ACTOR COLLABORATION

Governance networks are institutionalized patterns of interaction between public and private actors who may choose to collaborate in finding solutions to common problems. Sometimes the networked interaction merely provides a tool for exchanging information or coordinating action across different organizations and sectors, but it may also construct an arena for collaboration by creating the institutional conditions for different actors to join forces and cocreate public policies and services. Although some actors may join a particular governance network to prevent or obstruct a collective action that goes against their interests, the majority of the participants in governance networks can be expected to engage in a constructive management of differences and find a common ground for solving multiparty problems (Gray 1989). Actors often form or join networks when they realize that they cannot solve a particular problem or challenge alone because they do not have the necessary knowledge, skills, and resources. Some of the stronger actors may try to create their own solution to a joint problem and realize it through imposition. Such a unilateral strategy will not only encounter several constraints imposed by the other actors in the field but also create unwanted consequences for the other actors (Gray 1989, 1). The inevitable result is the development of conflicts. While the actors may choose to fight them, an adversarial approach to conflict resolution is often extremely costly and generates unsatisfactory outcomes and long-lasting mistrust, whereas a collaborative approach paves the way for win-win solutions and promotes trust and positive future relationships (Gray 1989, 50).

Consequently, governance networks tend to provide a collaborative alternative to command-driven public hierarchies and competitive private markets. In public bureaucracies higher-level agencies and managers govern lower-level agencies and street-level bureaucrats directly through budget allocations and regulatory rules and indirectly through formulating goals, norms, standards, and performance indicators. Sometimes the lower administrative levels in public bureaucracies are consulted and asked to provide information and feedback to the upper levels, but the formal differences in position and rank between the principals and their agents—at least outside those networked governance arenas that are deliberately established to level out these formal differences—often preclude proper collaboration.

In private markets, competition between sellers and buyers of goods and services is sustained by rules that aim to ensure free market access, full information about price and quality, fair and proper market conduct, and the honoring of contracts. The market actors compete fiercely with each other to sell or buy goods and services of a certain quality at the highest or lowest price, respectively. Buyers and sellers might negotiate the terms of market contracts with each other, but the negotiations tend to be short and episodic for two reasons: Prices are fixed, and dissatisfied buyers and sellers quickly move on to find alternative suppliers and customers who are perfectly substitutable. Collaboration among firms by forming strategic alliances and collaboration among customers by developing local retail cooperatives tend to endure and have a great potential for spurring innovation. Such collaboration, however, is not intrinsic to the competitive market logic and tends to reduce the internal competition among the buyers and the sellers.

By contrast, the interdependent relationships upon which governance networks are founded not only facilitate cooperation and coordination but also spur processes of collaboration. Hence, when actors recognize their mutual dependence and perceive the costs of sustaining a long-lasting conflict with an uncertain outcome, the probability that they will choose a collaborative strategy is high, especially if such collaboration is supported by a certain level of trust, by positive experiences with prior collaboration, and by rules, norms, and incentives ensuring reciprocity between the participants (Ansell and Gash 2007).

The horizontal relationships in governance networks are often asserted to be an important precondition for developing collaborative practices. Although the assertion is correct, the argument in support of this assertion is sometimes misconstrued. Hence, "horizontal" is often assumed to refer to the presence of a relatively even distribution of power resources in governance networks, and the symmetric power relationships are then supposed to create a situation in which the actors are eager to collaborate because they all have a fair chance of influencing the joint solutions. However, both the premise and the argument are wrong (Lake and Wong 2009). Governance networks are only horizontal in the sense that no single network actor has the formal authority to settle disputes that might emerge during the interaction. Plenty of power asymmetries exist in governance networks, but they do not seem to prevent collaboration. Indeed, the strong and resourceful actors are forced to show restraint when exercising their powers because the weaker actors might leave the network if they are bullied. Participation is for the most part voluntary, and continued participation is predicated on a positive evaluation of the interaction and the results it will help produce.

The goal of multi-actor collaboration typically is to build some degree of consensus about the problem or challenge at hand and the way it can be addressed (Ansell and Gash 2007, 5). However, the prevalence of conflicting interests and the absence of a common set of substantive values and procedural norms mean that collaborative arenas are frequently unable to reach a complete consensus, or unanimous support for a solution that satisfies and reflects the views of all stakeholders. When a seemingly unanimous consensus is reached, a closer inspection will reveal that the scope and ambition of the joint solution are limited and that controversial aspects are left out in order to secure support. Collaboration seldom leads to complete disagreement, however, because the actors may at least agree to disagree on some key issues while continuing to explore the prospect of agreeing on a solution that is better than what the conflict management literature refers to as the "best alternative to a negotiated agreement" (see Booher and Innes 2010). Thus, collaboration seems to move along a continuum from consensus to conflict without ever reaching the polar extremes of total consensus and total conflict.

Following this line of argument, we might view collaboration as a process through which a plurality of actors aim to arrive at a common definition of problems and challenges, manage conflicts in a constructive way, and find joint solutions based on provisional agreements that may coexist with varying degrees of disagreement and dissent. Collaboration involves forming a collective will through exercising political and moral-intellectual leadership (Gramsci 1971). Collective wills are shaped by seeking out areas of agreement and expanding these areas by offering new and persuasive redescriptions of the world that make a particular view look plausible and acceptable. The actors in this process interact with each other, explore and negotiate their differences, and search for solutions that go beyond their own limited vision of what is desirable and possible (Gray 1989, 5). They eventually come to an agreement about a certain set of issues, ideas, and options while disagreeing in other respects. Some actors might dissent and choose not to be a part of the agreement, and those actors who do participate might have different degrees of commitment, with some being strong supporters and others being slightly frustrated and plotting to challenge and change the content of the agreement at a later stage.

While the conception of collaboration as a process aiming to establish some kind of agreement in the face of persistent disagreement and dissent helps us to avoid conflating collaboration with total harmony and consensus, we should be careful not to miss the productive and transformative aspects of the notion of collaboration. The literal meaning of collaboration is "to work together." Hence, Roberts and Bradley (1991, 212) are right in pointing out the transmutational purpose of collaborative arenas, their explicit and voluntary membership, and the organization and temporal character of the interactive process. They combine these elements when they define collaboration as "a temporary social arrangement in which two or more actors work together towards a singular common end requiring the transmutation of materials, ideas and/or social relations to achieve that end" (212). The problem with this definition is that it does not address how actors with different ideas, opinions, and interests arrive at a "*singular* common end" (212, my emphasis) and whether they will all agree on this common end without any grievances and points of discontent. That being said, undoubtedly the productive aspect of collaboration is important—not least in relation to innovation—therefore, we should incorporate the transformative dimension in the conceptualization of collaboration presented earlier. In this book, we shall thus define *collaboration* as *a temporal process through which a plurality of actors work together in an organized way to transform problems and opportunities into joint solutions that rest on provisional agreements that are formed despite the persistence of various forms of dissent.* This definition both captures the productive aspect of collaboration and avoids conflating collaboration with complete harmony.

To further clarify the notion of collaboration, we should emphasize that collaboration involves more than consultation and responsiveness. Public agencies might consult other agencies or use consultative techniques such as stakeholder surveys and focus groups to elicit the views of private firms, nongovernmental organizations, or citizens, but that is not collaboration in a strict sense of the term. Collaboration involves a direct, two-way communication and a deliberative process through which a common object is defined, worked out, and transformed (Ansell and Gash 2007). Likewise, although responsiveness is a cherished norm that supports collaborative efforts, collaboration cannot be reduced to the kind of market-driven responsiveness to shifting demands that New Public Management promotes. Collaboration involves a direct engagement with citizens as "partners" rather than an indirect assessment of their needs as "customers" (Vigoda-Gadot 2002).

Finally, collaboration is not used in the negative sense of "collusion," as in working with the enemy. Rather, the term is used in the positive sense to describe a process that people use when working together to solve problems or to exploit new opportunities by making and implementing decisions through joint interaction (Straus 2002).

COLLABORATIVE INNOVATION IN THE PUBLIC SECTOR

Governance networks may limit themselves to knowledge sharing and attempts to enhance pluricentric coordination, but network actors will often want to go a step further and turn networks into arenas for interagency and cross-sector collaboration. Indeed, collaborative problem solving might be the key purpose of forming and participating in a governance network. The collaborative aspect of governance networks is important because multi-actor collaboration stimulates public innovation. The strenuous attempt to integrate the views and opinions of different actors tends to produce a synergistic and creative result that would be impossible for the participants to achieve on their own (Straus 2002). Therefore, collaborative forms of network governance are potent levers for the innovation of policy, organization, and service in the public sector. The argument in support of this claim is that each of the constitutive phases in the innovation cycle can be strengthened through collaboration between relevant and affected actors from the public and/or private sector (Bommert 2010, 22–23). The argument rests on five propositions that are introduced here and further elucidated in the following chapters.

First, the *understanding and framing of problems and challenges in need of innovation* are enhanced when the knowledge, experiences, and assessments of actors with different backgrounds and vantage points are aggregated and integrated. The competing problem definitions are then scrutinized and assessed in and through collective processes of reflection and sense making.

Second, the *generation of new and creative ideas* is spurred when a joint momentum for change has been generated, and different ideas, views, and suggestions are circulated, challenged, merged, expanded, and transformed through institutionalized processes of collaboration. These processes bring together empowered actors and facilitate the mutual, reflexive, and transformative learning that challenges habituated practices, common wisdom, and the identity of the actors.

Third, the *selecting, prototyping, and testing of the most promising ideas* are improved when actors with different perspectives and forms of knowledge participate in a joint and cross-disciplinary assessment of the content, feasibility, and potential gains and risks of competing ideas, options, and solutions and their practical embodiment and application. Hence, including a greater number and variety of actors in the selection phase is likely to increase the chance of avoiding "group think" (Bommert 2010, 23). In addition, collaborative interaction facilitates compromise and agreement, thus preventing stalemates and mitigating the role of veto players.

Next, *implementing the selected ideas, options, and solutions* is enhanced when collaboration creates joint ownership of new and bold solutions and spreads the inherent risks to a larger group of actors, thus reducing implementation resistance. Collaboration in the implementation phase also helps to mobilize resources, draw on specialized competences, make fast and flexible adjustments, and compensate eventual losers through a negotiated redistribution of costs and benefits.

Finally, the *dissemination of innovative practices* in the public sector is propelled by collaboration and knowledge sharing in social and professional networks. Networks with strong ties have a short and narrow reach but facilitate close communication and strong mutual support. Networks with weak ties have a longer and wider reach that enables dissemination of new ideas, but at the same time having a smaller bandwidth may hamper communication (Granovetter 1973).

The positive impact of collaboration on innovation is confirmed not only in studies of innovation in private firms (Powell and Grodal 2004) but also in empirical analyses of public sector innovation. A meta-analysis of studies of organizational innovation shows that a high degree of diversity among the involved actors, the dispersion of power, and both internal and external communication have a positive impact on innovation in both public and private organizations (Damanpour 1991). Apparently a variety of specialists broadens the knowledge base and facilitates the cross-fertilization of ideas. The dispersion of power in participatory arenas enhances the involvement and commitment of key actors, and internal and external communication facilitates the exchange of ideas and the dissemination of innovative solutions.

Another quantitative study supporting the relevance of the concept of collaborative innovation is Borins's (1998, 2001b) analysis of all the semi-finalists in the Innovations in American Government Award program between 1990 and 1994. His analysis shows that 29 percent of the government agencies whose innovation projects reached the semifinals reported that they coordinated with other organizations to deal with a problem that they sought to solve in an innovative way. In 28 percent of the innovation projects, a formalized public-private partnership was observed (Borins 1998, 19–29). A recent follow-up study comparing the semifinalists of 1990–94 with all of the 2010 applicants to the award program finds that the proportion of innovation projects with external interorganizational collaboration has increased from 28 percent to 65 percent, and the proportion of innovation projects concerning collaboration within government has increased from 60 percent to 80 percent (Borins 2014). The study also reports that both shared and overall funding of the participating innovation projects have increased and that the innovation agenda has expanded in every policy area.

Several qualitative studies confirm the positive impact of stakeholder collaboration on the ability to find new and innovative solutions in the public sector. A single US case study conducted by Roberts and Bradley (1991) shows that collaboration has a positive impact on policy innovation. Having failed to pass a new law about open enrollment in public schools, the governor of a state convened a group of representatives of the twenty-four stakeholders and asked the members to produce a visionary statement for state education. The sustained collaboration, which lasted longer than a year, resulted in an innovative policy proposal that was less radical than the governor had hoped for because the stakeholders had been constrained by the constituencies they were representing. Nevertheless, the networked collaboration constructed a broad ownership to new ideas that helped to bring about policy reform.

Another US case study confirms the role of collaboration in spurring innovation (Steelman 2010, 70–100). Population growth in the state of Colorado has put an increasing pressure on open land, farmland, and wildlife habitat. However, in a setting with strong political concerns about maintaining private property rights, preserving the ability to find local solutions, and preventing the "overregulation" of land use, the scope for determining effective land protection was rather limited and risked gridlock. Nevertheless, an innovative policy solution fostered by a collaborative citizens' committee brought together business, conservation, and political leaders from across Colorado in a constructive and creative dialogue. The citizens' committee found a way to work around the constraints as it proposed, lobbied for, and won the voters' approval to establish a trust fund, Great Outdoors Colorado. Financed by a dedicated funding mechanism, it has enabled local governments and nonprofit land protection organizations to purchase, enhance, and protect land.

A comparative case study of urban development in large cities in northern Italy finds that urban planning has been much more innovative in Turin than in Milan (Dente, Bobbio, and Spada 2005). The difference in the innovative capacities of the two cities is explained by the higher diversity and density of Turin's urban governance network. Urban policy ideas in Turin were richer because a greater number of different actors were involved in the urban governance network. At the same time, Turin's urban governance network also had a greater ability to develop innovative solutions through mutual learning and compromise formation because the public and private actors were better and more intensely connected over a longer period. In sum, the sustained collaboration between diverse social and political actors fostered the innovative urban planning.

A comparative case study from Britain concludes that local authorities with weak interagency and stakeholder networks tend to have less extensive patterns of innovation (Newman, Raine, and Skelcher 2001). The empirical analysis shows that governance networks and partnerships are on the rise and that collaboration between public and private actors enhances public innovation. However, the significance of networks and partnerships as drivers of innovation tends to be conditioned by the political culture in local authority. Hence, interagency and stakeholder networks had a greater impact on the ability to innovate where they were strongly embedded at different organizational levels, where public agencies were highly receptive to new ideas, and where local authorities took a positive stance toward partnership agencies.

These studies support the idea that the multi-actor collaboration provides an important source of public innovation (see also Ansell and Torfing [2014] for further examples of collaborative innovation). Sometimes multi-actor collaboration will fail, and where it thrives, it still may not foster innovation. Nevertheless, it seems plausible to assume that collaboration between a great many public and private actors carries significant potential for bringing about public innovation. If so, we need to explore the different *strategies for collaboration* that public agencies and private actors can apply to spur public innovation. For this purpose, Eggers and Singh (2009) provide a helpful overview of five different collaborative strategies that can enhance public innovation.

1. *The cultivation strategy* aims to facilitate collaboration between different kinds of public employees by creating spaces for interaction outside but close to the daily operations. This approach allows the participants to exchange and develop new and promising ideas and to test them directly in their everyday working life.
2. *The replication strategy* strives to build collaborative relationships between public agencies within and across different levels and jurisdictions that help them identify, translate, adapt, and implement the most successful innovations of other public agencies.
3. *The partnership strategy* tries to help public agencies develop innovative solutions by collaborating with private partners who have access to new ideas and technologies, are willing to share gains and risks, are not bound by red tape and onerous rules, and, therefore, may serve as an incubator or testing ground for new and creative ideas and practices.

4. *The network strategy* endeavors to facilitate the exchange of ideas, mutual learning, and joint action through horizontal interaction between relevant and affected actors who have different kinds of resources and expertise.
5. *The crowdsourcing strategy* seeks to produce innovation by using the Internet to invite anonymous experts and lay actors from all over the world to share knowledge and cocreate innovative solutions through online interactions based on free and open access to relevant information and resources.

Despite their different forms and labels, all of these collaborative strategies are based on some kind of networked interaction among different groups of actors. The number and type of actors and the form and character of the collaborative arena may differ, but the basic idea in all five strategies is to facilitate collaborative interaction between different nodes in a network.

Obviously the choice between the different collaboration strategies, or between different combinations of these strategies, depends on the character of the task of innovation, the political and institutional context, and the experiences and capacities of the public and private actors involved. If there is a lack of trust between the public and private actors, then the public agencies might prefer the cultivation or replication strategy. If public actors are receptive to ideas from the private sector and there is a tradition of public-private collaboration, then they might choose the network or partnership strategy. Finally, if crafting an innovative solution requires input from a large number of unidentified specialists or lay actors, then they might try the crowdsourcing strategy.

WHEN COLLABORATION FAILS TO FOSTER INNOVATION

Depending on a mix of traditions, cultural norms, and context-sensitive calculations, a group of interdependent actors will choose whether to collaborate and, if the choice is affirmative, then adopt a particular collaborative strategy or combination of strategies. As argued, there are good reasons to expect that this collaboration will spur public innovation. However, just as relevant and affected actors do not always choose to collaborate, collaboration also might fail to produce public innovation. Hence, public and private stakeholders might interact, share information, coordinate their actions, and aim to craft new solutions to wicked problems without ever succeeding in developing and implementing any new ideas. Collaboration is premised on developing a common set of norms, values, and routines, as well as on a particular distribution of roles and identities among the actors, but these institutional conditions for collaboration are sometimes disrupted by the search for and adoption of innovative solutions that break with established ideas and practices. The collaborating actors might agree that innovation is called for but oppose concrete attempts to implement innovative solutions that problematize their norms and identities. In other words, the attempt to secure the conditions for a stable collaboration may actually prevent innovation. In addition, collaborating actors who aspire to build a broad consensus may want to avoid radical and disruptive innovations because they prevent inclusive agreements. Thus, we can conclude that there is no natural, necessary, or intrinsic link between collaboration and innovation. Indeed, in several situations, collaboration will not foster innovation.

Empirical analysis suggests that a group of actors engaging in repeated collaboration in a closed and stable network over time will develop a more or less uniform worldview that will tend to stifle creativity and prevent new ideas from emerging (Skilton and Dooley 2010). When public authorities seek collaborative solutions to complex policy problems, for example, they often call upon the "usual suspects," and when the same actors have collaborated several times, they tend to form a cognitive and normative frame of reference that prevents them from exploring new and different solutions that challenge the implicit logic of appropriate action. Here, social and cognitive closure prevents collaboration from generating innovative ideas and solutions. Including citizens and users in the collaborative process may lead to questioning and challenging the established beliefs of the usual bunch of public agencies and organized interests and thus help open up new avenues, but often these groups are too disempowered to make themselves heard in formal arenas of networked collaboration (Young 2000).

Furthermore, in collaborative settings, strong veto players who want to preserve the status quo or favor a different kind of solution that better serves their interests might prevent the selection of new and bold ideas. Other collaborators may accept the vetoing of innovative solutions that they themselves support to avoid damaging conflicts and to keep in the network those veto players who control valuable resources upon which the network depends. Mediated negotiation and facilitation of face-to-face dialogue might overcome such obstacles by seeking to establish common ground, but the kind of compromise that can be formed might not even come close to an innovative solution. Bold and controversial ideas might be eliminated in order to foster agreement. Compromise formation often involves playing it safe and agreeing on the least common denominator, and the content of the agreement will thus consist of undisputed and well-tested ideas.

Although networks are important tools for implementing public innovations, they may heighten uncertainty, and their incomplete institutionalization may hamper the implementation of innovative ideas (O'Toole 1997). Uncertainty about the goals, commitment, and actions of the social and political actors who are collaborating in a network will tend to lower the level of mutual trust and, in turn, may give the actors reasons to withhold key resources. Moreover, the absence of institutional routines, command structures, and accountability mechanisms can make implementing new and bold solutions a difficult and risky business.

Finally, diffusing innovative practices within or across public organizations can be prevented when "structural holes" in the group emerge, and actors who could benefit from communication and knowledge sharing are not connected (Burt 1992). In other cases, innovation is stifled when an insufficient degree of homophily exists among the actors, discouraging communication among those who feel they are too different from each other in terms of norms, education, and worldviews (Rogers 1995). Hence, the structure and composition of collaborative networks may hamper disseminating innovation solutions in the public sector.

As we have seen, the causal link between collaboration and innovation can be problematized in all parts of the innovation cycle. Hence, collaboration may or may not spur public innovation depending on the nature and character of the collaborative efforts and the way that they are framed and facilitated. Nevertheless, there are reasons to expect that networked collaboration will enhance public innovation. Collaboration carries a strong potential for doing so, and leaders and managers of collaborative processes will aim to realize this potential while trying to avoid or mitigate the likely problems.

COLLABORATION, COMPETITION, AND BUREAUCRATIC ROUTINES

Under the right circumstances, multi-actor collaboration provides an important source of public innovation, but it is not the only lever of public innovation.

Indeed, many of the public innovations in the last thirty to forty years were fostered either by public bureaucracies or by publicly sponsored markets in which private contractors competed to deliver goods and services. Hence, the European Commission's Innobarometer survey of public sector innovation in four thousand public organizations in twenty-seven European Union member countries reveals that 75 percent of the organizations in the sample claim that they develop innovations themselves, while 31 percent of them developed innovations with private business actors through public procurement (European Commission 2013).

Public bureaucracies are staffed by highly committed public employees who are driven by professional norms and ambitions that urge them both to search for new solutions to urgent societal problems and administrative challenges and to produce innovations. Public organizations also have stable procedures for periodic policy reviews and routinized performance management that enable them to respond to changing environments and emerging problems (March and Olsen 1989). Finally, the quest for legitimacy makes public organizations eager to adopt new and innovative practices as a result of pressures from higher-level agencies, pressures to imitate other successful organizations, and pressures to apply the latest skills and ideas of the newly educated and recently employed staff (DiMaggio and Powell 1983).

On top of the bureaucratic drivers of innovation, the recent expansion of quasi-markets in which private providers compete for contracts to produce and deliver public services of a certain quality and at a certain price may stimulate the development of new and innovative methods that can give the private providers a competitive edge (Lubienski 2009). Moreover, the public procurement of goods from the private sector tends to stimulate innovation as the private producers compete to deliver innovative products with improved designs and functionalities. Last but not least, the corporate management ideas from the private sector that creep into the public sector put much more emphasis on the public managers' ability to drive innovation in public organizations and service delivery.

Collaborative innovation supplements bureaucratic and market-driven innovation in the public sector. However, this book boldly takes this point one step further: Collaborative innovation also has a comparative advantage in that it helps to overcome some of the problems and weaknesses associated with public bureaucracies and the new quasi-markets.

The problems are that public bureaucracies are rigid, risk averse, and lacking incentives to innovate and that the quasi-markets are difficult to create and sustain in a cost-efficient way. A more fundamental problem, however, is that public bureaucracy, with its hierarchy, silos, and institutional insulation from wider society, fails to mobilize and create interaction between all the relevant ideas and actors and to build a joint ownership for new and bold solutions. Likewise, the basic problem with quasi-markets is that competition undermines the mutual trust that is needed to ensure the emergence and circulation of new, creative, and still untested ideas. Competition also gives priority to short-term gains over long-term concerns in the hunt for innovative solutions to complex policy problems.

Developing collaborative innovation compensates for the problems inherent in public bureaucracies and quasi-markets. Collaborative innovation facilitates trust-based interaction between relevant and affected actors who are committed to exploring and exploiting new and innovative solutions to complex problems because the actors recognize their mutual resource dependency. This comparative advantage justifies the attempt to advance collaborative innovation as an interdisciplinary research field that can help to provide a new and potent tool for reinvigorating the public sector. Such an endeavor should be informed by a theoretical framework that can guide our exploration of the intricacies of collaborative innovation. Chapter 3 takes the first steps in developing such a framework.

CONCLUSION

Public innovation is a tool for enhancing efficiency, improving quality, and solving wicked and unruly problems. This chapter has argued that multi-actor collaboration in networks, partnerships, and other forms of interactive governance is a key lever of public innovation. Collaboration strengthens all the different parts of the innovation cycle, and the networked character of collaborative innovation makes the recently developed theories of governance networks a crucial stepping-stone for developing a theoretical framework for analyzing processes of collaborative innovation in the public sector. The research on governance networks emerged in response to the growing recognition of the limits of hierarchical and market-based forms of governance but has hitherto neglected the role that collaborative forms of multi-actor interaction can play in spurring public innovation. There are different strategies for enhancing collaborative innovation and many examples of successful outcomes. Nevertheless, there is no guarantee that multi-actor collaboration will lead to innovative solutions, and innovators may sometimes rely on the hierarchies and markets to spur the development and implementation of innovative solutions. However, as this chapter has shown, when it comes to enhancing public innovation, both hierarchies and markets have some inherent limitations that a collaborative strategy for creative problem solving may help to overcome.

3

TOWARD A THEORY OF COLLABORATIVE INNOVATION

DESPITE THE URGENT NEED for innovative solutions in public policy, organizations, and service production, the study of public innovation is a relatively new and undeveloped endeavor, and the study of collaborative efforts to spur innovation in the public sector is even less developed. Empirical studies and experiences suggest that networked collaboration contributes to the enhancement of public innovation, but they also point to limits and constraints of collaborative innovation (Ansell and Torfing 2014). Nevertheless, there are very few theoretically informed studies of the processes, outcomes, and conditions of collaborative innovation in the public sector. Therefore, to advance collaborative innovation as a new field of research, and to deepen our knowledge about the conditions, drivers, and barriers of collaborative innovation, we need to develop a theoretical framework for studying collaborative innovation.

The goal here, however, is not to develop a comprehensive theory based on a few analytical assumptions from which a coherent set of hypotheses covering the key aspects of collaborative innovation can be derived. The attempt to elaborate such a theory not only would be premature but also would tend to be totalizing and reductionist and fail to appreciate the complexity and contingency of real-life processes that cannot be adequately described from a single theoretical vantage point. Therefore, at this point and in this book, the goal is to piece together an analytical framework that can help us ask some good and relevant research questions, conceptualize and categorize the main determinants in processes of collaborative innovation, and understand network-based collaboration and innovation processes. Given the complex and multifaceted character of collaborative innovation, the theoretical framework must necessarily be interdisciplinary. It must draw on insights from different kinds of theories to capture the ambiguities, dilemmas, and contradictions that emerge in the field of collaborative innovation.

This chapter takes the first steps in elaborating a theoretical framework for studying collaborative innovation in the public sector. Section 1 clarifies the role that theory might play in analyzing collaborative innovation. Section 2 then considers the inadequacy and limits of current public management theory, which would otherwise seem to provide an obvious starting point for analyzing collaborative innovation in the public sector. As we shall see, the real source of inspiration is found in other bodies of theory. Hence, section 3 reviews some important precursors to a theory of collaborative innovation and reflects on their theoretical contributions and weaknesses. The limitations of these precursors force us to look for and combine a range of different theoretical building blocks when piecing together a theoretical framework. These building blocks are briefly summarized in the fourth section. The final section draws on central insights from this theoretical inventory to sketch the contours of an analytical model that will inform the analysis presented in the remaining chapters of this book.

WHY DO WE NEED A THEORY?

As Lord John Maynard Keynes once claimed, "There is nothing more practical than a good theory." Theory helps us understand the world, define key concepts and categories, and ask interesting research questions that enable us to produce knowledge that goes beyond a singular case or event. It provides an analytical lens that brings certain things into focus, shapes our preunderstanding of what is going on, and helps us categorize, analyze, and interpret empirical data. Theory also enables us to determine, and even sometimes explain, the connections between different observations and incidents. In short, theory helps us avoid *impressionistic descriptivism*, which is the fallacy of believing that a genuine understanding of the world can be achieved through an unmediated description of empirical facts and personal impressions. However, we also should beware of falling into the opposite trap of *theoretical reductionism*, which is the fallacy of subsuming a complex and rich reality to a pre-given theoretical scheme by way of reduction, thus producing an unrecognizable caricature of the processes through which situated actors interpret, reproduce, and transform social structures.

To avoid the Scylla of impressionist descriptivism and the Charybdis of theoretical reductionism, we must adopt a retroductive approach to the study of politics, administration, and society. Whereas the *inductive approach* to social inquiry aims to identify general patterns on the basis of observing singular empirical cases and to use these patterns to develop theoretical stipulations, the *deductive approach* aims to test theoretically deduced hypotheses with empirical data. In contrast to both of these approaches, the *retroductive approach* seeks answers to specific, contextual problems through an iterative process that combines theoretical insights and empirical findings in a way that modifies both (Howarth and Glynos 2007). Such problem-driven research rejects the false choice between data- and theory-driven approaches and insists that the task of scientific research is to answer important and relevant questions through theoretically informed studies of empirical findings. Ideally the research problems should be rooted in puzzles, anomalies, critical investigations, and societal needs, and they should be answered through a pragmatic articulation of theoretical and empirical reflections that aim to modify both in the pursuit of new insights. In this process, theory becomes a tool for crafting specific understandings and explanations and for answering problems that are important to researchers as well as practitioners. Theory provides concepts, analytical categories, and pre-understandings that guide empirical analysis, but the initial concepts, categories, and understandings are challenged and transformed in the course of the investigation.

The choice of a problem-driven approach to the study of collaborative innovation in the public sector immediately throws up a question about which problems we should try to answer. Both practical experiences from the public sector and scientific studies of empirical cases identify stumbling blocks and generate unexpected results that raise problems for further investigation. In the field of public innovation studies, we can distinguish different sets of problems related to different phases and aspects of the collaborative innovation process.

One set of problems relates to the question about *what triggers processes of collaborative innovation*. Both routines and shocks seem to be able to foster collaborative attempts to find new and innovative solutions, but as not all routines and shocks result in collaborative innovation, we need to dig deeper to uncover its triggering causes. The hunch is that collaborative innovation is stimulated by particular discursively constructed problematizations of existing practices and that past experiences sedimented into a perceived "tradition," norm-based calculations, and certain dramaturgical aspects of the governance process likely play a key role in bringing actors together and creating a joint quest or search process that spurs public innovation.

Another set of problems is concerned with *how the relevant actors are mobilized and empowered and how their collaborative interaction is ensured and institutionalized*. First of all, recruiting and mobilizing all the relevant actors needed in processes of collaborative innovation are not easy. In addition, while some actors must become empowered in order to participate in collaborative processes and use their knowledge and experiences to create new and bold solutions, other actors need to be disempowered so that they will not monopolize the collaborative arena and marginalize the other actors. Finally, when empowered actors are mobilized to participate in collaborative processes, the next problem is how to institutionalize these processes. Institutionalization lowers the transaction costs, reduces uncertainty, and helps to build trust, but too much institutionalization may create cognitive closure and stifle creative processes.

A third set of problems concerns *how to create the conditions for mutual learning and the creative development of new and promising ideas*. Not all forms of learning will enhance creativity and innovation, and mutual learning through network-based interaction is different from the kind of individual learning that is the key focal point of most learning theories. Transformative learning based on critical reflection may help us think and act in new and creative ways, and trust-based collaboration may allow the actors to think aloud and challenge and sharpen each other's ideas in a constructive way.

Yet another set of problems raises the question of *how bold and creative decisions are made and implemented*. There is always a risk that multi-actor collaboration will result in endless discussions or lead to dull and uninspired decisions that aim to preserve the status quo. Deliberation can be helpful in overcoming conflict, stalemate, and risk aversion in decision-making processes by engaging the actors in a serious, sincere, and responsive dialogue, but deliberation tends to rely on unrealistic assumptions about everybody behaving nicely and respecting the "force of the better argument." Thus, we have to look for an alternative understanding of how social and political actors can come to agree on a common solution that will bring about disruptive change. Even when the actors agree on an innovative solution, it might not be implemented because of technical problems, bureaucratic resistance, or the lack of funding. In this situation, implementing innovative solutions may be facilitated by joint efforts to remove obstacles, but obstacles may also be treated as challenges that trigger innovative reformulations of the chosen solutions.

A fifth set of problems relates to the question of *how to disseminate innovative solutions within or across public organizations.* One challenge is to properly understand the kinds of network structures that support the diffusion of innovation practices. Another problem relates to understanding how interpretation, translation, and bricolage help to make new ideas work in different contexts. Finally, there is the whole question of interorganizational communication, which is necessary to disseminate innovation but is complicated by the existence of different cultural and institutional codes.

The sixth set of problems arises in relation to the important question of *how we can lead and manage processes of collaborative innovation in order to improve the conditions, enhance the drivers, and reduce the barriers of collaborative innovation.* Leadership and management of innovation call for proactive rather than reactive actions and involve facilitative and inspirational leadership of interactive processes. One of the key dilemmas is that while collaborative innovation needs careful governance, it is important also to leave considerable space for voluntary collaboration and creative processes of innovation. How can we understand the delicate efforts to govern self-regulating network governance? Which tools can we use to metagovern collaborative innovation, and what does it take to become a metagovernor?

The final set of problems revolves around the question of *how to organize, govern, and manage public sector organizations to further accelerate public innovation in general and collaborative innovation in particular.* Both the ideal-typical model of bureaucracy associated with classical public administration and the recent forms of New Public Management provide drivers and barriers to public innovation. The common weakness is their failure to promote the crosscutting collaboration that can spur the innovation process. The current advancement of New Public Governance compensates for this problem by emphasizing the role of networks, partnerships, and active citizenship, but it also contains several unintended disadvantages in terms of enhancing innovation. So the big question is really determining how we can transform governance to enhance innovation.

The attempt to refine and address all these important questions calls for an interdisciplinary approach that makes it possible to attack the problems from different angles and to combine different insights when constructing plausible answers. To ensure theoretical consistency and to avoid eclecticism, the interdisciplinary approach draws on theories that are compatible with four basic assertions: The social and political actors are acting on the basis of socially constructed identities, interpretations, and reasons for action; the actors are situated within discursive and institutional contexts that provide the conditions of possibility for how they are thinking and acting; the discursive and institutional contexts are ambiguous and thus open to different interpretations that lend support for different kinds of action; and the contexts in which the social and political actors are situated are subject to dislocations that problematize and destabilize the sedimented conditions of their thoughts and actions and open up spaces for political struggles that eventually lead to the construction of new solutions and new contextual environments. The basic thrust of these assertions is that actors are internal to discursive and institutional structures that are shaped and altered by social action and political battles that not only exploit the ambiguity of relatively sedimented meanings, rules, and resource distributions but also aim to produce a new and relatively stable order when the existing order is destabilized by contingent events that reveal its limits and contingency. The strength of this theoretical point of departure is that it both allows for stability and change and places social and political agency at the center for social transformation while recognizing its institutional embeddedness.

Since the focus of this book is on public innovation, the obvious starting point for articulating an interdisciplinary theoretical framework is provided by public administration theory. However, as we shall see, traditional strands of public administration theory have several limitations that prevent it from playing a pivotal role in theory building in the area of collaborative innovation.

THE INADEQUACY AND LIMITS OF TRADITIONAL PUBLIC ADMINISTRATION THEORY

When it comes to understanding and analyzing public innovation and the role of collaboration in triggering innovation, traditional public administration theories generally have little to offer. Hence, public administration theory tends to hold a rather pessimistic view of the prospect for innovation in the public sector, and it has difficulties accounting for the numerous empirical examples of policy transformation, organizational reform, and service innovation.

The virtue attributed to stability in the public sector emanates from Max Weber's extremely influential notion of bureaucracy. According to Weber (1922), bureaucracy is the preferred organizational model in modern societies, which are dominated by rational-legal authority. Public bureaucracy is based on hierarchical and centralized rule, horizontal divisions of labor, meritocratic employment of professional civil servants, rational decision making, and rule-based service production that ensures legality, transparency, and predictability.

Given their efficiency, pertinence, and continuity, which is ensured by their hierarchical, specialized, professional, and rule-oriented decision-making processes, bureaucratic organizations are technically superior to other types of organizations. Bureaucratic governance is justified by its impartiality and technical supremacy, which first and foremost is predicated on the recourse to a relatively coherent system of written rules. The civil servants follow formal, consistent, and explicit rules that result from rational and knowledge-based decision making, and they have only a limited scope for professional discretion.

Rules are not necessarily rigid and unchangeable, but when civil servants are trained and expected to meticulously follow a set of explicit rules, they have little opportunity for creativity and hardly any motivation to search for alternative solutions. Innovation would presuppose that civil servants were considered capable both of responding to unforeseen events and changes without looking in the rule book and of acting independently and creatively without fearing reprimands from their superiors. But because they lack the latitude to creatively transform established practices, bureaucracy is associated with a slow and dull decision-making process in which different bureaucratic agencies mechanically apply a certain set of rules that are ill-adapted to new demands or expectations (Crozier 1964). In addition, the prospect for innovation is hampered by the hierarchical structure of public organizations, with policy decisions being made at the top of the organizational hierarchy but implemented at the bottom. New problems and ideas thus fail to reach the top-level managers while new objectives and rules are not always properly communicated to the frontline staff. Finally, the division of public bureaucracies into special-purpose branches inhabited by different kinds of professionals tends to prevent interorganizational learning and interaction with relevant actors in the external environment. Weber (1922) himself warned against the risk of being trapped in an "iron cage" of bureaucratic, rational control. He insisted that political reformers and entrepreneurs must counteract the implicit danger of the ongoing bureaucratization and rationalization of society, but he said little about how these actors bring about change and innovation.

Indeed, with the growth of the public sector in the 1950s and 1960s, the size of public bureaucracy came to be seen as an independent factor preventing change and innovation. This argument is clearly expressed in *Inside Bureaucracy* by Anthony Downs (1967), who claims that large bureaucracies tend to become increasingly rigid and ossified. Public organizations grow and grow until they suddenly begin to stagnate. This stagnation results when public bureaucracies lose sight of their mission and core objectives, leading them to become less and less effective. Stagnation is perceived as a threat against survival and is counteracted by accelerating the formation of formal rules to help strengthen goal achievement and to enhance efficiency. The proliferation of rules results in a growing institutional and organizational rigidity that blocks change and innovation. This tendency is exacerbated by the continued growth of internal coordination problems and external turf wars that reduce the amount of resources available for developing new and innovative ideas and practices. The lack of innovation leads to a gradual ossification of public bureaucracies, which then fail to deliver and are in constant danger of being terminated. The answer to this threat is reorganization, but that process tends to affect only the outer layers of public bureaucracies and seldom reaches their core. Thus, reorganization can hardly counteract the tendency of public bureaucracies toward rigidity and inflexibility that is a result of the tremendous public growth in the postwar era.

If Weber's rule-bound bureaucratic machines tend to stifle public innovation, then his emphasis on rational decision making points in the opposite direction. Rational decision-making processes indeed may spur public innovation. This is especially true whenever decision makers face a problem that cannot be solved by the existing rule set, and they start from scratch, carefully calculating the costs and benefits of all possible options and choosing the one that optimizes the achievement of some predefined goals. However, the rational decision-making model, which urges us to adopt a new and untried solution whenever our calculations say it is the right thing to do, has gradually been taken apart by mainstream public administration theorists.

The first blow to the rational decision-making model came from Simon (1957), who problematizes the idea that public decision makers have full information of all alternative options and all their positive and negative effects. In addition, he challenges the idea that public decision makers have sufficient time and resources to process all the available information and make the right optimizing decision. The social and political actors only have a "bounded rationality," for the lack of full information and sufficient cognitive capacity means that they cannot identify the optimal solution. Instead, they will have to be content with finding a satisfactory solution based on standard operational procedures and rules of thumb that short-circuit the rational decision-making process by telling the actors what kind of solutions are likely to work in a particular situation. The implicit reduction of the scope for rational decision making hampers the promotion of innovative solutions that could have been the result of rational optimization processes.

Lindblom (1959) also questions the rational, scientific decision-making model, according to which a large number of alternative options are thoroughly analyzed in order to determine their consequences vis-à-vis different public values and objectives. In most cases, civil servants make decisions on the basis of an experience-based comparison of a few alternative options. If positive outcomes are expected to a chosen solution, then it is tested and evaluated as a part of the next step in the decision-making process. If the positive expectations are confirmed, then civil servants might want to take additional steps in that direction. In a negative evaluation of the new steps, they will consider slightly adjusting the course and seeing what happens. Hence, instead of starting from scratch and evaluating the pros and cons of all possible solutions, public decision makers tend to make small, stepwise changes that are shaped by past experiences of what works. The resulting incremental transformation process may lead to progressive change and improvement but seldom to innovation. Public decision makers only take small steps forward, and each step is carefully evaluated on the basis of the experiences with the last one, thus creating a strong path dependence. A series of small incremental policy changes may sometimes amount to a significant policy change (Lindblom 1979), but most often the outcome is rather a disjointed pattern of policy adjustments and reversals than an innovation.

Both Simon's notion of "bounded rationality" and Lindblom's theory of the "science of muddling through" portray public decision making as a process in which deviations from the rational decision-making model narrow the scope for public innovation. However, paradoxically, the continued problematization of the rational model tends to widen the scope for public innovation. Kingdon (1984) adapts the original garbage can model that questioned the rationalistic idea that the problem always precedes the solution (Cohen, March, and Olsen 1972). His "multiple stream model" describes a world in which policy problems, policy solutions, and political actors with different agendas float around, combine, split, rise, and sink in popularity. In particular situations, policy entrepreneurs might be able to draw attention to a certain agenda item and link a particular solution to a specific problem. If they succeed in creating support for their precise alignment of problems and solutions, then they may promote incremental policy change that also includes the possibility of policy innovation (Kingdon 1984, 124). The "decision opportunity" that triggers the contingent alignment of problems and solutions is provided either by a routinized policy review or by some kind of scandal that shows the existing policy is not working. Hence, innovation is occasional and depends both on the emergence of particular events that open the window of opportunity and on the presence of capable policy entrepreneurs who successfully exploit that window of opportunity. Little suggests that stability-seeking Weberian bureaucrats, or elected politicians for that matter, will become more than "ad hoc innovators" who will eventually develop into "serial innovators."

Some public administration theorists combine arguments about the structure and functioning of public bureaucracy and the limits to rational decision making in their analyses of policy implementation. Politicians and executive public managers may try to exploit every decision opportunity to launch new, ambitious policies in response to the rising expectations of the citizens, but there is no guarantee that the new policies will be implemented in the ways that the central decision makers plan and expect. Indeed, many innovative policy proposals are never implemented, or they are implemented in a way that preserves the status quo. Pressman and Wildavsky (1973) claim that there is a large implementation deficit in the public sector, and they offer a top-down explanation of the gulf between stated policy objectives and actual policy outcomes. Public organizations are characterized by long decision-making chains that link the top, which is responsible for developing new policies, to the bottom, which is charged with their implementation. As new policies work their way down the bureaucratic decision-making chain, they are modified and transformed. Most often the final result at the local level is not as innovative, efficient, and effective as intended by the central policymakers, who designed the new policy on the basis of a rational reflection on means and ends. Distorted communication, insufficient coordination, no incentives, resource shortages, mission creep, goal displacement, and straightforward political resistance at lower levels—all may turn even the most ambitious and innovative policy ideas into small-scale adjustments of existing practices.

Lipsky (1980) criticizes Pressman and Wildavsky's top-down approach to the study of implementation problems for reducing public administrators to veto players who consciously obstruct or oppose new policy decisions from above. Instead, Lipsky's bottom-up analysis aims to understand the pivotal role of street-level bureaucrats in public policymaking. Street-level bureaucrats are the vehicle for policy implementation, but they are not passive tools for ensuring the implementation of public policies coming from above. Public policies are often founded on diffuse and conflicting objectives, as well as uncertain knowledge and program theories, and their implementation will therefore tend to rely on a series of discretionary decisions that are difficult to monitor and control. Thus, street-level bureaucrats have considerable leeway for influencing the form and content of public policy.

However, street-level bureaucrats cannot do as they please. As professionally trained public employees who act on behalf of their political principals while at the same time working in close contact with citizens and users, they are caught in a cross pressure between their own professional standards and values, the laws and regulations issued from above, and the urgent demands from citizens they are serving. To handle this highly frustrating cross pressure, they develop a variety of coping strategies that aim to limit the demand for public services, ration access and usage, routinize production and delivery, and control the users. The main objective of the various coping strategies is to protect the street-level bureaucrats and provide tolerable and manageable conditions for their work life by alleviating the pressure from the many conflicting demands and expectations. Thus, strong contradictory demands do not trigger attempts to think and act creatively and to produce innovation; rather, they lead to the development of defensive strategies that lower demands, reduce activities, simplify processes, and standardize the needs of clients and users. Hence, in this view, street-level bureaucrats have considerable power, but they use it not to produce public innovation but to ensure their own acceptable working conditions.

Principal-agent theory (Weingast and Moran 1983; Miller 2005) can be seen as a reaction to the observation that public agencies are not always delivering what their principals expect. It is assumed that the principal and the agent are mutually dependent on each other. The principal (e.g., an elected politician or an executive manager) needs to employ the agent (e.g., a public agency or a street-level bureaucrat) to produce and deliver public services and regulations, and the agent needs funding and a salary to survive. The principal and the agent have different and conflicting preferences when it comes to allocating resources. They also have asymmetric information as the principal lacks sufficient knowledge about the real competences, capacities, and efforts of the agent. When the agent acts opportunistically and aims to exploit the asymmetric information to maximize its utility, that action leads to inefficiency. The principal's rational reaction is to install a strict auditing regime that issues detailed targets and indicators, documents activities, benchmarks results, controls the budget, and sanctions bad performance. However, such an auditing regime is likely to hamper public innovation because it ties resources to documentation and control and limits the scope for entrepreneurship. Performance management systems tend to be self-reinforcing, and poor performance often leads to more rules that stifle creativity. The principal might also react by creating performance-enhancing incentive schemes to spur innovation, but such plans often have a limited impact (Whitford 2002). Incentive schemes tend to crowd out one of the key drivers of innovation in public service organizations—namely, the public service motivation of public employees.

The alleged absence of innovation in the public sector is explained not only as a function of bureaucratic structures and the limits of rational decision making but also by the nature and character of public services and the ways that they are produced. Theories of path dependence explain the failure to reform public policy as a result of adhering to a particular policy path (Thelen and Steinmo 1992; Pierson 1994, 1997; Torfing 2009). Contingent events establish a policy path based on a particular set of problem definitions, policy solutions, administrative procedures, and interlocking service delivery agencies. Once the policy path is established and becomes institutionalized, it generates increasing returns to scale—for example, in terms of learning effects and lower coordination and unit costs. Should the increasing return produce positive feedback from users, public employees, and agency managers, the institutional path becomes self-reinforcing and almost impossible to change, even when more efficient alternatives are available (David 1985; Arthur 1994). Only dramatic external events are capable of disrupting the existing policy path and creating a critical juncture, or branching point, which facilitates a departure from the old path and the shaping of a new one (Collier and Collier 1991). Hence, as we saw with Kingdon (1984), public innovation is, at best, a rare incident tied to cataclysmic shocks (Mahoney and Thelen 2009).

Path-dependence theory locates the source of institutional transformation in the external environment and tends to perceive change as an exception to the rule of stability. However, institutional change is also determined by internal dynamics, which are shaped by conflicts and experiences as well as by stable procedures that respond routinely to the changes in their environment (March and Olsen 1995). As March and Olsen put it: "[Public institutions] anticipate their futures and act to shape it. They contemplate their pasts and learn from them. They observe the actions of others and reproduce them. They engage in discourse, debate, and discussion and derive insights from conflicts and contradiction. They experiment with competing alternatives and preserve those that show the best results" (197).

Thus, institutional change in policy, organization, and services is a relatively permanent activity in modern public bureaucracies. This optimistic conclusion goes against the grain of much of the traditional public administration theory, which holds a more pessimistic view of the prospect of public innovation as seemingly only possible in exceptional moments and as a result of the efforts of willful entrepreneurs. The limitation in March and Olsen's work is that there is no explanation of the role of politicians, administrators, experts, citizens, and private stakeholders in bringing about institutional change and no account of how these actors may interact and collaborate in adapting policies and institutions to external and internal pressures.

PRECURSORS TO A THEORY OF COLLABORATIVE INNOVATION IN THE PUBLIC SECTOR

Despite March and Olsen's recognition of public innovation as a permanent and institutionally embedded activity, we have to look elsewhere for inspiration to develop a theoretical framework for studying the drivers of public innovation and especially the crucial role of collaboration. Some recently developed social science theories have come close to providing such a framework, although they are not quite there. Let us briefly review four of the most important precursors to a theory of collaborative public innovation in terms of theories of collaborative planning, theories of economic innovation systems, participatory theories of technological development, and the new and increasingly popular "design thinking."

Theories of Collaborative Planning

In planning theory we have seen an interesting intellectual development from rational and procedural planning via strategic planning to collaborative planning (Geertman 2006). *Rational planning theory* aims to produce a blueprint for the future development of urban and rural spaces through a technical-scientific process based on rational and instrumental decision making and on knowledge provided through the extrapolation of demographic and socioeconomic trends (Banfield 1973; Faludi 1973). The planning process is hierarchical as politicians and public planning experts treat citizens and private stakeholders as passive objects of public planning practices.

Procedural planning theory abandons the idea of constructing an optimal blueprint for the future development of physical space. The big, comprehensive master plans seldom produce the predicted outputs and outcomes because they lack knowledge about the local conditions and dynamics and because of the political resistance from citizens and organized interests. Therefore, planning should be more of an incremental process guided by procedures and methods for making local planning decisions. The procedural planning model must include consultation processes with the local stakeholders who can qualify the public planning decisions by providing relevant information about the local context. These processes will also help build support for local development projects (Sager 1999).

Strategic planning theory criticizes the procedural planning model for focusing too much on procedures and methods that organize day-to-day planning and too little on the overall visions for future planning (Faludi and Van der Valk 1994). The alternative planning model is characterized as "mixed scanning" (Etzioni 1967). Public planning should take the available knowledge and information as the point of departure, explore available future options, and select a few promising options for closer scrutiny—for example, through the construction and comparison of different scenarios in light of some overall planning objectives. When one of the available options for the future development of urban and rural spaces is chosen, it should be implemented and adjusted incrementally (Bryson and Roering 1988; Kaufman and Jacobs 1996).

Collaborative planning theory provides an alternative to all the aforementioned planning theories. It claims that knowledge and information about planning problems and planning solutions are socially constructed and subject to contestation and reasoned debate. It insists that planning processes should include all the relevant and affected actors in the deliberative processes that result in joint planning decisions. Last but not least, it perceives planning as a pragmatic process that involves learning and experiments and creates continuous coordination and overall direction in decentered and emergent development processes (Innes 1995; Healey 1997; Forester 1999; Brand and Gaffikin 2007).

Collaborative planning theory appreciates the importance of local and regional contexts and recognizes their uncertainty, complexity, and uniqueness (Booher and Innes 2010). Attention is drawn to the construction of collaborative forums and arenas that comprise a large number of social and political actors connected through multiple networks. The method for arriving at planning decisions is deliberation, which should be based on inclusive dialogue between different actors with different forms of knowledge. All actors must be free to express their views and be listened to, whether they are powerful or not (Booher and Innes 2010, 6). The deliberative process should have a holistic and strategic focus and aim to solve problems and conflicts by discovering new and innovative solutions that meet the interests of different stakeholders. Innovative solutions are fashioned through the exchange of ideas, transformative dialogue, and processes of mutual learning that also tend to create joint ownership of new ways of thinking and acting. The discursive framing of collaborative planning processes can stimulate innovation (Fischer and Forester 1993), and the professional facilitation of the joint search for new solutions proves to be highly important (Metze 2010).

Theories of collaborative planning offer crucial insights into how collaboration can foster innovative solutions, but they tend to have much more to say about collaboration through deliberative processes than about public innovation. Another weakness of collaborative planning theory is its somewhat naive Habermasian belief in the force of the better argument and the quest for "authentic dialogue" and "genuine consensus." There are many other forms of power than the power of good and persuasive arguments, and the quest for consensus based on reasoned dialogue may exclude certain actors and eliminate dissenting views that could potentially spur innovation (Young 2000). The strength of collaborative planning theory, however, is the great attention it pays to including stakeholders and facilitating dialogue between experts and lay actors. We can also learn a great deal from the theory's focus on the institutionalization and management of collaborative planning processes; it is slightly more pronounced in the European than in the North American theories of collaborative planning (Pløger 2002).

Theories of Economic Innovation Systems

Schumpeter (1934) claims that innovation is the primary source of economic growth and development. Inspired by Karl Marx, Schumpeter perceives innovation as a disruptive force that undermines the neoclassical equilibrium theory that was becoming increasingly fashionable in the 1920s and 1930s. Innovation is created by individual entrepreneurs who are the source of creative labor and who ensure that new ideas are transformed into new processes and products (Hagedoorn 1996). Investors, banks, and other financial institutions support industrial entrepreneurs, whose efforts give rise to periods of innovation-driven economic growth. Periods of imitation and eventually stagnation follow when the new economic growth potential is exhausted. With the advent of monopoly capitalism and the formation of large-scale corporations, individual entrepreneurs are transformed into a collective entrepreneurship. Innovation then becomes the responsibility of large R&D departments, which are financed by corporate profits. These departments bring together different kinds of experts who deploy scientific methods in the search for new innovations.

Schumpeter's pioneering work on economic innovation was later criticized for its linear and supply-driven view of innovation. His work too readily assumes that scientific research leads to new technology and that the new technology satisfies market needs (Edquist and Hommen 1999, 64). This criticism paved the way for developing a system-oriented perspective on technological innovation that emphasizes the existence of feedback loops from public and private consumers to business firms, from technical engineers to scientists, and from scientists to the public authorities who fund scientific research. From this perspective, innovation can also be demand driven. Innovation is increasingly seen as a result of interaction between a broad range of public and private actors who have different demands, ideas, and resources and who are collaborating within a complex and evolutionary system (Freeman 1974, 1991; Rosenberg 1982).

The logical extension of this new system-oriented perspective on economic innovation was the development of the concept of "innovation systems." An *innovation system* is defined as *the complex set of relationships and interactions between the actors who are determining the pace and direction of economic innovation*, and it is characterized by its specialization, institutional structure, and relationship to its environment (Lundvall 1992). Innovation systems can be identified at the national or regional level, and some of them are tied to particular sectors—for example, biotechnology. The term "innovation systems" is sometimes used in a narrow sense that focuses on the interaction between public research policy, universities, and the R&D departments of large private corporations. This is often the case in North America and mirrors how the United States produces a large number of radical, science-driven innovations that have a huge impact on its economy (Lundvall 2011).

In the broader sense of the term, innovation systems tend to include interactions with consumers and users, and the emphasis on the vertical relationships between different actors in the innovation chain is supplemented with a new emphasis on the horizontal relationships within different groups of actors. For example, Lundvall (1985) attempts to explain product innovation as a result of communication between producers and consumers that gives rise to "organized markets" based on interactive learning between the producers, who are eager to hear about the needs of the users, and the consumers, who want to discover the qualities of new products. Likewise, Hippel (1988) has developed "the distributed innovation model," according to which product innovations originate from any one of at least three distinct sources: suppliers, producers, and users. The particular combination of these innovation sources in a specific product field depends on the predominant incentive structure. Sometimes scientists, producers, or users will not have all the knowledge necessary to initiate and produce a particular innovation. This situation opens up the opportunity for horizontal networks to form among researchers, competing firms, or users. Hence, research consortia, strategic alliances, and user organizations are becoming increasingly important as sources of innovation.

Innovation systems theory provides an important source of inspiration for understanding collaborative innovation in the public sector. Its main strength is the evolutionary perspective on innovation that emphasizes the random and time-consuming processes of collaborative innovation and the institutional embeddedness of these processes. That being said, for our purposes, this theory has two crucial limitations. First, the innovation systems approach seems to be more of a conceptual framework than a theory that aims to explain the drivers and barriers of collaborative innovation. Second, its focus is on collaborative innovation in the private sector rather than in the public sector.

Participatory Theories of Technological Development

As with innovation systems theory, the theories of technological development also highlight the role of interaction and user participation in innovation processes. The focus of these theories, however, is exclusively on developing new technologies, and the analytical perspective is more sociological and ethnographic and oriented more toward the micro level (Jæger 2011). At the most general level, the *theories of science, technology, and society* criticize the traditional view of innovation as a technical-scientific process that develops new technologies that, in turn, determine the development of society (Bijker 1995). This linear and deterministic conception of technological development perceives innovation as an exogenous determinant of societal development. Hence, it fails to understand innovation's social embeddedness and how different actors—elected politicians, experts, interest organizations, and users—influence the development of new technology. By contrast, the science, technology, and society perspective claims that technology is socially constructed through a complex and networked interaction between a plurality of actors and the technology they are trying to develop (Latour 1987; Pinch and Bijker 1987). Social and political actors will often have competing interpretations of the function and uses of the new technologies, but controversies are resolved over time as a hegemonic interpretation is formed and gains momentum. This interweaving of technical and social processes means that we cannot separate the analysis of technological innovation from the analysis of society (Bijker 2010). Hence, *theories of the social construction of technology* insist that technological innovation is shaped in and through social practices in which social and political actors engage in hegemonic struggles.

On a more concrete level, proponents of *theories of participatory design* have studied actual processes of technological innovation, especially in the field of information and communications technology (ICT). They find that although it is common for both private firms and public organizations to carefully specify their demands for new ICT, these specifications are not enough to ensure that the users' demands are met. The problem is that demand specifications tend to focus on technical issues such as the capacity for processing different kinds of data, and they fail to take the practical and organizational aspects of the new ICT into account (Kensing 2003). To remedy this problem, the employees and managers should be invited to participate in an interactive innovation process (Ranerup 1996). The participatory design approach offers a method for developing ICT in an iterative process where demands are identified, ideas and solutions are tested, conflicts are solved, and new demands are uncovered (Granlien 2010).

The attempt to democratize the process of technological innovation has also played a role at both the practical and theoretical level in the *democratic technology assessment approach*. Since the 1970s people in the Western world have been increasingly skeptical about the consequences of technological development, and demands for establishing procedures for technological assessment have been growing. In the United States this demand led Congress to form the Office of Technology Assessment. In Denmark the Technology Board was formed in 1986 and has played a leading role in designing deliberative processes ever since, despite consecutive cuts and reorganizations. The Danish Technology Board is based on the principle that affected citizens have a right to participate and be heard in the process of technological innovation and that their views should be reflected in the advice given to policymakers. In accordance with the *theories of deliberative democracy* (Dryzek 2000), it is assumed that citizens can develop an informed opinion about new technologies through dialogue with key actors from a particular field of technological innovation. A widely debated Danish method for facilitating democratic deliberation is the so-called consensus conference in which a selected panel of citizens addresses invited experts. The citizens formulate questions about a particular technological innovation and cross-examine the experts. The panel then discusses the consequences of technological innovation based on the input from the experts and submits a consensus report with political recommendations to the politicians in the Danish parliament.

The social construction of technology, participatory design, and democratic technology assessment approaches all agree that technological innovation is not an autonomous scientific process but a social and political process with many different participants. They all emphasize the importance of involving users in technological innovation processes and provide concrete examples of how collaborative innovation can be studied and designed. However, despite their frequent references to actor network theory (Latour 1987) and theories of deliberative democracy (Dryzek 2000), the theoretical contribution of the three approaches is modest. Still the theories of participatory technological development have managed to set a new agenda in the field of technological innovation, and they have much to offer in terms of process design.

Design Thinking

Design thinking has become increasingly important in business management and in relation to processes of public innovation. In the past, design was a downstream step in product development aimed at enhancing the attractiveness of a specific product. Today design has become more of an upstream practice as designers are asked to build entire systems that can meet the explicit or latent needs of customers by offering new and innovative goods and services (Serrat 2010). Simultaneously, the scope for applying design thinking has become wider; so it not only includes product design, architecture, and applied aesthetics but also attempts to solve societal problems and create new futures (Banerjee 2010).

Simon (1969) defined *design* as *the changing of existing conditions and properties into preferred ones*. Thus, design can be seen as a deliberate attempt to create innovative solutions in response to particular needs and specific problems and challenges. Like innovation, design involves various processes: framing, researching, forming ideas, prototyping, selecting, implementing, and learning (Serrat 2010). Thus, design processes are problem driven and firmly anchored in an abductive mode of reasoning that aims to establish the conditions for problems to emerge and to be framed and solved. Finding innovative solutions to wicked problems begins with a deep understanding of the users' needs and involves experimentation and iterative rounds of generating ideas, prototyping, testing, and reformulating. Design processes are collaborative. Designers can therefore play a crucial role in facilitating collaboration between different actors with disparate disciplinary backgrounds, because they are used to working in an interdisciplinary environment and know that the right design can only be developed by reaching across disciplinary boundaries (Banerjee 2010).

The strength of design thinking is its acute observation of the importance of an empathetic engagement with users and its insistence that innovation is based on multi-actor collaboration (see Stickdorn and Schneider 2011). However, design thinking is primarily concerned with changing the way that innovation processes in private businesses are managed and with reforming the curriculum of master of business administration programs so that design thinking features more prominently (Dunne and Martin 2006). Design thinking features many good ideas—for example, the use of heuristic devices and cultural probes to make the future concrete. However, while the notion that design is coterminous with innovation is interesting, design thinking has yet to establish itself as an academic field of research with a clear set of research questions, a theoretical underpinning, and a methodological toolbox that facilitates empirical studies of design processes.

SOME KEY THEORETICAL BUILDING BLOCKS

Each of the four theoretical perspectives provides valuable insights into how collaboration can foster innovation, but none of them provides a full-fledged framework for analyzing collaborative innovation in the public sector. In constructing such a framework, we can draw on elements from each of them as precursors, but we will also need to look to other theoretical building blocks to cover the many different aspects of collaborative public innovation. Let us briefly review some of the theories that can help us piece together a theoretical framework for analyzing collaborative public innovation.

Innovation Theory

Innovation theory emerged in the late 1960s as a subfield of economics. It shifted the scholarly focus from the factors driving capital accumulation and the determinants of market behavior to the study of innovation, which traditionally has been treated as a "black box" in economics. The study of what happens inside the black box has attracted scholars from different fields such as organization studies, business economics, management, and economic geography. Innovation studies have thus had a strong cross-disciplinary character (Fagerberg 2004).

Building on Schumpeter (1934), several scholars focused their analysis on the uncertain processes of innovation in private firms (Nelson and Winter 1982; Nonaka and Takeuchi 1995; Van de Ven et al. 2008), and, as noted, others studied the role of networks and multi-actor systems of innovation (Asheim and Gertler 2004; Edquist 2004; Powell and Grodal 2004). The role of business management, the organizational structures of private firms, and the institutional norms in particular sectors for facilitating or hampering the exchange of knowledge and the process of creative learning—all have received considerable attention. Finally, many have studied the differences in the innovative capacities of different geographical regions and industrial sectors (Malerba 2004), and several have explored the impact of science, technology, and innovation policies on the form and level of business innovation (Lundvall and Borras 2004).

The main focus of innovation theory is on the process of economic innovation and how it can be facilitated and accelerated. *Innovation* is defined as *a new combination of new and old elements*, and the innovation process is depicted as an open-ended search procedure that runs through different iterative stages. In relation to the present study of collaborative innovation, it is particularly interesting that innovation theory has increasingly emphasized the innovative gains made from tapping into the experiences, ideas, and resources of economic and social actors across different organizational boundaries. Chesbrough (2003) thus claims that the era of closed, intra-firm innovation is over as knowledge has become dispersed among a large number of companies, suppliers, universities, national labs, and customers. In this situation, private firms must open up the innovation process to systematically source external ideas and to disseminate their own ideas externally. Further, actors with different forms of knowledge and expertise should be involved as collaborators in distinct stages of the innovation process depending on the problem that needs to be solved. The argument in favor of such "open innovation" is also sustained by Hippel (2005), who claims that firms should learn from "lead users" who experience needs that many users in the market will later have.

Howe (2006) holds a less selective view of who can contribute to the process of innovation. His notion of *crowdsourcing* is defined as *the act of a company or institution taking a function once performed by employees and outsourcing it to an undefined and generally large network of people through the issuing of an open call.* Crowdsourcing is predicated on the idea that crowds of people are often smarter than the smartest individuals in the group.

The argument about opening up the innovation process is developed in innovation theories focusing on private enterprises, but the argument is also relevant for the public sector. However, the conditions for innovation in the public sector are different from those found in the private sector. New theories of public innovation have noted the obstacles in the public sector—that is, bureaucratic rules, weak economic incentives, and the presence of a risk-averse political leadership (Halvorsen et al. 2005)—as well as its drivers, such as the large size of public budgets, the huge in-house expertise available, and the recent focus on enhancing cost-efficiency. When it comes to collaboration, the public sector has undergone significant changes in the last decades that make open innovation through collaboration with relevant and affected actors a likely scenario. Given the emphasis on contracting out, knowledge-based decision making, and empowered participatory governance, public administrators have much more interaction with private stakeholders today than they did previously. With these important qualifications, innovation theory seems to have much to offer when it comes to understanding the process of collaborative innovation in the public sector.

Discourse Theory

The underlying assumption of poststructuralist theories of discourse, which have been advanced since the mid-1980s, is that social meanings and political identities are not determined by a privileged and pre-given essence in terms of God, reason, nature, or the laws of capitalist accumulation (Torfing 1999a). Rather, they are contingently constructed on the basis of *discourses*, or *relational systems of signifying practices that combine semantic and pragmatic aspects* (Laclau and Mouffe 1985). In structural linguistics, discourse was originally defined in terms of language (Saussure 1981), but Barthes (1987) expands the notion to include social systems of signification such as advertising, mass media, military parades, and public administration. Hence, in line with Wittgenstein's (1958) notion of language games, it is argued that language and action are intertwined in the production of social meaning and identity. Speech can be a way of acting, and actions are loaded with meaning.

Discourses are *relational systems unified around nodal, or reference, points that are relatively empty expressions capable of partially fixing meanings to so-called floating signifiers.* To illustrate, in many European countries "welfare" is a nodal point that helps shape the meaning of other terms—such as "state," "right," "equality," and "citizenship"—that are so rich in meaning that they lend themselves to competing interpretations. According to Laclau and Mouffe (1985), discourses are constructed through *articulation*, which is defined as *practices that establish an internal relationship between dissimilar elements such that their identities are mutually modified.* Articulations that involve the construction of social antagonisms that divide the discursive space into opposing camps of "friends" and "enemies" are defined as *hegemonic articulations.* Hegemony is seen as a political practice aiming to construct a political as well as a moral-intellectual leadership in a group consisting of diverse social and political actors with different demands (Gramsci 1971). Thus, hegemonic discourses define the conditions for thinking and acting in a particular context, and they are often stabilized by totalizing ideologies. Ideology naturalizes meanings and identities by denying their contingent and political character and by presenting them as natural facts and eternal truths that capture the essence of the world. However, the stable and totalizing discourses are dislocated by new and disruptive events that they fail to domesticate and give meaning to, and the dislocation opens a space for new articulations and hegemonic struggles aiming to create a new order (Laclau 1990).

Discourse theory does not say anything per se about governance networks, collaboration, or public innovation, but poststructuralist theories of discourse advance some relevant concepts and arguments for analyzing public governance in general and collaborative public innovation in particular. First of all, the notion of dislocation is important for understanding how sedimented systems of meaning become destabilized and subject to change. Discourses are flexible and will often be capable of explaining and giving meaning to new and potentially disturbing events, but discourses will eventually encounter events that problematize the hegemonic meaning system and question its underlying assumptions. Think about how the phenomenon of stagflation, for example, dislocated the discourse of Keynesian economics in the mid-1970s. The dislocation of established meanings and identities is a precondition for thinking of and constructing something new and innovative. Hence, we would not have seen the rise of monetarism in the 1980s if the discourse of Keynesian economics had not been dislocated. Discourse theory not only helps us understand the conditions for articulating new meanings and identities but also enables us to grasp how new policy discourses manage to create a relative unity of dissimilar elements by positing an external threat to the discursive system. The construction of social antagonism is crucial for creating political frontiers in the public realm and thus for allowing new ideas to become hegemonic.

Second, when actors with different values, views, and interests are joined in a network, they are often held together by the discursive construction of mutual dependencies and by the formation of a common story line that defines their problems and possible solutions in a condensed, metaphorical manner, one that implies a certain sense of urgency and builds momentum for change (Hajer 2009). The discursive framing of networked collaboration may also involve different dramaturgical ploys in terms of a particular staging or scripting of the networked interaction that serve to facilitate collaboration and spur innovation.

Finally, discourse theory insists that social relations, meanings, and identities are shaped by politics and power. It reveals a "fourth face of power" in addition to the three faces of power that Lukes (1974) has already identified. Hence, power is not merely exercised by strong and resourceful actors who can prevail in an open conflict, suppress conflicts by means of controlling the political agenda, or manipulate other actors' perception of their preferences and interests so as to avoid conflicts altogether. There is also a discursive power that cannot be traced back to a willful and self-interested actor aiming to get his or her way (Foucault 1990). Discursive strategies, which neither emanate from nor are controlled by a particular actor, represent a crucial dimension of power because they define how actors perceive themselves, each other, and the terrain in which they operate. Discourses structure the conditions for thinking and acting, but that does not mean that the social and political actors are reduced to passive discourse *takers*. The ambiguities and constant dislocations of the hegemonic discourses create a space for political action that permits social and political actors to become discourse *makers* by reinventing traditions and creating new meanings and identities.

Institutional Theory

Whereas innovation theory recognizes the danger that innovation may be stifled by the traditions, habits, rules, and taken-for-granted knowledge found in all organizations, discourse theory perceives how institutions and other forms of sedimented discourse give rise to routinized behavior that is oblivious of its political origin and therefore prevents social actors from recognizing its contingency. Both insights attest to the relevance of institutional theory for understanding processes of collaborative innovation.

Rational choice institutionalists believe in the efficiency of history and tend to view innovation as common and unproblematic. When the external environment of particular institutions changes, the preferences of social and political actors will shift, and, as a result, they will start bargaining with each other to design a new set of institutions that matches the new external environment. If institutions are not adapted, they are expected to become obsolete and gradually wither away (March and Olsen 1995, 39–42).

Historical institutionalism tends to see the prospect for institutional change and innovation as much more limited. Not only are most institutions partially shaped by internal dynamics and power relations but they also seem capable of surviving for a long time despite their apparent ignorance of external pressures and their failure to respond to them. Furthermore, the idea of a single institutional equilibrium is problematic as institutions often have a choice of different institutional designs. The presence of multiple equilibriums reinforces a path-dependent lock-in when, despite the availability of more efficient designs, the current institutional design generates strong enough positive feedback to preserve it (Thelen and Steinmo 1992; Pierson 1994). The path-dependent preservation of the status quo, however, can be disrupted at critical historical junctures where cataclysmic shocks break down the existing order and mobilize resources for constructing a new one.

The sociological institutionalist response to the theory of punctuated equilibrium, which contrasts long stretches of stability with brief moments of instability and change, has been to emphasize the ambiguity of rules and norms that enable the continuous transformation of institutions through reinterpretation. It also emphasizes the existence of stable institutional procedures for change and adaption based on a regular scanning and testing of alternatives (March and Olsen 1995). In this literature a crucial question becomes how to balance exploration and exploitation when resources are limited (March 1991). An overcommitment to the exploration of new ideas might prevent exploitation and vice versa.

A more recent response to the innovation-skeptical theory of path dependence claims that network-based collaboration can stimulate innovation. Policy paths tend to be multilayered as new layers of policy are added on top of existing layers, creating different kinds of conflict and tension (Thelen 1999, 2003). In this situation multi-actor networks may function as a kind of collective memory that can help to revive and bring into play dormant and half-forgotten options that are buried under several layers of policy. Hidden alternatives might be chosen if they have the potential for resolving tensions and problems in the existing policy path and if the actors agree to adopt a long-term perspective. Collaborative networks might also address the problem that institutional paths are often reinforced by policy interlocks involving a broad range of public and private organizations, which may have different interests in preserving the existing policy path. Governance networks provide institutionalized arenas for agreeing upon and coordinating the shift from one path to another while compensating those who stand to lose the most (Considine 2009). Hence, institutional paths often lead to the formation of interactive arenas that facilitate a collective action that overcomes inertia and creates change.

In sum, institutional theory can help us understand both the conditions for stability and the conditions for change. Institutionalization of social and political practices seems to enhance stability, but institutional paths may also contain mechanisms that drive change and innovation.

Theories of Learning

A key idea of collaborative innovation is that collaboration facilitates mutual learning, which can produce new ideas and improve the way they are implemented and diffused. Theories of learning can help us better understand these learning effects. Learning theory aims to describe and comprehend the process through which people acquire, enhance, or revise their knowledge as a result of cognitive, emotional, or cultural influences. Whereas *behavioral learning theory* focuses on how learning is manifested in changing social behavior and *cognitive learning theory* studies how brain-based learning brings about new gestalts, *constructivist learning theory* analyzes how learners actively build novel concepts and ideas based on new and existing knowledge and experiences and how they apply these concepts and ideas in specific real-life contexts. *Social constructivists* perceive learning as a social practice that unfolds when learners engage in social interaction with other people. For example, Lave and Wenger (1991) emphasize that learning is situational and involves participation in communities of practice that use mutual learning as a tool for solving the problems that a team of coworkers encounter in daily operations.

Of particular relevance for studying collaborative public innovation, we find a number of social constructivist learning theories that focus on those forms of learning that produce new ways of thinking and acting and that restructure the relationship between the social actors and their social environment. Bateson (1972) distinguishes between different learning processes on the basis of their transformative capacity. The first and simplest form of learning involves acquiring incorrigible knowledge in terms of factual information that we take for granted and act upon. Hence, the first day in a new workplace you need to know which person to consult for your initial briefing, what time you break for lunch, where the break room is, and what to do when your computer malfunctions.

A second and more advanced form of learning occurs during socialization processes through which we internalize rules and norms and acquire certain habits that structure our actions in a particular context—for example, a workplace or a voluntary organization. Here corrective change is possible, but we can only choose between those rule-bound actions that are specified by the context.

A third learning process involves changing the range of alternative actions that we can choose from through a conscious attempt to revise those norms and habits that are deemed inappropriate in light of new problems or challenges. This kind of learning involves developing new practices either through processes of trial and error or through more strategic forms of experimentation. Incremental innovations might emerge as a result of this kind of instrumental learning, where new problems trigger a search for a new kind of rule-bound action.

Finally, another learning process takes us one step further into creative problem solving as it involves reframing both problems and solutions. Here we aim to learn not only new ways of doing things or dealing with a given problem but also new ways of thinking about and defining the problem or challenge that confronts us. We strive to transgress the context that constrains our choice of rule-bound actions by searching for images, metaphors, and narratives that help us make sense of the situation, understand what we fail to comprehend, and solve puzzles. Engeström (1987) labels this kind of learning, which involves further developing the usual context for thinking and acting, as "expansive learning." Spinosa, Flores, and Dreyfus (1997) call it "reconfiguration"; Schön and Rein (1995), "framer realignment." Emphasizing the role of critical reflection and the need for going beyond affirmative thinking, Mezirow (2000) talks about this "transformative learning" as the key to radical innovation. Dialogue, boundary crossing, and multi-actor collaboration are seen as key features of both expansive and transformative learning processes.

Innovation always involves some degree of creativity. Some researchers associate creativity with the presence of particular intellectual or artistic capacities. Learning theory takes a different route as it links creativity to the process of learning. According to Wakefield (2003), creativity involves identifying problems that cannot be answered immediately but call for an explorative learning that aims to change our basic assumptions about the world. This understanding of creativity has a lineage that can be traced back to Dewey's (1938) concept of learning, which also emphasizes the role of problem identification, critical reflection, and experimental testing of hypotheses. From this perspective, creativity is not a personal capacity but a certain way of thinking. Creative thinking depends on the social actors' motivation, expertise, and ability to combine different experiences and insights in new ways (Amabile 1998). It can be either an individual or a collective endeavor. If creative thinking is a collective and collaborative enterprise, it becomes important to create cultural and institutional conditions that motivate the actors to work together to find creative solutions, that provide a trust-based environment in which they feel safe to voice incomplete and uncertain ideas, and that stimulate the use of fantasy and imagination (Lund and Jensen 2011).

In sum, learning theory enables us to understand those kinds of learning that stimulate innovation. It also helps us develop a deeper appreciation of what creativity is and how it relates to learning and innovation. Finally, it helps us recognize the conditions for enhancing creative thinking in collaborative arenas.

Systems and Complexity Theory

The institutional arenas of multi-actor collaboration can be characterized as systems. They have boundaries and external environments, and we can describe their operations in terms of the inputs they receive, their internal processes, their resulting outputs and outcomes, and the positive and negative feedback that these processes engender (Katz and Kahn 1978; Koliba, Meek, and Zia 2011). The systems perspective helps us understand that various sorts of input trigger processes of collaborative innovation that result in the production of innovative solutions, whose evaluations differ depending on the system or subsystem that makes the assessment. These collaborative arenas are also seen as "complex adaptive systems." They consist of multiple actors linked by complex patterns of interaction that lead to dynamic processes with many feedback loops (Morçöl and Wachhaus 2009). These systems have a self-organizing capacity in that they can define their own organizing principles and thereby enhance their own complexity (Meadows 2008). This capacity for self-organization is important as it permits systems to adapt to changes in their environment. However, the system interprets and filters the inputs from the environment on the basis of the system's own internal communicative codes, and the specific coding of inputs determines whether a response is needed and what kind of response is appropriate (Luhman 1995). The complex interactions within self-organizing and self-referential systems also tend to produce emerging features, ideas, and solutions that are not initiated by a particular input.

All of these qualities of complex adaptive systems help us to understand the complex character of institutional arenas of multi-actor collaboration that cannot be grasped using linear models. The description of collaborative arenas as complex and adaptive systems provides a non-reductionist perspective on collaborative innovation. Complexity is a feature we have to live with and learn to take advantage of by "deliberately changing the structure of a system in order to increase some measure of performance" (Axelrod and Cohen 1999, 9). Complex systems thus can be manipulated to enhance innovative outputs. Exactly how this manipulation occurs, and who is responsible for it, is not particularly clear although adaptation has traditionally been considered a key function of social and political systems.

Theories of Network Governance

The contribution of different strands of governance network theory has already been discussed extensively in the book's introduction. Therefore, it is sufficient to simply remind the reader of a few key points about what governance network theory may contribute to the study of collaborative innovation. First of all, the concept of governance networks offers a way of understanding the organization of collaborative interaction in and through multi-actor networks that combine strong and weak ties as well as formal and informal relations in a flexible manner. The adjacent research field of social network analysis provides the tools for mapping the patterns of interaction in collaborative innovation processes, thus permitting us to identify central and peripheral actors, network brokers, and structural holes (Considine, Lewis, and Alexander 2009).

Second, governance network theory assumes that networks are formed in response to particular problems, which they aim to solve. It also assumes there is often a great deal of uncertainty about the nature of the problems, the scientific knowledge surrounding them, the strategies of the public and private actors inside and outside the network, and the relative importance of different decision-making arenas (Koppenjan and Klijn 2004). In this situation, innovation can only be achieved by redefining the problems; treating knowledge as tentative, frame bound, and divergent; ensuring goal intertwinement; and creating crosscutting and multilevel governance networks. This work will lead to innovative solutions that not only are richer and more creative than those solutions that the actors originally imagined but also match the complexity of the problem at hand.

Next, governance network theory can help explain why actors may want to take a collaborative approach to problem solving. Public and private actors are likely to interact and exchange resources because they recognize their mutual dependency (Kickert, Klijn, and Koppenjan 1997). Interdependence is not an objective fact that is fully visible to, and perceived by, all actors. It must be discursively constructed, pinpointed, and demonstrated, and sometimes it must even be created and supported by institutional incentive schemes (Scharpf 1994). When actors first recognize their interdependency vis-à-vis a certain problem or challenge, they may be keen to share knowledge, exchange ideas, and pool resources to formulate and implement new and bold solutions.

Last but not least, governance network theory recognizes the need to manage or metagovern governance networks (Kooiman 1993, 2003; Kickert, Klijn, and Koppenjan 1997; Jessop 2002; Agranoff 2003; Milward and Provan 2006). The attempt to govern governance networks is referred to as metagovernance, and those who exercise metagovernance are called metagovernors (Torfing et al. 2012). In respect for the self-regulating character of governance networks, metagovernors should aim to influence governance networks without reverting too much to traditional hierarchical forms of governing-based command and control. Instead, they should use other metagovernance tools such as institutional design, storytelling, incentives, process management, conflict mediation, and direct participation in policy deliberation to spur collaboration and enhance the creation of innovative solutions.

Governance network theory seems to be compatible with all the other theoretical approaches to collaborative innovation presented here. It therefore provides a good starting point for theory building.

A SIMPLE ANALYTICAL MODEL

The theoretical building blocks capture different aspects of the processes of collaborative innovation in the public sector. Drawing together their different insights helps us develop a simple model for analyzing collaborative innovation. It is inspired by the model of collaborative governance advanced by Ansell and Gash (2007) and the institutional analysis and development framework elaborated by Ostrom, Gardner, and Walker (1994). As indicated in figure 3.1, the underlying assumption is that collaborative innovation processes, which produce specific public innovation outputs that can be measured and evaluated in different ways, are embedded in institutional arenas of networked interaction with a contingent set of drivers and barriers that facilitate and hamper collaboration and innovation (Sørensen and Torfing 2011). The institutional arenas of interaction, and thus the processes of collaborative innovation, are shaped by some initial conditions and proactive forms of leadership and management that can be understood as a form of metagovernance. Here, metagovernance is defined *as the attempt to govern interactive governance arenas without reverting too much to traditional forms of command and control.*

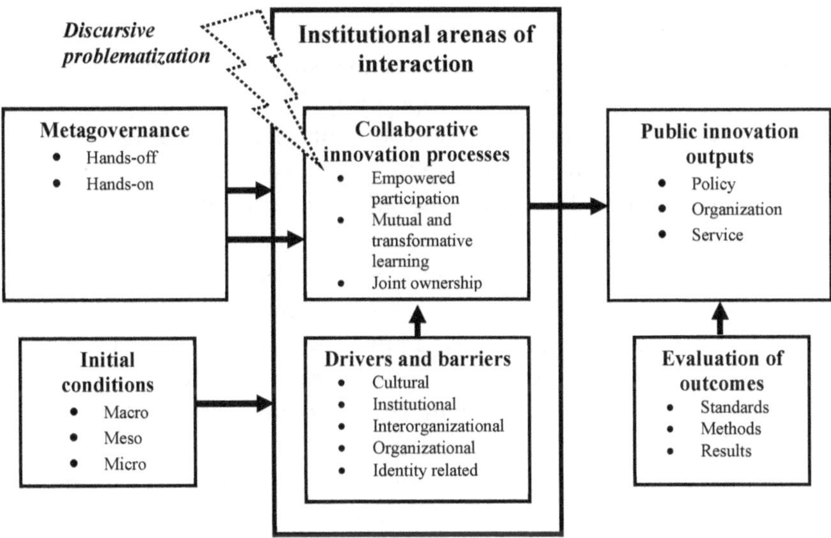

FIGURE 3.1. Analytical model for studying collaborative innovation

The model displayed in figure 3.1 maps the interplay between the different factors that may lead to the production of specific *public innovation outputs.* These outputs may involve reformulating policy problems, policy objectives, and policy tools; developing new forms of governance, organization, and work processes; or creating new kinds of public service. Public innovation outputs may produce different outcomes that can be evaluated by a broad range of actors who will apply competing standards, use different methods, and arrive at different conclusions about the results of public innovation. Evaluation of these outcomes may either spur the diffusion of a best practice or, after the creative destruction of existing solutions, stimulate the search for a next practice in terms of new and better solutions for the future.

Public innovation is a result of open-ended and nonlinear innovation processes that can be more or less collaborative. The study of collaborative innovation processes focuses on the participation of empowered actors with different identities, roles, and resources; on the processes of mutual and transformative learning through which new ideas are generated, tested, and selected; and on the development of joint ownership, which helps to overcome implementation resistance and to ensure the coordination and flexible adjustment of innovative practices.

The extent to which interdependent actors work together and use collaboration as a vehicle for public innovation is conditioned by a number of context-bound *drivers* and *barriers* that either stimulate or hamper the processes of collaborative innovation, respectively. The drivers and barriers may arise from cultural norms and values, institutional logics, interorganizational relations, organizational routines, or the identities of the key stakeholders.

The processes of collaborative innovation are embedded in institutional arenas of interaction that can be analyzed as governance networks. The institutional arenas provide rules, norms, routines, cognitive scripts, and discourses that structure the actions of the social and political actors who are linked because they recognize their mutual dependency. In relatively self-regulating governance networks, the actors will negotiate and amend the rules of the game, and the institutional arenas may therefore be gradually transformed over the course of the interaction.

The attempt to create and sustain institutional arenas of interaction that facilitate collaboration and public innovation depends on a number of initial conditions. At the macro level, we might find different traditions for stakeholder involvement in different countries and in different parts of the public sector. At the meso level, there will often be different legal and institutional conditions for participatory governance in different policy fields. At the micro level, the presence of strong power resource asymmetries, the lack of clear incentives, and negative past experiences with cooperation might prevent collaborative interaction (Ansell and Gash 2007). Analyzing the impact of the initial conditions is particularly important in comparative case studies of collaborative innovation.

The institutional arenas and the drivers and barriers that they engender can be influenced by proactive forms of metagovernance that aim to regulate the self-regulatory arenas of networked interaction through a combination of hands-off strategies, such as institutional design and network framing, and hands-on tools, such as process management and participatory engagement. Metagovernance can be exercised by legitimate and resourceful actors who are willing to take responsibility for the reflexive monitoring and strategic management of processes of collaborative innovation so that they can remove the obstacles and enhance the drivers.

This simple analytical model provides a heuristic tool for mapping the basic factors and dynamics that condition and shape collaborative innovation in the public sector. The connections between the different components are not deterministic but strive to capture the possible conditions for spurring public innovation through collaborative interaction. While simple, this model can be expanded depending on the research question being addressed.

The analytical model, however, will not be treated as a reified mechanism or a recipe for stimulating collaborative innovation in the public sector that we have to elaborate in greater and greater detail to enhance its explanatory and predictive capacity. The logic of the argument underlying the analytical model does inform the theoretical discussion and empirical exploration in this book and thus helps give direction and coherence to its findings and arguments. In subsequent chapters we first take a closer look at the triggers of innovation and collaboration and then review the institutionalization of arenas for collaborative innovation. Next we study the different aspects of the process of collaborative innovation such as learning, decision making, implementation, and innovation diffusion. Finally, we explore the role of metagovernance in terms of innovation leadership and governance reform for stimulating collaborative innovation.

CONCLUSION

The discovery of the intrinsic link between collaboration and innovation prompts the search for a theoretical framework for analyzing the complex and contingent processes of collaborative innovation. As we have seen, the theories of public management and administration that developed after the Second World War have surprisingly little to offer in terms of explaining the creation of public innovation and of understanding the processes of collaborative innovation. However, this chapter has identified a number of important precursors to a theory of collaborative innovation in terms of theories of collaborative planning, theories of economic innovation systems, participatory theories of technological development, and the new design thinking. It has also assembled and presented some of the main theoretical building blocks that help us create an analytical framework for studying collaborative innovation. The following chapters introduce more theories that further explore the different aspects of public innovation processes based on multi-actor collaboration. Nevertheless, the core arguments of the theories presented so far are summarized in the simple analytical model and inform the discussions in the next chapters. Rather than attempt to refine the analytical model and specify the conditions for its application, the idea is to use the model to open a new field of study and to structure the analysis of the key aspects of collaborative innovation.

4

TRIGGERING INNOVATION AND COLLABORATION

A LARGE NUMBER of public policies, organizations, and services tend to be fairly stable and experience very little change over time. The stability of the public sector is positive insofar as it creates a high degree of predictability and security for citizens, private firms, and other stakeholders. Welfare recipients can safely rely on getting the same benefits and services tomorrow as they received yesterday, and private contractors can plan ahead, knowing that they will provide the same kind of garbage collection and hospital cleaning in coming years. In some areas, such as the regulation of traffic, the control of nuclear power plants, and the taxation of pension schemes, we would consider experimental changes and rapid reforms as unwelcome and perhaps even dangerous (Mulgan 2007, 5).

Nevertheless, as tax payers and engaged citizens, we expect the public sector to adapt, change, and innovate in response to new conditions and developments, to emerging problems, and to bold political ambitions for improving social and economic life, meeting new demands, and strengthening democracy. Ideally public organizations that face serious problems, or new challenges and opportunities, should look for an innovative response that enhances their performance and helps them realize their goals. Moreover, since multiparty collaboration and cocreation are likely to spur public innovation, efforts should be made to bring together relevant and affected stakeholders in collaborative arenas that can stimulate the development and realization of innovative designs. In reality, though, neither innovation nor collaboration arises spontaneously in the public sector. Many public organizations avoid the risks and uncertainties associated with innovation, and the high transaction costs and potential conflicts associated with cooperation across institutional and sector boundaries tend to limit the use of collaborative approaches to fostering public innovation. In other words, the link between emerging problems, challenges, and opportunities; the search for innovative solutions; and the rise of multi-actor collaboration are contingent and, at best, dependent on a number of administrative and political factors. Therefore, we need to study the conditions for problems, challenges, and new opportunities to trigger innovation processes and for collaborative efforts to create innovation.

This chapter aims to provide a systematic study of the factors triggering innovation and collaborative innovation in the public sector. The first step is to look at the impact of both crises and routines on public innovation. As we shall see, there is no clear trigger of public innovation. In most cases the trigger is simply the identification of problems, challenges, and opportunities, no matter whether they stem from a crisis or emerge as a part of a routinized performance assessment. The second step consists of showing why some problems, challenges, and opportunities rather than others stimulate the search for public innovation. The context in which certain problematizations emerge seems to be an important factor in this regard, as well as the discursive construction of the relative importance of the problems, challenges, and opportunities. The third step is to identify and discuss the factors that inform the decision on whether to take a collaborative approach to public innovation. Traditions, calculations, story lines, and the dramaturgical articulation of the innovation challenge are key determinants in this regard. The final section discusses the power effects of including and excluding actors from the collaborative arenas that want to produce public innovation. The convener decides which actors to include or exclude from processes of collaborative innovation and thereby sets the course of the innovation journey, but the collaborative arena and the discursive framing of this arena may also influence which actors are involved in the collaborative efforts to renew the public sector.

CRISES, ROUTINES, AND BEYOND

There seems to be little agreement in the public innovation literature about which situations trigger innovation processes in the public sector. Most of the time, we act in accordance with unconscious habits and customary ways of thinking about the tasks that we undertake. Sometimes new knowledge, accidents, or newcomers to the organization make us reflect on what we are doing and why we are doing it in a certain way, and that reflection may sometimes lead to innovation. However, because change and transformation are painful and risky, the initiation of innovation processes cannot be reduced to a question of stimulus and response. Something more than a disturbing incident is needed for social and political actors to give up their habitual ways of doing things and to invest their time and energy in developing and implementing new ideas and practices.

Innovations are often triggered by *crises,* which are defined as *unstable situations where things are not going well and the survival of a particular public program, organization, or service is at stake* (Levin and Sanger 1994). Without clear performance measures and competition from other providers, public agencies could possibly perform poorly for a long time without making any improvement until they suddenly become involved in a public crisis that forces them to reconsider and adjust their methods. Such a crisis can be caused by new societal developments that render existing policy programs obsolete, goal displacements that create a clear and visible discrepancy between the stated and the pursued objectives, failures to adhere to particular technical standards or normative values, or public detection of underperformance caused by bad management or a lack of coordination. A crisis situation is often characterized by the increasingly intense internal and external critiques, the rise of tensions and conflicts, and a general recognition that something must be done as the costs and risks of not doing anything are too high. Radical innovations that promise to fix the crises-ridden situation by redesigning policies, organizational procedures, or the content of concrete services will clearly offer a way out of the impasse, but smaller, less ambitious, and more symbolic innovations will often be enough to resolve the crisis.

Although crises may trigger innovation, Borins's recent study of several samples of public innovations in the United States shows that crises only appeared in about 30 percent of the public innovations that were analyzed (Borins 2001b). According to Borins, "The relative infrequency of crisis-driven innovation . . . suggests that crises are not a necessary condition for public sector innovation" (Borins 2001b, 314). Apparently public innovators often respond to problems and challenges before they reach crisis proportions. They also seek to exploit new opportunities on a regular basis and are often supported by established procedures that allow them to identify, develop, and adopt new ideas that enhance their performance. This interpretation squares well with the argument of March and Olsen (1995) and the ideas of Polsby (1984) that tend to see administrative and political *routines* as crucial triggers of public innovation. Crises might force public organizations to innovate, but innovation can also be a part of institutionalized procedures and routinized behavior.

According to March and Olsen (1995), not only do public reforms and innovations occur at the exceptional, critical junctures and breaking points of history, where we look for a new path because the old one is no longer viable, but they also emerge as a result of stable procedures that routinely evaluate established practices, monitor the results, and identify and test alternative options. Such procedures for exploration and exploitation are inherent features of public organizations, and their role and impact as triggers of incremental forms of innovation have been strengthened by the growing emphasis on strategic leadership, performance measurement, and performance management associated with the concept of New Public Management. Public managers regularly change the structure, practices, and outputs of public agencies as a result of periodic reviews, adjustments to external developments, and institutionalized processes of experimental learning. The executive public managers involve politicians when necessary to obtain clearances and secure resources for pursuing and realizing new ideas that might entail significant repercussions. Public managers at lower levels aim to negotiate their room for maneuver with their superiors, and this leeway allows them to create incremental innovations as a part of daily operations without seeking permission from above.

Similar routines are found in political life. Particular routines and rituals prompt politicians to develop and present new and innovative ideas. Inaugural speeches in parliament, publications of election campaign manifestos, press briefings after important cabinet meetings, televised addresses to the population, and so on, are examples of well-established routines that urge politicians to advance new ideas and innovative solutions and show that they are capable of exercising a proactive political leadership. In these situations, they will often look to their administrative staffs for new ideas that, if they catch on and are successfully implemented, become public innovations (Polsby 1984).

Whether uncertain crises or stable routines are the key triggers of public innovation is difficult to determine empirically. The problem is that crises and routines are often combined in ways that make it hard to say whether one or the other is triggering innovation processes. Hence, a public crisis may surface during a routine review when it is suddenly revealed that public performance has dramatically declined or is unexpectedly low or poor. Take, for example, the reaction to the Programme for International Student Assessment's annual publication of its rankings of all countries according to the proficiency of their schoolchildren in reading, writing, and calculus. Although it is a fairly routinized performance review, a drop in ranking can sometimes create heated debates about a "crisis in the national school system" that are likely to trigger strong political demands for innovation. Likewise, even stable routines in place that help handle public crises can facilitate policy innovation. For example, a public crisis caused by a critical news report that reveals alarming service gaps in the local public care for elderly people may be solved by referring the problem to a standing committee responsible for the oversight and development of municipal elderly care. The committee might even have a standard procedure in place for describing and analyzing problems and how to search for new and better solutions. In short, crises can emerge from routine reviews, and routines can be mobilized to solve public crises.

The failure to determine the relative importance of crises and routines in triggering public innovation forces us to find another starting point for analyzing when and how public innovation processes are triggered. Instead of looking for more or less crisis-ridden situations or routinized practices that may or may not initiate the search for innovative solutions, we should look instead for particular push or pull factors. *Push factors* are at work when we seek to escape the present predicament, or perhaps a situation in the near future, that is perceived to be unsustainable due to the emergence or aggravation of some serious problems. *Pull factors* are at work when we want to go in a new and attractive direction in response to positive and ambitious challenges that dare us to realize our dreams or by means of exploiting new opportunities that are revealed to us. Let us explore these push and pull factors a little further.

On the one hand, organizations are seemingly *pushed* down the innovation road when they face sizable and manifest problems that are not likely to go away in the foreseeable future and when they problematize existing practices and the way they are organized and governed. Serious and enduring problems put pressure on public organizations to innovate. To illustrate, reports showing that long-term training and education programs for unemployed people appear to increase the duration of time that they are unemployed and receive unemployment benefits are likely to trigger a search for new ways of enhancing the competences of the unemployed so that they can return to the labor market as quickly as possible. Rising costs in the health care sector tend to stimulate the development of new and innovative attempts to prevent lifestyle-related diseases. Reports of corruption and fraud in the contracting out of public services lead to calls for innovative control mechanisms if the present procedures have failed. A growing frequency of cloudbursts caused by global warming drives big cities, whose existing sewer systems cannot cope with such large amounts of water, to seek to create innovative ways of handling them.

Public awareness of policy problems is important for triggering the search for new and innovative solutions. In Oakland, for instance, several thousand people mourned the death of a hardened criminal who had controlled a public housing project for many years through a combination of violence, threats, and handouts. The sizable crowd gathered at this infamous drug lord's funeral showed the city council that the problem with drugs and criminal gangs was out of control. Likewise, the general public clearly saw that the time for change had arrived and that a window of opportunity for policy innovation had opened. Similarly, an attempt to shoot down a Danish gang leader as he was drinking coffee in a crowded café in the inner city demonstrated that Copenhagen was no longer a safe and peaceful city and that steps needed to be taken to curb gang-related violence. The sensationalized bullet hole in the café's window epitomized the public's recognition that the community faced a serious problem that called for policy innovation.

On the other hand, organizations and people seem to be *pulled* toward innovation when they face *new challenges* that urge them to pursue hopes and dreams in a world of perils and constraints. At all levels, realizing that new and ambitious goals and objectives cannot be reached by relying on established ideas, practices, or forms of organization makes innovation an attractive and desirable response. When US president Barack Obama announced that the United States aspires to send a manned spaceship to Mars, the project called for developing new and creative solutions. When a government wants to ensure a greener and more sustainable future and decides to reduce carbon dioxide emissions by 30 percent by 2020, it needs to produce major innovations in the energy and transport sector. When a regional authority aims to create regional growth and prosperity in the face of economic globalization, it must find new and innovative ways of connecting public institutions in the field of research and technology with private firms and financial institutions. When a local municipality wants to eliminate illiteracy among groups of poor refugees and immigrants and turn them into an asset for the local labor market, it calls for innovative measures to reach and enroll the adult population in educational programs. When a local planning agency wants to gain widespread popular support for a new urban development plan in a city with little trust in government, it requires innovative ways to organize public participation in planning processes.

New opportunities provide another pull factor that can trigger public innovation processes. Sometimes we innovate, not so much because we face a problem or want to take on certain challenge, but because new opportunities permit us to do new and desirable things. When new opportunities are revealed to us and we realize that we can now do things that we did not think were possible, we begin to consider how we can exploit the new opportunities in and through innovative projects and solutions. The development of new information and communication technologies has enabled the public sector to innovate its modus operandi by creating fast and decentered communication flows that facilitate an easy method of disseminating and retrieving information, a transparent access to government data, the coordination of initiatives and actions of different agencies, and a democratic dialogue with citizens and private stakeholders. To illustrate, Dutch health care employees now use digital technologies to empower chronically ill patients, who can create their own virtual hospital experience through which they can interact with experts, caregivers, and other patients and gain control over their treatment and their lives.

Many other opportunities can trigger public innovation. Organizational reforms that create larger and more resourceful organizations, or facilitate the formation of joined-up government, may persuade public organizations to embark on new and ambitious innovative projects that require a larger institutional capacity than was previously available. In a similar way, relaxing central government rules and providing special-purpose funding may trigger local experimentation and innovation. Rumors and reports that public organizations have succeeded in solving intractable problems or in improving public performance in new and disruptive ways prompt other public managers to replicate those successful innovations and transform the prevailing ideas and practices in their own organizations. When public managers learn about how other organizations have gained legitimacy by adopting innovative solutions that are recommended as best practices, they might even construct or pay attention to problems that had not previously been on their agenda. Sometimes the changes prompted by the circulation of best practices take the form of a garbage can process (Cohen, March, and Olsen 1972), whereby the knowledge of innovative solutions creates a problem that was not there beforehand but leads to the adoption of a new solution inspired by the best practice.

In sum, problems may serve as push factors that call for the development of innovative solutions, and challenges and opportunities may serve as pull factors that make the search for innovative public solutions more attractive. In some public organizations, it may not be considered appropriate for public managers and employees to focus on problems. Instead, problems will be talked about as "challenges" and "opportunities" because these terms have a more positive ring. However, when the public media reports that outdated and malfunctioning government programs fail to meet politically agreed standards, targets, and goals, the public agencies responsible for the underperforming programs will soon realize that they have serious problems that call for innovation.

WHEN DO PROBLEMS, CHALLENGES, AND OPPORTUNITIES TRIGGER INNOVATION PROCESSES?

The mere presence of problems, challenges, and opportunities does not always generate sufficient will and determination to change the current state of affairs and to search for new and innovative ways of doing things. Emerging problems might be met by indifference, resignation, or shrewd blame avoidance strategies; new challenges might be seen as minor, uncertain, or distant; and opportunities might be passed over because they are considered trivial, insignificant, or difficult and costly to exploit. As not all problems, challenges, and opportunities trigger processes of public innovation, we need to look more carefully at the conditions under which they will initiate change processes and have an innovative impact.

The search for innovative solutions only begins when it becomes clear that continuing along the established path is impossible, or at least highly problematic, and that a new path can and should be developed to improve performance and goal attainment. The discursive construction of the nature and character of problems, challenges, and opportunities is crucial in this regard. Hence, when problems are framed as "burning platforms," the preservation of the status quo clearly is not an option. When challenges are depicted as "well recognized," "scientifically proven," and "expedient," the scope for not responding to and acting upon them narrows. Finally, when opportunities are constructed as "unique," "strategic," and "irresistible," the idea of not exploiting the fertile ground to produce new, innovative, and highly attractive solutions will appear as unforgivable, because standing still will make public organizations appear to be falling behind.

The framing of problems, challenges, and opportunities takes place in and through a series of loosely connected language games that involve a plurality of actors—politicians, lobbyists, experts, and mass media—and are shaped by the power strategies and rhetorical devices that these actors deploy. There is probably no better example than the discursive construction of the greenhouse effect. In Europe the ill effects of concentrations of carbon dioxide in the atmosphere are constructed as an urgent problem that threatens the survival of humankind, and a veritable race is on to exploit new opportunities to develop low-emission technologies and use renewable energy sources. By contrast, lobbyists and right-wing politicians in the United States have managed to portray the greenhouse effect as a minor problem by insisting that the scientific evidence is uncertain. The result is that the United States as a whole has been doing much less than the European Union has in terms of crafting innovative policies that promote the development of green technologies.

The sense of importance and urgency ascribed to problems, challenges, and opportunities depends on the context in which the issues emerge. A relatively small problem might be seen as a serious incident that calls for creative thinking and bold action if it is perceived as an unacceptable development or if it problematizes the current ways of doing things. To illustrate, a shooting in Oakland, which has close to a hundred homicides per year, will not cause much alarm, whereas the attempted murder of a gang leader in Copenhagen, which is considered one of the safest cities in Europe, appeared on the front pages of every newspaper and triggered a search for an innovative policy response. In much the same way, Denmark, Sweden, and Norway, with their high degrees of ethnic homogeneity and highly skilled labor forces, face the emerging challenge of integrating increasing numbers of refugees fleeing from war-torn Syria and must develop innovative solutions. The same goes for new technological opportunities that facilitate treating cancer patients in their own homes, an option that has been discussed for some time but was previously considered impossible given the therapy's dependence on once-immobile and expensive hospital equipment. Thus, exploiting new opportunities also requires developing innovative services and forms of organization. Context, therefore, conditions and shapes the impact of emerging problems, challenges, and opportunities.

The construction of problems and challenges as a problematization of existing practices and the creation of new opportunities for change provide a necessary but insufficient condition for initiating public innovation processes. It also requires some legitimate, energetic, and resourceful entrepreneurs who assume responsibility for responding to the problematizations of the existing practices and who seek to exploit the new opportunities in the search for innovative solutions (Doig and Hargrove 1990). Such entrepreneurs will often play an active role in the discursive framing of problems, challenges, and opportunities as innovation triggers. Then they will use the momentum that these triggers create to put innovation on the agenda, to mobilize resources, and to generate support for the idea of changes so that the innovation journey can begin.

The social and political actors who seize the moment and set out on the long, hard, and perilous innovation journey are driven by a mixture of curiosity, good intentions, professional ethics, career ambitions, institutional incentives, organizational goals, and so on. Assessing the risks associated with innovation and the likely consequences of such risks will also be a key parameter in the calculations of the innovation entrepreneurs. Here it is important that the actors do not focus exclusively on the negative outcomes of risk and the need to reduce these risks. There is always a chance that innovation will fail to solve the problem, meet the challenge, or exploit the opportunities. In addition, the costs of innovation might be considerable, and people might dislike and criticize the results. However, it is important not only to refrain from exaggerating these negative results but also to ensure the assessment of all the things that might go wrong is balanced by an assessment of the positive gains and potential spin-offs from innovation (Renn 2008; Osborne and Brown 2011). A narrow focus on the negative possibilities and the attempt to minimize them will tend to deter policy entrepreneurs from embarking on the uncertain and troublesome journey to public innovation.

Sometimes diverging perceptions of the size of negative risks and the possibility for risk management deter innovation. For example, in innovative urban development projects, the technical experts and the regulatory agencies might believe the negative environmental risks can be mitigated and are therefore negligible or acceptable, whereas the local community actors might think the environmental risks are imminent and call for independent monitoring, and the conservationists tend to distrust both the mitigation efforts and the detection systems. Reaching an agreement about the size of and prospect for managing risks thus requires collaboration and trust-based dialogue between multiple stakeholders (Gray 1989, 251–53, 274–75).

In sum, as illustrated in figure 4.1, the context-dependent framing of problems, challenges, and opportunities that are taken up and acted upon by legitimate, energetic, and resourceful entrepreneurs triggers public innovation. Social and political actors also may be motivated to move on particular issues and thereby trigger processes leading to public innovation, but the big question is whether these actors will take a collaborative approach to developing and realizing their new ideas.

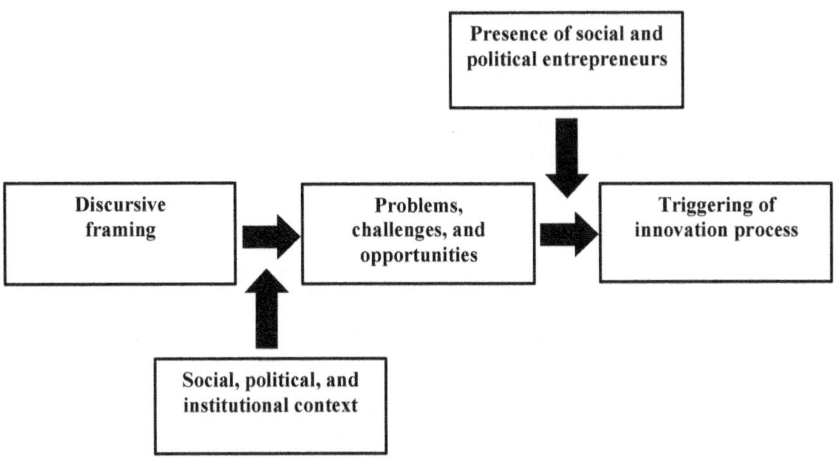

FIGURE 4.1. Model of factors triggering innovation processes

TAKING A COLLABORATIVE APPROACH TO INNOVATION

Depending on the circumstances, numerous stakeholders can initiate the search for innovative solutions and practices: political leaders, policy experts, public managers, public employees, users, civil society organizations, and private firms. Politicians might see policy innovation as a means of demonstrating their initiative, responsiveness, and political leadership and thus of helping to ensure their reelection. An innovative policy proposal that is successfully transformed into legislation can make a political career.

Policy experts are keen to use their professional and scientific knowledge to identify problems, point out new challenges, and urge the political decision makers to exploit particular opportunities to produce policy innovation. Experts work in a growing number of private think tanks and on public committees that advise government officials about the urgency of different problems and challenges. They inspire politicians to find new and innovative solutions on the basis of scientific research.

Public managers in a New Public Management environment tend to view the initiation of public innovation as both an obligation and a chance to display their strategic capacities for managing change and producing results. However, middle managers often have little time to initiate and participate in innovation projects because they are busy running their organizations, supporting and monitoring their staffs, and feeding the elaborate systems of performance management. The time pressure under which they work is revealed in a survey of Danish public managers conducted by the research project on Collaborative Innovation in the Public Sector in 2010. The survey reveals only 12 percent of the managers feel that they have time to pursue innovation, and 47 percent of them spend less than five hours per week on tasks and issues related to innovation (FTF 2010).

According to the same survey, 73 percent of the public managers claim that it is rather the public employees who are the primary source of public innovation. This finding can be explained by the fact that public employees are much closer to the problems and challenges that call for innovation. Further, they have the practical knowledge required to exploit the available opportunities to develop and implement new ideas. Frequently they do so in an incremental way and under the radar so that top managers and politicians cannot block their service innovations.

Users, citizens, and their different associations and organizations can also initiate public innovation on the basis of their unique experiences and knowledge about the effects of public regulation and services. Their impact, however, will rely on support from public officials that can be hard to get and often only obtained after persistent lobbying efforts. The new emphasis on user-driven innovation—which assumes that lay people are competent interpreters of their own lives and capable of developing new and innovative solutions together in close cooperation with public employees—might help users, citizens, and their different organizations to be heard in the future.

Finally, private firms might be able to stimulate public innovation processes by showing public authorities, who either are contracting out public services or are responsible for the public procurement of particular goods, how new technologies or designs create opportunities for innovation in goods and services. Marketization strategies associated with New Public Management also aim to strengthen the role of private firms in initiating public innovation, although we lack clear empirical evidence confirming whether this effort has been successful.

Some innovation entrepreneurs may have considerable success with adopting a "go-it-alone" strategy in pursuing particular innovations. Some politicians and public managers not only have the knowledge and capacity to develop innovative ideas and solutions by themselves but also have the power and leverage to impose them in their jurisdiction or organization. Likewise, public employees will frequently be able to create small, everyday innovations in the content, production, and delivery of public services. These innovations will often take place without the direct involvement of top-level public managers and elected politicians, although the employees might act on the basis of a broad mandate from public managers and political leaders or at least try to anticipate their wants. By contrast, policy experts, users, interest organizations, and private firms do not have the same capacity to foster public innovation all by themselves. They can try to set the agenda and initiate innovation processes, but their role and impact depend on their collaborating with other actors.

Despite this asymmetry, all the different actors stand to benefit from taking a collaborative approach to public innovation. As argued in chapter 2, collaboration may generate better and more creative ideas through cross-fertilization and mutual learning. It may also help select the most promising and feasible ideas, ensure that they are implemented on the basis of joint ownership and flexible adjustment, and see to it that they are disseminated throughout and across public organizations. By comparison, go-it-alone strategies will not only lead to more narrow-minded and less innovative solutions but also generate externalities and conflicts that may be extremely costly and impede implementation and diffusion (Gray 1989).

Now simply because one can reap some significant benefits from collaboration, there is no guarantee that social and political actors will choose to adopt a collaborative approach to public innovation. Whether particular actors decide to include and interact with other actors in the pursuit of innovation depends on a number of factors.

The first factor concerns the structural conditions for collaboration. According to Gray (1989, 28–54), collaboration provides an antidote to increased turbulence in the social, political, and economic environment as it enhances the collective capacity for responding to structural changes and mitigating their negative effects. Turbulence is enhanced by a rapid economic and technological growth, declining productivity, and increasing competitive pressures; the expansion of the horizon of strategic action to the global level; the blurring of the boundaries between the public and private sectors; the shrinking public revenues for public programs; and a dissatisfaction with juridical processes for problem solving. The presence of one or more of these structural conditions will intensify the pressure to collaborate, and collaborative innovation will help create new and stable solutions that alleviate some of the stress that is felt by the social and political actors in turbulent environments.

The second factor in whether actors will collaborate is the tradition for and experience with collaboration (Ansell and Gash 2007). The tradition for collaborating with other actors in adjusting, changing, and innovating public policies, organizations, and services varies among countries, levels, and policy areas. More cross-sectorial collaboration occurs in northwestern European countries with strong neo-corporatist traditions than in other countries. In addition, countries in which political power and public service provision are devolved to the local level create good opportunities for sustained collaboration because there are many contact points for private stakeholders and good chances that collaboration will have a significant impact on policymaking, societal regulation, and service delivery. Some policy areas also seem to be more open to collaboration than others. Frequently welfare areas such as health, education, social policy, and employment policy will have stronger traditions of collaboration than the more technical and economic policy areas, although business development, environmental protection, and urban planning also exhibit a considerable degree of collaboration between public and private actors. Positive experiences with collaboration will encourage actors to take a collaborative approach to innovation, whereas negative experiences will inhibit collaborative innovation. A proactive strategy for bringing the different stakeholders together again by building trust and healing wounds, however, might break the negative spiral.

The third factor influencing collaboration is the existence of social capital, which has two important dimensions. The first dimension relates to the individual actors' contacts and connections with other actors that can help give them access to relevant resources embedded in social networks (Lin 2001). The second dimension of social capital relates to the level of generalized trust within the social network that the actors can draw upon when collaborating (Putnam 2000). For the actors to choose a collaborative approach to innovation, they must know and, preferably, have some prior contacts with other actors. Moreover, they must also have a certain level of trust in these other actors in order to overcome collective action problems and to facilitate mutual learning, coordination, risk sharing, and joint implementation of new and bold solutions. Weak ties to other actors may be enough to initiate collaboration (Granovetter 1973), but the chances of developing a high level of generalized trust are improved as ties become stronger. The real danger to collaboration is the presence of structural holes in the web of social relations as they can prevent actors from identifying and collaborating with others who might hold key innovation assets (Burt 1992).

A fourth factor involves the actors' calculation as to whether they want to spend the necessary time and energy to become involved and collaborate with other actors in order to cocreate innovative solutions. According to Gray (1989), this calculation involves a series of judgments about whether the alternative to collaboration is acceptable, whether other relevant actors will agree to collaborate, whether parity exists among the potential collaborators, whether it is likely that collaboration will produce positive outcomes, and whether reaching a fair agreement is possible. Although the first judgment hinges on a pretty rational calculation of how one's interests are best served, the subsequent judgments tend to rely on interpreting the different degrees of trust on the part of the potential collaborators. In a sense it all boils down to one question: Does the actor trust that the others are prepared to collaborate, overcome power asymmetries, and find fair solutions to the problem or challenge at hand?

The pursuit of individual interests and the actors' trust in the commitment, sincerity, and generosity of other actors are not the only parameters when calculating whether to collaborate with other actors. In most cases these calculations will be influenced by the way that social and political actors perceive themselves. Some identity constructions might hinder collaboration (March and Olsen 1995). For instance, some politicians perceive themselves as the only legitimate decision makers and oppose the idea of consulting other actors to generate public innovation. Many policy experts do not want to deliberate with citizens, civil society organizations, and other "amateurs" who fail to understand the experts' scientific approach and their demand for evidence-based knowledge. Some public managers and public employees have an identity as fast-moving entrepreneurs, and it makes them perceive collaborative arenas as mere talk shops that will slow them down and dilute their brilliant ideas. Others believe that their professional training and knowledge mean that they have all the answers; thus, they maintain consulting with citizens and users is a waste of time. Some users like to raise complaints and advance their demands, but they do not see engaging in collaboration to find new solutions to public problems as their task. Some social movements will even insist that collaborating with the "system" will compromise their autonomy. Finally, a fair number of private firms will have strong prejudices against collaborating with public agencies that they see as slow-moving bureaucracies burdened by red tape. We shall revisit how the role and identity of the various actors can act as both a barrier and a driver of collaborative innovation in chapter 5.

A fifth factor in whether actors will interact with others in the pursuit of innovation is the extent to which potential collaborators are united by a particular story line or metaphor. As we have seen, the public and private actors who can contribute to collaborative public innovation are rather diverse, and they often have conflicting interests and different frames of reference. Eventual communication failures, disagreements, and open conflicts constitute a fundamental barrier to collaborative innovation; however, this barrier can be overcome with story lines and metaphors that create and sustain collaborative coalitions of actors who are committed to a common mission and recognize their mutual dependence vis-à-vis that mission (Hajer 2009). Story lines are short, condensed statements that summarize a particular account of what the problem or challenge is and how it can be responded to or solved. For example, the assertion that "the rising costs of health care should be curbed by focusing more on preventive health care" is a good story line that links problems and solutions in a narrative structure. Sometimes a story line can be further abbreviated into a metaphor that captures the entire mission of potential collaborators. The declaration of "the war on drugs" constructs a mission-defining metaphor that signals the serious commitment on the political leadership's part and calls for the mobilization of a broad range of actors (Hajer 2009, 61).

Story lines and metaphors derive their political effect from their ability to galvanize, bring together, and tendentially unify a range of actors who respond to the socially constructed idea of a common mission. The trick of story lines and metaphors is that the key terms are often so vague and ambiguous that the actors can read different things into them. The actors might have different opinions and frames of reference, but they will agree that a particular story line or metaphor describes an urgent task or mission that they want to be a part of. Hence, as Hajer (2009) concludes, "The multi-interpretability of metaphors and story lines is a vital aspect of their political efficacy" (62).

To illustrate this important conclusion, the mobilization of a broad range of Danish public and private actors in a national governance network behind the active labor-market reforms of the early 1990s was facilitated by the gradual emergence of a story line that claimed "structural employment should be reduced through activation." Despite interpreting the key terms differently, all of the key actors subscribed to this story line. The actors told disparate stories to their various constituencies about what the terms "structural unemployment" and "activation" meant and implied, but they all agreed on the particular framing of the problem and the solution. Thus, their broad agreement facilitated collaboration, mutual learning, and compromise (Torfing 2007).

The last factor concerns the dramaturgical effects of multi-actor interaction. These effects, which are created through the setting, staging, and scripting of the interaction, can play a decisive role in determining the fate of collaboration. Collaboration often begins, naturally, with some kind of meeting. It might be a planned and formal meeting convened by a public manager, a workshop or (video) conference that provides opportunities for unstructured dialogue, or a spontaneous gathering that permits an informal exchange of views and opinions in relation to an issue that calls for joint action. Whatever the meeting's form, its location and the way it is organized and conducted are key determinants in the social and political actors' decisions about whether to collaborate (Hajer 2009, 65–67).

Often the study of the dramaturgical aspects of the interaction process is neglected to focus on analyzing the motivations of the actors and the level of internal conflicts. However, the setting of the social and political interaction—that is, the physical venue for the meeting and the artifacts that are brought to the venue—is frequently important in determining the prospect for collaboration. For example, if the meeting is held in the city hall and perhaps even uses the city councilors' assembly room as the meeting place, some actors will likely feel too intimidated to attend. Thus, the politicians will continue their internal party-political battles and make the other actors feel that the meeting is a complete waste of time.

The interaction's staging—the temporal and symbolic organization of the interaction and the attempt to arrange and divide the participants into different groups with different roles in the process—can also influence the actors' willingness to collaborate. For example, long and formal meetings with highly technical content might scare off the innovation entrepreneurs. A court-like division of the participants into a small group of active players, a few expert witnesses, and a large passive audience is also likely to prevent future collaboration.

Finally, the scripting of the actors' performance, or the attempt to determine the character of the actors and to provide cues for their appropriate action, is also paramount for determining future collaboration. For example, on the one hand, presenting the actors as antagonistic enemies who confront each other at a negotiating table during strategic bargaining will reduce the preference for collaboration. On the other hand, the appropriate cultivation of agonistic relations that make the actors see each other not only as opponents with equally legitimate demands and ideas but also as part of a joint search for new and better solutions will tend to stimulate collaboration. Thus, instead of asking the private stakeholders to state their views and placing the public actors in the role of mediators, beginning the meeting with a joint exploration of the problem or challenge at hand may build a common ownership of it and prove much more conducive for spurring collaboration.

THE POWER OF INCLUSION AND EXCLUSION

Although innovation offers an intelligent alternative to across-the-board cuts and persistent policy deadlocks, and collaboration appears to be a potent driver of public innovation, there is no guarantee that collaborative innovation will be the preferred response to emerging problems, challenges, and opportunities. Both the willingness to innovate and the preference for a collaborative innovation strategy rest on a number of contingent factors that might prevent collaborative innovation. Nevertheless, public innovation is a relatively frequent phenomenon, and it is seldom a result of the genius and heroic action of a single entrepreneur who acts like a lone wolf. Instead, politicians, public employees, users, and private stakeholders seem to have a strong preference for solving problems, responding to challenges, and exploiting new opportunities by creating new and innovative designs. Moreover, the presence of professional, interorganizational, and cross-sectorial interdependencies tends to stimulate crosscutting collaboration between a plurality of actors with different roles, ideas, and resources. A comprehensive Danish survey of 1,255 public workplaces, for instance, shows that 86 percent of them have produced innovation in terms of having introduced significantly new and different solutions and that 79 percent of these innovations were a result of collaboration with one or more external actors (National Centre for Public Innovation 2015).

In the considerable number of cases where public innovation is driven by multi-actor collaboration, we should bear in mind that collaboration is always based on processes of inclusion and exclusion, two processes that have important power effects. Collaboration is often discussed in pragmatic and managerial terms and as a matter of "who can help to get things done." Thus, it is frequently asserted that the strength of collaboration comes from inclusion, not exclusion (Straus 2002): "When the full range of differing interests and points of view is involved in solving a problem or making a decision, the solution is likely to be much more comprehensive and creative than if a small group of like-minded individuals acted on its own" (39). However, inclusion always has its limits. To suggest that all relevant stakeholders should be involved in all aspects of collaborative governance and policymaking is naive.

Limits on time and resources force us to be selective, to include some actors rather than others, and to involve them in some processes and arenas rather than others. The inclusion and exclusion of actors will often depend on their access to relevant resources, their commitment to finding a joint solution, and their relative degree of affectedness.

By contrast, the decisions about whether to involve relevant and affected actors in different parts of the innovation process tend to be based on both political and tactical concerns. For example, when public political control is considered important, the tendency is to involve stakeholders in the problem-framing, implementation, and dissemination phases rather than in the formulation and selection of innovative solutions. However, the drawback of this strategy for stakeholder involvement is that the relevant innovation assets are not fully present when formulating and selecting innovative solutions. Finally, whether the public and private stakeholders are included in collaborative arenas such as steering groups, plenary meetings, task forces, or outreach activities will depend on both pragmatic concerns about where the different actors can make the largest contribution and political struggles about who gets to influence what and when and how.

To influence the outputs and outcomes of collaborative innovation processes, it is important to gain access to the different collaborative arenas. Public innovation is not inherently good; therefore, the ability to shape the content of innovative solutions is decisive for ensuring the production of desirable outcomes. In the initial phase of collaborative processes, the convener plays a pivotal role in determining who should be invited to participate and in which phase and to which arena. Over time, however, the collaborative arenas will gradually enhance their role in governing the processes of inclusion and exclusion. The participating actors will also begin to negotiate on who should be included and where and when, and who should not. Actors inside or outside the collaborative arenas will advance claims about which interests, viewpoints, competences, and so forth, should be represented (Saward 2006). The collaborators will discuss, and perhaps validate, the relevance and legitimacy of these claims vis-à-vis the problems, objectives, and tasks they are facing. As new actors are included, others will leave the table, changing the composition of the different collaborative arenas. The negotiated validation of representative claims and the broadening of the range of participants will normally take place in the initial, formative phase of the collaborative process. Later in the process, the pattern of inclusion and exclusion will typically become rather sedimented, although its political character can suddenly become reactivated in a moment of crisis or stalemate in the collaborative arena. This does not, however, prevent the number of collaborators from shrinking over time. Especially in the implementation phase, bureaucratic actors tend to take control of the process and exclude the private actors to ensure operational efficiency.

Thus, besides the convener or the participating actors, who make conscious political decisions about inclusion and exclusion from the collaborative arena, the discursive framing of the innovation process also has a crucial impact on the relative influence of social and political actors. In the beginning the actors might have a relatively open discussion in the collaborative arena about the nature and character of the innovation in question, because the actors bring their different experiences, viewpoints, and ideas into play in open competition with each other. After a while as a hegemonic discourse that defines the problem setting and the range of feasible options is constructed, the formation of the discourse will have an important effect on the participating actors' relative influence. Those participants who disagree with the hegemonic discourse or have little to offer in the particular way that the problems, constraints, and solutions are framed will become marginalized and lose influence. Thus, despite being formally included in the collaborative process, they will be "internally excluded" (Young 2000).

It is worth noting that the discursive construction of the innovation process exerts power over all participating actors as any ideas and arguments that are not in line with the hegemonic discourse will be considered illegitimate and unwelcome (Torfing 2007). Even those actors who play an active or leading role in the process will be constrained by the hegemonic discourse, which might hamper the innovation process. If it is too narrow and rigid, the hegemonic discourse could prevent an open-ended search for new ideas that challenge conventional wisdom and established practices.

CONCLUSION

This chapter analyzes the triggers of collaborative innovation. It argues that instead of seeing public innovation as solely triggered by either crises or routines, we should also look for push factors in terms of specific problems and pull factors in terms of new challenges and opportunities. The context-bound discursive construction of the importance and urgency of problems, challenges, and opportunities is a necessary but not a sufficient condition for triggering the search for public innovation. Indeed, the presence of legitimate and capable innovation entrepreneurs who actively engage in risk management is a sine qua non for embarking on a public innovation journey. Focusing on the role of social and political actors counters the tendency to see public innovation as solely driven by technological inventions and new scientific insights learned during the search for evidence.

Social and political actors are decisive for triggering public innovation, but whether they choose a collaborative strategy over a go-it-alone approach is an open question. As we have seen, the choice of a collaborative approach to innovation is contingent on numerous factors such as the amount of social capital, the tradition for and prior experience with collaboration, the roles and identities of the actors, and the impact of unifying discourses and story lines, as well as the dramaturgical effects created through the setting, staging, and scripting of multi-actor interaction. Exploring these crucial factors reveals the relevance of network theory, institutional theory, and discourse theory for the study of collaborative innovation.

Last but not least, the chapter shows that the collaborative innovation process cannot be seen merely as a practical and pragmatic activity that includes the relevant, affected actors from the public and private sectors in order to enhance the wealth of ideas and to mobilize pertinent knowledge and resources. The triggering of collaborative innovation is imbued with power as external and internal exclusions from the collaborative arena prevent certain actors from influencing particular parts of the innovation process. Further, a discursive regulation of what can be said and done in the collaborative arena points to the relevance of studying the structural forms of power that pervade the collaborative arena and narrows the scope for how the social and political actors can use their free, responsible, and empowered actions to reinvigorate the public sector through different kinds of innovation.

5

MOBILIZING AND EMPOWERING ACTORS AND INSTITUTIONALIZING INTERACTION

WHEN THE momentum for collaborative innovation is created, a plurality of actors with different ideas and competences must be mobilized and empowered, and their interaction must be institutionalized to facilitate mutual learning and collaborative innovation. To illustrate, when the government asks the police force to find new and innovative solutions to address the rising problems of gang-related crime, the force may want to initiate a collaborative process to enhance its limited cognitive and ideational capacity for designing and implementing new measures. It must recruit and motivate a number of relevant and affected actors and institutionalize the process of interaction to create a stable process of collaboration that can facilitate cognitive and ideational exchange.

To better understand how the momentum for collaborative innovation is transformed into actual processes of collaborative interaction, this chapter draws on governance network theory and institutional theory to explore the factors that determine the empowerment and disempowerment of social and political actors in collaborative arenas. The chapter also analyzes the processes of institutionalization and de-institutionalization of collaborative endeavors to develop and implement new designs. The argument here, supported by empirical cases, is that collaborative interaction requires a certain balance between empowerment and disempowerment and between institutionalization and de-institutionalization. The chapter concludes with a discussion of how to facilitate collaboration between relatively empowered actors in relatively institutionalized arenas. The roles of trust, process management, and game structuration are emphasized in this regard.

MOBILIZING RELEVANT ACTORS

The political will to find innovative public solutions through collaborative efforts must be backed by concrete attempts to mobilize social and political actors who hold important and applicable innovation assets that enhance the collective capacity to design innovative responses to the problems, challenges, and opportunities at hand. This situation immediately prompts the question of how we conceptualize the different actors who should be mobilized in collaborative innovation. The literature on this subject commonly invokes a conceptual distinction between the relevant and affected actors. The *affected actors* are *those social and political actors who have concrete experiences with particular problems and who are either helped or harmed by the existing solutions or the lack of solutions.* The group of affected actors also includes those who will be impacted by the crafting of new and innovative designs that will change the output and outcomes of public policies, organizations, and services. In many mature democracies, it has become a well-established norm that affected actors have the right to participate in decision-making processes that deal with issues that somehow affect them. Citizen hearings about new local neighborhood development plans are fairly common, and parents are usually represented in school boards that influence the quality of the education offered to their children. Also, private companies affected by new economic or environmental regulation are normally given a chance to comment on such regulations before they are passed into law. Hence, the affected actors are frequently invited to participate in public decision-making processes and given the opportunity to shape and modify the impact of innovative solutions.

The ultimate goal is to include all the affected actors in order to provide a pluralistic and comprehensive understanding of the problem at hand and to fully grasp the stakes involved in constructing an innovative solution. However, because involving all the affected actors might prove impossible, we often have to content ourselves with bringing in the most intensely affected stakeholders or finding representatives for different affected constituencies. In policy innovation the number of affected actors included is often higher than those for service innovation, which can be rather technical in nature and tends to be less preoccupied with creating legitimacy through participation and inclusion. Indeed, sometimes the affected citizens, such as the potential users of particular services, are not even considered as legitimate stakeholders in collaborative innovation.

Hence, the collaborative arenas involved in designing new innovative measures to curb gang-related violence in Oakland and Copenhagen hardly made any efforts to involve the at-risk youths in their respective deprived neighborhoods. Likewise, the criminal gang members were not invited to participate in the collaborative innovation process. These groups were treated as policy takers rather than policymakers. As a general rule, youth groups and gang members were not considered as resourceful, trustworthy, and legitimate participants in collaborative innovation. A local project in Oakland called Youth UpRising, however, provides a positive exception to the rule. From the start, it involved a group of at-risk youth in the conceptualization of the project, which offers educational leisure activities to local youths and recruits and trains a new generation of community leaders who can build a safer and more prosperous neighborhood. The director was disappointed with the input from the usual suspects who had been invited to help formulate and design the new crime-prevention project, so she recruited local at-risk youths who, after a series of competence-building activities, became a real asset in developing a creative solution to local problems.

The example from Oakland is clearly a positive exception to the general rule that collaborative innovation in crime prevention fails to bring those people who are affected by the problem into the processes that define the problem and craft the innovative solution. New studies suggest that this rule also applies to other policy areas. Hence, when affected citizens are involved in collaborative innovation, they tend to be involved as co-implementers rather than as codesigners and co-initiators (Voorberg, Bekkers, and Tummers 2013). This is problematic because unfortunately the affected actors do not contribute to the understanding of the problem or to the design of the innovative solutions. Important knowledge and information are thereby lost.

If mobilizing affected actors with firsthand knowledge about problems and challenges is important, then mobilizing those actors with relevant innovation assets that can help generate innovative solutions is even more so. *Relevant actors* are *those social and political actors whose knowledge, competences, and ideas are essential for formulating, implementing, and diffusing new and innovation solutions.* Affected actors are relevant because they have valuable experiences and might be able to assess the potential impact of different innovative solutions. However, the forms of expertise needed in processes of collaborative innovation go beyond the experiences, ideas, and suggestions of the affected actors. Hence, there is strong demand for including social and political actors with skills and competences for handling technical and scientific analysis, creative and imaginative thinking, interdisciplinary problem solving, designing and testing prototypes, conducting risk assessment and risk management, planning and coordinating implementation processes, and communicating results.

Actors who might try to block or veto new and bold solutions out of interest-based political disagreement might also be considered as relevant actors who should be included in the collaborative process because their objections might provide a valuable input. However, the decision to include oppositional actors depends on whether the potential damage they can do to the collaborative innovation process is more significant if they are included or excluded from the collaborative processes. If the antagonistic actors can be persuaded to influence rather than block innovative solutions, then including them is probably a good idea as their critical stance might force the other actors to consider those objections and to revise their own ideas. However, if their presence will stall the decision-making process and prevent an open-ended search for new solutions, then it is probably better to exclude them from the collaborative arena.

A key objective when trying to mobilize relevant actors is to provide sufficient knowledge and various capacities so that in formulating innovative solutions they can draw on multiple perspectives while producing public value (Gray 1989, 64). Diversity, however, is not the only concern and can even be dangerous if the different actors are unable to communicate in a meaningful manner and thus enter into a dialogue of the deaf—that is, talking to but not with each other. To avoid that risk, it is essential to recruit a number of intermediaries and boundary spanners who are both capable of translating and linking different kinds of knowledge and expertise and proficient in creating synergy between different skills and competences. *Boundary spanners* are *competent people with an interdisciplinary background, a general knowledge of the field, and an extensive toolbox that enables them to mediate between different groups of professionals, forms of knowledge, and types of actors* (Williams 2002). Facilitating exchanges between different actors requires a profound understanding of each actor, of what they can bring to the table, and of how to prompt them to share their knowledge, resources, and ideas with other actors.

Having drawn up a list of relevant and affected actors that one wants to include in processes of collaborative innovation, the next question becomes how to mobilize all these actors as active and constructive contributors to collaborative innovation. The ability to approach and engage different kinds of actors depends on the social capital of the conveners, and the ability to actively engage the potential collaborators is conditioned on the tradition for and the evaluation of prior experiences with participation and collaboration. Bad experiences with collaboration and lacking social capital are two factors that are difficult to overcome in the short run. By contrast, conveners can influence the various actors' context-bound ideas and calculations about whether to participate in collaborative endeavors. Let us see how it can be done.

First of all, if we want to mobilize relevant and affected actors as a part of a collaborative process aiming to foster innovation, it is important to emphasize the urgency of the issue at hand and the desirability of finding innovative solutions. Portraying the current situation as detrimental to the interest of these actors and imagining the benefits of a new future are paramount for spurring the actors' motivation to participate in innovation processes. Rhetorical devices might be useful in producing such a motivational effect, but they also risk overselling the role and impact of public innovation. Emphasizing the political issues at stake in the search for public innovation may also prompt participation, but the dilemma is that it might not spur collaboration. People may then participate to safeguard their political interests rather than to cocreate innovative solutions.

Second, some actors may want to change things and create innovation, but they might doubt that collaboration is the right mechanism for producing the innovative solutions that they desire. These actors might be persuaded to participate in collaborative arenas if conveners highlight the advantage of collaboration vis-à-vis other options, such as authoritarian ruling by state agencies, market-based competition, adversarial court processes, or uncoordinated go-it-alone strategies (Roberts 2000; Gray 1989, 48–53). Collaboration might be filled with disappointments and compromises, but it will tend to provide a better understanding of the problem at hand, generate a broader range of ideas, and facilitate implementation of robust and workable solutions with widespread support. Perhaps most important, it will help prevent the upsurge of costly and long-lasting legal disputes that often follow attempts to single-handedly impose a particular solution on the other actors in the field.

Next, given that many actors worry that collaboration will be too demanding and take too much time, their motivation to collaborate can be augmented by the development and display of an explicit remit and process plan that specifies what participation in the collaborative process entails, how it is organized, and what it demands from the participants (Straus 2002, 81–105).

A clear and transparent picture of the collaborative process may help convince some actors that the benefits will supersede the efforts required. Dividing the collaborative innovation process into separate stages that involve different constellations of actors and that are tied to particular milestones, which allow the actors to exit the process in a meaningful way, will also help the potential participants to view collaboration as more manageable.

In addition, actors sometimes fear that they will not be listened to and will have no real influence on the joint decisions. The way to circumvent this obstacle to collaboration is to establish and publicize a set of explicit and enforceable rules of conduct to ensure that everybody will be heard and will be able to make a difference, despite persisting resource asymmetries. Being able to write and submit a positional statement that will be properly assessed and included in a joint report or policy paper will help to increase the actors' democratic efficacy, or their belief in their ability to influence a process of democratic decision making. For low-trust actors, being able to veto particular aspects of an innovative plan before it is implemented may convince them that it is worth participating in the collaborative innovation processes.

Further, sometimes conveners encounter a collective action problem. Some actors will refrain from participating in collaborative processes either because they lack confidence that other actors are fully committed to participation or because they rely on other actors to do the job so that they will have the benefits from the new solutions without paying the costs of contributing to its development. A convener might overcome this obstacle by asking key actors to publicly announce their commitment to participate and collaborate and act as front-runners. If a few key actors declare their willingness to participate and engage in collaboration, it may drag others along and create a bandwagon effect. In the end, nobody wants to be left on the platform as the train of collaborative interaction is leaving.

Finally, the dread that collaboration will lead to imbalanced and one-sided solutions that benefit the strong and loudmouthed actors may prevent weaker and less articulate actors from participating in collaborative processes. Weak actors who lack important skills and resources might fear that their goals and interests will become marginalized. However, making deliberate efforts in advance to clarify the common goals and standards that the joint solution must meet and to signal that all contributions are valuable and will be taken seriously might help to remove this barrier to participation. Actors will mobilize if they recognize the urgency of the problem and if they believe that collaboration will result in a fair solution that corresponds with a number of common goals and standards and reflects a broad range of ideas and demands.

As we have seen, the decisions of relevant and affected actors to engage in processes of collaborative innovation can be affected and encouraged in different ways. However, ultimately, the inclination of relevant and affected actors to become actively involved in collaborative innovation processes is shaped by the ways in which their particular identities as social and political actors are framed and articulated. (Identity is here defined as *a relative coherent bundle of identifications that help social and political actors answer the question, who am I?*) The contingent, changing, and multilayered character of the identities of different actors creates dilemmas when making their decisions about whether to participate in collaborative arenas. As we shall see, the mobilization of actors, therefore, calls for particular ways of addressing the different social and political actors.

First of all, many *elected politicians* tend to see themselves as sovereign decision makers who sit at the top of the governing pyramid and have all the power and all the responsibility. They can see no reason to engage in collaborative policymaking that will force them to share power with non-elected actors. However, politicians also tend to see themselves as "organic leaders" who are capable of listening to the man on the street, of engaging with stakeholders, and of providing a unifying sense of purpose and direction in multi-actor arenas. Emphasizing their role as organic leaders of the social and political community rather than as sovereign decision makers will help to mobilize politicians as active and constructive participants in collaborative innovation processes. While deliberating in collaborative arenas, politicians will be able to exercise political as well as moral-intellectual leadership by tapping into and molding the ideas, opinions, and sentiments of lay actors.

Policy experts tend to perceive themselves as privileged providers of critical scientific diagnoses and proponents of evidence-based solutions that are both ready-made and nonnegotiable. This self-perception of research-based policy experts as guardians of scientific truth, who are far removed from mundane political battles, does not encourage their engagement in interactive arenas of collaborative innovation. However, since the mid-1980s, the identity of policy experts has been problematized by post-positivist critiques of the idea of an indisputable scientific truth (Lyotard 1984), and a more pragmatist conception of scientific experts as coproducers of knowledge and ideas has come to the fore (Fischer and Forester 1993). The more this latter identity is accentuated, the more policy experts will tend to participate in collaborative settings. Discussions of Mode 2 research and the triple helix model seem to take us in that direction by insisting that scientific knowledge may benefit from interacting with other and equally legitimate forms of knowledge (Etzkowitz and Leydesdorff 2000).

Some *public managers and employees* will see themselves as old-school public bureaucrats who should follow the rules and orders and stay within their administrative silo, while others will see themselves as public entrepreneurs who introduce, adapt, and implement new ideas in the pursuit of radical efficiencies (Roberts and King 1996, 10–18). Emphasizing the entrepreneurial identity of public managers and employees might spur public innovation but not necessarily their participation in collaborative processes. These public entrepreneurs often fear that collaboration with self-interested stakeholders will slow them down and/or politicize the process of innovation. However, those public entrepreneurs who have been constructed and praised by the New Public Management reform movement are now competing with a new type of entrepreneur, one who is focused more on processes and outcomes than inputs and outputs and on having an interorganizational rather than an intraorganizational perspective on institutional change and public innovation (Osborne 2006).

The new breed of network entrepreneurs highlighted by New Public Governance seem to be more convinced about the advantages of collaboration, and they will be much more inclined to collaborate with different kinds of stakeholders than the bureaucratic entrepreneurs are. A special problem arises in relation to professionals, however. They may have a more positive view of collaborating with private stakeholders, but they often fail to do it in practice (Tait and Lester 2005; Langton et al. 2003). Their lack of time and resources, their concerns about the users' lack of representativity, and their fear of losing power and influence in the seemingly "uncontrollable" processes of collaboration are the frequent explanations for the discrepancy between their intentions and actual practices (Langton et al. 2003; Bovaird 2007). Developing new professional identities that emphasize the role of professionals as facilitators, translators, and mediators and that stress their collective identification with the task at hand is paramount for engaging professionals in collaborative processes (Swan, Scarbrough, and Robertson 2002; Bovaird 2007; Suter et al. 2009; Mitchell et al. 2010).

Citizens have been constructed first as clients of bureaucratic welfare systems and then as customers with a free choice between public and private service providers. Neither identity is conducive for participating in collaborative innovation. *Clients* are disempowered actors subjected to the benevolent power of public authorities, whereas *customers* are focused on their own individual demands and their access to and the quality of public services. Both clients and customers are placed in the receivers' end and generally do not perceive themselves as active contributors to public solutions or even to solving their own problems. Fortunately the new discourses on recognition, empowerment, and active citizenship tend to transform the identity of citizens by emphasizing their competences, capacities, and public orientation. Citizens are perceived as knowledgeable, competent, and capable of pursuing their own interests and acting as cocreators of public services. Conscious and active measures to build a new kind of engaged citizenship will help mobilize what British prime minister David Cameron talks about as the "hidden wealth of society."

It is not enough to talk about citizens and civil society in a new way, however; the public sector must play a crucial role in mobilizing this hidden wealth of society. New platforms for cocreation must be built and new strategies for inviting and encouraging participation must be developed, and here public professionals can play a key role. But if the new discourse on active citizenship and on the construction of resilient communities is used as an excuse for making huge public spending cuts—cuts that will reduce the capacity of the public sector to facilitate citizen engagement in cocreation—the result might be a decline in civil society activity and citizen participation in collaborative innovation (Bartels, Cozzi, and Mantovan 2013).

Interest organizations see themselves as legitimate pressure groups that pursue the interests of their members through different lobbying activities, while *civil society organizations* such as community organizations, grassroots movements, and charities perceive themselves as autonomous, authentic, and alternative providers of public goods that the systemic actors in private markets and public bureaucracies either fail to deliver or do not deliver in the expected way. Both of these identity constructions insist on maintaining a certain distance between the private organization and the public authorities. Political demands and requests for support can be directed to public authorities, but close cooperation either might make them responsible for solutions that their members dislike or might threaten or compromise their autonomy and authenticity. While the pressure group identity of some interest organizations and the systemic-critical identity of at least some civil society organizations may prevent them from supporting and participating in collaborative endeavors, the alternative construction of the same actors as responsible social partners working in tandem with public organizations to achieve common objectives carries a huge potential for mobilizing key resources in the pursuit of public innovation. Both the classical ideas from the corporatist tradition and the current praise of the positive impact of public-private partnerships seem to take us in this direction and will allow us to realize the potential of new identity constructions.

Finally, *private firms* also respond to different identities, some of which may hamper or stimulate their mobilization as active participants in collaborative innovation. The traditional corporate understanding of private firms is that they are only concerned about boosting profitability, supporting deregulation, and rolling back the welfare state. This neo-liberalist identity construction of private firms has recently been challenged by the discourse on Corporate Social Responsibility (CSR). This discourse claims that private firms not only should be concerned about their shareholders but also should be accountable to their stakeholders, including the employees, the customers, the local community, and the political authorities. CSR encourages firms to partner with these different actors and find joint solutions to common problems (Scherer and Palazzo 2011). The new CSR identity opens the possibility for a close collaboration with private firms and the creation of public-private innovation.

Mobilizing social and political actors in collaborative arenas is a question of influencing the calculations and identities of the various actors in a positive direction, but the process also depends on how the relationships between the actors are forged and how the bond between them is construed. Hence, governance network theory argues that networked interaction is a negotiated response to the presence of interdependencies between public and private actors with different stakes, roles, and resources (Rhodes 1997; Kickert, Klijn, and Koppenjan 1997). This argument is well illustrated in the observation of a key actor in the stakeholder network that successfully pushed for public school reform in Minnesota in the mid-1980s: "No one person has all the requisite skills or resources needed to engage in large-scale policy change and we need each other to distribute the workload" (quoted in Roberts and King 1996, 93).

When the relevant and affected actors realize that they cannot produce new and creative solutions all by themselves, they will consider whether to exchange or pool resources with other actors. The social and political actors will begin to contact each other, and if the contacts are positively evaluated and the exchange relations are deemed valuable, they might result in the construction of a network of engaged and resourceful actors (March and Olsen 1995). Sometimes the formation of networks, partnerships, and other collaborative arenas through a bottom-up process based on the need for exchanging and sharing knowledge, ideas, and resources is supported and sustained by isomorphic pressures that promote "multi-actor collaboration" as the proper, or legitimate, tool for enhancing coordination and solving complex problems (DiMaggio and Powell 1983; Skelcher and Torfing 2010). Thus, in gaining legitimacy, this bottom-up formation of networks of collaborating actors follows the current fashion and works with other coercive, mimetic, or normative pressures to adopt a more collaborative approach to public governance and innovation.

As we saw in chapter 4, the interpretative and constructivist strands in the theories of networked governance supplement the resource-interdependency argument by emphasizing the crucial role of discourses and story lines in creating a momentum for collaboration and innovation by framing problems and solutions in certain ways (Hajer 2009). For example, the discourse on global warming and climate change mitigation not only has brought governments together in a community of destiny but also has fostered a platform for large cities to form networks (Bulkeley and Betsill 2003). Further, it has mobilized private corporations in public-private partnerships that want to develop new clean technologies and innovative environmental solutions (Pattberg 2010).

The discursive construction of the political space and opportunities for influencing public policies, organizations, and services is also important. Local and regional governments that brand themselves as open and responsive will encourage the mobilization of private actors, whereas those governments that emphasize the role of professional norms and technical expertise will have some difficulties getting people to trust that their participation is welcome and will have a real impact. Thus, choosing the right venues and forms of interaction is also consequential when mobilizing relevant and affected actors. Participating actors must find the venues attractive and encouraging. Also a willingness to meet people outside government offices and signaling a commitment to sustained two-way interaction based on deliberative norms will encourage potential stakeholders to participate in collaborative processes.

Because the mobilization of relevant and affected actors is important in developing a proper understanding of the issues at stake, in harvesting a sufficient number of creative ideas, and in building joint ownership, the efforts to recruit actors must pull all the levers. It is also essential to influence the context-bound calculations of the actors as well as their identities and relationships. Finally, shaping the public discourse and the institutional arenas for participation is also crucial. However, mobilizing social and political actors is only the first step in initiating processes of collaborative innovation. We also have to think about what the actors bring to the table and how they can contribute effectively and constructively to the collaborative process and the cocreation of innovative solutions. Hence, mobilizing actors is one thing; empowering them so that they can make a real contribution is a separate task that we shall explore next.

EMPOWERING AND DISEMPOWERING ACTORS

As Cruikshank (1999) observes, empowerment emerged out of the 1960s as a strategy for constituting citizens out of subjects and for enhancing their political participation and impact. Thus, empowerment was seen as a progressive strategy for enabling people suffering from various forms of oppression to put up resistance and emancipate themselves. For many years, people on the left talked about the need to empower women, minorities, postcolonial subjects, and the poor so that they could rise and claim their right to free, equal, and prosperous living. Today empowerment has become a polyvalent strategy that political forces at both ends of the political spectrum use. Right-wing politicians talk about the empowerment of private market actors and civil society organizations as alternative welfare providers, and they propose setting up voucher schemes that permit welfare recipients to freely choose their service providers. Similarly the idea of empowering the poor has been advanced by right-wing policy entrepreneurs as a part of neoliberal attempts to privatize public housing projects and turn tenants into homeowners. The will to empowerment is no longer solely a question of emancipating the oppressed; now it is evoked as a way of legitimizing privatization, cutting public spending, and rolling back the welfare state.

Between these extreme conceptions of empowerment as a tool for emancipation or as the human face of spending cuts and privatized welfare, we find a continuum of differing empowerment strategies that are regularly deployed in public governance. At the one end, we find attempts to empower welfare recipients as rational consumers who are exercising their right to free consumer choice. The welfare recipients are informed about their right to a free choice of service provider, encouraged to compare service quality across a broad range of public and private providers, and make informed choices in their own interest. Next to this empowered consumer-choice strategy we find attempts to empower people so that they can take care of themselves, even when they are old and weak, rather than becoming dependent on public welfare services. Some local governments run programs for educating senior citizens so that they can help themselves and stay as long as possible in their own homes rather than attending a public care facility. Farther down the road we find attempts to empower citizens as competent interpreters of their own lives and as important resources for determining what kind of help or service they need to improve their situation. Dialogue with social clients and users of public service facilities is considered a key tool for providing the right service.

At the more participatory end of the continuum, we find attempts to empower citizens so that they can master and optimize their involvement in the production of public services (Bovaird 2007). The idea is that the public effort to help people get a job or an education, escape a criminal environment, or recover from illness will be much more efficient and have greater impact if it actively involves the citizens. Thus, public authorities should facilitate the coproduction of public services by urging the citizens to take responsibility for their own situation and draw on their own competences, resources, and sheer wills to improve their living conditions. Giving the unemployed personal responsibility for their labor-market participation by providing digital tools and counseling so that they can craft their own job plan, with specific measures that can help them gain employment, is a good and illustrative example of empowerment in the coproduction of public service.

Finally, empowerment might involve attempts to empower users of public services and facilities as cocreators of public policy, organizations, and services. Here it is not only a question of encouraging citizens to contribute to the implementation of certain measures but also a question of involving them in developing policies, designing institutionalized forms of service delivery, and shaping the content of particular public services. In this instance, citizens are empowered as competent collaborators in developing and transforming the public sector. The idea here is not to emancipate people; rather, it merely gives them a say in the political and administrative processes that shape and reshape the public sector.

What underlies the different attempts to empower people as active and responsible citizens is a political strategy in which somebody (usually experts or public employees) interacts with others (typically lay actors or welfare recipients) and prods them to act in their "own interest" by working toward appropriate and desirable societal ends (Cruikshank 1999, 67–76). In talking about a strategy for constituting and regulating the political subjectivities of those who are empowered, we are clearly talking about a power strategy. Empowerment is a productive rather than a repressive power strategy as it aims to develop the resources, rights, capacities, and identities of social and political actors (Foucault 1990). The precondition for the emergence and recent deployment of this power strategy is the problematization of the liberal concept of citizenship and the advancement of a new concept of *active citizenship* that is rooted in the republican tradition. The liberal concept of citizenship tends to define *citizens* as *passive individual bearers of legal rights.* This notion of citizenship has been criticized for being too individualistic and for not recognizing that citizens are members of a particular community that they are dependent on and contribute to (Mouffe 1992). The republican notion of active citizenship expands the liberal concept of citizenship, viewing citizens as active participants in social and political life and perceiving their civic engagement as founded on a number of political, social, and cultural rights (including the right to participation), as well as a set of moral obligations—for example, taking responsibility for society and the environment (Gaventa 2002). Active citizenship is often associated with the idea that citizens must learn how to make use of their skills and competences in public life. Thus, empowerment and active citizenship are closely linked.

"Empowerment" and "active citizenship" are political buzzwords promoted by politicians, public managers, policy advisers, and social scientists who seek to mobilize the resources of civil society to improve public governance. In this current embrace of empowerment strategies and active citizenship, we should not forget that we are dealing with a power strategy that skillfully combines two governmental technologies. The empowerment of social and political actors and the emphasis on their rights and obligations are part of the construction of free, capable, and responsible citizens through the deployment of what has been referred to as technologies of agency (Dean 1999). However, instead of using their knowledge, energy, and free action to do whatever they please, the actors are called upon to promote and achieve a predefined political objective defined by technologies of performance (Dean 1999). To illustrate, citizens are encouraged to participate in local neighborhood committees that are part of the city of Oakland's community policing program and to spend their time and energy enhancing local security. At the same time, these citizens' voluntary participation is shaped and given direction by a set of politically defined performance indicators that aim to measure the effects of these local efforts in terms of whether they contribute to a growing feeling of security and lead to decreasing crime rates.

Now given our interest in exploring the conditions for enhancing collaborative innovation in the public sector, we shall focus here on the empowerment strategy that seeks to turn social and political actors into cocreators of public innovation. This empowerment strategy strives to create political subjectivities that have the possibility, motivation, means, and capacities to form and engage in sustained collaborative exchanges with other actors while pursuing individual or collective goals in ways that facilitate the constructive management of differences. We cannot assume that social and political actors are naturally endowed with the capacity to engage in such processes of collaborative innovation. Hence, they must be empowered.

Empowerment generally involves enhancing the rights, resources, competences, knowledge, organizational skills, and political know-how of social and political actors (March and Olsen 1995, 91–95). First of all, actors are empowered when political constitutions, institutions, and traditions give them rights that are embedded in formal or informal rules. Public actors must be given rights to act and take authoritative decisions, whereas private actors need to be given rights to participate while retaining their personal or organizational autonomy. Rights are protected, interpreted, and enforced in daily political life, and their existence depends on continued political support. The right to act and participate, however, is not enough to create empowerment. In striving for empowerment, the actors must also have resources. They require not only key assets—such as money, information, special equipment, and access to particular facilities—but also personal attributes such as energy, curiosity, resolve, legitimacy, and creativity. To use their resources to exercise their rights, the actors must also possess competences—analytical skills, strategic intelligence, political flair, social skills, and the ability to communicate with others and get a point across—and knowledge. The kind of knowledge that the actors need can be general or specific, based on analysis or experience, substantial or procedural, and explicit or tacit. Knowledge is contingent rather than absolute as it depends on what counts as relevant and true knowledge in the specific context or collaborative arena (March and Olsen 1995).

Finally, the efficient utilization of rights, resources, competences, and knowledge depends on the organizing capacities and political astuteness of the actors. Organizing capacities include the ability to convene and conduct a meeting, plan ahead, manage projects, and establish a rudimentary communication system, and political astuteness involves an intuitive understanding of whom to consult, how to mediate conflicts, how to build a winning coalition, and how to communicate to different audiences. These qualities will help the actors enhance their internal and external efficacy by heightening their trust in their own ability to make a difference and by reinforcing their belief in the responsiveness of the social and political system in which they are acting. Improving these capacities, furthermore, is paramount so that the actors can exploit their rights, draw upon their resources, and use their knowledge and competences to make a difference in the collaborative arena.

Thus, empowerment not only increases the power of the actors in a quantitative sense—that is, ensuring they have more resources than before and that they are more capable of using them—but also shapes and reshapes the actors' identity to enhance their feelings of empathy and their commitment to public value production (March and Olsen 1995, 103–7). As we have seen, certain identities may encourage social and political actors either to engage in collaborative processes or to remain passive spectators. Their identities also shape their preferences and determine their position with respect to society's center of gravity.

Empowering citizens and private stakeholders is extremely important if the collaborative processes of innovative policymaking and service development are going to have a real impact. However, the attempt to empower private actors has two important limitations. The first concerns the nearsighted nature of political processes. Our heavily mediatized Western democracies tend to focus on current political pressures and forget about the long-term empowerment strategies that can build capacities for collaborative innovation in the distant future (March and Olsen 1995, 98). The second and related limitation is that although elected politicians and public managers may want citizens to play a more active role in public governance, they still want to be in control. Thus, they are so reluctant to empower private actors that might end up becoming too strong and autonomous vis-à-vis the public decision makers (Dean 1999). Fortunately, empowerment does not always require a proactive and long-lasting effort from politicians and public managers because many of the components of empowerment are self-reinforcing and augmented by use. The more social and political actors engage in processes of collaboration and creative problem solving, the more their right to participate in and influence social and political outcomes is recognized. Crucial assets, such as information, and personal attributes, such as legitimacy, may also be enhanced by usage, and as a result of active engagement, competences and knowledge are also bound to increase over time.

Empowerment is important, but so is disempowerment. When one actor has a strong and unchallenged power to influence a particular domain and dictate the solution to a given problem, collaboration does not make sense and is unlikely to occur. Collaboration thrives in interactions between actors with countervailing powers, and it has the best results when the distribution of power resources in a network of actors is not too imbalanced (Gray 1989, 112). As Gray argues, "Parties will be understandably reluctant to collaborate if they are at a disadvantage to adequately represent their interests or if they believe their interests will be deemed secondary to more powerful ones"

(250). Thus, weaker parties must develop their capabilities as stakeholders to match the power of other actors—for example, by developing complementary resources and forms of knowledge that other actors will need and want to share. Furthermore, in disempowering very strong actors, their command and authority should be weakened relative to that of the other actors, and their resources should be more widely shared and perhaps dispersed for a more even distribution.

Creating the conditions for successful collaboration involves empowering some actors while disempowering others, but it can be quite a challenge to strike the right balance between empowerment and disempowerment. On the one hand, we would want to empower particular actors so they can participate in collaborative processes, engage in a constructive exchange of resources and ideas, and have a real impact on the outputs and outcomes. On the other hand, we do not want actors to become so strong that they are tempted to go it alone and that collaboration becomes problematic due to large and insurmountable power asymmetries.

INSTITUTIONALIZING AND DE-INSTITUTIONALIZING INTERACTION BETWEEN EMPOWERED ACTORS

When relevant and affected actors are mobilized and empowered, the problem then becomes one of how to ensure a sustained interaction that facilitates collaboration and innovation. Creating stable and enduring processes of interaction, collaboration, and creative problem solving requires some degree of institutionalization. The institutionalization of social and political action is analyzed using institutional theory, which aims to understand the stable conditions for acting alone or together (Peters 2012). In the beginning, political science tended to focus merely on the formal, constitutional rules that regulate interaction in well-established political systems. After the Second World War, the behavioral revolution almost eliminated the institutional focus in social and political analysis (Rhodes 1995). However, institutional analysis survived, resurfaced, and gained increasing importance from the end of the 1980s. Gradually the definition of *institutions* has been broadened to include *the rules, norms, values, ideas, symbols, rituals, and cognitive frames that in various ways define what appropriate action is for different actors in particular situations* (March and Olsen 1995). Departments and agencies within the public sector, the corporate structures of private firms, and civil society organizations can be seen as institutional settings in which action is shaped by particular logics of appropriateness.

As soon as we move from the relatively clearly defined organizational units within the public and private sector to messy interorganizational and cross-sectorial interactions, however, things become more complicated. When interactive arenas are initially formed and the different actors gather around the table, they do not have a common constitution and a stable institutional logic of appropriate action as different public and private actors will invoke different ideas, values, and forms of knowledge and draw on different rules and resource bases (Hajer and Versteeg 2005). Consequently, we cannot talk about networked forms of interaction as institutions in the same way that we talk about the ministry of finance, the city planner's office, the headquarters of a corporation, or the local chapter of a nonprofit as institutions.

As noted, there is no common constitution in terms of a generally accepted institutional framework when different actors are first brought together and begin to interact with each other. Over time, though, the emerging patterns of exchange, the distribution of resources, and the common repertoire of ideas, values, and forms of knowledge become more and more sedimented, and the involved actors take them for granted. While the increasingly stable and rule-bound interactions might not yet constitute a full-fledged institution, at least we can say that a relative institutionalization of the networked interaction has taken place.

Olsen (2009, 199; 2010, 126–28) defines institutionalization as *a process that implies the increasing clarity, agreement, and formalization of the content, explanation, and justification of behavioral rules and the allocation, access to, and control over legitimate resources.* Consequently, de-institutionalization implies that existing rules and resource distributions, and the reasons for considering them as legitimate, have become more unclear, contested, and uncertain.

The different strands of institutional theory offer different analytical perspectives on the process of institutionalization (Peters 2012; Sørensen and Torfing 2007). *Rational choice institutionalism* recognizes the limits of formal rules in ensuring compliance in interactive settings. It tends to view the formation of particular incentive structures as the principal means by which to attract and involve relevant actors. *Historical institutionalism* explains the institutionalization of interactive arenas in terms of the presence of a positive feedback loop that reinforces the initial pattern of interaction. *Sociological institutionalism* emphasizes the role of socialization in creating a commitment to the basic structures of interactive arenas and in providing institutional stability. Finally, new forms of *ideational institutionalism* stress the role of discourses, narratives, and story lines in building stable coalitions of actors and providing a unified, but also somewhat ambiguous, framework for concerted action.

Whereas institutional theory tends to see institutionalization as a process that takes place behind the backs of the social and political actors, some collaboration theorists highlight the role of these actors in the process. For one, Gray (1989, 228–29) claims that collaboration involves the formation of a negotiated institutional order that emerges among a set of stakeholders. The institutional order is negotiated but not invented by these actors. According to Trist (1983), an institutional order gradually evolves through a process of joint *appreciation*. "Appreciation involves assessing a current course of activity in light of current norms and beliefs about what is possible and desirable for the future" (Gray 1989, 229). Through the process of appreciation, actors craft agreements about the norms and beliefs that are supposed to regulate their collaborative interaction.

An important result of the institutionalization process in interactive arenas is the formation of formal or informal ground rules, which may help the actors mediate conflicts that are bound to emerge while defining problems and developing and realizing new and bold solutions (Gray 1989, 75–79). Ground rules include procedural methods for regulating the access to the collaborative arena; the frequency and scheduling of meetings; the process of agenda setting; the handling of complex, confidential, and controversial data; the provision of input from external sources; the decision-making process; the procedures of conflict resolution; the system for record keeping; and the use of third-party mediation. Sometimes ground rules are supplemented by normative standards of conduct that guide appropriate behavior inside and outside the interactive arena. They typically recommend basing collaborative interaction on mutual respect and recognition, openness and transparency, procedural fairness, the possibility for dissent and for "exiting with honor," the avoidance of dogmatism and extremism, and so on. Last but not least, the actors often need to clarify rules for allocating resources—that is, procedures for exchanging and pooling resources and agreements on how to share the costs and benefits of collaboration and the production of innovative outputs and outcomes.

By defining some commonly acceptable rules of the game, the institutionalization of multi-actor interaction does the important work of lowering the transaction costs, reducing uncertainty, and preventing conflicts.

Hence, institutionalization provides the conditions for a stable, enduring interaction among empowered actors that facilitates collaboration and creative problem solving. However, it is important to bear in mind two points: The stability of interactive and collaborative arenas only exists as a partial limitation of instability, and de-institutionalization is the ever-present counterpart to institutionalization. De-institutionalization can emerge as a result of various conditions: New actors challenge the institutional order, internal power struggles erupt over questioning accepted rules, the task or purpose of interorganizational interaction is reformulated, or external events proliferate that problematize the modus operandi of the interactive arena.

Despite the unmistakably positive impact of institutionalization, de-institutionalization might sometimes be desirable and a result of intentional action. Some have argued that the institutionalization of networked interaction has its limits, after which further institutionalization becomes detrimental and begins to undermine the performance of interactive arenas (Torfing et al. 2012). Institutionalization might help stabilize precarious forms of networked interaction so that we can harvest the flexibility and innovation gains associated with interactive governance (Milward and Provan 2006, 12). If the degree of institutionalization becomes too high, however, then it will seriously reduce those gains and subvert the raison d'être for interactive governance. Hence, public authorities and other actors capable of governing interactive arenas should aim to balance the processes of institutionalization and de-institutionalization. Striking the right balance is a difficult task that often requires a good deal of trial and error to get the right mix of stability and flexibility.

The negotiated order perspective also has an eye for the processes of de-institutionalization and re-institutionalization that become possible given the emergent, contingent, and developmental character of the negotiated order (Gray 1989, 230–36). The developmental tendency toward an increasing institutionalization can be weakened, problematized, and reversed precisely because it is tentative, rests on compromise and tacit agreements, has a relatively informal character, and is not backed by formal sanctions. The ongoing processes of institutionalization, de-institutionalization, and re-institutionalization make collaborative interaction a highly complex and dynamic phenomenon. As we shall see, this observation has important consequences for exercising leadership and management in collaborative arenas as it points to the strategic importance of institutional design.

CHAPTER 5

FACILITATING COLLABORATION BETWEEN EMPOWERED ACTORS IN INSTITUTIONALIZED INTERACTION

Collaborative innovation hinges on the expectation that actors who have been mobilized and empowered as participants in relatively institutionalized arenas of sustained interaction will not only share knowledge and coordinate their actions but also collaborate in developing and implementing new, bold, and creative solutions. As interaction will not necessarily lead to collaboration, we need to further explore how it is possible to facilitate collaboration between empowered actors in institutional arenas. In chapter 4 we listed a number of factors that might help trigger collaboration. Here we take the argument another step and look at how proactive measures can enhance collaboration. The focus is on trust building, game structuration, and network management, which are measures emphasized by governance network theory (Koppenjan and Klijn 2004; Sørensen and Torfing 2007). The argument is straightforward: Social and political actors in interactive arenas are inclined to collaborate if they trust each other, if the game-like interactions are structured to favors collaboration, and if the processes are properly managed.

The development of trust is crucial for promoting collaboration between well-motivated and empowered actors in interactive arenas. *Trust* is commonly defined as *the stable expectation that other actors will refrain from opportunistic behavior when the opportunity occurs* (Nooteboom 2002; Koppenjan and Klijn 2004). It can be directed to a specific individual or group of people and tied to a specific situation, but it can also be a more general perception that we can depend on other people. Institutional arenas, or particular policy fields, can be pervaded, to a greater or lesser extent, by the feeling of generalized trust. Both individual trust and generalized trust are important in lowering transaction costs, facilitating the exchange of knowledge, and pooling resources and ideas. Social and political actors will not want to invest time and energy in collaborative processes if they are uncertain about the other actors' behavior and fear that they will be self-seeking, uncompromising, and unwilling to share the costs of joint solutions. Trust building is, therefore, extremely important. Actors can enhance it through recalling positive past experiences, engaging in informal social interactions, making joint calculations that everybody will benefit from collaboration, and developing procedures for sanctioning opportunistic behavior (Koppenjan and Klijn 2004, 86–87). In the beginning, people need to have reasons to trust each other, and if their positive expectations are repeatedly confirmed, then a more general trust will emerge that, in turn, will facilitate and sustain their collaborative interaction.

Game structuration and process management are equally important conditions for the development of collaboration. *Game structuration* involves constructing game-like structures that provide incentives for collaboration (Scharpf 1994), and *process management* involves both designing clear, meaningful, and useful interaction processes and mediating emerging conflicts (Kickert, Klijn, and Koppenjan 1997). Whereas the former involves hands-off governing of the interactive arenas, the latter involves hands-on governing of the collaborative processes.

Game structuration is favored by rationalistic approaches that explore how it is possible to construct collaborative interaction by creating particular incentive systems (Hertting 2007). Game structuration may involve producing plus-sum games such as the famous "split-a-dollar" game in which all the participating actors are rewarded if they agree about how to split the dollar but receive nothing if they disagree. As the total sum increases, the actors will usually accept a more uneven distribution because even if their share is disproportionably smaller than the other actors' share, they will still get a sizable reward for supporting a joint solution. Collaboration can also be stimulated by setting up a collective incentive scheme that ties the future influence of the interactive arena to the relative success of the current forms of collaboration. The formation of informal and secluded structures of negotiation will also tend to enhance collaboration as the actors will have more freedom to maneuver and will no longer fear that their constituencies will criticize their concessions. Finally, segmenting collaborative games to reduce their complexity or linking games to expand the choices of governance networks will also increase the prospect of collaboration (O'Toole 1997).

Whereas game structuration is concerned with shaping the type of games that rational actors play, process management aims to organize and change the actual process of interaction to facilitate a constructive management of differences. It also works to prevent the centrifugal forces of conflict and dissatisfaction from outweighing the centripetal forces of common understanding and the mutually supportive exchange and pooling of resources. Process management involves creating organizational arrangements such as steering groups, task forces, sounding boards, and so on, that permit a flexible integration of actors in relation to more or less clearly defined tasks. It also entails regulating and guiding the process of interaction by designing a process map and clarifying the ground rules. Joint production and sharing of knowledge and information are also important. To ensure a constructive exchange of knowledge and resources and to produce a certain degree of reciprocity, activating particular actors and their resources in certain situations is sometimes necessary. Process management also involves mediating conflicts and developing goal-oriented strategies aimed at creating divergence and convergence in problems and solutions (Klijn and Edelenbos 2007, 203).

Both game structuration and process management presuppose the presence and intervention of strategic actors with sufficient legitimacy, reflexivity, and organizing capacity. The research on governance networks talks about these strategic actors as metagovernors because they are involved in the governance of more or less self-regulating governance arenas (Jessop 2002; Kooiman 2003; Sørensen and Torfing 2009).

CONCLUSION

Rather than assuming that multi-actor collaboration will emerge by itself because it carries a large potential for generating public innovation, this chapter has focused on factors that either prevent or spur the development of collaborative arenas. The first one concerns how to mobilize the relevant and affected actors who can contribute to collaborative innovation. The second component involves how to empower and disempower social and political actors so that they can contribute effectively and constructively to the collaborative process. Next we need to determine how to ensure sustained interaction that facilitates the emergence of collaboration and innovation through processes of institutionalization and de-institutionalization. The final factor examines how interactive arenas can be turned into arenas for collaboration.

The conclusion is that the context, framework, calculations, perceptions, and identities of social and political actors should somehow be influenced and transformed in ways that create active engagement, empowered participation, sustained interaction, and constructive collaboration. Although we have not yet discussed who will do the job of influencing the actors and shaping the conditions for interaction and collaboration, we do discuss different forms of leadership and management in chapter 9.

6

ENHANCING MUTUAL, EXPANSIVE, AND TRANSFORMATIVE LEARNING

THE COLLABORATIVE EFFORT to enhance public innovation involves a plurality of public and private actors who hold different assumptions, views, and interests that inform their individual and joint attempts to solve urgent problems, respond to future challenges, and exploit emerging opportunities. In the process of collaboration, the actors advance and discuss their differing views, assumptions, and ideas. If the interaction is constructive and conflicts are successfully mediated, then they will be able to reach a common understanding of the issues at stake, one that can serve as the basis for envisioning different solutions and strategies. Iterative rounds of analysis, idea generation, testing of prototypes, and decision making will eventually produce joint solutions based on a "rough consensus," which is a provisional agreement that the participants think they can live with despite minor grievances.

Sometimes collaboration merely aspires to find simple solutions to simple problems; at other times it aims to find innovative solutions to wicked problems and crosscutting challenges. When the latter is the case, what aspects of the collaborative process help foster innovation? A key part of the answer is learning. Collaboration stimulates learning processes through which the actors acquire, enhance, or revise their knowledge, beliefs, and goals; and these learning processes prompt the development of new and creative solutions. Other drivers are important when it comes to implementing and diffusing innovative solutions, but without mutual learning, the collaborative arenas are unlikely to produce any new and creative solutions that can be used and shared and thus make a difference.

CHAPTER 6

Drawing on recent developments in learning theory and a number of empirical case studies, this chapter analyzes the nature and character of mutual, expansive, and transformative learning and explores the conditions for such learning processes to emerge in collaborative arenas. The chapter first discusses the importance of circulating information to trigger and foster innovation in the public sector. New and relevant information given to the right actors at the right time tends to spur public innovation by means of inspiration, imitation, and instructive learning. Yet despite the importance of organizing and managing information streams, not all kinds of information encourage innovation. For instance, circulating information about best practices might prevent the creative development of a next practice, despite its contribution to enhancing innovation diffusion.

The second section explores the role of and conditions for mutual learning in communities of practice. The processes of mutual learning are pitted against individual learning, detached learning, and unidirectional learning, all of which do not rely on interaction and mutual exchange. As some forms of learning stimulate innovation more than others, the third section looks at the relative impact of different kinds of learning. Types of factual, normative, and instrumental learning are discussed, but the main focus is on how expansive and transformative learning condition and spur innovation. The next section focuses on creativity, which is a constitutive element of innovation. Learning theory shows that creativity is not a stroke of genius on the part of a daring, skillful, and artistic inventor but a feature of collaboration that gives rise to creative processes of bricolage through which new qualities emerge from the recombination of existing elements. The chapter concludes by arguing that learning is not merely a product of collaborative innovation processes but also a tool for reforming and improving these processes. Learning from critical evaluations of collaborative innovation processes will help us build future capacities.

INFORMATION MATTERS

Gaining access to new information can be seen as a basic form of learning. When we stumble on new and relevant information, our experience is that we have learned something that opens up new possibilities: "Wow, I didn't know this, and it really changes my perspective on what we are doing." Access to new information occasionally arises from reflection on past experiences, analysis of data and statistics that reveals patterns and trends, or careful scrutiny of the current state of affairs. Most often, however, we simply plug into an available stream of information and extract some new and interesting information that seems to be relevant for what we are doing. Alternatively people will deliberately pass new information to us because they believe it might be useful or because their job is to circulate information and keep others informed. Nevertheless, the new information imparted might inspire us to think and act differently, and it may even spur public innovation as new problems, ideas, solutions, and resources come to the fore. As a result, new information may have an immediate learning and innovation effect, and we can begin to think and act in different ways. If the new information problematizes the common wisdom, views, and habits in a particular organization, service area, or policy field, it might even give rise to deeper and more elaborate learning processes based on systematic research, consultation, and dialogue.

The kind of information that makes us feel that we have learned something new is more than a random collection of brute facts. Information is constructed through processing facts and findings into specific data and forms of knowledge that reflect particular values, discourses, and ideologies. Information can be quantitative or qualitative or a particular combination of the two. Sometimes information has been aggregated or synthesized into an insight, a story, or a normative lesson or statement; at other times, it is a singular observation, evaluation, or event that is reported in a factual way.

Sources of information exchange are numerous. The Web, printed and electronic mass media, social media, newsletters, meetings and conferences, managerial networks, and personal contacts—all are constantly bombarding us with new information. In today's information society, we deal with massive, overlapping, and competing streams of information. Some flow vertically from the top to the bottom of public and private organizations and back, whereas other information streams flow horizontally, connecting actors and agencies at more or less the same level within or across different jurisdictions, sectors, and countries. Some streams are restricted in the sense that only a few actors are authorized to circulate and receive information, while other streams are more open in terms of access and thus involve all-to-all communication. No matter how the streams of information are organized and regulated, the big challenge is to filter the endless stream of information, to identify the information that seems relevant, and to discard the useless information. This difficult task requires both experience and intuition.

Information is circulated in wide-ranging networks of public, private, and nonprofit actors. The seminal work of Walker (1969) demonstrates that the decisions of states and local authorities to adopt particular policy innovations are influenced by the information that public administrators gain through networked interaction with other administrators, professional associations, and policy experts. On the basis of this insight, Hale (2011) has conducted an interesting study of the impact that a national information network has on diffusing and institutionalizing policy innovation in the field of crime prevention. Since the late 1970s, "tough-on-crime" policies in the United States have imprisoned greater numbers of drug offenders and increased the length of their sentences. Recidivism is high, however, because incarceration often does not curb drug addiction among offenders (Hale 2011, 32–34). Hence, the political and professional demand for more humane alternatives to incarceration has been growing, and since the establishment of the first drug court in Miami in 1989, the number of US drug courts has exploded. Drug courts provide an innovative approach to drug-related crime based on therapeutic jurisprudence. Interdisciplinary teams of professionals provide an innovative service that combines the effort to protect public safety with the promotion of personal accountability and the treatment of drug addiction. Hale's analysis shows that a nationwide network of professional associations, state offices, and local administrators and programs helped drive the adoption of the new and innovative drug courts. The network provided a persistent information flow that circulated general knowledge and concepts as well as concrete models and templates that facilitated the implementation of the new design. The vertical flow of information successfully combined with a horizontal exchange of experiences across states and local programs.

The core of Hale's (2011) study identifies different positions in the information network in terms of champions, supporters, challengers, and bystanders and how they contrast based on their preferences and the strength of their engagement in the information exchange (22–28, 53–61). Particularly interesting is the dynamic interaction of the various types of actors in the information network. Champion organizations advance a new and innovative policy solution as well as a series of prototypes that local authorities can develop. Supporters are keen to evaluate the results derived from testing the prototypes, and the champion collects and generalizes the results of the evaluations, often in ways that emphasize the successful aspects. The skeptical challengers usually conduct their own critical evaluations and force the champions to fine-tune their information about best practices. Bystanders watch with great interest and compare results and recommendations with their own ideas and missions. Gradually they transform into supporters, challengers, or even champions in the process (178–79). Each of the actors contributes to the production and dissemination of information in the network.

Hale (2011) analyzes a national information network that disseminated highly synthetic and normative information consisting of evidence-based knowledge, recommendations of best practice, model programs, pilot projects, and so on. This kind of information is very helpful in diffusing policy innovation, but the prescriptive, closed, and definitive character of this information might hamper adaptation and prevent further experimentation and innovation at the local level. To facilitate local exploration of a next practice, the circulation of different kinds of knowledge and the dissemination of open-ended pathfinder projects are needed (Mulgan 2007, 21). However, the study of the drug courts shows that the information network created a language for interagency collaboration that facilitated crosscutting interaction among the network actors, and that, in turn, stimulated learning processes and produced further innovation. We shall now examine these collaborative learning processes and their potential for fostering innovation in greater detail.

DIFFERENT KINDS OF MUTUAL LEARNING

As we saw with the drug court case, the *circulation of information* can spur learning by means of instruction and interaction, and it can enhance innovation through inspiration and imitation. Local practices were transformed because the local actors interacted, received new knowledge and ideas, and learned how to adopt and adapt new formats that were developed elsewhere. However, learning cannot be reduced to a stimulus-response model where the infusion of new information triggers new behavior and practices (Piaget 1954). At its core, learning involves *reflections upon empirical and theoretical experiences*. Through reflection we craft new understandings and develop new ways of doing things in the hope that they will provide intelligent solutions to specific problems and challenges and will help us take advantage of new opportunities (Dewey 1916, 1922). This kind of learning through reflection is situated in a specific cultural and historical context that conditions and shapes our reflections, and it tends to transform the identity of those involved in the learning process because they are encouraged to reflect upon and adjust their own role and expectations.

Learning can be a result of *individual reflection*. We develop our individual skills and competences and engage in social activities, and through that process we create a personal knowledge of the world. Our personal knowledge might differ slightly from the culturally embedded knowledge found in the context in which we are situated, and reflecting on this difference may lead to revisions of our personal knowledge or attempts to change the culturally embedded knowledge. Our own interpretation of social and political events will sometimes challenge our personal knowledge and give rise to critical reflections and revisions that, perhaps, create more conflicts with the culturally embedded knowledge. Although some people are prepared to accept quite a bit of dissonance between their personal knowledge and culturally embedded knowledge, reflection on different kinds of knowledge discrepancies provides a constant source of individual learning. Sometimes we do not want our knowledge to be disturbed either because we might believe our knowledge is adequate or because we dread going through another complicated and uncertain reflection process. At other times, though, we do make a conscious effort to confront and absorb new forms of (inter)cultural knowledge and reflect on how it challenges our own understanding of the world. Public employees attending training courses, searching the Internet, going on excursions to other countries, and reading new scientific reports and scholarly books provide a good example of the latter.

Individuals learn when they mull over their social experiences, but this kind of individual learning is often embedded in more *collective forms of learning* that emerge when we relate to and assess each other's reflections on both practical experiences and theoretical insights. Collective learning is interactive because it compares, juxtaposes, and aligns the reflections of different actors to produce new and more informed understandings that match their different experiences. Some reflections will support each other, whereas others will be contradictory and problematize each other. The context and the varying positions of the different actors will also mean that certain reflections will appear as more central and authoritative than others. Collective learning does not take place in a power-free zone; rather, it is premised on a particular truth regime that is constructed through power struggles and has some clear and discernible power effects (Foucault 1980).

To further explore the different forms of collective learning, we shall take a closer look at the well-known situation in which public managers and employees want to improve a public service, organizational design, or policy program through innovation, and they have decided to seek inspiration from the users' experience in order to examine the current service, design, or policy. We shall adopt this user-driven, or citizen-centered, innovation perspective to develop a clearer picture of what mutual learning through collaborative interaction entails.

Users of public services, institutions, and policy regulations can be defined broadly as including the politicians, public managers, and administrators who utilize particular administrative tools, service standards, and institutional set-ups to produce public value. In the following discussion, we shall more narrowly focus on individual citizens, private organizations, and business firms as the chief end users of particular public services, institutions, and policies. There has been a growing interest in taking users' experiences and ideas into account when producing new public solutions. The underlying idea is that a better understanding of these users' needs and demands, and the degree to which existing policies and services meet them, will help improve the public sector by triggering a step change in the way things are done. Feedback on new and alternative solutions from potential users can also help prevent the adoption of innovations that nobody will use. The procedures and methods for involving the users in learning-based innovation processes differ in terms of how much and how actively the users are involved. We shall distinguish here between different forms of mutual learning in terms of whether they are detached, unidirectional, or cocreated.

The first method aims to learn about the users: what their situation is, what their needs and wishes are, how they gain access to different kinds of service, how their services are delivered and received, how they experience the quality and impact of the services, and whether any service gaps leave their needs and wishes unfulfilled. Learning about the users is achieved in a rather indirect way that strives to minimize the active and direct participation of the users, and public administrators often considered this method as a source of unconstructive criticism and complaints (see Bason 2007). The resulting *detached learning* allows us to learn about the users' experiences with public services, institutions, and policies while keeping them at a distance and not asking the users directly about their opinions.

A typical way of learning about the users without involving them too much and too directly is to observe their behavior through anthropological studies. Anthropologists may use shadowing, for example, to passively observe citizens arriving at a public service center and register key aspects of their meeting there, including how they find their way, how different staff members help them, and how they perceive and react to the help they receive. Brief talks with the users and public staff members about what happened in the encounter, and what they thought about it, add further depth to the observations. Anthropologists may also follow individual users such as chronically ill patients over a short time and see how they deal with the many health agents they had to contact or visit during a typical week. Analyses of these so-called user journeys can help map the users' road through the jungle of public service agents and reveal the service gaps, the bureaucratic obstacles to service access, or the lack of coordination, integration, and holistic treatment.

Some user studies have aimed to analyze the social and cultural context of different user groups and how it shapes their interpretation and acceptance of public service offers. A Danish study based on so-called ethno raids showed that some unemployed youths did not respond to written invitations from the local job center to appear for a "job interview" because they mistakenly thought it was for a formal interview with a potential employer rather than merely an informal talk about job and career opportunities. Some unemployed youths even thought that the job center had offered them a job and judged, from their cultural perspective, that it was not the right job for them. In another instance, if the users of a public service cannot be identified, that service might apply the mystery shopper technique. A local municipality that wants to observe how private firms are treated and what they are offered when they call and make inquiries at the municipal business center might hire someone to call their own and other similar municipalities and act as if he or she were a private firm needing services. A comparison of the services offered by one's own municipality with those of other municipalities might reveal problems and potential service gaps that call for innovation.

A second method of learning about the users is to learn from them by asking them to respond to some direct questions regarding their opinions of existing or prospective public services and policies. The absence of dialogue and mutual exploration turns this method into a form of *one-directional learning*, although the users are more actively and directly involved than they would be in a mere observational study. If there are only a few users or it is possible to select a small representative sample of users, their experiences and perceptions can be elicited through a focus group interview during which the users negotiate their answers to different questions. If there are many users, and the criteria for assessing whether a purposefully selected sample is representative are unknown, a user satisfaction survey of the whole population of users can be conducted and analyzed statistically. If the public authorities already have some vague ideas about new initiatives and solutions and want to explore the users' preferences, they can conduct a stated choice analysis. This survey technique presents users with a series of choices between two clearly stated options and asks them in each case to choose the option that best reflects their individual preferences. This method may lead to conclusions such as "60 percent of the commuters are willing to pay a dollar more for the ticket if there is free Internet access in the train" (see Bason 2007).

Citizens' opinions about new policy ideas can also be elicited via the Internet or social media. Another example can be taken from some municipalities in Scandinavia. They have established permanent citizen panels that permit a group of citizens with a changing composition to express the members' views on new policy ideas and policy proposals on a regular basis. Finally, users can also be asked to produce their own data as a way of probing what they like. Asking pupils to take pictures of what they like in their school, and then possibly writing a short commentary to accompany the pictures, is a way of learning from users who seldom have a voice in innovation processes. Other such cultural probes may also include diary writing, logbooks, drawings, model building, and so on. The quality of this kind of material may vary, and structuring the input and transforming it into information and knowledge can be time consuming. Nevertheless, cultural probes might be used to highlight dos and don'ts.

The third way of learning about the users is to establish a continuous dialogue with them. This technique can be viewed as a form of *cocreated learning* as it is based on the active and direct involvement of users in a two-way discussion through which problems are assessed and new and creative solutions are formulated. If a group of lead users can be identified (Hippel 1986), they can be invited to participate in interactive workshops or camps. Given their frequent and engaged use of a certain public service, lead users tend to experience problems and needs still unknown to the general public. Lead users stand to benefit greatly from the provision of new solutions and will be able to offer informed ideas and opinions about alternative solutions. Because of their particular expertise, involving lead users as partners in mutual learning processes based on collaborative interaction makes good sense.

Another category of users includes those who have a representational role because they are elected, or perhaps appointed, to a user board. Found in schools, kindergartens, elderly care homes, and other public service institutions, these boards generally have few formal powers and mostly function as information channels and complaint services. However, they might sometimes play a role as arenas for collaborative innovation that involve public managers, professionally educated public employees, and users in creative problem solving. Public innovation has a more strategic character and greater impact if it results from collaborative processes that cut across public institutions. Therefore, if the goal is to enhance strategic policy innovation in elder care, public schools, and watershed management, user boards might be a good supplement to thematic town hall meetings focusing on a certain policy problem and bringing together relevant public actors and interest organizations that represent different stakeholders and user groups might be a good supplement to user boards.

Finally, there are the "ordinary users" who are neither particularly engaged nor elected to a representational body. When it comes to small and incremental innovations in producing and delivering public services, these users are still important partners. They can contribute to interactive learning by helping to clarify problems and challenges and by providing continuous feedback on experiments and prototypes. Some users, such as patients at the hospital or parents with children in public day care, have daily contact with public employees that can spur collaborative learning processes. Other user groups, such as commuters driving on public roads or small firms filling out their tax returns, do not have regular contact with public employees, but using social media or online feedback systems can facilitate their communication and dialogue. The use of social media in the public sector is still at an experimental stage, but it might prove an effective means of communication in the future. In some Danish kindergartens, the staff sends a text message about the children's daily activities to the parents before they pick up their children. This arrangement enables the parent to ask informed and qualified questions about the day care service that has been provided, and the resulting discussions may lead to small, incremental innovations.

Cocreated learning through continuous dialogue with different kinds of users is an important lever for public innovation because it facilitates a mutual exchange of experiences, knowledge, and opinions and a joint transformation of preferences, ideas, and visions into new and better solutions. However, collaborative learning should preferably include all affected actors in order to harvest all the relevant input that is necessary for innovating public services, organizations, and policies. Depending on the issue at stake, the interaction between public managers, public employees, and different user groups should be expanded to include politicians, policy experts, think tanks, private firms, and civil society organizations. Every one of these actors may have ideas and resources that can contribute to public innovation. Empathic involvement of users is a necessary but not a sufficient ingredient of collaborative innovation in the public sector.

FROM INTRA- TO INTERORGANIZATIONAL COMMUNITIES OF PRACTICE

We can understand the processes through which different groups of actors within and across organizations engage in and produce collective learning and innovation from the perspective of those learning theories that focus on communities of practice (Wenger 1998). The central concept in these learning theories is *practice*, which is defined as *an active engagement with the world that leads to a social construction of meaning*. The construction of meaning, in turn, is a result of context-dependent negotiations between different actors and leads to the production of concrete reified interpretations, classifications, conventions, and rituals. Communities are formed on the basis of social practices. *Communities of practice* develop among people who *do things together and are mutually engaged in work-related activities whose meanings they negotiate with one another* (Wenger 1998, 73). The actors define a joint enterprise in response to the complex situations and conflicting pressures that they encounter. Over time they develop a shared repertoire of routinized actions, stories, gestures, symbols, and other devices that give the community of practice a relative coherence. Their shared repertoire of actions and artifacts is also supported by specific discourses and styles of communication that enable the actors to make meaningful statements and express themselves in particular ways when they work together (Wenger 1998, 83).

Communities of practice are vehicles of learning. Learning takes place in and through social practice and draws upon the communicative styles, discourses, and repertoires of the actors. For the community of practice, this learning in practice has three consequences. First, it further develops and sustains the mutual engagement of the actors by redefining their identities and changing the terms of their interaction. Next, it provides a common understanding and practical fine-tuning of their joint enterprise by aligning activities, creating mutual accountability, and reconciling conflicting interpretations. Finally, it transforms the repertoire, discourses, and styles of the members of the community of practice. In short, learning alters the identities, interaction, discourse, and activities of a community of practice in ways that improve its performance.

Newcomers to a community of practice are granted the status of legitimate peripheral participants and serve as apprentices. The apprentices learn from their participation in the social practices of a certain community, but in the beginning their tasks are few and relatively simple, and they have little responsibility for the activities as a whole (Lave and Wenger 1991). Gradually as their understanding of the joint enterprise deepens, their proficiency, workload, and responsibility are enhanced.

Communities of practice tend to emerge spontaneously from the informal networking of groups of actors that engage in the same kind of work-related activities. A community of practice may be formed among the managers and social workers in a local job center who work together to help unemployed people enter training programs or find a suitable job. Such a community of practice will often "help foster an environment in which knowledge can be created and shared and, most importantly, used to improve effectiveness, efficiency and innovation" (Lesser and Everest 2001, 41). Communities of practice create and sustain flows of knowledge that are linked to social relationships developed through shared practices. They become sources of innovation because their members constantly improvise and adapt their behavior to overcome limitations imposed either by the formal organization and its canonical practices or by changes in the environment (Brown and Duguid 1991; Swan, Scarbrough, and Robertson 2002). The common meaning system of a community of practice enables the members to communicate and make sense of the world, and the situated learning processes allow them to transform their repertoire, discourse, and styles of expression together with their joint enterprise and relational identities.

When the situated learning processes and the creation and circulation of knowledge lead to significant transformations in their work-related activity system, they spur innovation in communities of practice. To illustrate, groups of schoolteachers may tackle motivation problems in the classroom by creating partnerships with private firms or public utility companies, which supply real-life problems for the pupils to solve using their skills in math and science. However, communities of practice may simultaneously constrain innovation because their social and cognitive closure prevents the integration of knowledge from outside the group. Research suggests that whereas the learning processes within a particular community of practice facilitate incremental innovation, more radical innovations tend to rely on assimilating specialized and distributed knowledge that a range of different actors working across different communities of practice possess (Swan, Scarbrough, and Robertson 2002, 480–81). Therefore, if the goal is to spur public innovation in schools, hospitals, elderly care facilities, and the local police forces, we should not only support the development of local communities of practice but also pursue alignment and foster collaboration across these communities. The public managers and employees in a local job center, for example, should be encouraged to collaborate with other public as well as private agencies that are providing services for job seekers. Further, they should engage trade unions, unemployment insurance funds, local employers, and researchers in a search for innovative solutions to emerging problems and challenges.

The formation of what might be termed interorganizational, or cross-sectorial, communities of practice and the use of such communities as vehicles for public innovation call for an increasing emphasis on multidisciplinarity, mutual recognition, and problem-oriented communication, and it highlights the crucial role of boundary objects and boundary spanners in facilitating crosscutting deliberation. Working with professionals from other disciplines to deliver collaborative solutions requires a willingness to look at problems and solutions from a multidisciplinary perspective that permits the creation of synergies and the exploitation of productive tensions between different perspectives. It also entails the development of specific competences such as the ability to understand, recognize, and appreciate the role of other professionals and multiple private stakeholders and the ability to ensure effective communication among different professional groups as well as between public providers, users, and citizens (Suter et al. 2009).

Finally, collaboration and learning across different communities emphasize the crucial role of objects and subjects that facilitate collaborative interaction (Wenger 1998, 104–21). *Boundary objects* are defined as *artifacts, documents, concepts, and story lines that help connect people from different communities of practice because they attract their attention and call for joint action* (see Star and Griesemer 1989). Boundary objects that succeed in engaging actors across different professional communities in collaborative innovation lend themselves to different interpretations and usages, and they tend to abstract from specific details and provide standardized information that increase their accessibility. Whereas boundary objects provide a common focus for interorganizational communities of practice, *boundary spanners* facilitate dialogue between different actors of different backgrounds and worldviews. Hence, boundary spanners are essentially brokers who help translate different views and vocabularies so that actors can relate to each other, coordinate their efforts to deal with a common problem or challenge, and align perspectives and interests so that they support or complement each other.

Although the recipe for success is relatively clear, creating well-functioning interorganizational, or cross-sectorial, communities of practice is difficult, and even more so are the communities' attempts to reap the fruits of their interaction in terms of ensuring the creation of innovative outcomes. Multidisciplinary teams are often formed to facilitate the development of innovative solutions, but disciplinary diversity may not always benefit a team and lead to the desired innovation outcomes. Maintaining a positive bias toward the contribution of one's own disciplinary group and perspective while discriminating against the input from other groups with different disciplinary perspectives impairs the exchange of information, views, and ideas (Gray and Ren 2014). According to Fay et al. (2006, 555), this problem might be offset by high-quality team processes that are characterized by the pursuit of a shared vision, a high frequency of interaction, and the development of trust and reflexivity. A multiple case study of team innovation in the United Kingdom's health care sector supports this hypothesis for the quality, but not for the number, of innovations (Fay et al. 2006). Another study in the field of health care, however, confirms that the multidisciplinarity of interprofessional teams does not always produce synergistic innovation effects (Mitchell et al. 2010). Cognitive heterogeneity may eventually give rise to misunderstandings that limit the sharing and integration of knowledge, and disciplinary attempts to protect knowledge monopolies tend to prevent open-minded discussions.

If it is somewhat difficult to establish well-functioning interprofessional teams, it is even more difficult to involve users in cross-sectorial communities of practice. User involvement is costly in terms of time and resources, and often concerns arise about the representativeness of individual users. In addition, many professionals strongly resist the idea that users possess a special expertise that can enhance innovation (Tait and Lester 2005). Hence, when users are invited to participate in concrete development projects, the users and the professional providers often encounter huge difficulties in forging a constructive dialogue.

In a study that compared two cases of user involvement in the planning and delivery of mental health care services in London (Rutter et al. 2004), considerable differences between the professional health providers and the users impaired collaboration. The staff wanted the users to address the strategic and managerial agenda of the health trusts and tended to see user involvement as a goal in itself, whereas the users wanted to change and improve user-identified services and were looking for concrete results. The staff also sought to involve the users through consultation, whereas the users wanted to be involved in a partnership based on a shared policy-making framework. Finally, the nursing staff complained about their added burden in having to engage with the users, and they thought that the users' views were given too much credibility. Nevertheless, despite the poor returns and the personal costs in terms of time and efforts, the users voluntarily participated and collaborated in the existing decision-making structures. The conclusion is that the future sustainability of user involvement in communities of practice requires increased transparency and a better alignment of the expectations of staff and users (Rutter et al. 2004, 1982). Another study of user involvement in health care identifies many similar barriers and, to overcome them, recommends further education for the health staff, especially with regard to their communication skills (Langton et al. 2003).

In sum, a discrepancy exists between the innovative potential of interorganizational, or cross-sectorial, communities of practice and the actual attempts to bring together different groups of professionals and involve different kinds of users in collaborative innovation processes. The empirical research, however, is inconclusive. Studies also indicate a clear correlation between diversity and innovative outcomes in teams, work groups, and networks (Jehn, Northcraft, and Neale 1999). Others show process management and education can help overcome the barriers to collaborative innovation (this will be further discussed in chapter 9).

THE FORM AND CHARACTER OF THE LEARNING PROCESS MATTERS

There are many hindrances to collaborative learning in interorganizational and cross-sectorial settings, but when actors with different perspectives and ideas are brought together in joint learning processes, the prospect for producing innovative outcomes is great. However, first we need to understand what collaborative learning entails and to grasp when and how learning leads to innovation. As we shall see, the form and character of learning matter if the goal is to foster innovative policies, organizations, or services.

Engeström (1987, 2008) is one of the key figures in current attempts to understand the nature of joint learning processes, and his work provides a good start for pinpointing the kind of mutual learning processes that sustain innovation. Engeström and his associates focus on collective forms of learning in private firms where craft production, mass production, and customized production gradually and unevenly give way to more innovation-driven production based on knowledge and learning. Business firms are conceived of as activity systems that have a complex relational and mediational structure (Engeström 1987). In a specific work-related activity, there is interplay between a subject and an object. Any given member of the community of actors involved in a joint collaborative project can assume the subject position in a specific action that works upon and transforms a particular object to produce a certain outcome. The relationship between subject and object is mediated by the subject's material or immaterial instruments: practical tools, machinery, computer programs, modes of calculation, and specialized vocabularies. The subject-object relationship is also mediated by the community, which establishes a collaborative structure that organizes the collective attempts to transform objects and constructs a certain division of labor among the actors. The subject's relationship to the community is mediated by rules, norms, and traditions that provide particular and sometimes competing scripts for the subject and regulate the interactions.

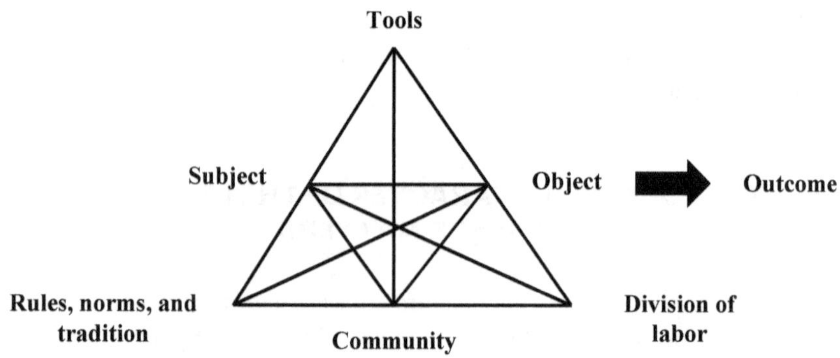

FIGURE 6.1. Engeström's model of the activity system
Source: Engeström (1987, 78). ©Yrjö Engeström. Used with permission.

Engeström's (1987) model of the activity system in a workplace is shown in figure 6.1. While the theory of activity systems focuses on individual subjects and their mediated relationship to the objects that they want to transform, we should not overlook the fact that activity systems are multivoiced, multitiered, and sources of social conflict as well as collective achievements based on seamless teamwork (Engeström 2008, 27). The activity system model seeks to capture the different components of the production process in private firms, but it may also be applied to public organizations that produce public goods and services. Thus, the model can help us understand the conditions for mutual learning processes in the private as well as the public sector.

Situated actions can be understood as manifestations or instantiations of an activity system. All actions will have an effect on the activity system. Some actions will reproduce the system, while other actions will transform it. The kinds of action that have the largest transformative effect are those that are classified as *disturbances*. According to Engeström (2008), "disturbances are essentially actions that deviate from the expected course of normal procedure. They can be interpreted as symptoms or manifestations of historically evolving *inner contractions* in a given activity system" (27). Contradictions within, but also between, activity systems can be sources of trouble and decay, but they also carry a potential for development and innovation. The potential for innovation is often realized by a task force or work team. Workteams have always played a role in organizing, but work teams responsible for driving innovation seem to be gaining importance (Engeström 2008, 17). In fact, teams gradually develop into collaborative communities that transgress the traditional notion of "teams" in the sense of small, homogenous, and well-defined groups (Adler and Hecksher 2006, 44; Engeström 2008, 18). Hence, teams and task forces tend to include a growing number of actors from inside and outside the organization to gain access to relevant innovation assets—namely, knowledge, ideas, political support, and money. They also seek to accommodate diverse competences and knowledge bases to facilitate learning and joint problem solving. Finally, their boundaries are becoming less fixed as they aim to integrate development and production and to align different and shifting knowledge projects.

Engeström discusses the development of teams from coordination to cooperation to collaboration as an *expansive transition*. In teams based on *coordination*, the actors follow their scripted roles when dealing with each of their specific objects while mutually adjusting their actions to prevent overlaps and clashes and to produce linkage and synergy. In teams based on *cooperation*, the actors focus on a shared problem and, without questioning or reformulating their respective roles, go beyond the confines of their scripted roles to find acceptable ways to define and solve it. Finally, in *collaborative* teams, the actors deal with a shared object while reconceptualizing both the common problem and their different scripts in the course of the interaction. The collaborative reframing of the problem and the scripted roles, norms, and routines is an expansive response to disturbances and provides a fruitful alternative to the disintegration and contraction of the action system (Engeström 2008, 50–51).

On the basis of these stipulations, Engeström (2008, 130–31) develops the cycle of expansive learning, or an ideal-typical sequence of epistemic actions that drives innovation in collaborative settings:

1. Question, criticize, or reject certain aspects of established practices and common wisdom.
2. Conduct either historical-genetic or actual-empirical analysis of the critical or problematic situation to discover explanatory mechanisms and new solutions.
3. Construct a simplified model of the new ideas that explains and offers a solution to the problematic situation.
4. Examine the model to identify its dynamics, potentials, and limitations.
5. Implement the model in practice.
6. Reflect on and consolidate the model to optimize its functioning and ensure the desired outcome.

Engeström's cycle of expansive learning is similar to the innovation cycle presented in chapter 1, but it pays more attention to the learning aspects of the process of innovation. The idea that innovation involves questioning, analyzing, modeling, examining, and so forth, however, does not really capture the distinctiveness of the learning processes that drives innovation. All learning processes seem to involve elements of questioning established truth, of analyzing the causes of problems and new solutions, of figuring out the designs of these solutions, and so on.

This problem can be solved by taking a closer look at Engeström's elaboration of Bateson's (1972) hierarchy of learning that reveals that only particular advanced forms of learning enable social and political actors to create innovation (Engeström 1987; Roepstorff 2001). At the bottom of the learning hierarchy, *factual and normative learning* helps the actors in a particular institutional context function and operate in ways that are considered appropriate. Learning is based on a corrective change of behavior prompted by signals from the social environment and institutional context that tell us how to think and act in different situations. As we unconsciously adapt to positive and negative sanctions, what we learn becomes an acquired habit.

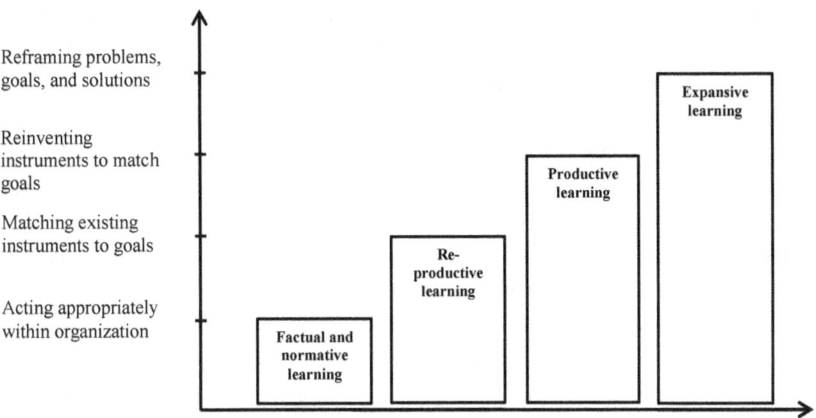

FIGURE 6.2. Representation of Engeström's elaboration of Bateson's hierarchy of learning

At the next and higher level, learning processes take the form of *reflexive problem solving*. Learning here begins with an urgent or deep-seated problem that we aim to solve by reflecting on a range of options based on our knowledge of how the system works. This level has two different kinds of learning—reproductive and productive. In *reproductive learning*, the instrument by which we achieve our goal is found through processes of trial and error that involve a blind search among a broad range of more or less well-known alternatives. In *productive learning*, the instrument used to achieve the goal is reinvented and adjusted through experimentation.

At the highest level of Bateson's hierarchy is *expansive learning*. Here the learning process is less instrumental, for the problem, the range of alternative options, and the criteria for evaluating them are reframed and expanded. Productive learning carries an expansive potential, but it is only realized if the contextual boundaries for thinking about the problem and for crafting and evaluating alternative solutions are transgressed. Hence, in processes of expansive learning, the subject envisages and aims to manipulate the entire activity system—its past, present, and future (Roepstorff 2001). Expansive learning tops the hierarchy of learning that is displayed in figure 6.2.

To grasp the distinctive character of the learning processes that spur innovation, we should distinguish between instrumental and expansive learning. *Instrumental learning* about causes and effects facilitates practical problem solving through an experience-based revision of strategies and procedures in order to produce a known and desired outcome. By contrast, *expansive learning* aims to construct a coherent understanding of complex social contexts, problematic and crisis-ridden conjunctures, and new horizons and possibilities through a communicative search for concepts, narratives, and ways of thinking that can give meaning to the unknown and thus extend our previous knowledge. In short, expansive learning permits us to imagine and do new things and thus leads to innovation.

However, although expansive learning broadens our knowledge base by mapping unknown territory through the development of new discourses, the risk is that the new knowledge will be continuous with the past and result in an affirmative worldview that preserves rather than transforms the status quo. Human beings have an urgent need to understand what they experience and to integrate new information with their knowledge so they can avoid dissonance and chaos. Hence, to develop innovative solutions to the problems and challenges that we encounter, our *critical reflection* is what frees us from those beliefs and practices that are problematized and contested by new events and understandings. When social actors enter the mode of critical reflection, they begin to question tacit assumptions, challenge acquired procedures and habits, and use metaphors that create new interpretations and new ways of making sense of the world. In short, critical reflection gives rise to problematizations of accepted knowledge and revisions of the old repertoire of goals and solutions that, in turn, may foster some bold and creative ideas.

Critical reflection as a tool for revising one's basic assumptions is the key focus point in the theory of *transformative learning* that Mezirow and his colleagues have advanced. "Transformative learning refers to the process by which we transform our taken-for-granted frames of reference (meaning perspectives, habits of mind, mind-sets) to make them more inclusive, discriminating, open, emotionally capable of change and reflective so that they may generate beliefs and opinions that will prove more true or justified to guide action" (Mezirow 2000, 7–8). It is commonly asserted that learning involves four steps: establishing and maintaining intersubjectivity; relating actions to contextual events, utterances, and behaviors; making normative evaluations of actions in relation to common goals and standards; and decontextualizing meanings through propositional statements based on inference or logic (Bruner 1990). To this list Mezirow (2000, 4) adds a fifth element in terms of transformative learning, which he defines as *the practice through which one becomes critically aware of one's own and others' tacit assumptions and problematizes their relevance for interpreting and acting in the world.*

According to Mezirow (2000, 8), transformative learning is not achieved through individual self-reflection; rather, it involves participating in the construction of a collective discourse through communicating with other actors. In the process of communication, the actors use each other's experiences to test the reasons justifying different assumptions and to make action decisions based on the resulting insights. Mezirow holds a rather Habermasian view of the communicative process of transformative learning as he claims that, ideally, the social actors will have complete information, the freedom from coercion that distorts communication, an ability to weigh evidence and assess arguments in objective ways, and a general feeling of trust, solidarity, security, and empathy (10–16). At the same time, he recognizes that learning processes are both enabled and constrained by the power-knowledge networks in which they are embedded and that many people will feel threatened and act emotionally when their basic assumptions are questioned. However, while Mezirow tends to see the presence of power and conflict as a problem that should be eradicated, we might also see powerful alliances of social and political actors as vehicles for overcoming conservatism and perceive conflicting views and cognitive dissonance as catalysts of change. Mezirow's argument does not logically depend on the Habermasian preference for power and conflict-free deliberation. Further developing the role of power-knowledge networks might actually strengthen his argument as it will enable us to see how different groups of actors struggle to protect or transform the basic assumptions that are pervading a certain field action.

According to Mezirow (2000, 22), the process of transformative learning follows some variation of the following phases. Social actors first confront a disorienting puzzle or dilemma. Their individual examinations of the problem generate feelings of fear, anger, guilt, or shame. Next they undertake a critical assessment of their assumptions. When the actors recognize that the feeling of discontent and the process of transformation are shared, together they explore new roles, relationships, ideas, and actions. They then agree upon a joint course of action and acquire the skills for implementing it. As they test their new roles and solutions, the process results in building new competences and self-confidence. Finally, they evaluate, adjust, and mainstream the new course of action.

What is interesting in this process is the implicit transition from individual to collective learning and the built-in emotional triggers of transformative learning. Because the theory of transformative learning developed in the field of adult education, it also has a strong emphasis on its personal rewards in terms of empowerment, self-confidence, and even emancipation. As Mezirow (2000) notes, the theory of transformative learning "shares the normative goals of the Enlightenment of self-emancipation through self-understanding, the overcoming of systematically distorted communication, and the strengthening of the capacity for self-determination" (xiv). However, when it comes to enhancing public innovation through processes of transformative learning, the emancipatory perspective is perhaps less relevant due to the predominance of a systemic perspective in public policies, organizations, and services. Hence, when functioning as a vehicle for public innovation, transformative learning serves the achievement of systemic goals such as efficiency, improved service quality, democratization, and enhanced capacity for problem solving rather than the individual goals of personal growth and emancipation that are inherent to adult education. To this empirical reservation we could add that the emancipatory perspective is heavily indebted to the Kantian idea of true knowledge as the force of self-emancipation that completely overlooks the constant interweaving of power and knowledge (Foucault 1980).

Nevertheless, we should be careful not to neglect the roles of the individual's motivation for and rewards from participating in collaborative processes of public innovation. Further, although there is no such thing as achieving emancipation from power, the moment when well-established routines and forms of knowledge are problematized and new forms of knowledge and courses of actions are developed will always appear as an empowering revelation to the actors involved. So, despite its Enlightenment bias, the theory of transformative learning provides an important elaboration on the theory of expansive learning by emphasizing the role of problematizations for triggering more discontinuous forms of innovation. The argument's credibility depends on how we account for the kind of critical reflection that problematizes our basic assumptions. Mezirow sides with Kant, who defines *critical reflection* as *reason's reflection on its own principles and categories* (Mezirow 2000, xiii). We might instead think of critical reflection in less rationalistic terms and view it as the experience of a radical incompatibility and epistemic clash between new events, experiences, and information, on the one hand, and our otherwise rationalized and accepted assumptions about the social world, on the other hand. In this sense, critical reflection is not a matter of reason reflecting on itself but an experience of the limits of reason.

COLLECTIVE CREATIVITY

Problematization and the transformation of the basic assumptions that pervade a certain field of knowledge and action are linked to the question of creativity. Creativity is often associated with the idea of a creative individual whose personality, genius, and intellectual and/or artistic capacity facilitate the generation or visualization of something new and valuable (Lund and Jensen 2011). Creative persons aim to influence the field in which they are situated (science, arts, entertainment, industrial production, or public administration) by advancing new ideas and influencing other actors to confirm the originality and appropriateness of their ideas. Hence, according to Csikszentmihalyi (1996), creativity involves not only one or more persons with creative ideas and disruptive propositions but also the particular intellectual and practical domain that is being transformed and, within this domain, those people who assess the new ideas and validate them as a creative contribution to the field.

In a similar vein, other creativity researchers claim that creativity cannot be reduced to a particular mode of thinking, for a broad range of factors such as the sociopolitical context, the cultural environment, the access to knowledge, and the acquired expertise of specific individuals tend to influence the production of creative ideas and solutions (Woodman, Sawyer, and Griffin 1993; Weisberg 2006). In this highly interesting literature, the focus is on the drivers of processes that generate creative results. Amabile (1983, 1998) explores the role of the individual's ability to identify and combine different kinds of knowledge and use a variety of heuristic devices to gather information and experiment with new solutions, the role of formal and informal expertise and the cross-disciplinary interaction between complementary forms of expertise, and the impact of the intrinsic and extrinsic motivation of the social actors that is sustained by specific cultures and institutional frameworks. Within this triangle of creativity-enhancing factors, motivation is by far the most important, because without motivation the different forms of expertise and the personal capacity for creative thinking will not be mobilized and exploited. Hence, if the leaders in the Oakland Police Department are not motivated by a mixture of professional ambitions and politically sanctioned systems of performance management, then they will not spend the sufficient time and energy on activating the internal and external knowledge and capacities when searching for creative ways of curbing gang-related crime.

Following these lines of thought, an emphasis on *collective creativity*, through either open sources or some kind of collaborative interaction, has been growing. Creativity does not only happen inside a person's head; it also grows out of interactions between actors within or across different sociocultural contexts. Individuals become part of a collective mind that is more than the sum of the individual parts because the processes of interaction transform individual creativity into collective creativity (Weick and Roberts 1993). Creativity becomes collective when the individual contributions shape the subsequent contributions of others and, at the same time, give new meaning to and rearticulate the past contributions of others. In the literature we find two important, but familiar, arguments in favor of this recent movement toward collective creativity. The first is that individual actors rarely possess all the ability, expertise, and motivation needed to foster creative solutions to complex problems; therefore, they must rely on exchanges with other relevant actors such as scientific experts, customers, or users (Hargadon and Bechky 2006). The second argument is that interactions between actors who are distant from each other in terms of cognition, culture, functionality, and so on, will tend to prevent the lock-in that is often a problem in closed circles (Parjanen, Harmaakorpi, and Frantsi 2010). From this perspective, creativity based on an individual stroke of genius is the exception to the rule of creativity generated through collective coproduction.

Based on this insight, Hargadon and Bechky (2006) have developed a model of collective creativity that explains how the locus of creative problem solving shifts from the individual to the interpersonal interactions within a collective. Four types of activities seem to play a role in triggering the emergence of collective creativity: help seeking, help giving, reflective reframing, and reinforcing. *Help seeking* is when individuals request others' assistance in solving complex problems. In large organizations help-seeking activities typically involve initiating casual hallway conversations, but they may also include calling ad hoc meetings or tapping into personal networks. Help seeking tends to be inhibited if it signifies personal ignorance, inability, and failure, but the need to overcome deadlocks or threats can prompt individuals to overcome this barrier.

While help seeking invites other people to participate in finding a creative solution to a particular problem, *help giving* is the positive response to an explicit or implicit invitation and involves a willingness to devote time and attention to assisting others in exploring the problem and developing a creative solution. Helpful collaboration is when the help givers provide a timely and empathic response that brings forth relevant knowledge and useful ideas that may help to solve the problem at hand in a new and creative way.

Because the question posed by the help seeker is sometimes unclear, ill-founded, or posed in a wrong way, it is important for the participants in this social interaction to engage in *reflective reframing*. In this process, the problem can be reinterpreted in light of joint discussions, and the conditions for solving it can be expanded, challenged, or rethought (see Schön and Rein 1995). Reframing the task at hand may promote a reevaluation of existing knowledge or recombinations of old ideas and established practices.

Reinforcing refers to those activities that strengthen the organizational norms and values that support engagement in help seeking, help giving, and reflective reframing. Reinforcement may be either a direct result of positive experiences with producing collective cognition and creativity or a more indirect result of management strategies aiming to increase the status and ensure the promotion of those who help each other solve complex problems in creative ways.

The model of collective creativity provides a good and simple representation of the process through which collections of creative individuals become creative collectives, but it has two clear limitations that call for further development of the model. First of all, it tends to narrow the social interaction that spurs creativity to a singular transient moment (Hargadon and Bechky 2006, 489). Second, it defines creativity as a recombination of existing ideas while excluding the more challenging aspect of developing new ideas based on new interpretations and discoveries (485). These two limitations are related, for the development of new ideas requires more than a one-off exchange of knowledge and ideas. By removing these inherent limitations, the initial encounter between help seekers and help givers can be seen as a contingent prelude to more sustained processes of interaction, and the roles of help seekers and help givers are blurred, or abandoned, as the actors recognize or construct a mutual dependence and perhaps even a community of destiny that enables them to explore new avenues and develop new ideas.

LEARNING FROM PROCESSES OF COLLABORATIVE INNOVATION AND BUILDING FUTURE CAPACITIES

For multi-actor collaboration to foster innovative solutions, it must give rise to some kind of mutual, expansive, and perhaps even transformative learning that fosters collective creativity. That being said, we should remember that learning is not only an essential part of the process of collaborative innovation but also a valuable tool for improving the functioning and outcomes of such processes. Thus, learning is both a practice embedded in the process of collaboration and a strategic reflection on the current and past performance that enables the actors to enhance their capacities for collaborative innovation.

Learning through either simultaneous or ex post evaluation of collaborative innovation requires measuring the actual processes and results as well as the informed reflections about the drivers of and barriers to different parts of the process and the production of desired outputs and outcomes. In the current audit regime, associated with New Public Management, the demands for quantitative measurement are strong and pretty hard to satisfy when it comes to measuring innovation and the processes of collaboration and mutual learning that aim to produce it. The element of subjective interpretation is too large. What can and should be measured in quantitative terms, however, are the outcomes of innovation. User satisfaction surveys can establish whether the quality of public services is improved. Productivity statistics and fiscal accounts can tell whether service production or public regulation has become more efficient. Performance studies can help assess whether the problem-solving capacity has actually increased as a result on innovation. Finally, quantitative surveys can reveal whether the democratic legitimacy of public governance has improved due to the creation of new arenas for participatory governance and the cocreation of public solutions. While the measurement of the desired outcomes can be done in relatively rigorous ways, the measurement of the innovative output and the processes that have produced it will, to a large extent, have to rely on a qualitative assessment. The important step here is to ask the right kind of questions.

Evaluating the production of innovative outputs may involve asking the following questions. What initiated the process, and what was the output? To what extent is the form and content of the output breaking with common knowledge and established practices in the field of application? What kind of innovation was produced, and how was it implemented, consolidated, scaled up, and diffused? Did the results match the expectations? Were there any bottlenecks in the innovation process that need to be eliminated? Which drivers and barriers to innovation affected the innovative output, and how can the drivers be sustained and the barriers removed through joint initiatives and the exercise of innovation management?

Asking questions can also help assess the collaborative processes that produced the innovative solutions. How was the process of mutual exchange organized? Who participated, and what kind of knowledge and resources did they bring to the table? Did the actors merely coordinate and cooperate with each other, or did they actually collaborate in ways that involved the constructive management of differences to find joint solutions to common problems? What triggered, sustained, or impeded the process of collaboration? How were conflicts managed throughout the process of mutual exchange?

This chapter has highlighted learning as an essential aspect of multi-actor collaboration and the production of innovative outputs. The learning aspect can be improved by engaging in *meta-learning*, which aims to discover how learning is best sustained (Biggs 1985). Several key questions can be asked in this regard. Which implicit and explicit learning processes took place, and what was the result of these processes? Did the actors engage in interactive, expansive, and transformative learning? What spurred the learning processes, and what blocked or slowed them down? How could the learning processes have been accelerated and deepened?

It is important that the actors who participate in collaborative innovation and those who manage the process learn from their experiences so that they can enhance their future capacity for collaborative innovation. Both simultaneous and ex post learning are crucial tasks for researchers and consultancy houses that are often directly involved in ongoing innovation processes and have the capacity for generalizing the experiences across many different cases into a set of tentative recommendations. Successful cases of innovation may also serve as benchmarks and beacons that inspire and set the standard for future attempts to create innovation through collaboration, but the successful cases should be complemented with a scrutiny of unsuccessful cases in which the potential for collaboration, learning, and innovation was not fully realized. Too often the successful cases of collaborative innovation are canonized as best practices without checking whether the same basic practices are also found in unsuccessful cases.

Ex post learning seems to be informed by a rationalistic perspective that holds out the promise that we will be able to optimize the processes of collaborative innovation if we measure and assess what has happened, identify and reflect on the barriers and drivers, search for supporting or complementary evidence from other cases, and use the generated insights in future processes. A somewhat less rationalistic and more pragmatic approach to simultaneous in situ learning is to use design experiments to enhance innovative outputs and desired outcomes of collaborative processes. Design experiments were developed in the field of aeronautics, but they are increasingly being used in the study of social and political processes (Stoker and John 2009). Iterative rounds of problem diagnosis, generation of tentative hypotheses about what might stimulate collaboration and enhance innovation, incremental change of institutional and process designs, and systematic evaluation of the resulting change in performance—all contribute to the development of situated knowledge about what works in a specific context. Design experiments aiming to enhance the capacity for collaborative innovation should be theoretically informed and can be used to develop and test new ideas about how to design collaborative processes that spur public innovation.

CONCLUSION

This chapter has focused on a highly important aspect of collaborative processes that plays a key role in triggering the development of innovative solutions. While innovative solutions can be the result of accidental events and chance discoveries, they are usually a product of learning that is stimulated by the exchange of information, views, and ideas between multiple actors with different knowledge bases and forms of expertise. The chapter has shown that the circulation of prefabricated information to the right people at the right time may create an immediate learning effect that can trigger innovation. However, it has also argued that the most important learning processes are those procedures that actively involve social and political actors in reflections through which they can acquire, enhance, or revise their knowledge, beliefs, and goals, as well as their ideas about how particular goals should be achieved. Collaborative interaction stimulates these active learning processes. Research suggests, however, that while communities of practice in public service organizations or in regulatory agencies may create incremental forms of innovations, interorganizational and cross-sectorial communities may give rise to more radical innovations because local forms of knowledge challenge each other and help foster new ideas about specific work-related problems and challenges.

Collaboration stimulates learning, but as the chapter also shows, not all forms of knowledge lead to innovation. Learning may have a socializing effect and help actors do what is appropriate for them to do in a certain context and situation. It may also be instrumental in helping actors solve puzzles and problems by means of drawing on a particular repertoire of more or less well-defined tools and actions. By contrast, those forms of learning that stimulate innovation take the form of either expansive learning, which aims to explore and give meaning to the unknown, or transformative learning, which involves critically reflecting on and revising the framework that informs social action.

The chapter has also revisited the recent studies of creativity and has shown that creative processes tend to be collaborative. Hence, instead of looking for creative individuals who can reinvent the public sector, we should try to create and sustain creative milieus. Last but not least, it has been underscored that not only is learning an inherent feature of collaborative innovation but it also involves a strategic reflection upon the processes of collaborative innovation in order to improve them and enhance the future capacity for collaborative innovation. Researchers, think tanks, and consultancy firms may contribute to this kind of strategic learning.

7

MAKING AND IMPLEMENTING BOLD AND CREATIVE DECISIONS

MUTUAL LEARNING makes actors engaged in collaborative problem solving wiser. Further, it broadens and revises the knowledge base that actors can draw upon when they seek to craft innovative solutions to wicked and unruly problems. Expansive and transformative learning problematizes tacit and taken-for-granted knowledge and utilizes metaphors that stimulate creative problem solving. As a result, collaborative processes that stimulate this kind of learning generate a number of new and creative ideas and solutions. Unfortunately, many problem-driven search processes in the public sector stop here and fail to do the hard work of singling out the most promising solution and implementing it so that it can prove its value. Consequently, these new and bold ideas do not lead to proper innovations as the selection and realization processes are not carried through. This can be explained, to a certain extent, by the actors' perception of the different parts of the innovation process and what the steps demand from them. Usually the creative phase of collaborative exchange, learning, and idea generation is perceived as constructive, rewarding, and filled with positive energy, whereas the decision-making and implementation process is experienced as uncertain, risky, and complex and as ridden with interest conflicts, antagonism, and power games. Hence, the trouble and pain awaiting innovators in the selection and implementation phase sometimes make them shy away.

This chapter aims to show how collaborative processes can help overcome the difficulties associated with selecting and implementing creative and promising ideas. It spells out the nature of the problems that confront innovators when they try to turn good and promising ideas into innovative solutions that work. It then problematizes the rationalistic idea that the successful promotion of bold and creative decisions results either from cost-benefit analysis or from undistorted deliberation based on the force of the better argument. By contrast, this chapter suggests that the mobilization of passion and the exercise of political as well as moral-intellectual leadership are the true allies of the collaborative decision making that aims to break new ground by fostering innovation. The chapter also takes issue with the rationalistic idea that implementing bold and creative solutions is a matter of eliminating obstacles and breaking down the barriers and resistance to change in order to secure an unfettered realization of new ideas. Alternatively, it argues that decision making and implementation are intertwined and that dealing with obstacles in a constructive way often triggers a creative reformulation of the solution that has been selected. The chapter concludes with some cautious remarks about the implementation problems facing collaborative innovators.

WHY ARE MAKING AND IMPLEMENTING BOLD AND CREATIVE SOLUTIONS SO DIFFICULT?

Although the collaborative search for new knowledge and the development of bold and inspiring ideas might produce cognitive dissonance and problematize the roles and habits of the actors involved in the process, the joint experience of discovering new understandings and possibilities is exciting, liberating, and rewarding. Indeed, when new insights and unforeseen options dawn on a group of actors, it constitutes a moment of truth. It is suddenly revealed that things can be different and perhaps better, cheaper, and more satisfying. By contrast to the complex problem that triggered the search process, the newfound solutions look simple and self-evident. The nature and size of the potential effects of the new ideas and solutions might still be unclear, but the lack of precise knowledge of the effects will merely enhance the expectations and promise of progress and improvement.

As the initial excitement fades and the actors take a more sober view of the range of possibilities that the new ideas and insights bring into play, a series of difficult questions comes to the fore. Which of the new and bold options is the most promising in terms of its effects and its feasibility, and what are the risks associated with different options? How should the preferred option be designed to work properly in the given environment? Who has the authority to approve the experiments and the testing of prototypes? Who will bear the costs of the innovative policy, service, and/or organization? How can the new design become implemented and consolidated without compromising its innovativeness? Who will take responsibility for its implementation and any failure thereof? Are the actors involved in the implementation process properly skilled and educated? Underlying all these questions is perhaps the most important one: What kind of political games and professional conflicts will emerge in the difficult transition from the ideation stage to the selection and implementation stages in which one new idea rather than another is selected and realized in practice? We can think more systematically about all these challenging questions that threaten to bring the innovation process to a premature halt under the headlines of "uncertainty," "risk," "complexity," "collective action problems," and "power."

Uncertainty becomes an issue because it is difficult to know whether new and daring options will actually work in practice and whether they will produce the desired effects or perhaps some undesired ones. It is also hard to tell whether the new solutions will fit into and function properly in the political, social, and administrative context in which they are going to be implemented. In addition, their results and effects are difficult to measure because the innovative designs have not yet been tried out in the specific context, and simulations are impossible, or at least extremely complicated, given the lack knowledge of the behavioral impact of the new designs. To reduce the uncertainty associated with selecting and implementing innovative solutions, the actors will frequently seek to develop and test prototypes in an experimental process of trial and error, perhaps in a small part of the organization. A thorough testing of prototypes is indispensable to public innovation because it gives a glimpse of the likely effects and reveals unexpected problems that can be avoided through a redesign of the innovative solutions before they are realized at full scale. Public money is frequently wasted due to the lack of proper testing.

Two problems inherent to testing prototypes, however, prevent a complete elimination of uncertainty—Hawthorne effects and learning-curve effects. *Hawthorne effects* refer to the performance improvements that result, not from the innovation or pilot itself, but from the fact that the piloting organization has been subject to extraordinary attention and maybe even has received extra funding to pay for the pilot. The presence of Hawthorne effects will result in an overly positive evaluation of the pilot and an underestimation of the risks and costs. *Learning-curve effects* refer to the performance-improving changes in organizational behavior within the piloting organization that result from learning during the process of testing innovative designs. If the learning curve slowly rises and the time frame of the test is short, the pilot will not be able to realize the full potential of the innovative solutions and thus will tend to underestimate their positive functioning and outcome. Thus, both the Hawthorne and the learning-curve effects may cloud the real performance and effects of the innovative designs that are being tested and may make eliminating the uncertainty about future outcomes of the innovation difficult (Mulgan and Albury 2003). Nevertheless, in collaborative settings these problems can be partly overcome.

Comparing the positive evaluations of public leaders and staff against the more critical views of users, citizens, and private stakeholders may create a fuller and more balanced picture of the problems and risks associated with innovative designs. In addition, mutual learning will contribute to realizing the full potential of a particular prototype within the time frame of the pilot. More generally, trust-based exchanges of information, knowledge, and evaluative judgments between actors with different backgrounds, experiences, and vantage points will help to uncover hidden and unforeseen outcomes and turn uncertain factors into known and calculable risks (Koppenjan and Klijn 2004).

Risk is another hazard associated with selecting and implementing innovative public solutions. Risk should be clearly distinguished from uncertainty. Whereas *uncertainty* concerns decision making in the context of relatively unknown outputs and outcomes, risk is relevant to decision making in the context of likely results and probable effects (Brown and Osborne 2013, 195). When trying to produce a step change in the form and content of public policies, organizations, and services, there is always a chance that something will go wrong. There is a risk that implementing the innovative designs will fail because of the impact of habits and institutional inertia or because of active opposition from actors with vested interests in preserving established practices. There is also a risk that the innovative solutions will not solve the problem or challenge at hand in the expected way because the underlying program theory does not hold up in practice due to unforeseen interaction effects or the absence of triggering conditions. Finally, there is a risk that an innovation, despite its beneficial effects, will create unacceptable externalities that will harm service staff, individual users, or the wider community. The risks associated with public innovation are unavoidable and impossible to eliminate because innovative policies, organizations, and services are a part of an open system based on interaction between multiple public and private actors who are coming from different sectors and are operating at different levels and scales. A plausible and attractive strategy in this situation is to try to minimize risk, but if this strategy is carried to the extreme by risk-averse public leaders, it will prevent innovation. Because innovation and risks are intrinsically related—you cannot have one without the other—innovation necessarily involves some degree of risk-taking (Borins 2001a).

Risk management offers an alternative to risk minimization. It involves identifying and calculating the likelihood of different kinds of risks, assessing the scope and character of the potential damage caused by the most likely risks, and considering the options for mitigating, containing, or compensating the potential damage. Although this approach sounds attractive, because it is carried out in a rather technocratic manner, its one-sided focus on the assessment of risks and their potential damages also tends to limit the amount of public innovation. Hence, we should bear in mind that risks are socially constructed and that social and political actors might be prepared to bear a certain level of risk in exchange for access to particular benefits (Renn 2008). Determining the acceptable trade-offs between risks and benefits calls for a collaborative strategy by which the actors construct and evaluate different combinations of risks and benefits (Brown and Osborne 2013). In this manner, risk negotiation is preferred to both risk elimination and risk management.

Complexity is another troubling factor. The process of deciding which of several creative solutions to adopt in practice is complex in at least three different ways (Koppenjan and Klijn 2004). When the most promising innovations are to be selected, there will often be competing decision-making arenas with an unclear division of labor. Some arenas are formal and associated with government and public authorities, while others are less formal and sites of collaborative interaction between a host of public and private actors. To further complicate matters, the decision-making arenas might exist at different levels and in overlapping jurisdictions. The interplay between these arenas makes the decision-making process very difficult.

Complexity also springs from the fact that many different actors will be involved in the decision-making process. Public actors will interact with and seek support from private for-profit and non-profit actors. The various actors will have contrasting, as well as sometimes unclear and vague, agendas and preferences, and they will apply various strategies to influence the decision-making process. Some of them will be supportive of particular innovations, while others will be unsupportive and critical and perhaps act as veto points. Some private actors might also bring their own innovative ideas and proposals to the table and try to win support for these proposals from particular public agencies. When the actors begin to adjust their strategies in response to each other, or even in anticipation of the strategic actions of other actors, the process becomes even more complicated. This interplay provides a third source of complexity in the decision-making process and makes it hard to predict the winning solution because alliances will be unstable and shifting until hegemony for a particular solution is established through a combination of force and consent (Gramsci 1971).

The implementation process is equally complex, for the division of labor between the many actors who have collaborated in developing the innovative design is often unclear. Should they all participate in implementing the new design? If not, then who should participate and who should not, and what should the various participants do and in which order? The relationship between the collaborative arena and the operational agency responsible for delivering the policy or service in a certain area is often complex. It may become a source of dispute, because the collaborating actors might want to see the innovative design through to the implementation phase, while the operational agency will insist on its autonomy, competence, and responsibility for making the innovative design work in practice.

Whereas New Public Management aims to eliminate complexity by creating separate agencies with their own distinct and singular purpose (Koppenjan and Klijn 2004), collaborative governance aims to harness it by matching the complexity of the decision-making process with a complex governance structure based on multiple interactions and feedback loops. If the processes of decision making and implementation are complex, there is only one thing to do—facilitate the crosscutting dialogue and pluricentric coordination that allow the actors to find flexible solutions based on mutual learning and simultaneous engineering (Pedersen, Sehested, and Sørensen 2011).

Collective action problems are well described in the literature (Olson 1971). They are likely to assert themselves in the decision-making and implementation phase when actors have to agree on a more or less innovative solution and spend time and resources on its realization. While it is relatively free for the actors to partake in the mutual learning processes through which new and interesting ideas are developed, decision making and implementation tend to distribute costs and benefits of innovative solutions unevenly. The actors will most likely try to maximize their benefits while minimizing their costs, and these maneuvers may lead to problems such as joint decision traps (Scharpf 1988), prisoner's dilemmas (Poundstone 1992), and free riding (Olson 1971).

Should such issues arise and hamper the decision-making and implementation process, they tend to be mitigated by the fact that collaborative arenas aim to reduce the pursuit of individual interests in two ways—by building relationships of mutual trust and by constructing a collective "we" that is supported by a joint narrative and a broad range of social norms and sanctioning mechanisms such as "naming and shaming." Hence, relying on collaborative strategies to construct a particular innovative solution is a win-win opportunity. Arriving at a fair distribution of costs and benefits that takes into account the authority and resources of various actors will help facilitate the decision-making and implementation process.

This brings us to the last factors complicating the decision-making and implementation phase in collaborative innovation processes—*power struggles* and *conflicts*. Such problems are likely to arise when an important matter such as designing innovative public solutions in the field of health, education, or environmental protection is at stake, and the actors have different interests, opinions, and preferences regarding the outputs and outcomes. These issues can lead to a stalemate and/or antagonistic clashes and make the actors leave the decision-making arena. Innovative solutions challenge existing ideas, norms, and procedures and disrupt the status hierarchy among different actors in the field (Klein and Sorra 1996). They also generate different kinds of outcomes that affect the resource distribution among the actors in an asymmetric way. Actors who want to preserve the status quo or have a strong preference for a particular outcome will exercise their power and try to block the innovation process or shape the innovative design in accordance with their ideas and preferences.

In the ensuing power struggles, all the different faces of power will become visible (Lukes 2005). Stronger actors will prevail over weaker actors in open disputes, although the blunt display of direct power will not be considered legitimate in collaborative arenas. A more subtle way to exercise power in the decision-making process is to set the agenda and ensure that the favored innovations are placed high on the program and the less favored ones are not considered at all. If this tactic fails to produce an acceptable result, actors may try to prevent the implementation of unfavorable innovations by stalling or systematically underfunding them. To avoid the overt or covert conflicts in these forms of decision and nondecision making, actors may also try to shape the preferences of the other actors by creating a consensual view of the premises for developing innovative designs and selecting an innovative solution that will be implemented in practice. An even subtler and more ambitious power strategy involves transforming the entire discourse in and through which problems are defined and solutions are discussed. This can hardly be done by a single actor, no matter how willful and skillful, but coalitions of actors may successfully change the vocabulary and way of thinking in a particular decision-making arena by plugging into new, specialized forms of knowledge advanced by experts, mass media, and the like.

In collaborative settings when many different power strategies will be exercised at the same time, conflicts between different groups of actors are likely to erupt. Some conflicts will be productive, forcing the actors to revise and improve the innovative solutions that they are advocating and demonstrate their effects. Other conflicts will be disruptive and either prevent the actors from making decisions or lead to vague compromises based on the least common denominator, thus bringing us back to the joint decision trap.

In sum, there are good reasons for innovators to tremble when anticipating the difficult task of selecting and implementing innovative solutions in the public sector (Klein and Knight 2005). However, as hinted earlier, collaboration might alleviate some of the problems and worries in this part of the innovation process. First, the joint assessment of information and knowledge gathered by collaborating actors with different perspectives will shed light on the hidden costs and benefits of innovative solutions. Collaborative arenas based on generalized trust may be able to manage risks by forging an agreement about how to share those costs and benefits. They may also agree to take a calculated risk on a particular innovation if they think that it is compensated by some highly desirable benefits. Next, creating and institutionalizing a complex set of interactions that connects the various arenas, actors, and strategies to facilitate the production of pluricentric coordination can moderate the complexity of arenas, actors, and strategies in innovation processes. In addition, jointly formulating an overriding story line, which constructs the social and political actors as a part of a community of fate, may help reduce collective action problems. Last but not least, combined efforts to civilize antagonistic conflicts and power struggles may help turn destructive confrontations between enemies into a constructive rivalry between adversaries (Mouffe 1993). However, the challenges to collaboration will not be entirely eliminated. Consequently, we must think more carefully about how collaborating actors arrive at an agreement concerning which innovative designs they want to realize in practice and how they will implement such designs in the face of institutional, economic, and political obstacles. The next two sections discuss these two important questions.

CHAPTER 7

CHALLENGING THE RATIONALISTIC APPROACHES TO COLLABORATIVE DECISION MAKING

The rationalistic decision model that perceives the definition of problems, decision making, and practical implementation as temporally ordered stages of collaborative innovation processes has been subjected to fierce criticism (Van de Ven et al. 2008). Although defining problems, selecting solutions, and implementing them are indispensable moments of any innovation process, there are many examples of solutions that look for or construct particular problems and of implementation issues that lead to adjustments and revisions of the solution. Hence, the idea that the collaborative decision-making process is segmented into clearly separated phases that neatly follow each other in a fixed temporal sequence has little empirical support. Thus, Kingdon's (1984) famous "organized anarchy model" provides a more adequate description of multi-actor decision making than those traditional theories that insist that problems always precede solutions. Streams of problems, solutions, and events that make it possible for entrepreneurs to adopt and implement a new and creative public solution run their own parallel courses, but they are occasionally joined into a single channel that may produce discontinuous change. Similarly, design thinking challenges the idea that the crafting of innovative solutions precedes their implementation (Ansell and Torfing 2014). The implementation process is bound to produce other learning that alters the innovative solution in fundamental ways.

Nevertheless, there still is a moment in decision making when the actors decide which innovative solution to pursue. Most often they will make a series of decisions in different arenas and at different levels. The decision-making process will have a certain extension in time and can be more or less formal. In those cases that require a formal decision to pursue a particular innovative solution, an informal process of discussion and persuasion normally precedes it, and sometimes the formal decision is merely a final endorsement of the many smaller decisions that already have been made in a number of small, informal discussions and forums.

This section aims to problematize the core of the rational decision-making model by looking at how multiple actors decide which among several alternative options they want to pursue and implement to foster public innovation. How can social and political actors with different ideas, opinions, and forms of knowledge come into agreement and align their views about which innovative solution they are going to realize? The rationalistic answer to this question is to conduct a cost-benefit analysis of all possible solutions to the problem or challenge at hand (Boardman et al. 2006). However, this decision method has well-known problems. Limited cognitive capacities and decision-making resources mean that we cannot specify all possible solutions and will not be able to list all the potential costs and benefits (Simon 1957). We only have information, analytical capacity, and time enough to review a few alternative solutions, and in choosing between them, we rely on shortcuts in terms of intuition and rules of thumb as we look for a satisfying rather than an optimal outcome.

The presence of uncertain and intangible effects and high risks add to the problems associated with a systematic impact analysis and make it almost impossible to precisely estimate the costs and benefits of the actual and available alternatives (Stacey 2012, 54–65). Even in those cases where relatively reliable information about the likely effects is available, the idea of translating the qualitative assessments of costs and benefits into quantitative figures that can be tallied in a single number representing the net present value of an innovative solution has little purchasing power because too many intangible effects cannot be priced. Last but not least, a cost-benefit analysis completely glosses over the fact that decision-making processes are pervaded by political conflicts and power struggles that constantly shape and reshape the innovative solutions and seek to contest and reinterpret their impact by invoking competing goals and standards. The result is that innovative solutions are a moving target with ambiguous and unpredictable effects.

Now some people claim that deliberation can overcome the problems associated with limited capacities, uncertainty, intangibles, risks, and power struggles. Dreyfus and Dreyfus (1986) recommend that we move from a *calculative rationality*, which aims to predict outcomes on the basis of data gathering and rule following, to a *deliberative rationality* that seeks to make practical judgments about what is likely to work in a certain context on the basis of experience, intuition, and collective reasoning. Strong and convincing arguments favor such a move. Deliberation in collaborative settings will engage actors with different kinds of expertise who will use heuristic rather than analytical tools to narrow down the range of options. In addition, these actors will assess the impact of the alternative solutions based on their past experiences with similar attempts to break new ground, arguments about the context-dependent validity of the new program theory, and intuition nurtured by a deep understanding of the social and political context in which the innovative solution will be implemented. Hence, continued talk and argumentation that draw on the individual expertise of the speakers as well as on the collective intelligence of a group of relevant actors are good alternatives to analytical decision-making tools that aim to analyze and discount the costs and benefits of all possible solutions. Deliberation might not produce an unequivocal conclusion based on a rigorous comparison of different innovative solutions, but it gives us reasons for adopting a particular solution that has been developed, scrutinized, and revised through a lengthy debate by professional experts and lay actors with different forms of expertise.

Deliberation among multiple stakeholders in collaborative arenas is a well-known and frequently applied decision-making tool for collaborative innovation, but its success depends on the kind of deliberation that is applied. Since Habermas's path-breaking account of public deliberation based on communicative rationality (Habermas 1981), many social science researchers have recommended that deliberation take place in accordance with a particular procedural discourse ethic in which the claims advanced in a face-to-face dialogue between two or more actors will only be deemed valid if the speakers are sincere and legitimate and if their statements meet certain requirements (Forester 1989; Healey 1992; Dryzek 1990): They are comprehensible by the other actors, they are true in the positivist sense of relying on adequate logic and evidence, and they are normatively justifiable in relation to the common good. In a deliberation based on valid claims, the truth emerges through the formation of a consensus between the speakers. A consensus is formed during a process that fuses the speakers' statements and is governed exclusively by the "force of the better argument." Statements that are backed by more and better reasons than other statements will prevail, and they may integrate aspects of other well-argued points. Power exercised through the exclusion or silencing of speakers, the withholding or manipulation of information, or the use of peer pressure should not play a role in the communication process. When it does, it distorts the communication process and prevents the production of rational and socially valuable outcomes of the decision-making process.

In reality, however, public deliberations about the selection and realization of innovative solutions to societal problems seldom take place in power-free spaces safeguarded from the influence of the political system of government and the pressures from the economic market system. Indeed, government actors and private firms are often key participants in collaborative innovation processes. Booher and Innes (2010) discuss this problem in their recent attempt to develop the Habermasian model of communicative reason into a more practical model that can be used in the study of complex planning processes. What they term "collaborative rationality" is based on the inclusion of diverse interests; the interdependence of the actors, thus ensuring their enthusiasm for engaging with each other; and an authentic dialogue based on reciprocity, learning, and creativity (35). Empirically, there will be cases where powerful actors prevent affected stakeholders from participating in the decision-making process, threaten to go solo and find their own unilateral solution, or manipulate the dialogue and compromise the principles of ethical discourse. According to Booher and Innes (2010, 36) these cases fail to meet the criteria of collaborative rationality and will be unsuccessful in producing rational and socially valuable outcomes. It follows that, ideally, coercive use of power should be eliminated, although it is difficult to do so in reality.

This point is where the limitations of the Habermasian interpretation of deliberation become visible. Most people would probably agree that deliberative decision making that excludes affected actors and permits large power asymmetries among the included actors might lead to biased outcomes that fail to exploit the collective intelligence of the actors in the collaborative arena. Nevertheless, the idea that we should strive to eliminate all traces of power from the deliberative process to ensure a reasoned debate based on a universal discourse ethic is problematic for at least three reasons.

First, we should not judge empirical reality against an ideal that is almost impossible to realize; rather, we should work from a realistic assumption that deliberations take place in a political environment where social and political actors with different attributes and relational positions advance crosscutting power strategies. Assuming that power is ubiquitous, the deliberative decision-making process can work well and produce successful outcomes if it meets the following conditions. It must first include countervailing political power holders with different interests, views, and opinions and with sufficient leverage to back them and prevent political and cognitive closure. Next, the interdependency among the participating actors must be strong enough to prevent the more powerful actors from steamrolling the weaker actors so that they are not silenced or leaving the table. Finally, all participating actors must negotiate, approve, and agree to abide by the democratic rules that govern their interaction. Thus, deliberation does not require the eradication of power but merely that the exercise of power be regulated and constrained.

Second, the demand that all participants in deliberative decision making should be reasonable and only advance arguments that are polite, moderate, well-articulated, dispassionate, disembodied, and logical and that appeal to the common good may lead to the unintended and undemocratic exclusion of those who are loud, radical, inarticulate, passionate, and physical; who invoke rhetorical ploys to influence other people; and who deny the existence of an all-encompassing common good (Young 2000, 39–51). To avoid such a performative contradiction, in which a procedural ethic that aims to ensure justice may lead to injustice, we need to relax the strong ethical demands of Habermasian deliberation and give room to less exalted forms of discourse.

Third, relaxing the strict demands of Habermasian discourse ethics not only will make the process of deliberation more inclusive and more pluralistic but also will enhance innovation. Since innovation is not about what *exists* but about what might *emerge*, we should welcome speech acts that are not merely factual, analytical, evaluative, and pervaded by reason. Indeed, we should salute the advancement of speech acts that use gestures, pictures, models, and figurative language to produce concrete and persuasive images of possible futures and to advance bold ideas, captivating metaphors, and appealing story lines that breed enthusiasm, courage, and hope. In other words, the decision to realize a new and innovative idea in practice depends on a successful attempt to win the hearts and minds of the relevant decision makers and to mobilize broad support among the affected actors. In fact, one might argue that the adoption of an innovative solution is predicated on creating a hegemony—defined here as *political as well as moral-intellectual leadership* (Gramsci 1971)—that ensures support and consent through the construction of fantasies, desires, and narrative accounts of how we get from here to there and why it is important to do so.

The greatest barrier to innovation is lacking confidence in the collective capacity to change things. Believing that we cannot transform the current state of affairs no matter how hard we try will preserve status quo. We cannot overcome that barrier merely by accumulating factual evidence of the current predicament and good reasons for adopting new and innovative solutions. We need to build a visionary and passionate discourse that recruits and empowers a number of change agents who not only want to change the current state of affairs despite the considerable uncertainty and risks but also want to go all the way and prove the skeptics and the critics wrong. The more bold and disruptive the innovation is, the stronger the hegemony of the innovation discourse must be. The challenge is, of course, to build a compelling and convincing innovation discourse without overselling it and losing credibility. The protagonists of innovation must strike a balance between providing factual evidence and good reasons to support the adoption of a particular innovative solution and backing it with a hegemonic discourse that invokes passions and visions that take us beyond what is normally considered as amenable to reason.

Underlying this last argument is the idea found in the works of Foucault (1990), who writes that power is not merely prohibitive, repressive, and based on discipline but also productive, formative, and based on the proliferation of knowledge, identities, and practices. Thus, both the development of innovative solutions and the selection of the most promising one through deliberation hinge on exercising power based on the latter sense of the term. Power may exclude, silence, and control social actors, but it also involves the production of knowledge, local truths, new identities, and persuasive narratives that call upon the social actors to act and do new things.

In sum, deliberation provides a good alternative to cost-benefit analysis when we have to select a particular solution from among several alternatives. However, we have also seen that the rationalistic interpretations of the deliberative decision-making model are problematic and should be replaced with a less rationalistic model that is not premised on eradicating power but aims to constrain and regulate power and harness its productive aspects to build support for innovation. Although deliberation can be "rescued" from its most rationalistic interpretation, the preceding discussion clearly reveals a certain disappointment with the rationalistic approaches to decision making. This does not mean, however, that we should abandon the pursuit of intelligent change; rather, we should apply a deliberative model that recognizes the impact of power as sine qua non and supplement this model with other intelligent but less rationalistic decision-making instruments.

With respect to intelligent decision making, it has been suggested that "among the instruments of intelligence that have been 'discovered' as a result of the disappointments with rationality none is more prominent than learning from experience" (March and Olsen 1995, 199). As March and Olsen eloquently put it, the vision of experiential learning is "one of contemplating the past rather than anticipating the future, of adapting to changes rather than trying to guess what they will be, of developing capabilities to respond to various possible worlds after one of them is realized rather than gambling on the ability to forecast which of them will occur" (199). Hence, we can deliberate and try to predict and calculate what might happen if we put an innovative idea into practice, but we can also test it on a small scale and evaluate the experience. Then we can redesign the format and test it again until it finally works and produces a desired outcome.

Experiential learning builds on risk taking and resilience in the face of early adverse signals, and the evaluation of the success and failure of provisional designs is a social construction that results from competing interpretations of what has happened and what was hoped for (March and Olsen 1995, 200–201). The impact of an experiment often causes considerable confusion because many different actors judge its effects and because its many different factors cannot be controlled. There is also great confusion about the goals because they are often ambiguous, conflicting, and changing. However, social and political actors engaged in experiential learning impose some order and meaning on events, and they deliberate with each other to learn from the experience and to discover how they are going to proceed in the future. Thus, as clearly demonstrated by North American pragmatism, deliberation and experiential learning seem to go hand in hand (Ansell 2016).

CREATIVE REFORMULATION WHEN FACING OBSTRUCTIONS TO IMPLEMENTATION

Whether a bold and relatively path-breaking innovation in the public sector is fully realized or ends up as a half-hearted or abortive attempt to produce step change ultimately depends on the implementation process. When there is significant pressure to find a new solution and subsequently an innovative solution is designed and has managed to capture the hearts and the minds of a broad coalition of relevant and influential actors, there is a fair chance that the new policy, service, or organizational design will become implemented and produce additional public value. However, implementing innovative solutions will meet much more resistance than routine adjustments and incremental changes because they aim to break away from the established path and disrupt the common wisdom, trusted habits, and entrenched rights that many people rely on, cherish, and want to maintain. Implementation is further complicated if the proper organizational and institutional capacity for executing policy and service innovations are not in place and need to be established. That step takes time and requires a great deal of leadership, patience, and resources.

Multi-actor collaboration might contribute positively to implementing new solutions owing to its ability to mobilize resources and facilitate the interorganizational coordination and negotiated adjustment of the solution (Boyne 2003). Empirical studies indicate that the more complex the implementation of public innovations, the greater the significance of collaboration and networking will be to the implementation's success (Meyers, Sivakumar, and Nakata 1999; Valente 1995). However, the positive effects of collaboration are sometimes undermined by the destabilizing effects of strategic uncertainty in collaborative settings that may encourage the actors to shirk in low-trust environments. Also, the lack of institutionalization in these settings produces an unclear division of responsibilities and makes it difficult to protect the actors from the overwhelming complexity of the context of implementation (O'Toole 1997). Hence, the successful implementation of bold and creative solutions requires a good deal of determination, the ability to think through and solve emerging puzzles, and a willingness to adapt to unforeseen events and conditions.

Few of the classical implementation theories can help us understand the perils of implementation in processes of collaborative innovation. *Top-down implementation theory* stresses the presence of long decision-making chains in public bureaucracies and highlights the negative, cumulative effect of the goal displacement, underfunding, and vetoing that occur as we move from the top to the bottom of public bureaucracies (Pressman and Wildavsky 1973). This perspective may help us appreciate why government-driven policy innovation is difficult to forge at the local level or why great expectations in Washington are then dashed in Oakland. Pressman and Wildavsky (1973) assume, however, that the actors in the long-stretched decision-making chains are placed at different organizational levels between which there is little mutual interaction and communication. Thus, their theory has limited relevance for understanding the implementation problems confronting policy innovation advanced by collaborative networks of interdependent actors who make joint decisions about how to implement innovative solutions.

In opposition to top-down implementation theories that emphasize the role of formal hierarchies in structuring the implementation process (Mazmanian and Sabatier 1981, 1983), *bottom-up implementation theories* emphasize the crucial role of street-level bureaucrats for implementing public solutions (Lipsky 1980). Street-level bureaucrats are public professionals with considerable room for discretionary decision making, which they can use to further, redefine, or block the implementation of new and innovative solutions. Street-level bureaucrats are caught in an intolerable cross pressure between public policy goals, their own professional norms, the demands of the users, and the lack of adequate resources. Torn between these different norms, demands, and constraints, they use their mandated and legally regulated but relatively uncontrollable room for discretion to develop and deploy a series of coping mechanisms that enable them to manage the cross pressure and create an acceptable working life.

From this perspective, the failure to implement innovative solutions can be explained by the fact that street-level bureaucrats will view innovative policies, services, and organizational designs coming from above as yet another external pressure that they either have to fend off or find a way of coping with simply to maintain a tolerable working life. For this reason, in public organizations subject to successive waves of reform, change, and transformation, the front line is likely to oppose or even sabotage additional innovations. However, if public employees are brought into the collaborative innovation network, then this kind of bottom-up implementation theory becomes less relevant as the discretionary power of street-level bureaucrats is bounded by their moral obligation to the other participants in the network and the joint solution that they have designed and are trying to implement. Even if the frontline personnel are not entirely satisfied with the innovative design, they are less likely to block its implementation if they have participated in the collaborative innovation process, have thus established a joint ownership to the solution, and understand its importance. In that scenario, they will not construe innovative solutions as an external pressure but as an integral part of what the public employees, and other actors in the collaborative process, want to achieve.

A third set of implementation theories seems to be geared more toward the study of implementing collaborative innovation. Rather than looking at how the attempt of central government to implement innovative policies and service programs is hollowed out as it moves down the decision-making chains of public bureaucracy or at how street-level bureaucrats become the ultimate stumbling block in attempts to implement policy and service innovations, the so-called *bottom-up theories* are interested in the role that local networks of public and private actors play in implementing new solutions to joint policy problems (Hjern and Porter 1981; Hull and Hjern 1987). The local implementation networks are identified through a backward mapping of all the actors who have somehow contributed to the production of policy outcomes. Networked implementation of public innovation is highly complex as it involves forming governance structures, strategic planning, mobilizing resources, fund-raising and budgeting, training staff and helpers, constructing administrative routines and incentive structures, establishing interorganizational and cross-sectorial coordination, jointly evaluating results, practical learning, and making mutual adjustments in a relational structure with varying levels of trust, experience, and legitimacy. As for the choice of governance structure, appointing a lead organization or constructing a network administrative organization (Provan and Kenis 2008), which can manage the network and assume the main responsibility for organizing and monitoring the implementation process, may help to reduce the degree of complexity as not all decisions are subjected to endless negotiation between all the participating actors in a shared discussion forum. In addition, the lead agency or the network administrative organization may succeed in advancing and gaining support for a particular story line, a number of fundamental ground rules for the interaction, and a particular way of mediating conflicts.

Nevertheless, networked implementation of innovative solutions remains a formidable challenge as a great many things can go wrong or create problems and severe challenges (Klein and Knight 2005). The construction of a clear governance structure that reduces complexity may be impeded by an internal rivalry between different administrative silos or different groups of professionals who believe that only they know how to implement the new and bold solutions. The strategic planning of the who, what, when, and how of implementing the innovative solution also might lack proper attention if the project's key actors lose interest when the final agreement about its content and design is made and if they assume, incorrectly, that the implementation process will take care of itself. Given that the mobilization of resources from public budgets and of special-purpose funding for new and exciting things is limited in times of austerity and fiscal constraint, private collaborators may only have their knowledge, competence, and enthusiasm to offer. While these contributions are vital in the long run, they will not pay for the initial investment in new facilities, equipment, and staff training. Budgeting is normally straightforward in a public bureaucracy; however, it is really difficult to predict how much time and resources voluntary organizations and citizens will contribute and how their voluntary contribution will develop and fluctuate over time. Training the core staff, and perhaps the auxiliary and voluntary staff, is important in order to change the members' mind-set and to empower them to operate in a new way. Still training is costly and sometimes considered a private good appropriated by those who receive the training, and these factors tend to reduce the willingness of other actors to pay for it. Constructing administrative routines and incentive structures is crucial to move from idea to realization; however, in a multi-actor context, the risk is that routines and incentives will become politicized and subject to intense discussions that might stall implementation.

The devil sometimes lies in the detail. Constant coordination between public and private stakeholders to avoid gaps and overlaps and to create flow and synergy is a key to implementation, but it is hard to achieve and maintain when many actors—some of whom are inexperienced and uncertain about their role—are involved in the process. When the innovative solution is in place, feedback and systematic evaluation are necessary to facilitate learning and adjustment. The challenge then is to agree on appropriate measures of success and to retrieve and synthesize the evaluations of all the relevant actors including politicians, administrative staff, users, citizens, volunteers, and local stakeholders.

In addition to all these internal barriers, the project might also encounter an external resistance, or opposition, from those actors who are not convinced that change is for the better and who want the innovative solution to fail. To illustrate, the transition to the online procurement of public goods based on just-in-time delivery may be fiercely resisted by trade unions that fear layoffs in the public warehouses that stock and distribute goods to public agencies and by local vendors who will face increasing competition and lose the lucrative business of moving goods in and out of the warehouses (Eggers 2003). Sabotage of the implementation process is far from infrequent and can take many forms: public protests, legal battles, attempts to deprive innovative projects access to relevant knowledge and resources, demands to continue funding for the old solution, or leaking reports about an initial underperformance.

Faced with all these challenges to collaborative implementation, the rational response is to think through the different steps in the implementation process, to try to avoid or eliminate the obstacles, and to break down the opposition to change in order to secure an unfettered realization of the innovative solutions. This task will surely be difficult, and some of the hurdles on the way to successfully implementing innovative solutions may seem almost insurmountable unless the advocates of the new solutions mobilize all their strength, skills, and courage. Clearly, if the attempts to remove hindrances and to deal with those actors who are trying to block or derail the implementation process were unsuccessful, then public innovation would hardly occur. We owe the relatively high rate of innovation in the public sector to determined leaders, resilient public employees, patient users, and open-minded publics who are eager to reap the fruits of innovation. These groups often work together to overcome roadblocks in the implementation process.

However, the attempt of innovators and innovation managers to circumvent or remove all obstacles to innovation and silence critical voices is not always the best solution. An alternative strategy worth considering is to face the obstacles and treat them as challenges that call for a creative response involving the reformulation of the original ideas or of the strategy for implementing them. Dealing with obstructions in a constructive and creative way will produce deviations from the designated course of action, but often in such cases, new and truly innovative developments emerge. Hence, we should remember that innovation is a contingent and open-ended process, and we should be careful not to "freeze" an agreed-upon innovative solution and inflexibly try to implement it at all costs. Rather, we should look at the emerging barriers to implementation and judge whether they can and should be removed or, alternatively, whether we should rethink the innovative solution and its implementation in ways that might improve its chance of success.

By changing our perspective on the obstacles that we face in the implementation phase and perceiving them as triggers of creative puzzle solving rather than as roadblocks that prevent us from moving forward, we will frequently discover that hurdles can be overcome quite easily with the right strategy. Hence, faced with the apparently impossible task of defeating Goliath in a duel, David used his slingshot to bring down the giant before their dual had even begun, producing an extraordinary result by relatively new and ordinary means. David did not stand a chance in directly confronting the giant, but as soon as he cleverly changed his strategy, it took little effort to deal successfully with the problem he faced. In fact, as Michelangelo captures so well in his famous *David* statue, displayed at the Accademia di Belle Arti in Florence, David could relax in front of the giant because he knew an alternative to wrestling with him. While other Renaissance artists such as Donatello and Verrocchio portrayed the hero standing victoriously over the head of Goliath, Michelangelo presents David alone in the moment before the battle. David is ready to fight his foe and has an intense expression, but having already decided what to do, he adopts a relaxed and almost nonchalant pose as he stares beyond the spectator.

What we can learn from this analysis is that obstacles are not, first and foremost, something to avoid or eliminate but something that can lead us in new and unforeseen directions that may transform and improve the initial version of an innovative solution. If obstacles, through such a change of perspective, can be redescribed as "creative constraints" (Ibbotson 2008) and turned into "opportunities" (Stoltz 1997), we might even begin to invent obstacles in addition to those that we have already discovered in the course of implementation. Indeed, many artists subject themselves to self-imposed constraints because they find that the constraints stimulate their creativity and inventiveness. One example is a set of rules for filmmaking that the group of Danish film directors known as Dogme 95 established in 1995. Among other directives, their so-called oath of chastity prohibited the use of artificial sound and light and required that their movies had to be shot on location with a handheld camera. The rules inspired a generation of Danish filmmakers to produce brilliant and much-appreciated movies such as Thomas Vinterberg's award-winning film *The Celebration.*

To further illustrate the point, let us look at some empirical examples of how obstacles to public innovation have been turned into creative constraints that supported rather than impeded implementation. The first examples concern the legal and bureaucratic rules that seemingly prevent the implementation of an innovative solution. Here it is always a good idea to first check whether the alleged hindrance is real or simply imagined or anticipated. For example, a large proportion of the Danish municipalities that applied to the Ministry of Social Affairs and the Interior to become an official "enterprise municipality"—thereby exempting them from a particular set of legal and administrative rules so they could enhance public innovation—were told that the legal and administrative rules did not prevent them from doing what they wanted to do. However, in many other cases, legal and administrative rules may actually hamper innovation, and exemptions will offer a way out. Exemptions to the law prohibiting the sharing of personal information about individual citizens among administrative units, for instance, have enabled Danish police, social authorities, and local school officials to collaborate and find innovative solutions to the problems experienced by at-risk youths.

Sometimes, however, winning such exemptions from legal rules is impossible. Then the only way forward is to think constructively about what methods can be used to secure the implementation of an innovative solution. To illustrate how it can be done, the US government's attempt to halt global warming by developing carbon capture and geologic sequestration is likely to trigger liability and reporting requirements under existing environmental protection statutes, such as the Resource Conservation and Recovery Act; the Comprehensive Environmental Response, Compensation, and Liability Act; and the Clean Air Act. In fact, myriad legal regulations may prevent concrete carbon dioxide capture and geological sequestration projects. However, instead of abandoning this new and innovative strategy for combating global warming, scientific experts and policymakers have called for establishing a comprehensive permitting regime that streamlines the rules for capturing, transporting, and placing carbon in geological sequestration to replace the patchwork of regulations that is currently applied. Thus, innovation in climate policy seems to be triggering innovation in the regulatory framework governing the entire field of environmental protection (Jacobs et al. 2009).

The next group of examples concerns the lack of public funding, which is a typical problem in the implementation phase. An innovative crime-prevention project in Denmark offering a range of leisure activities to at-risk youths in a deprived neighborhood was only made financially viable because local volunteers ran the youth center. Involving local citizens as volunteers in the youth center helped to empower the neighborhood and improved intergenerational relationships. It also encouraged immigrant parents to become active in organizing leisure activities such as traditional dances, which became a big hit, and increasing numbers of youths frequented the youth center. A lack of funding was also the problem in Oakland when the local government sought to implement its new crime prevention strategy Measure Y. Legal constraints forbad the local government to pay for the policy initiative by raising income taxes, but the government found a creative way out of the impasse by establishing a public fund financed by a flat tax on each parcel of real estate and by a parking surcharge on commercial lots. That solution created a stable funding stream that cannot be squeezed by other fiscal pressures because the money is earmarked for crime prevention. Last but not least, an international aid program that sought to build new and better houses for Chilean citizens in an earthquake-devastated region found that it was impossible to build everyone suitable, good-quality homes with the money available. The project's innovative solution was to build one-story houses with all the basic amenities and prepare them so the homeowners could construct an additional floor later.

A third kind of example relates to the problems of reaching the target group and ensuring that innovative solutions are adopted. A public-private innovation project to improve health in developing countries disseminated information about hygiene, health, and disease control but soon realized that most of the people in the target group could not read and benefit from the written material. People were dying, not because they lacked medical staff or medicine, but because their illiteracy prevented them from learning how to improve their health, prevent diseases, and take prescribed medicine. The Speaking Book provides an innovative solution to this obstacle to health campaigns. Its concept is fairly simple: The Speaking Book incorporates an electronic device powered by a small long-life battery that allows it to speak to the reader. In contrast to other awareness texts, the sixteen-page, brightly colored and simply worded text also has a button placed on the page, and when pressed, it plays a corresponding soundtrack of the text. Hence, no matter the reader's reading proficiency, the information contained in the book can be read, heard, or both. The Speaking Book covers public and personal health issues, including how to prevent and treat diarrhea, malaria, tuberculosis, HIV, and AIDS, as well as more socially focused issues such as how to apply for benefits.

Another example shows that not only developing countries have difficulty reaching the target group. The municipality of Copenhagen has tested a prototype of an innovative scheme that encourages unemployed job seekers to use the Internet and, as much as they can, fill out an individual action plan for returning to the labor market before they have their first meeting with a job consultant. The consultant would then help them finalize the action plan, which gives them access to counseling, education, and job training. When it turned out that few job seekers had drafted their action plans before arriving at the job center, the scheme was redesigned. Now when they arrive at the Job Center, the unemployed can use the center's computers, and this new kind of guided self-service allows them to make a draft of their action plan before they meet with a job consultant. This solution has increased not only the take-up rate but also the unemployed's engagement in drafting their action plans, thus enhancing their ownership of the plans and, in turn, the plans' impact.

A final example shows how opposition to innovation can trigger reinventions. In Rotterdam the citizens opposed the construction of an innovative "water square" to prevent flooding of lower-lying areas because it would have created a large rainwater storage basin in a small square located in a densely populated neighborhood. Moreover, the local square had recently been renovated, and the citizens could not bear another two years of construction work. Instead of panicking, the public-private partnership behind the innovative water square adjusted its implementation strategy and looked for another square that was still in the planning stage. By integrating the storage facility's construction with the plans for building a new green square next to a public school, the water square became a functional and aesthetic success (Bressers 2014).

These examples support the earlier proposition that obstacles to implementing novel ideas can be used creatively to reformulate and even improve innovative solutions. However, we should not be overly optimistic and draw the conclusion that barriers to the implementation of innovative solutions can always be turned into positive reinventions; instead, we should seize the opportunity to turn obstacles into possibilities when it comes. This requires mental agility in the sense of being able to adapt new ideas to the shifting and unforeseen circumstances discovered in the process of innovation. Drawing on Stoltz (1997), we need to turn "quitters" and "campers" into "climbers" if we want to surpass the mountain that blocks our way to the development and implementation of new and better solutions.

THE TENSION BETWEEN INNOVATION AND OPERATIONS

In the daily operation of public service institutions, key goals are stability and predictability ensured by the application of clear and explicit rules. By contrast, innovation aims to destabilize and disrupt routinized practices and create new and perhaps better ones. Hence, it is understandable if an unresolved tension between operations and innovation becomes visible in the implementation phase when new designs are introduced. Let us briefly look at three paradoxical relationships between operations and innovation.

On the one hand, the conventional wisdom is that we should avoid separating innovation too much from operations and from the people who both understand the problems at hand and have the power to make suitable changes (Eggers and Singh 2009). Thus, separate R&D departments and centrally located strategic innovation units are often too far removed from the daily operations to identify the problems that call for innovation and offer helpful solutions. In addition, many public organizations have an unfortunate tendency to create special task forces, project groups, and other "ad-hocracies" that are completely divorced from the operational level and its leaders, managers, and employees. When the innovation task force comes back after several months of search and exploration and reports that it has found an innovative solution, the people in daily operations have frequently moved on or forgotten the problem. Moreover, if they have not participated in the innovation process, they will feel limited ownership over the new solution and thus be reluctant to implement it.

On the other hand, we should be careful not to assume that the people in daily operations will produce a sufficient amount of innovation. Learning processes in local communities of practice may spur collaborative innovation, but public employees are often too busy to consider what public service provision or regulatory policies could be like in the future. Radical forms of innovation will often require applying different methods and forms of knowledge than the ones used in daily operations; therefore, the solution is to create spaces for collaborative innovation that are close to but outside operations. Thus, innovation teams bringing together public employees with the right kind of innovation assets should be given extra resources so that they can spend time collaborating with each other and with relevant actors, such as users, civil society organizations, and private firms, to develop new and promising ideas. However, the teams should report regularly to the leaders and colleagues of their respective organizations and strive to develop and test a prototype of the most promising solution directly in the daily operations within a short time frame. This strategy has been pursued with great success at some of the most innovative hospitals in North America. They set up small innovation teams of relevant employees that report to operational managers at weekly meetings, and the teams are terminated if they do not manage to develop and test a prototype of an innovation solution within three months.

Another dilemma concerns the limited time, resources, and attention spans in public organizations. Many examples show the effort to develop and implement innovative ideas in public organizations is crowded out by the demands of daily operations and the need to meet the growing demands of citizens and the performance targets coming from above. To illustrate, a technical school offering vocational training for young people in Denmark had an alarmingly high and rising dropout rate. When they were confronted the managers' immediate reaction was that they did not have time to find an innovative solution because they were under pressure to deliver a large amount of teaching and solve an increasing number of administrative tasks including documenting their performance and results.

By contrast, there are also examples of innovation projects crowding each other out and requiring so much time, energy, and attention that the daily operations begin to suffer. This problem is standard for small public organizations. They have trouble shouldering the burden of managing or participating in large-scale innovation projects over longer periods because the resources available for these kinds of activities are scarce. The paradox is that public organizations subjected to spending cuts will urgently need to find innovative ways of producing more for less, but they will have almost no resources to invest in the search for innovative solutions. One answer to this problem could be to create what people from the consultancy house Deloitte call a GovCloud, where highly competent, knowledgeable workers are placed in a central talent pool that public agencies can tap when they occasionally need experienced entrepreneurs and innovation managers to work with their staffs for a certain period (Tierney, Cottle, and Jorgensen 2012). The two main attractions of the GovCloud are that it provides scalable support to frontline organizations with scarce resources while facilitating learning and knowledge sharing across public service organizations.

Finally, the bureaucratic logic that dominates service production seems to be both the condition of possibility and the impossibility for innovation. Implementing innovative solutions requires the invention of new bureaucratic rules, routines, and divisions of labor to ensure that the staff knows what to do and who should do it. By contrast, the open and creative search for disruptive ideas may be hindered by using formal bureaucratic language to describe and operationalize the emerging ideas in minutes and policy briefs. In addition, implementing the new ideas may be jeopardized by early performance measurements that will often show a dip in the overall program performance because the innovative solutions have not been properly implemented and routinized and "infantile disorders" are not yet cured. This paradox can be resolved by developing an innovation culture that enables situated actors not only to use bureaucratic tools to secure the implementation of innovative solutions but also to avoid them when they prevent creative thinking and pragmatic problem solving. Maneuvering in such an organizational culture demands a high degree of reflexivity on the part of public managers and employees.

CONCLUSION

This chapter has identified and described the problems that hamper the selection and implementation of innovative solutions in the public sector. These problems consist of a mixture of uncertainty, risk, complexity, collective action problems, and power struggles. Although they are not easily overcome, their negative impact can be mitigated in and through multi-actor collaboration. The chapter has challenged the rationalistic approach to selecting innovative solutions that relies on either cost-benefit analysis or deliberation based on communicative rationality. Thus, when it comes to promoting innovative solutions, deliberative processes must combine the accumulation of arguments based on reason with the articulation of a hegemonic discourse that is capable of mobilizing passion and constructing visions. Further, deliberation in collaborative arenas pervaded by conflicts and power struggles can pursue intelligent change by facilitating experiential learning based on pragmatic experimentation. When it comes to implementing innovative policies, organizational designs, or services, the rationalistic idea of removing all obstacles and steamrolling the opposition is quite limited. Indeed, sometimes obstacles cannot and should not be removed; rather, they should be treated as "opportunities" or "creative constraints" that spur the development of innovative designs and redesigns.

Last but not least, the efforts to create innovative solutions should not be divorced from the daily operation of public bureaucracies. Instead, we should aim to integrate innovation and operations, for example, by making it possible for frontline personnel to seek support from highly competent knowledge workers who can help them initiate and manage innovation processes that take place outside but close to operations. Finally, we should prevent bureaucratic language and demands for a "business plan" from stifling creative thinking and innovative learning processes by instead cultivating a flexible application of bureaucratic rules and procedures so that they support rather than impede public innovation.

8

DIFFUSING PUBLIC INNOVATION THROUGH COLLABORATIVE NETWORKS

GRANOVETTER'S (1973) seminal work has convincingly demonstrated the strength of weak ties when it comes to spreading new ideas and solutions between social actors and within and across public and private organizations. For example, if an ambulance service in Stockholm seeks an innovative way of reducing its response time to life-threatening calls, it may benefit from looking outside its immediate surroundings and drawing on the experiences of another ambulance service. A Swedish staff member attending an international conference for medical response teams may have heard about a British ambulance service in the West Midlands that had put its paramedics on motorbikes. Chasing down the speaker from the conference will prove more valuable than contacting the neighboring ambulance services in and around Stockholm that most likely follow the same standard procedures as the team that looks to improve its service. However, to get the full story about the innovative strategies pursued by the West Midlands' Ambulance Service, the weak tie between the supplier and the potential adopter must be developed into a strong tie. That could be done by organizing a face-to-face meeting with the British colleagues in order to fully gasp their innovative solutions and their effect on response time. Strong ties are important here because they expand the bandwidth of communication and allow the transfer of tacit knowledge about implementing the innovative ideas that improve public services.

This example illustrates the importance of diffusing innovative ideas and solutions. We do not always have to invent things ourselves to produce public innovation; instead, we can replicate innovations that come from elsewhere.

CHAPTER 8

Innovation diffusion is an important way of creating a more innovative and better public sector, and it is spurred by interaction, networking, and collaboration (Rogers 1995; Albury 2005, 54). The more public and private actors who participate in creating and implementing public innovations, the greater the chance that some of them will have weak and strong ties that give them access to new and inspiring ideas and the larger the number of ambassadors who can broadcast the news about an innovative solution and its achievements.

This chapter first looks at the process of diffusing innovation in the public sector and then discusses the role of innovation diffusion networks and the impact that network structures and interpersonal relations play in diffusing public innovation. From there it argues that innovation diffusion seldom involves a simple transfer of innovation solutions from one public agency to another. Rather, it results from the complex and conflict-ridden selection, negotiation, translation, and transformation of creative ideas through a process of bricolage that aims to combine new ideas with old ones and make them work in new and different contexts. The final sections challenge the pro-diffusion bias found in much of the innovation literature and considers the problems with measuring outcomes of collaborative innovation. Through this analysis, the chapter reveals some of the key dilemmas of innovation diffusion in the public sector.

INNOVATION DIFFUSION

Public organizations can gain a great deal from replicating the innovations of other organizations because they reap all the potential benefits of the innovative solution while saving the development costs. Second movers might even enjoy greater benefits from an innovation than the first movers because they can learn from the experiences and mistakes of the latter. Finally, adopting well-tested and seemingly successful innovations helps reduce the political uncertainty that often prevents risk-averse public organizations from innovating. However, on the one hand, the attempt to import and deploy innovative solutions from other organizations is often met with strong objections from people who either claim that they should be "pioneers and front-runners rather than imitators and laggards" or insist that they are "too special" to benefit from innovations created elsewhere. Such objections are widespread and serve as fundamental barriers when public agencies try to benefit from innovation diffusion. On the other hand, the absence of market-based, cutthroat competition between public agencies tends to make them more amenable to collaboration, knowledge sharing, and mutual learning than private firms are. Public agencies seldom protect their innovations with patent rights, and the adopters are not forced to use industrial espionage or reverse-engineering techniques to uncover the contents of innovative solutions invented by other agencies. In fact, it could be argued that public agencies have a moral obligation to spread information and knowledge about innovative solutions and to explore and exploit such solutions to the benefit of the citizens and users. Indeed, the citizens of Birmingham have the right to enjoy the same smart solutions in elderly care as the citizens of Bristol.

Now while replicating simple product innovations such as electronic travel cards in public transportation and discrete service innovations such as hand washing in hospitals is relatively unproblematic, the attempt to reproduce complex and multidimensional innovations, like energy policies, garbage collection systems, or collective traffic solutions, is extremely challenging. Public innovations are multifaceted and hard to demarcate because they tend to combine new policy objectives with changes in the form and content of public services and in the organizational system through which these services are produced and delivered. For example, the innovative "workfare policies" that spread to most Western countries during the 1990s aimed to move unemployed people into gainful employment as quickly as possible through different combinations of benefit reductions, enhanced control with labor-market availability and job-seeking behavior, and an increased use of job counseling, education, and training (Lødemel and Trickey 2001). In some countries, providing active educational opportunities and subsidized jobs to the unemployed spurred the contracting out of job services and led to the creation of new network-based governance structures (Damgaard and Torfing 2010). Therefore, the adoption of the innovative workfare policies had widespread repercussions throughout the administrative system, making it difficult to describe and delineate the new policy model.

Another related challenge to replicating public innovations is that separating the innovative solution from its wider institutional and political conditions is often difficult. To illustrate, other European governments have been interested in replicating the Danish flexicurity model that combines the relative freedom of employers to hire and fire employees with the unemployed's easy access to relatively generous social benefits. In turn, the unemployed have both a right and an obligation to receive education and job training that can help bring them back into the labor market. In Denmark, this model has created a hyper-flexible labor market, a high degree of social security for the unemployed, and a strong program for unemployed people to regain employment.

This carefully calibrated flexicurity model gave rise to an unprecedented high and stable job growth from 1993 to 2008 that was also accompanied by a very low inflation rate (Torfing 1999b; Damgaard and Torfing 2010). Thus, other European governments are tempted to adopt the flexicurity model in the hope that it will produce an active job market similar to the one Denmark experienced after implementing the labor-market reforms in the early 1990s. However, the Danish model rests on a political compromise between the peak labor-market organizations and the government that has taken a century to forge and is supported by a large number of regulatory institutions. For other countries to replicate the Danish flexicurity model would be extremely difficult. Hence, we can conclude that although innovation diffusion in the public sector is not prevented by the same kind of cutthroat competition that is found in private markets, it is still complicated because the complex and multidimensional innovative practices rest on specific conditions that are hard to reproduce.

Central government agencies constantly try to push innovative ideas and solutions down the chain of command to regional and local governments and service institutions through a combination of legislation, regulation, guidance, and dissemination of authoritative recommendations and inspirational information. However, despite the existence of successful dissemination strategies, such a top-down "innovation-push strategy" has major limitations. First of all, when lower-level organizations are told what they should do without first being asked about their problems, needs, and ideas, they tend to resist the adoption of new practices in order to preserve their autonomy. Second, evidence suggests that dissemination strategies have the most purchase with striving organizations in the mid-range of performance. High-achieving organizations are often far ahead of the recommended practices, whereas weak or failing organizations do not have the organizational capacity to adopt new ideas. Finally, what is considered a best practice in one context does not always work in other contexts, and public agencies are often better off searching for and developing their own innovations through close interaction with other agencies (Albury 2005, 54). These limitations explain why the recent research on replicating public innovation has focused on demand-driven diffusion rather than supply-driven dissemination.

The focus on *dissemination* takes a managerial perspective on the need of central governments and executive managers to ensure that field agencies and frontline personnel adopt particular practices. In this perspective, government officials and public managers identify and evaluate different innovative designs and decide which ones should be disseminated, and the general idea is that lower organizational levels will comply and adopt the innovative design. Within the professional communities and organizations of planners, teachers, nurses, and doctors, the focus is less on dissemination and more on *knowledge transfer*. Technical knowledge of new projects, procedures, and methods is generated in accordance with professional standards, and the knowledge is transferred to all colleagues in the profession through specialized journals, magazines, websites, and conferences. Compared with the managerial focus of dissemination and the professional focus of knowledge transfers, the emphasis on *innovation diffusion* has a broader and more social focus on how networks within and across organizations facilitate a decentered circulation and adoption of innovative ideas and solutions. Innovation diffusion is based on the potential adopters' demand for innovative solutions and the process through which these demands are satisfied by the constant supply of innovative ideas and practices. It is less formal and more chaotic than the processes of dissemination and knowledge transfer. The criteria for validating the diffused knowledge and information are also more diverse, fluid, and conflict ridden than the criteria applied in practices associated with dissemination and knowledge transfer.

Public innovation diffusion is driven by intentional actions on the part of the suppliers and adopters of innovative ideas; thus, it is distinguished from the passive spread of innovation that occurs as a result of natural or automatic responses to changing conditions and environments. Public leaders and employees do not passively accept innovative solutions and uncritically adopt them to marginally improve their organization's chance of survival. Instead, public leaders and employees who face problems and challenges search for innovative solutions by drawing on their vast network of contacts and the multiple streams of information in which they are immersed. Here, innovation diffusion is a two-way street in which potential adopters proactively—though often in informal and unplanned ways—seek innovative solutions to the problem or challenge at hand and in which other actors supply, circulate, relay, and mediate more or less promising and ready-made innovations in a complex and multitiered system of interorganizational and interpersonal interaction (Greenhalgh et al. 2004, 601).

According to the groundbreaking work of Rogers (1995, 5), innovation diffusion connects suppliers of innovative solutions with potential adopters and facilitates a complex and contingent circulation of innovative solutions through different communication channels in time and space. To ensure the circulation of innovative solutions, a supplier must be capable of identifying and conceptualizing new ideas and practices as innovations, assessing their problems and merits, and communicating with the external environment to make the knowledge and information about the innovation solutions and their merits available to potential adopters. These adopters must also be looking for innovative solutions or at least be open to new ideas and methods. They need to be competent, motivated, and curious to be able to scan their surroundings for innovative designs and to explore their content. As important, they must also be capable of tolerating ambiguity, for the coexistence of new and old practices in the implementation phase may generate tensions and grievances and cause frustration.

The suppliers and potential adopters of innovative solutions are connected in and through different communication channels—either print or electronic mass media with large, anonymous audiences or interpersonal networks of people who know each other or are somehow acquainted (Rogers 1995 18). Change agents and opinion leaders who act as gatekeepers, broadcasters, and knowledge brokers often mediate the diffusion processes within the different communication channels. Whereas change agents work professionally with identifying, clarifying, and circulating innovative solutions to facilitate or promote change, opinion leaders have a particular influence on the beliefs and actions of their colleagues through their perceived authority and status.

The time it takes for an innovative solution to travel from one public organization to another can vary from days, weeks, and months to several years. Some public organizations quickly identify and adopt innovations that they judge as promising, whereas other organizations stick with inefficient practices for many years either because they are out of the loop or because they do not have the courage to implement the innovative solutions that they encounter. The spatial distance may also vary greatly as innovative solutions can be diffused from one part of an organization to another, from one local or regional jurisdiction to another, or from one country or continent to another. The rise of supranational regional institutions such as the European Union, the North American Free Trade Agreement, and the Mercado Común del Sur is likely to stimulate cross-national innovation diffusion.

ROGERS'S INNOVATION DIFFUSION MODEL

Rogers (1995) developed a widely recognized model for analyzing the process of how innovations are diffused. The model tends to view innovation diffusion as a process of communication in which a series of actions and decisions by the adopter lead to the adoption of innovative solutions. The innovation diffusion model consists of five stages (169):

1. *Knowledge* occurs when a social actor becomes aware of the existence of a particular innovation and begins to understand how and why it works.
2. *Persuasion* results from forming a favorable or unfavorable opinion about the innovation.
3. *Decision* takes place when a social actor engages in activities that lead to a determination about whether to adopt or reject the innovation.
4. *Implementation* occurs when a social actor aims to realize the innovative idea, method, or design in practice.
5. *Confirmation* takes place when a social actor seeks to reinforce the decision to adopt an innovation based on positive feedback or reverses the decision due to negative or conflicting feedback.

In the *knowledge phase* we gain knowledge about an innovation—for example, about how it works and what it achieves. Sometimes we have a more or less well-defined and deep-seated need or problem that prompts us to search for an innovative solution, while at other times our exposure to information about an innovation creates a new need or makes us invent a present or future problem that the innovation will be able to solve. An important driver of the search for innovation knowledge is that being an early knower yields social status and professional prestige. According to Rogers (1995, 174), early knowers tend to be more educated, better connected, and more cosmopolitan than later knowers are.

In the *persuasion phase* we actively seek information about the innovation, assess the credibility of different reports and messages, and interpret their meaning to form an opinion about the innovation. The crucial questions are, What will happen if we implement this innovation in the present context? Which advantages and disadvantages will the innovation bring in the present situation? What are the inherent risks, and how can we possibly eliminate, mitigate, or manage them?

In the *decision phase* we make up our mind and decide whether to adopt or reject an innovation. To cope with the inherent uncertainty, we will often try out the innovative idea on a partial basis. For example, we make it possible for users to choose a new and innovative service over the old one and carefully evaluate their satisfaction and the impact of the new service on their needs and problems. If either the initial assessment of the expected results or the results from the trial turn out negative, the innovation will be rejected. By contrast, positive expectations and a successful trial will increase the chance of its adoption. However, sometimes there is no clear or final verdict as the assessment of the consequences of an innovation is ambiguous. This situation will lead to a passive rejection because the lack of a decision will prevent adoption.

In the *implementation phase* we aim to put the innovative solution into practice, and in the public sector this process will involve the coordination between many different actors and often people who were not present in the decision phase. This phase requires that we find answers to questions about how the new ideas can be realized in practice and how to solve the operational problems that are likely to emerge. Modifications, adjustments, and changes of the innovative design of policies, organizations, and services are an essential part of the answer to these pertinent questions. Implementation also involves knowledge sharing, unlearning old practices, and training staff members to ensure that they have the skills and competences that the innovative solution requires. Last, institutional embedding through retention and routinization, aligning the new practices with the old ones, and managing political and organizational tensions also occur during this phase.

Finally, in the *confirmation phase* we review our decision to adopt and implement new ideas and innovative solutions in light of the feedback we receive. Positive feedback will urge us to consolidate or even upscale the innovation, whereas negative feedback or conflicting reports that create cognitive dissonance will make us reverse our prior decision to adopt an innovation. The decision to reject an innovation that had previously been adopted is called *discontinuance*. According to Rogers (1995, 190), discontinuance can take two different forms. *Replacement discontinuance* is a decision to reject an innovation in order to adopt a better one, whereas *disenchantment discontinuance* is a decision to reject an innovation due to dissatisfaction with its performance.

Adopting a new idea or solution depends on a number of decisions on the part of the potential adopter, who in each stage of the innovation diffusion process must decide whether to reject the innovation or move on to the next stage. Despite the adopter's pivotal role, other factors influence the innovation diffusion process as well and lead to different innovations having different chances of passing through its separate stages. The innovation itself, and the way it is constructed in and through the multiple streams of communication, is an important factor. The relative advantage of a new policy, service, or organizational design is the sine qua non for innovation diffusion. Hence, innovations that clearly demonstrate and document their ability to cut public expenditures and to improve the performance of policies, organizations, and services are more likely to be adopted than innovations that cannot demonstrate such advantages. Other important attributes of an innovation that increase its chances of being adopted are its compatibility with the professional norms, values, and opinions of the adopting organization; a low degree of complexity, thus making it simple to implement; the possibility of experimenting with the new idea on a limited basis to see how it works; the ability to make adjustments to suit the local context; and its discursive construction as promising, feasible, appropriate, and politically legitimate (Rogers 1995, 219–65; Greenhalgh et al. 2004, 594–98). Innovations with these features are likely to be adopted because they increase the chances that potential adopters will hear about the innovations and will let them pass through the persuasion, decision, and implementation stages.

In the public sector, adopters are not lone wolves who single-handedly decide whether to adopt a new and promising solution. The adopters are individuals or groups of people who are part of a bureaucratic organization that, in turn, greatly influences their ability to support new ideas. Hence, the organizational capacity for absorbing new knowledge and the readiness for change matter. Open-minded and externally oriented organizations that are equipped with procedures and routines that enable them to identify, capture, interpret, adjust, and apply new knowledge are better able to assimilate innovative ideas. The same goes for organizations with a strong strategic leadership, visionary staff members in key positions, and a culture characterized by experimentation and risk taking (Greenhalgh et al. 2004, 606–7). Tight budgets, growing demands, and the urgent need to "do more with less" are often seen as the key drivers of innovation adoption, but organizational energy in terms of a motivated and engaged staff, curious and entrepreneurial leaders, and a positive climate for learning and innovation seems to be equally, if not more, important.

The external context and environment of the organizations and persons that contemplate the adoption of innovative solutions may also have a profound influence on innovation diffusion. Shifting political goals and policy agendas are crucial in the public sector as they define what is legitimate for public service organizations to pursue. Political directives accelerate the search for and adoption of a particular kind of innovative solution, especially if the new policy objectives are combined with dedicated funding streams (Greenhalgh et al. 2004, 610). Other important external factors are the presence of public pressures from citizens and users who demand new services;

the media's attention to best practices that tends to enhance the pressure to adopt such practices; and the rivalry between public agencies that want to achieve a competitive advantage or avoid falling behind. The introduction of performance measurement systems, award schemes, and a culture of peer recognition stimulate interagency rivalry. While rivalry may motivate public agencies to seek and adopt innovative solutions, it also reduces trust and increases defensiveness, two factors that may prevent interorganizational learning. At a more macroscopic societal level, political discourses on global competition may construct public innovation as a way to enhance the efficiency of the public sector and free resources that can be transferred to the private sector in order to boost its competitiveness. Indeed, political discourses may construct public innovation as a necessity without which it becomes impossible to ensure public welfare as well as private growth and prosperity (Griggs and Sullivan 2014).

In sum, we can say that innovation diffusion hinges on a number of actions and decisions on the part of the would-be adopters. These actions and decisions are conditioned by the innovation itself, the organization in which the adopters are situated, and the external environment of the organizations. All of these factors interact in producing different rates of adoption and different kinds of adopters. Rogers finds that over time the cumulative number of innovation adopters forms an S-shaped curve, indicating a slow rise at first, followed by an acceleration as the rate of adoption increases, and finally the flattening of the curve as the number of new adopters falls. The cumulative S curve and the bell-shaped frequency curve, which can be derived from it, permit us to divide the adopters into different categories that range from the well-connected and well-respected leaders over the cautious but striving early followers, the skeptical but resourceful late followers, and the traditional and parochial laggards (Rogers 1995, 282–85). When classifying adopters as leaders and laggards, however, it is important not to think of the various labels as being essential characteristics of individuals or groups. The personal traits and structural position of the adopters may influence their decision on when to adopt a new idea, but the complex interrelation of the different factors determining the innovation diffusion process means that the time from knowledge to implementation may vary from innovation to innovation. For example, strong political pressures to adopt an innovative solution in a public health organization may help to overcome diffusion barriers in terms of personal skepticism and the presence of a risk-averse culture.

THE ROLE OF DIFFUSION NETWORKS

Having established the basic parameters of innovation diffusion from the point of view of the adopters, we shall now take a more decentered approach to innovation diffusion that emphasizes the role of diffusion networks. Adopters, suppliers, and different kinds of mediators interact and collaborate in these networks to spread innovative solutions within and across public organizations and sometimes even from private firms or civil society to the public sector. To clarify how the network perspective on innovation diffusion differs from other perspectives, we shall begin with a brief discussion of different theoretical explanations of the spread of innovation in the public sector.

Dobbin, Simmons, and Garrett (2007) compare different theoretical perspectives on policy diffusion between nation-states, but their categorization of different theoretical explanations, and the diffusion mechanisms that they identify, has a general relevance for understanding innovation diffusion within and between public organizations. In discussing the diffusion of economic policy and human rights among countries and global regions, they identify four different theoretical approaches: theories of coercion, theories of competition, theories of global norms, and theories of organizational learning.

Political science explains policy diffusion as a result of *coercion* exercised by governments, international organizations, and nongovernmental actors through the use of military threats, the imposition of loan and aid conditionality, the manipulation of economic costs and benefits, and the monopolization of expertise and policy advice (Dobbin, Simmons, and Garrett 2007, 454). There are many examples of regional superpowers aiming to force other states to adopt particular policies (Owen 2002), and many have criticized the World Bank for making loans to developing countries conditional upon particular economic and political reforms (Mosley, Harrigan, and Toye 1995). The United States sometimes uses the promise of a favorable trade status in return for tariff reductions to influence the policies of countries that are dependent on trade with the United States, but coercive policy diffusion can also take place within supranational organizations. In some areas, the European Union makes majority decisions and forces the opposing member states to adopt particular policies, while in other areas it has created voluntary policy standards that the member states comply with because they fear being named and shamed for not meeting the targets. The theories of policy diffusion through coercion build on a realist approach that views policy choice as a calculated response to sanctions and incentives. The limiting case is the attempt to coerce nation-states to adopt a particular policy by using authoritative, uncontested, and biased expertise. Here adoption is voluntary but premised on manipulation.

Political economists see *competition* rather than powerful hegemons as the key driver of international policy diffusion. Governments have little choice, so it is argued, but to adopt new market-friendly policies to attract direct foreign investments and keep their export sector competitive (Dobbin, Simmons, and Garrett 2007, 457). Today the notion of economic competition has been redefined to include not only low wages and a stable and relatively well-educated workforce but also the availability of a broad range of direct and indirect production factors such as research, technology, labor-market flexibility, tax policies, child care, health insurance, political stability, and human rights (Jessop, Nielsen, and Pedersen 1991). Now there is almost no limit to the kind of policy innovations that a country can adopt with the ambition of enhancing the structural competitiveness of its economy. The mechanism of policy diffusion arises when a country's competitors adopt a new market-friendly policy and that country feels pressure to follow suit (Dobbin, Simmons, and Garrett 2007, 457). Competition might trigger a "race to the bottom," through which corporate taxes and environmental standards are lowered to attract footloose capital, but competition need not lead to policy convergence. Global firms have different needs and may prefer having access to highly skilled laborers and new research and technology than to lower corporate taxes and the absence of environmental regulation.

The sociological perspective emphasizes the role of *global norms and hegemonic ideas* that are socially constructed and change over time. "Policy choices are based on fads, revered exemplars, or abstract theories, rather than solid evidence" (Dobbin, Simmons, and Garrett 2007, 451). Neither actual needs nor concrete experiences with new ideas and innovative solutions play a significant role in diffusing policy. What matters is that particular norms and ideas become socially and politically accepted. This can happen in three ways: Leading countries define exemplary policies that inspire other countries to follow them, well-reputed experts theorize the effects of new policy norms and thereby provide plausible reasons to adopt them, and countries with perceived similarities tend to like and do what the other countries like and do. DiMaggio and Powell (1983) refer to these three mechanisms as *isomorphic pressures*, which are defined as *external pressures to adopt certain policies that are accepted because there are good reasons to do so*. It results in a relatively homogenous field of organizations. The argument behind this homogenizing mechanism is that, in the long run, it is more important for public organizations to be legitimate than efficient. In their quest for legitimacy, public organizations accept the norms defined by higher-level organizations (coercive isomorphism), expert groups (normative isomorphism), and neighboring organizations with which they share key characteristics (mimetic isomorphism). An example of this isomorphic pressure is reflected in how the system of New Public Management spread in the 1990s. International organizations, leading countries, and esteemed public choice theorists recommended adopting its principles, and gradually it became the new fad that all countries had to implement in order to appear as legitimate.

Compared to these political, economic, and sociological theories, organization theory has a rather different take on the diffusion of policy innovation that emphasizes the role of *organizational and interorganizational learning*, or the individual and collective learning processes that are part of organizational and interorganizational practices (Rashman, Withers, and Hartley 2009, 472–75). From this perspective, government institutions and public organizations are not seen as passive targets of hierarchical, competitive, and normative pressures from the outside. Rather, they are reflexive entrepreneurs that aim to improve their performance and outcomes by learning from their own experiments as well as from those conducted by other countries or organizations. Learning is driven by dissatisfaction with existing policies in light of rising and changing ambitions and the development of new ideas. It occurs when new knowledge transforms the policy objectives and changes the beliefs about the likely effects of different policy tools (Dobbin, Simmons, and Garrett 2007, 460).

Public organizations mobilize actors from different levels and units of their own organization as well as from interest organizations, private firms, universities, and think tanks to enhance mutual learning (Rashman, Withers, and Hartley 2009). They also look to other countries for inspiring ideas and for evidence that implementing new policies has proven successful (Hall 1993). Public organizations participate in international conferences and are part of national associations, governance networks, and strategic alliances through which they gain knowledge about innovative solutions that further stimulate their internal learning processes (Knoepfel and Kissling-Näf 1998). They interpret reports of new policy initiatives and policy experiments in other countries in light of domestic conditions and experiences, and they use these findings as evidence for or against the realization of innovative ideas that are invented by and circulated among national policymakers. Thus, organizational learning brings together public and private actors and links national and international experts and decision makers. In short, organizational and interorganizational learning processes are based on the formation of domestic and international innovation-diffusion networks.

The analytical advantage of the organizational learning perspective is that it addresses both the *internal* search for innovative solutions through the creation and mobilization of intraorganizational networks and the *external* contacts and interorganizational relationships that provide access to new knowledge that can spur public innovation. The main problem is that the organizational focus tends to prevent the appreciation of inputs from and dialogue with individual users and citizens although they may have experiences, ideas, and resources that are vital to producing public innovation. However, from the perspective of organizational learning, nothing in its notion of innovation diffusion networks prevents the inclusion of individual and unorganized social actors. Indeed, innovation diffusion networks are both organizational and personal networks.

There are many empirical examples of the importance of innovation diffusion networks. In San Francisco, the STOP AIDS Project, which used small-group meetings to help change the behavior of gay men, grew through an interpersonal network and reached about 20 percent of the target group in 1984–87 (Rogers et al. 2005). In the British National Health Service, forming collaborative networks brought together a large number of public managers and professionals to develop, spread, and implement health care innovations. In much the same way, the British Talking Heads network (2000–2004) assembled more than ten thousand heads of schools in an online interorganizational community of practice that supported the diffusion of innovation in primary education (Mulgan and Albury 2003). A study of Education Network Australia shows that collaboration was a key driver of the diffusion of information and communications technology in education (White 2010). Finally, as noted previously, a national information network of public and private actors was a crucial vehicle for policy innovation and the spread of drug courts in the United States (Hale 2011).

During the last decades, national innovation award schemes such as the Innovations in American Government Awards Program at Harvard's Kennedy School and the UK Beacon Scheme have proliferated and are now found in most countries (Borins 2008). Innovation award schemes play an important role in helping to identify, broadcast, and circulate knowledge about public innovations and thus to connect people and organizations that want to adopt new practices. From time to time governments create special public institutes such as the British Nesta and the Danish MindLab to accelerate public innovation diffusion through digital platforms, workshops, and seminars. However, innovation diffusion networks are not all formal, planned, and managed. Most networks are informal and grow from below when public organizations, managers, and employees contact other organizations, managers, or employees and perhaps even users, experts, or private stakeholders to probe whether they have new ideas or recommendations about where new ideas can be found (Considine, Lewis, and Alexander 2009). Such networks are small, loosely coupled, and contingent, but the advantage is that they are built for a particular purpose, and their density might increase if an innovative solution is identified and broadcasted. When that happens, many actors will want to know what the content of the innovative solution is, what it can achieve, and how it can be implemented.

ANALYZING INNOVATION DIFFUSION NETWORKS

If innovation diffusion networks are both ubiquitous and important, then a number of analytical questions demand our attention. The first question is, who is networking with whom and to what effect? The primary participants in innovation diffusion networks are those individuals and organizations that are the sources of innovative ideas and solutions and those that are recipients of such ideas and solutions. While the former supply new ideas and innovative solutions, either to gain status and a reputation as innovators or to help others improve their performance, the latter are either open to new ideas or actively searching for innovative solutions that they can adopt.

The secondary participants are the various types of mediators who are professionally engaged in circulating knowledge and in connecting suppliers and potential adopters of innovations. Network contacts may be initiated by the sources or the recipients or the mediators of innovative ideas. While some actors may be extroverts, interacting frequently with other actors, and others may be introverts who have less interaction with other actors, they have many different ways of initiating contacts with other actors. Suppliers and potential adopters of innovative solutions can broadcast their demands or solutions to a mass audience, and they can target a particular group of actors that they believe will either benefit from their innovation or have something to offer. They may also seek out venues where they can meet potential adopters or suppliers of innovations face to face. Finally, they can use existing networks as vehicles for innovation diffusions by redefining or expanding the agenda.

The mediators, meanwhile, harvest ideas from larger numbers of suppliers, publicize the results to targeted or mass audiences, and try to connect suppliers and potential adopters with one another.

An Australian study of innovation networks (Considine, Lewis, and Alexander 2009, 58–67) finds that although contact varies significantly across municipalities, the primary target and source of the external engagement of local government officials are bureaucrats in other local governments. The study also shows that it is the bureaucrats, closely followed by the politicians, who interact most frequently with external bureaucrats. The politicians, however, carry more weight when it comes to engaging with representative organizations such as municipal associations that have politicians from other municipalities as members. Thus, the general pattern is that bureaucrats contact other external bureaucrats while politicians contact other external politicians. Bureaucrats at all levels reported they had the most contact with external bureaucrats who were at the same organizational level as themselves.

The Australian study has also examined the external interaction with nongovernment organizations. Public officials in innovation networks communicate the least with trade unions and the most with residents' groups. The frequency of their contacts with community organizations and nonprofit organizations lies somewhere in between, while their level of contact with private business is not statistically significant. These results are, with a few exceptions, stable across municipalities. Breaking down these measures for politicians and bureaucrats reveals that elected politicians have more contacts with private business and residents' groups than the bureaucrats have, but there are no other significant differences between the two groups when it comes to contacting other nongovernmental organizations.

In the study of innovation diffusion networks, many have focused on the degree of similarity between the sources and recipients of innovative ideas and solutions (Rogers 1995). They explore the impact of *homophily*—the high degree of similarity in terms of the participating individuals' personal attributes, education, values, and opinions—and *heterophily*, which reflects a low degree of similarity and a correspondingly high degree of diversity. As argued earlier, collaboration between social and political actors with different backgrounds helps generate innovative ideas and solutions, but such differences may present obstacles to public diffusion of innovation. For example, the professionals in the public sector seem to be less receptive to accepting and implementing new ideas from other professionals. Hence, homophily is generally assumed to enhance external engagement, communication, and knowledge transfer whereas as heterophily presents a barrier (Darr and Kurtzberg

2000; Reagans and McEvily 2003). The paradoxical conclusion is that while the invention of innovative solutions in the public sector hinges on exchanges between diverse groups of actors with different experiences, ideas, and resources, innovation diffusion is enhanced by communication between like-minded people.

The second question in analyzing innovation diffusion networks concerns how the actors involved in innovation diffusion engage with one another. The networking is structured by different communication channels that play distinct roles in different parts of the innovation diffusion process. Thus, those channels based on mass communication play an important role in the knowledge stage as they help would-be adopters become aware of new and innovative solutions, and those channels based on mutual dialogue are important in the persuasion and decision stages because they widen the bandwidth of communication and help ensure that relevant knowledge is passed on to and properly digested by the potential adopter. Rashman, Withers, and Hartley (2009, 480) report that networks with high levels of interaction and reciprocity tend to enhance innovation diffusion. The drawback is that consensual networks of stable and relatively closed groups of actors may foster groupthink, which tends to reduce innovation diffusion. Hence, it is important that diffusion networks based on mutual exchange remain open to external actors and inputs that can challenge and disturb the consensual worldview of the networks' actors.

Evaluations of the experiences from the British Beacon Scheme emphasize the value of face-to-face interactions as one organization seeks to learn from another (Rashman and Hartley 2008). Web pages with evidence-based reports of best practices can help transfer the explicit knowledge about different innovations and their achievements, but they fail to capture and transmit the innovators' *tacit knowledge*, which is defined as *the know-how that is implicit to particular practices and experiences that have not been subjected to systematic reflection and therefore cannot be precisely expressed through formal language systems*. This tacit knowledge of the innovators is extremely valuable to the potential adopters because it not only helps them clarify and sometimes even eliminates their doubts and queries but also provides answers to their detailed questions about implementing the innovation. The exchange of this kind of knowledge requires forming trust-based communication and holding context-sensitive face-to-face meetings that permit informal interaction, practical demonstration, storytelling and anecdote sharing, and joint reflections on the prospect for adapting an innovative solution to different contexts. In the 2004 survey of learning through the Beacon Scheme, 79 percent of the politicians and public managers who had visited a Beacon council and engaged in informal face-to-face meetings reported that they had made changes in their own organizations that were wholly or mainly due to the visit (Rashman and Hartley 2008). This finding confirms the importance and impact of exchanging tacit knowledge through direct dialogue.

In intraorganizational networks of innovation diffusion, given their combination of proximity and interpersonal acquaintance, the possibility for exchanging both explicit and tacit knowledge through face-to-face meetings is much better than in interorganizational networks. Intraorganizational diffusion networks also tend to benefit from the fact that the suppliers and potential adopters share the same context and values and from the relative absence of competition. These positive features can be enhanced by constructing a "community of fate" that sees intraorganizational knowledge exchange as a crucial strategy for surviving in the face of external threats.

The third element in analyzing innovation diffusion networks involves their structure. Researchers have found that the structure of personal and organizational networks has a decisive influence on the diffusion of innovation (Valente 1996; West et al. 1999), and there are good reasons to expect that some network structures are more conducive for diffusing public innovation than others. Diffusion networks may privilege either horizontal or vertical communication, and that choice will have an impact on the way that they diffuse innovation. It has been reported that while horizontal networks between persons and organizations at the same level are effective for spreading innovation based on peer influence, vertical networks that cut across different organizational levels are more effective for cascading codified information and spreading new authoritative practices (Greenhalgh et al. 2004, 602).

The diffusion of innovation is also affected by the particular shape of innovation diffusion networks, and these shapes can be revealed through social network analysis (see Considine, Lewis, and Alexander 2009). Figure 8.1 shows the two types of networks. At an intuitive or commonsensical level, we should expect *star-shaped networks*—in which information flows from and through a number of *hubs*, which consist of minorities of strongly connected actors—to be more efficient in transmitting information and more robust to accidental failure than *diamond-shaped networks* in which everybody is connected with everybody else in a loose or decentered fashion. New research suggests, however, that hubs may create bottlenecks in networks that hamper the diffusion of new ideas (Baños et al. 2013). The hubs that play a crucial role in star-shaped networks may block, censor, or distort information about innovative ideas and practices and thus fail to convey knowledge and information about innovative solutions to potential adopters. This problem is solved in diamond-shaped networks, where suppliers of new ideas and the potential adopters are connected through many different indirect paths. Hence, redundancy in the diamond-shaped network enhances the chance that potential adopters will eventually hear about new and innovative solutions that are relevant to their undertaking.

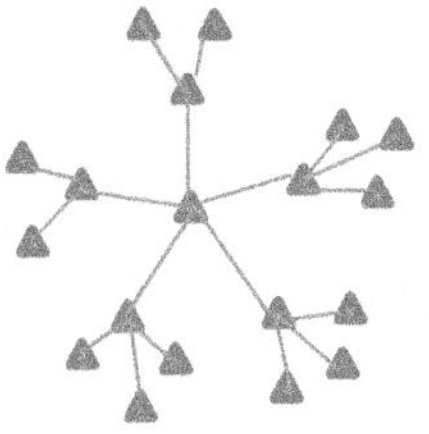

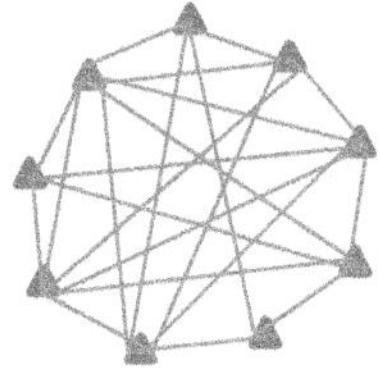

Star-shaped network

Diamond-shaped network

FIGURE 8.1. Star-shaped and diamond-shaped innovation diffusion networks

One drawback to the diamond-shaped network, where everybody knows each other and the actors have few or no external ties, is that there might not be many innovative ideas to circulate. Hence, Burt (1992) has drawn attention to the impact of structural holes between unconnected networks or subnetworks in which the actors cannot reap the fruit of innovative ideas from other networks or subnetworks because they lack crosscutting connections. In such situations, actors who manage to form a tie with one or more actors from another network or subnetwork will benefit all the members of their own network or subnetwork. The total benefit of forming a bridge between dissociated networks increases with the number of direct and indirect ties that the bridging actors have. The number of indirect ties is a measure of how many actors will become aware of an innovative solution if it passes the bridge from one network to another.

The last factor in analyzing innovation diffusion networks addresses the different roles that social and political actors perform in innovation diffusion networks. Networks are horizontal in the sense that nobody can use their formal authority stemming from their position in a vertical hierarchy to settle a dispute among the network actors. Still some actors will perform a leadership role because they are respected, are resourceful, and have a central position in the network that allows them to connect other people. Leaders in innovation diffusion networks play an important role in bringing people together and creating an environment conducive to mutual learning and the adoption of new ideas. Leaders may act as brokers who encourage relevant actors to contact each other and cross the bridge between networks to seek new knowledge. Brokers may also support innovation diffusion by creating arenas for mutual interaction and by building digital infrastructures. Another important leadership role is that of the champion, who is a charismatic, esteemed, and powerful individual who actively supports middle managers or staff members in adopting an innovative idea or practice that they have become aware of and want to pursue.

Change agents, opinion leaders, and role models also play a crucial part in circulating new ideas and enhancing the rate of adoption. In terms of public and private campaign organizations, change agents are found to be particularly effective if they take the need of the potential adopters into account and offer them persuasive and tailor-made solutions through appropriate communication channels and if they incorporate procedures for experiential learning and monitoring of performance and results (Rogers 1995, 373–88). Change agents can also maximize the impact of their scarce resources by recruiting and linking to opinion leaders. Expert opinion leaders use their scientific or professional authority and status to influence the spread of innovation by making persuasive recommendations, while peer opinion leaders draw on their central position in the network of potential adopters and their credibility as sources of good and reliable information to convince their colleagues that the innovation is worth trying. Finally, role models are individuals or organizations that have had the courage, skills, and perhaps luck to develop or adopt innovative solutions that produce the kind of results that other agencies crave. Role models are often serial innovators who have a track record of achieving above-average performance through innovation. They have acquired the status of beacons, and other striving organizations will want to copy their innovative efforts.

Despite the presence of brokers, champions, change agents, opinion leaders, and role models, the rate of adoption may not take off until a certain number of organizations recognizes the innovative solution as the new "normal." This situation holds true especially if the advantage of an innovative solution is uncertain or its acceptance depends on other organizations adopting it. The standard example concerns information technology systems that may not work properly in the beginning. They often will have greater impact as more agencies adopt them and begin to feed data into them. Diffusing such systems will often require that the number of adopters pass a certain threshold for the rate of adoption to grow.

FROM ADOPTION TO ADAPTATION OF INNOVATIVE SOLUTIONS

Central governments sometimes think of innovation diffusion as an engineering problem that can be solved by rolling out new innovative formats through organizational processes that first identify innovative designs, then provide evidence of their positive effects, and finally transfer new knowledge to target agencies to ensure adoption. In reality, not only is innovation diffusion less linear and more networked and collaborative, but it also rarely takes the form of "copy and paste" of ready-made innovations with a universal applicability. Hence, diffusing public innovations across organizations and sectors often transforms the innovative solutions to fit the specific demands and conditions of the recipient organization. The adopter translates and interprets an innovation in a certain way and adapts it to the local context to secure support and to enhance its chances of success. Sometimes the needs and experiences of the end users and frontline staff are taken into consideration. These contributions further modify the original innovation, which often ends up assuming the character of a vague, distant, and almost mythical reference point that only has a passing resemblance to the innovation that is implemented.

In Denmark, for instance, the national diffusion of a relatively successful attempt to train and support elderly people so that they can stay longer in their own homes resulted in the construction of numerous local variants based on highly different methods. The only thing the different variants had in common was that they sought to rehabilitate the everyday life of elderly people and thus cut the costs of public elderly care facilities. The example demonstrates that complex public innovations often have both a "hard" kernel and some "soft" elements. Whereas the hard kernel remains relatively unchanged, the soft elements are often modified according to circumstances (Denis et al. 2002). The changes of the soft elements are bound to affect the hard kernel, which, therefore, might also be subject to revision.

An empirical study of the British Beacon Scheme conducted by Hartley and Downe (2007) confirmed the idea that adoption involves creative adaptation. The study shows that 63 percent of the local government officials who participated created innovation in the local municipality by adapting a Beacon idea to their local context. Twenty-nine percent of the participants claim that knowledge of innovative solutions from local Beacon councils accelerated the implementation of ideas and practices that either already existed in their organization or were in the process of being developed. This finding indicates that innovation diffusion is often a question of "graft and grow" rather than copy and paste (Hartley and Benington 2006). Public agencies look for innovative ideas that resonate with their current thoughts and practices, and they graft these new ideas onto the emerging and embryonic practices in the organization to help them grow, gain acceptance, take new and more creative forms, and finally produce the desired results.

The shift from the linear engineering model to the collaborative graft-and-grow metaphor has important policy implications for governments. Instead of diffusing public innovation through pilots who provide detailed recipes for adopting innovative ideas, governments should use pathfinders who encourage local agencies to adapt new, innovative ideas and practices to their local conditions and context and thus inspire them to find their own way forward. Likewise, instead of trying to identify a set of best practices that all local agencies should adopt and then stick with, pathfinders should coax local agencies to use successful and promising innovations developed by other agencies to stimulate the development of their own next practices that take the adopted innovations a step further.

Adopting innovative ideas always involves some degree of adaptation, which sometimes leads to a reinvention in which key parts of the innovation are omitted, or transformed, and new elements are added. The distinction between adaptation and reinvention is a matter of degree. Hence, the term *reinvention* is used to describe a *thorough adaptation and modification of an innovative practice that radically changes or expands its functionality.* Whereas a creative adaptation of a particular innovation to the organizational and local context aims to enhance its chance for being successfully implemented, an innovative reinvention aims to further develop a given innovation in order to bring out new and unforeseen qualities and to improve its overall performance, sustainability, and effects.

Public innovations are reinvented in local public service organizations for many reasons. For one, they may need to meet conflicting political and administrative expectations for an innovation or to solve the problems of a variety of user groups with different demands. Attempts to enhance local ownership and to restore local pride when adopting an innovation that comes from the outside may spur attempts to transform it so that it appears as a local product.

Finally, after reviewing the experiences of earlier adopters, a local agency in the process of adopting an innovation might remove an innovation's negative side effects and highlight its desirable effects (Rogers 1995, 186–87).

Recombinant innovation is a special case of reinvention that *combines and adapts innovative practices from other sectors to suit a slightly different purpose in another sector.* In a well-known example, Henry Ford, in his revolutionary conception of car production, combined the use of interchangeable parts from the sewing machine industry, the continuous flow production from the soup canning business, and the assembly line from slaughterhouses. Instead of inventing a new production system from scratch, Ford thus used his many contacts to pull together ideas and methods in different ways to suit his purpose. The private sector is also a great source of innovative solutions for recombinant innovation in the public sector. Great Ormond Street Hospital for Children in London has drawn on the experiences of Ferrari's Formula 1 pit stop team, which completes the complex task of changing tires in merely seven seconds, to rethink the handover of patients from emergency to intensive care and has thereby reduced both the time and inherent risk of this task. In addition, many public organizations take inspiration from Toyota's use of lean manufacturing technology, but they twist the purpose of cutting different forms of slack from generating value for the customer to saving the public's money.

Finally, New Public Management can be seen as a recombinant innovation that takes innovative governance and leadership techniques from the private sector and uses them in new ways in the public sector. For example, the legal contracts used in the contracting out of public services often vastly differ from the contracts that regulate the relationship between private firms and their subcontractors. In the public sector, contracts with private service providers are often based on ongoing negotiations between the public purchaser and the private providers. The use of so-called relational contracts based on regular negotiations aims to compensate for the fact that services are complex and multifaceted, and it is consequently difficult to regulate outsourced service production on the basis of prices and expected service standards alone.

As we have seen, the result of collaborative and networked innovation diffusion varies over a continuum from duplicative imitation to creative adaptation, to innovative reinvention, and even to recombinant innovation. Which form it takes depends to a large extent on the knowledge base and learning capacity of the adopters (Kim 1998; Hartley and Rashman 2014). If the knowledge base is limited and the learning capacity is low, then the adopters will merely attempt to imitate the innovations created by other organizations. A greater knowledge base and learning capacity permit adopters to creatively adapt innovative solutions, while an extensive knowledge base and a large capacity for learning enable them to reinvent the innovations that they encounter. If the adopters also have a large and diversified network that gives them access to innovative ideas and practices from other sectors, then they can try to make recombinant innovations. As innovative reinventions and recombinant innovations can meet needs and demands that are specific to a particular organization, public organizations are clearly rewarded when they expand their knowledge base, enhance their learning capacity, and build networks that branch out in different directions.

BEYOND THE "PRO-DIFFUSION BIAS": FACING THE DILEMMAS OF INNOVATION DIFFUSION

Much of the innovation diffusion literature contains a "pro-diffusion bias"; that is, it readily assumes that innovation diffusion will always benefit the adopters (Abrahamson 1991). Moreover, the innovation diffusion literature tends to argue that more and faster innovation diffusion is better than less. The pro-diffusion bias is a product of the rationalist presumption that public innovations are diffused whenever they benefit the public organizations adopting them but are rejected when they do not. Two common observations, however, counter this presumption.

First, some innovations that are diffused through networked collaboration tend to be inefficient or, at least, do not fulfill the expectations. The successful diffusion of failed innovations occurs when innovative ideas and solutions become fads and fashions despite the failure to test them properly and document their beneficial effects (Park and Berry 2014). Even without compelling evidence of their relative advantage, public innovations are frequently adopted because they cohere with predominant beliefs, norms, and values and seemingly provide a solution to urgent and deeply felt problems. For example, the so-called matrix organization, which proved to be extremely demanding and time consuming, spread widely in public service institutions because it offered a fashionable solution to the much-discussed silo problems in public organizations and promised a more holistic approach to problem solving in large organizations. Another example is the current proliferation of public-private partnerships (PPPs) as an innovative method for constructing, maintaining, and running large infrastructure projects such as bridges and tunnels. Although their enterprises often end up being more expensive than publicly funded infrastructure projects, these partnerships are extremely fashionable due to their emphasis on the idea that a trust-based partnership creates mutual benefits to the public and private partners. The problem with diffusing public innovations that have the status of fads and fashions is not only that public employees waste precious time and energy on dubious projects with disappointing results but also that the adopted innovations tend to crowd out less fashionable but perhaps more efficient innovations.

The second observation is that given the urgent need of public organizations to appear legitimate by signaling their innovativeness and entrepreneurship, some organizations become so eager to adopt new and innovative solutions that they fail to reject potentially harmful innovations that do not fit the institutional context, carry many high and unmanageable risks, and are unlikely to outperform existing practices. The introduction in the Nordic countries of new governing practices associated with New Public Management is a case in point. Given the strong Scandinavian tradition for a low power distance and a low degree of work structuration, the initiation of an NPM system based on clear goals, detailed performance targets, prescribed methods, and regular evaluations linked to managerial sanctions was bound to generate resistance, to increase the transactions costs, and thus to undermine the potential gains of a stricter performance management. Nevertheless, New Public Management was launched for several reasons. The government faced mounting fiscal pressures, government officials and executive managers considered it the latest fad, and when operational public agencies adopted the new managerial techniques, it contributed to making them appear legitimate to the Ministry of Finance, which strongly believed in the program's wonders.

It is tempting to remove the importance and impact of administrative fads and fashions, as well as the persistent concern of public managers for the symbolic representation of their organizations as being ready for change, by insisting that public agencies should always look for solid evidence of the effects of new innovations before they are adopted. However, this move would merely reassert the two basic assumptions that are the root cause of the pro-innovation bias of innovation diffusion theory: Organizations in a larger group can freely and independently choose to adopt a new and innovative solution, and they are relatively certain about their goals and their assessment of how efficient the new, innovative solutions will be in attaining these goals (Abrahamson 1991, 590). If these assumptions are accepted, then the innovation diffusion will necessarily enhance the efficiency of public organizations. It will be rational for free and unconstrained public agencies with a clear perception of their goals and with reliable knowledge of the impact of innovative solutions to adopt only efficiency-enhancing innovations while rejecting all those that fail to increase goal achievement.

The problem is, of course, that the assumptions behind the belief that innovation diffusion is always beneficial to public organizations are unsustainable. Public organizations are part of an organizational field in which it is more important to be considered legitimate than efficient (DiMaggio and Powell 1983). Further, not only are the multiple objectives of public agencies relatively unclear and subject to political contestation but also, when evaluating innovative solutions, the knowledge and information at their disposal are often incomplete, unreliable, and anecdotal due to Hawthorne effects and learning curve problems. Hence, public organizations face two difficult dilemmas. They want to make independent decisions based on efficiency calculations but are bound by strategic concerns about doing what is generally considered correct. In addition, public agencies need reliable knowledge about their goals and the effect of new innovations, but that is exactly what they lack. Given these irresolvable dilemmas, public managers can only hope to find a pragmatic way of managing them by accepting that efficiency and legitimacy are competing but important objectives and by doing the best they can with the knowledge and information they have.

MEASURING THE OUTCOMES OF COLLABORATIVE INNOVATION

Measuring the outcomes of public innovation is difficult. It becomes even more complicated when innovation is created or diffused through collaborative processes because the actors involved in different parts of the innovation process may have different expectations and apply different standards for calculating whether the outcome is desirable. However, such problems should not check our ambition to measure the impact of collaborative innovation in the public sector.

In pursuing this task, the first issue concerns which outcomes to measure. Some actors may emphasize efficiency or quality gains, while others are more concerned with either the actual capacity and ability to solve particular problems or the contribution of the innovative solution to creating a more open, transparent, and democratic way of governing. If the objective of the collaborative innovation process has not been clarified in advance, the actors involved in the innovation process should voice their opinions, engage in deliberation, and develop an agreement about how different potential outcomes should be ranked and judged in relation to each other.

The next problem is how to measure the outcomes of an innovative solution. Agencies in the public sector often have standard procedures for measuring the efficiency and effectiveness of public policies and services, while determining the democratic effects of public innovation is more uncertain. However, no matter how the different outcomes are measured in the public sector, it is important to supplement the more or less objective measures used in the public sector with the subjective accounts provided by the users and the private stakeholders involved in the innovation process. They may see and evaluate things differently, and their reports may cover some of the blind angles such as the satisfaction of the end users.

The third problem is when to measure the effects of public innovations. To reduce the impact of the Hawthorne and learning-curve effects, supplementing the measurement of short-term effects with an additional measurement of the long-term effects is a good idea. It may take some time before the positive effects of new and innovative teaching methods kick in, for instance, because teachers need to be properly trained and perhaps change their mind-set before they can use the new methods correctly. A positive feedback loop between training, performance, and results may further enhance the methods' positive effects. Such effects obtained in the initial phase might also wane over time, though, if funding is cut in the expectation that a program can do more with less given the innovative design.

The final problem is how to handle the results of the measurement exercise. The outcome of a systematic measurement of the effects of public innovation will always be subject to interpretation and debate, and inviting different groups to participate in the discussion will help put the result in the right perspective and explain the relative degree of success or failure. Negative or disappointing results can either lead to the innovation's discontinuance or trigger efforts to scrutinize the implementation process and perhaps even to redesign the innovation in order to adjust or remove features that are malfunctioning.

On a final note, we should remember that in measuring innovation, we can also focus on the processes of collaborative innovation or innovation diffusion to learn how to improve them in the future. Such evaluations can be supplemented with measuring the innovation readiness and innovation culture of the public organizations involved in the innovation process. Assessing the quality of collaborative innovation processes and the conduciveness of the organizational and institutional designs is a crucial step in building long-lasting innovation capacities in public organizations.

CONCLUSION

Whether a result of chance discoveries, bold and creative leadership, or collaborative processes, public innovation will not realize its full potential if it is not disseminated in and across public organizations. This chapter has argued that although diffusing public innovation is difficult due to the complexity of the innovations and the great variation in the political, institutional, and cultural conditions among the potential adopters, the absence of cutthroat competition in the public sector provides a favorable condition for innovation diffusion. The chapter has introduced Rogers's classic diffusion of innovations model, which connects suppliers and potential adopters of public innovations through various communication channels and shows that innovation diffusion results from a series of discrete decisions on the part of the potential adopters that may either promote or halt innovation diffusion. The innovation itself, the organizational context of the adopters, and other factors in their external environment also condition the decisions of the potential adopters.

The chapter has aimed to demonstrate the positive role and impact of interorganizational and interpersonal networks on innovation diffusion. It has looked at the questions of who is networking with whom, how they are networking, and how different structures of diffusion networks are influencing the ability to diffuse public innovation. It has also considered the role of the different actors in the diffusion networks including innovation leaders, change agents, opinion leaders, and role models. The chapter has challenged the idea of innovation diffusion as a replication process based on copy and paste and explained why and how the adoption of innovative solutions from elsewhere are adapted to both the demands of the potential adopters and the political and organizational context in which the innovation is supposed to function and thrive. Last but not least, it has argued that the measurement of innovation outcomes is a crucial and complicated affair that contains several dilemmas.

9

ENHANCING COLLABORATIVE INNOVATION THROUGH LEADERSHIP AND MANAGEMENT

COLLABORATIVE INNOVATION is shorthand for innovation processes that are facilitated and accelerated by multi-actor collaboration. In other words, the notion of collaborative innovation refers to a causal relation between collaboration and innovation. In the previous chapters, we have seen how collaboration between public and private actors can help define and frame problems, challenges, and opportunities that call for innovative solutions; how relevant and affected actors can be mobilized and empowered in institutional arenas of interaction that facilitate expansive and transformative learning processes; how decisions to realize bold, creative, and promising ideas can be made and implemented in practice through multi-actor collaboration; and, finally, how the diffusion of innovative ideas and solutions depends on networked collaboration between suppliers and potential adopters of innovative solutions.

Bureaucracy can spur public innovation by setting the agenda, mobilizing resources for search and development processes, and triggering standard procedures for exploring and exploiting new ideas. Likewise, competition in publicly created quasi-markets coupled with enhanced emphasis on strategic leadership and performance management can provide important incentives for public managers to boost innovation. However, by comparison, collaboration offers a promising and somewhat underexploited tool for tapping into the competences, capacities, and ideas of public and private actors while, at the same time, facilitating mutual learning, coordinated implementation, and networked innovation diffusion. The question is, therefore, is it possible to make collaborative innovation the primary innovation strategy of public organizations, or will they continue to rely on internal bureaucratic routines for exploring and exploiting new ideas or on the incentives that develop when newly created quasi-markets and the elaborate systems of performance measurement generate competitive pressures?

This chapter addresses this pressing question by assessing the drivers and barriers of collaborative innovation in the public sector. The first section argues that despite the prevalence of bureaucratic and market-based logics in the public sector, collaborative innovation has several drivers. The second section analyzes the barriers to collaborative innovation from a process perspective and catalogs those aspects of public organizations and their immediate environment that may obstruct the different parts of the collaborative innovation process. Having identified the typical barriers to collaborative innovation in the public sector, the third section considers how they can be overcome by exercising a new kind of public leadership and management that enhances collaboration and stimulates innovation. Because collaborative innovation requires not only direct, hands-on innovation management to overcome the process-related barriers to collaborative innovation but also indirect, hands-off leadership to create the right institutional and cultural conditions for collaboration innovation, the fourth section provides a method for making public organizations conducive to collaborative innovation. The chapter concludes with a short presentation of some recent contributions to leadership and management theory that examine how concrete interventions on the part of administrative and political leaders strengthen innovation and collaboration processes. The theoretical overview introduces important insights from governance network theory that argue that collaborative networks must be metagoverned to produce the desired effects.

DRIVERS OF COLLABORATIVE INNOVATION IN THE PUBLIC SECTOR

The current *drivers of innovation* in the public sector are easy to spot. Internal pressures from budgetary constraints, policy failures, and high professional ambitions, as well as external pressures from needy citizens, demanding stakeholders, critical publics, inquisitorial mass media, and globalized markets that urge nation-states to boost their structural or systemic competitiveness—all have contributed to placing innovation at the top of the public sector agenda, where it is likely to stay for quite some time. The idea that trust-based collaboration between multiple public and private actors should drive public innovation might appear unrealistic and far-fetched, however, given two factors: Bureaucratic logics emphasizing stability, hierarchical rule, and compartmentalized decision making and service production have dominated the public sector, and executive managers have recently attempted to incorporate a market-based logic built on competitive tendering of public service production. Nevertheless, a number of inherent and deeply sedimented features of the public sector can be invoked to spur the future development of collaborative innovation.

The first of the inherent drivers of collaborative innovation is that the problems, challenges, and opportunities that are defined and recognized as "public" tend to invoke a collective ownership to the task of developing a new and innovative solution, thus creating a moral obligation to participate in processes of collaborative problem solving. If problems and challenges concern everybody and we have joint responsibility for responding to them, we should ask not only what the public sector can do for us but also what we can do for the public sector and its capacity for creative problem solving. From this perspective, those who do not in some way contribute when they are called upon to find innovative solutions to shared problems are considered illegitimate free riders. This driver of collaborative innovation is deeply ingrained in societies with a well-developed public sector and is supported by the republican tradition of Aristotle, Machiavelli, and Tocqueville. Hence, classical republicanism insists that citizens enjoy particular rights because they are members of a social and political community, but with those rights come certain obligations. These duties have traditionally been defined as paying taxes, serving in the military, providing for your family, and so forth, but they also include actively participating in public deliberation and collective efforts to find new solutions that benefit the community by solving public problems. An important liberalist amendment would insist that the social and political community comprises a variety of different actors who might agree on what is right but have competing conceptions of the good (Rawls 1971). The insistence on a liberal "pluralization" of the community is important because collaborative innovation thrives not only on active engagement but also on difference and contestation (Mouffe 1993).

The second driver of collaborative innovation is that public organizations and agencies are all parts of the same public enterprise. There are different levels of government, different jurisdictions, and a large number of departmental divisions, but public organizations and agencies in the same political territory share an identical legal foundation. They operate on the basis of the same rules, norms, and values, and they are all committed to producing public value and achieving the same overall political goals. In addition, internal competition is limited because although the transactions costs are sometimes considerable and public funding is scarce, there is a joint political and administrative leadership at the top of the public sector and much to gain from exchanging ideas and pooling resources with other public organizations or agencies. Therefore, despite interorganizational rivalry and persistent turf wars motivated by the quest for power, status, and recognition, the general and legitimate expectation is that public organizations and agencies will work together to find innovative solutions to shared problems. Public organizations might have difficulties communicating and understanding each other because they operate in different fields and comprise different professional groups, but in most cases, at least if the gains are significant and the transactions costs are low, they are committed to intra- and interorganizational collaboration to solve joint problems.

The third driver concerns the nature and character of the public sector's output. The public sector regulates particular parts of economic and social life, but it spends most of its resources on service production. This point is important because the citizens who benefit from public services are an integral part of public service production. Whereas the consumers of commodities purchased in private markets are not involved in producing the goods they buy, the users of public (or private) services participate in the production process as pupils in the schools, students at the universities, patients in the hospital, job seekers at the job center, and so on. Hence, the production of public services always includes some form of coproduction in that the service users contribute to the service production by doing their homework, studying for exams, exercising their bodies after an operation, or actively seeking jobs that have been recommended by frontline personnel at the job center. Because the service users regularly interact with public employees and are highly interested in service improvement, there is a good chance that the service users' coproduction of public services can be expanded to include the cocreation of services and perhaps even of new policies. At least with the right motivation, lead users can often be persuaded to participate in collaborative innovation and all because of the predominant service orientation of the public sector (Osborne, Radnor, and Nasi 2013).

The fourth and last driver of collaborative innovation in the public sector is found in the area of democratic governance. Involving intensely affected groups and individuals in political decision-making processes is a long-established democratic norm (Dahl 1961). In some countries, notably in the northwestern European countries, norms about the democratic participation of stakeholders have led to the establishment of formal systems of corporatism, but in most Western countries, affected actors are informally included in some kind of collaboration or consultation at the subsector level (Schmitter and Lehmbruch 1979; Goodin 2008). The idea that those actors who are affected by changes in particular policies, services, or governance arrangements should have the opportunity to voice their opinions and influence the decision-making process lies at the heart of collaborative innovation. In the case of collaborative innovation, the reasons for including private stakeholders are not only to strengthen democracy but also to facilitate participation in collaborative forms of governance that can enhance the innovative capacity of the public sector.

In terms of a public commitment to solve public problems, public value production, coproduced service production, and democratic norms, the list of inherent drivers could perhaps be expanded, but the important point is that collaborative innovation is by no means foreign to the public sector. Rather, collaboration finds support in key aspects of the public sector that, in turn, can drive the expansion of collaborative innovation in the future.

BARRIERS TO COLLABORATIVE INNOVATION: A PROCESS PERSPECTIVE

As we have seen in previous chapters, there are many barriers to collaborative innovation. Some of them are institutional or organizational, some are political or cultural, and others involve the constellation of actors and their resources and identities. Finally, the external environment of collaborative processes may also act as a barrier that prevents actors from collaborating and producing innovative solutions.

While some barriers hamper collaboration, others might impede innovation. For a clearer picture of where the different barriers kick in, we shall adopt a process perspective on collaborative innovation. Thus, collaborative innovation can be seen as an exercise where actors with relevant innovation assets are brought together in interactive processes through which they exchange experiences and ideas. The expectation is that the networked interaction between different social and political actors will eventually give rise to collaboration and that, finally, the collaborative process will generate innovative solutions and ensure their implementation in practice.

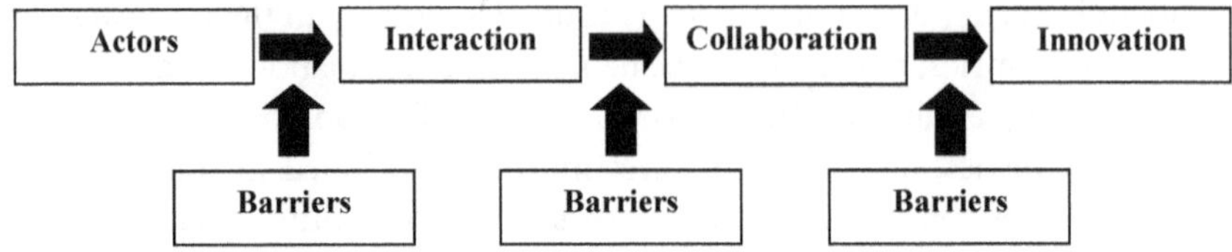

FIGURE 9.1. A process perspective on barriers to collaborative innovation

The process of collaborative innovation is depicted in figure 9.1. Collaborative innovation is predicated on constructing a continuous flow from left to right along the horizontal axis in the figure. However, as the vertical arrows in the figure indicate, different sets of barriers might interrupt the flow.

When the window of opportunity for collaborative innovation has opened and a number of relevant public and/or private actors have been identified, the first step in facilitating collaborative innovation is to encourage the actors to interact with one another. It is here that the first set of barriers arises and may block the process (Gray 1989; Ansell and Gash 2007; Hartley, Sørensen, and Torfing 2013). Bringing together relevant and affected actors in sustained interaction might fail for many reasons. First, if the actors do not have a sense of necessity or urgency regarding the problem or challenge at hand and do not recognize their interdependence, then they are not compelled to interact and exploit the window of opportunity. Second, there might not be a tradition for participation or sustained interaction in the policy area either because of the predominance of hierarchical decision making or because it might be highly technical, politically sensitive, pervaded by deep-seated conflicts, or perhaps concerned with classified information. Next, negative experiences with previous attempts to create participatory and interactive processes can lead to a lack of generalized trust among the actors. Fourth, a narrow scope for collaborative innovation and weak political support for the innovation process both tend to discourage the actors from participating in the interactive arena. Further, there is a demotivating uncertainty about who else wants to participate and what is required from the actors to participate in the interactive process. Finally, if the potential benefits appear to be vague and unclear and overshadowed by potential risks, then the potential participants will have little motivation to spend time and energy on formal and informal interaction.

Even with the unfavorable initial conditions and perhaps helped by deliberate attempts to eliminate particular barriers, if the social and political actors choose to interact and exchange their experiences, perceptions, and ideas, there is no guarantee that the interaction will lead to collaboration. A second set of barriers might lead the actors to leave the table, might foster a dialogue of the deaf, or might create insurmountable conflicts that prevent collaboration (Gray 1989; Straus 2002; Koppenjan and Klijn 2004; Ansell and Gash 2007). The transition from interaction to collaboration may be impeded by large power asymmetries that could tempt the strongest actors to go solo and develop and impose their own solution on the other actors or that could convince the weakest actors that they will have little, if any, influence in the interactive arena. A highly competitive environment that creates and sustains opportunistic behavior and prevents the development of mutual trust also blocks collaboration. Next, collaboration is stymied when complex strategic and substantial uncertainties paralyze the actors because they cannot properly assess the conditions for and outcomes of alternative actions. Other barriers to collaboration might include the predominance of mental and organizational silos that prevent fruitful communication and trust-based collaboration, the existence of different cognitive schemes and antagonistic conflicts of interest, and the lack of incentives, cultural norms, and a unifying story line that support the development of a collaborative approach to joint and creative problem solving.

Even if and when the actors engage constructively in collaborative processes, the procedure might not necessarily foster innovation because, for example, the deliberations are inconclusive, the solutions are not creative or novel, the innovative ideas cannot be realized in practice, or knowledge about the innovative idea is not disseminated to the relevant actors. Hence, as we saw in chapter 2, what amounts to a third set of barriers may prevent the conversion of the multi-actor collaboration into transformative learning and innovative solutions. A number of factors might be at play. The collaborative endeavor may round up the "usual suspects" who over time have developed similar worldviews and, instead of formulating new and bold ideas, merely recycle old complaints about the world and abstract wishes for a better future (Skilton and Dooley 2010). Veto players also may block the group's ability to make joint decisions in the face of persistent and deeply felt conflicts, or they might encourage the actors to settle for incremental solutions based on the least common denominator and avoid the battles and risks that follow attempts to develop bold and more innovative solutions (Scharpf 1994). Third, a high level of political complexity and operational uncertainty and the incomplete institutionalization of collaborative processes and arenas may prevent an effective implementation of innovation ideas (O'Toole 1997). Last, structural holes in the networks of communication may prevent knowledge transfer and innovation diffusion (Burt 1992).

In sum, given the three sets of barriers, the successive linkages between interaction, collaboration, and innovation are contingent and indeed highly precarious. The constant danger is that unfavorable conditions will act as stumbling blocks and prevent us from reaping the fruits of collaborative innovation. Not even good intentions to collaborate and a willingness to explore and exploit new, bold ideas are enough to ensure a successful outcome of the processes of collaborative innovation. However, the barriers to collaborative innovation are themselves contingent as their presence and impact varies in time and space and can be influenced and changed by situated social and political agency. Thus, removing particular barriers or at least mitigating their negative effects is possible through exercising public leadership or management. The private actors participating in processes of collaborative innovation can contribute to the exercise of leadership and management, but they will often lack the centrality, legitimacy, resources, and reflexive capacities that the public leaders and managers command. That being the case, it should be emphasized that assuming public leadership and management does not require a participant to have a formal role or position as a leader or manager. Indeed, a broad range of public employees can undertake the role if they have the necessary skills, competences, and experience. Hence, innovation management is often a distributed endeavor.

OVERCOMING BARRIERS THROUGH PUBLIC LEADERSHIP AND MANAGEMENT

To drive the process from the identification of relevant actors through interaction and collaboration and on to public innovation, leadership and management are urgently needed to remove barriers and drive the process forward. However, we should be careful not to believe that more and better public leadership and management can solve all problems. When it comes to stimulating collaborative and innovative processes, traditional forms of strong and resilient leadership based on command, regulation, and control will be counterproductive, and the processes depend on institutional, cultural, and environmental factors that are difficult to affect, at least in the short run.

Nevertheless, public leaders and managers who assume the role of conveners, facilitators, and catalysts can mitigate and perhaps even eliminate the barriers to collaborative innovation in the public sector (Straus 2002; Crosby and Bryson 2010; Morse 2010; Page 2010; Ansell and Gash 2012; Hartley, Sørensen, and Torfing 2013; Bason 2014; Gray and Ren 2014). As indicated in figure 9.2, the three roles performed by innovation leaders and managers help create an uninterrupted flow from left to right by addressing the different sets of barriers to the process of collaborative innovation.

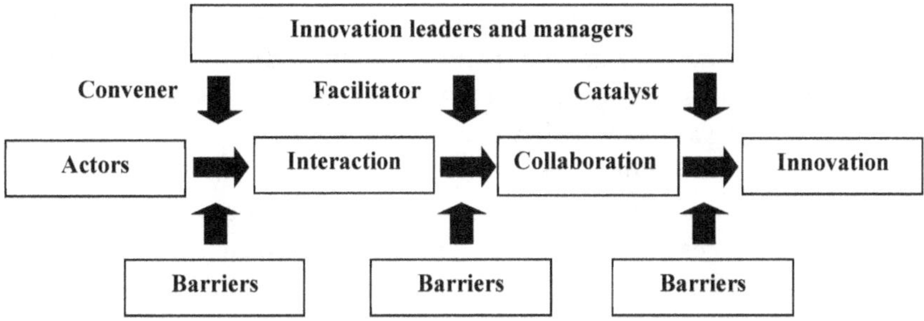

FIGURE 9.2. The roles of innovation leaders and innovation managers

The role of the *convener* is to bring together the relevant and affected actors and spur the interaction that triggers an initial exchange of information, views, and ideas. The convener must perform a number of different tasks:

- Select the team by mobilizing actors with relevant innovation assets and motivate them to participate in the innovation process by demonstrating the need for innovative solutions and by telling them how they can contribute to and gain from the collaborative innovation process.
- Clarify the roles and competences of the different participants and draw up a process map that delineates who participates when and how in the different phases of the innovation process.
- Encourage interaction and exchange between the participating actors by explaining and enhancing their mutual dependence with regard to solving the problem or challenge at hand.
- Secure political and economic support for the search for innovative solutions and protect the integrity of the group of actors by ensuring a scope for self-regulation and issuing a "license to innovate."
- Give an overall direction to the joint search for innovative solutions and align the various goals and expectations of the participating actors.

The role of the *facilitator* is to persuade the actors to collaborate. Thus they will manage their internal differences in a constructive manner and engage in processes of mutual learning and creative problem solving that bring them beyond the least common denominator. In doing so, the facilitator must undertake several important duties:

- Lower the transaction costs of collaborating by arranging good and effective meetings, ensuring smooth communication within the network of actors, and selectively activating those actors who are not contributing as much as they could and should.
- Enhance and sustain trust between the actors by creating venues for informal social interaction, encouraging the development of some common rules and procedures for interaction in the collaborative, and triggering a virtuous cycle of trust creation through a unilateral display of trust in the other actors.
- Develop a common frame of understanding that facilitates dialogue by creating a common knowledge base through knowledge exchange and joint fact-finding missions and by developing a common language based on jointly accepted definitions of key terms and ideas.
- Resolve or mediate conflicts so that they become constructive rather than destructive and ensure that irresolvable conflicts are depersonalized and conceived of as joint puzzles rather than as roadblocks.
- Remove obstacles to collaboration by securing support from the executive leaders in the participating organizations and by negotiating how costs and gains of innovative solutions are distributed among the actors.

The role of the *catalyst* is to create appropriate disturbances and encourage the actors to think outside the box and use their different competences and capacities to develop and implement new and bold solutions. In order to do so, the catalyst must perform various missions:

- Construct a sense of urgency either by invoking the sense of standing on a "burning ship" or demonstrating the presence of a "window of opportunity" that creates a unique possibility for changing the existing path and going in an entirely new direction.
- Prevent tunnel vision by encouraging the actors to change their perspective, including new actors with a different set of experiences and

ideas in the network of collaborators, or by bringing new and inspiring knowledge into play, for example, through the commissioning of expert reports.
- Create open and inventive search processes by changing the venue of the meetings, inviting guests, organizing excursions and using future workshops, brainstorming, scenario building, prototyping, and designing experiments and other heuristic devices that can facilitate divergent thinking and make the future concrete.
- Facilitate the management and negotiation of the risks associated with innovative solutions and coordinate the implementation process both to enhance synergy and to avoid gaps and overlaps.
- Ensure that the participating actors assume the role of ambassadors and use their strong and weak ties to disseminate knowledge about the innovative solution.

Although figure 9.2 indicates that the three roles of innovation leaders and managers must be performed sequentially—with leaders and managers first acting as conveners, then as facilitators, and finally as catalysts—in the real world, collaborative innovation processes are full of jumps, overlaps, and feedback loops. Sometimes it is necessary to combine the three roles because new actors are convened or conflicts erupt or reappear in the implementation phase. The contingent combination of the different roles and tasks is very demanding and requires a great deal of skill and experience. Leaders and managers of collaborative innovation must constantly monitor and reflect upon the process to judge which role must be invoked and which leadership tasks must be performed. In this process, dialogue with a team of leaders and managers or with other colleagues is invaluable for aligning perceptions and ideas and for coordinating interventions.

PREPARING PUBLIC ORGANIZATIONS FOR COLLABORATIVE INNOVATION

The kind of innovation leadership and management described in the previous section involves a hands-on attempt to "massage" actual processes of interaction to facilitate collaboration and enhance innovation. However, public leaders and managers need to supplement these hands-on efforts with a more hands-off attempt to build a stronger *innovation culture* in the public sector.

Such an endeavor involves persistent efforts to shape and reshape a broad range of structural, institutional, and cultural factors that affect the ability of the various actors within public organizations to collaborate and produce innovation.

Wang and Ahmed (2004) define *innovation culture* as *a multidimensional phenomenon involving the intention to innovate; the infrastructure to support innovation processes; the motivation, knowledge, and orientation of employees to support the thoughts and action necessary for innovation; and the general ability to implement innovative solutions that manage risks and reward compromise.* Building on this work, Dobni (2008) has tested a large number of items that are relevant to the definition of innovation culture using an exploratory factor analysis in order to identify and measure its key aspects. The result is a short list containing seven measures of innovation culture (Dobni 2008, 551). Dobni analyzed business firms from the service sector that in many respects are similar to public service organizations; thus, his results seem to be generally valid for the public sector as well. When reformulated with public organizations in mind, the measures of innovation culture can be defined as follows:

Innovation propensity—the degree to which the organization has a strategic focus on innovation that is communicated through its vision, goals, and objectives and supported by practical methods, procedures, and routines at the level of operations

Organizational constituency—the degree to which managers and employees have ownership of and are engaged in the innovation imperative and the way that they think about their individual and collective role in and contribution to innovation

Organizational learning—the degree to which the training and education of managers and employees is aligned with the innovation objectives of the organization and the degree to which mutual learning is encouraged and facilitated at different levels

Creativity and empowerment—the degree to which managers and employees are capable of thinking and acting creatively, are encouraged to do so in their daily work, and have opportunities to experiment with new solutions

Knowledge diffusion—the degree to which the managers and employees use (a) their external contacts and networks to discover and explore knowledge and ideas and (b) their formal and informal communication channels within their own organization to spread innovative ideas and solutions

Public value orientation—the degree to which managers and employees are sensitive to the changing demands of users and citizens and are focused on and engaged in creating public value

Implementation context—the degree to which the organization is capable of aligning and adapting systems, processes, and actors both to realize new and innovative ideas in practice and to ensure that they create added value

Public organizations that score high on these measures of innovation culture are more likely than others to produce different kinds of innovation and to engage public and private actors in the process. We can use these measures to draw up a checklist for public leaders and managers who want to strengthen the innovation culture of their organization. Such a checklist would include the following tasks:

1. Ensure that innovation is one of the key strategies to achieve the goals and objectives of the organization and translate the overall innovation strategy into everyday practices by developing a toolbox of innovation-enhancing methods, procedures, and routines.
2. Develop a common language that enables middle managers and employees to talk about innovation: what it is, how it is facilitated and hampered, and what it can achieve.
3. Provide targeted courses in organizing and managing change and innovation processes to managers and employees at all levels, and support the development and retention of organizational learning.
4. Empower the employees to develop and test new ideas and solutions, and create spaces where they can do so together without being trapped in bureaucratic rules and regulations.
5. Facilitate creative problem solving by ensuring a short power distance, a trust-based relationship between leaders and the led, a low degree of work structuration, and a high degree of internal mobility and flexibility.
6. Create incentives to collaborate and innovate by persistently praising efforts to drill holes in the mental and organizational silos and to think out of the box while simultaneously resisting the temptation to use individual bonus payments to stimulate creativity.

7. Institutionalize the use of problem-driven, interdisciplinary project work to ensure that the project organization model both is open for rethinking and reframing the problem and for adjusting the goals and is reduced to a process through which policies are executed and ready-made plans are implemented.
8. Develop an experimental culture in which tests and trials of new ideas are an integral part of the decision-making process.
9. Make sure that all leaders and managers are part of and participate in professional networks and that all employees have access to new knowledge and ideas through professional organizations, conferences, and relevant websites.
10. Build an internal communication system that ensures the dissemination of innovation knowledge between departments and between different organizational levels.
11. Encourage employees to learn about, from, and with users and citizens in order to better understand their needs and demands and to harvest their innovative ideas.
12. Create a clear understanding of the organization's key tasks and its contribution to producing public value and of how innovation can help improve organizational performance to benefit users, citizens, and society at large.
13. Do not try to eliminate organizational slack, but use it as a kind of "venture capital" that can be invested in promising innovations.
14. Involve relevant actors from inside and outside the organization in co-initiating, codesigning, and co-implementing innovative solutions so that their ideas and resources are mobilized and a joint ownership to the new designs is developed.
15. Establish a system for systematically evaluating innovative solutions in order to maximize the outcomes through adjustments and redesigns.

Those public organizations with a limited capacity for innovation leadership and management are forced to make tough priorities and decide where on the list to begin and where to end. Like the more capable public organizations, they have to measure and assess the innovation culture of the organization to discover critical areas that deserve special attention and call for immediate action. A flow perspective aiming to detect bottlenecks in processes of collaborative innovation will often be helpful.

THEORIES OF LEADING AND MANAGING COLLABORATIVE INNOVATION

The attempt to enhance collaborative innovation in the public sector requires the development of a new kind of public leadership and management. Since the early 1990s, public leaders and managers have been trained and encouraged to focus on inputs in terms of using different public resources and on outputs in terms of how their staff and agency perform (Osborne 2006). However, this backward-looking focus on resource consumption and performance will neither drive innovation nor initiate and orchestrate collaborative processes.

Leading and managing *innovation* require the ability to govern "emergence" and "potentiality" in the sense of the possible future development and realization of new and creative solutions that break with and perhaps outperform the existing practices. When attempting to govern the potential for the future emergence of new and desirable but as yet unknown practices, it is not enough to use *transactional leadership*—that is, recruiting, instructing, and correcting public employees in order to motivate them to do their jobs. Nor is it sufficient to inspire, motivate, and incentivize the staff to pursue a commonly defined mission rather than their individual interests through what has been termed *transformational leadership* (Parry and Bryman 2006). Transactional and transformational leadership continue to be important in ensuring an efficient implementation of predefined, collective goals through planned and well-described bureaucratic practices, but they have limited value in rethinking goals and practices and in changing the way that problems and goals are defined and that new routines are established, tested, and adjusted.

Instead, enhancing public innovation requires a combination of adaptive and pragmatic leadership. *Adaptive leadership* determines which activities to maintain and which to adapt and transform. It then develops new practices based on new ideas by crafting and testing prototypes. Finally, it endeavors to align people, processes, and goals across institutional and organizational boundaries to ensure the execution and to facilitate the integration of the new activities with the old ones (Heifetz, Linsky, and Grashow 2009). *Pragmatic leadership* attempts to transform the culture of public organizations in order to enhance learning by doing and to encourage the development and testing of prototypes and the use of experimentation. This kind of leadership increases the organizational and individual capacity for single- and double-loop learning (Argyris and Schön 1978). It also spurs transformative learning, which produces new metaphors and narratives that enable us to understand what we fail to comprehend, to imagine new ways of doing things, and to change our roles and identities (Mezirow 2000). Adaptive and pragmatic leadership mutually reinforce each other because creating a culture of organizational learning spurs the development and adaptation of new ideas that can be tested in practice and because aligning different actors, processes, and goals will stimulate learning.

Public leaders and managers will also be able to benefit from a closer acquaintance with *design thinking* (Bason 2010, 2014), which responds to real-life problems by questioning assumptions, focusing on outcomes, and redesigning practices and artifacts. It uses heuristic devices such as scenario building, interdisciplinary workshops, prototyping, design experiments, and role playing to make new and emerging futures concrete and tangible. Most important, managers inspired by design thinking promote collaboration and cocreation through the construction of interactive forums and arenas. Collaboration is also enhanced in order to achieve both *divergent* thinking, which uses logical analysis as well as intuition and association to generate large numbers of creative ideas, and *convergent* thinking, which synthesizes the new ideas into feasible and workable solutions that actually solve the problem at hand (Ansell and Torfing 2014).

Further, Boland and Collopy (2004) talk about how some public managers have developed a *design attitude*, which "views each project as an opportunity for invention that includes a questioning of basic assumptions and a resolve to leave the world a better place than we found it" (9). In an empirical study of design consultants, Michlewski (2008) has identified five dimensions of this design attitude: Designers reconcile different meanings and objectives; bring new ideas to life through visualization and prototyping; embrace the challenge of working in an environment characterized by uncertainty, risks, and loss of control; use an aesthetic sense and pragmatic judgment to merge form and function; and have an engaging personal and commercial empathy that enables them to tune in to people's needs. Bason (2014) has studied the presence of design attitudes in public managers who are leading and managing collaborative innovation processes and finds that they tend to challenge basic assumptions, focus on outcomes, steward the unknown, and seek to make the future concrete. Hence, according to his study, the new design thinking is gradually finding its way into the public sector.

Leading and managing *collaboration* also pose a huge challenge to public leaders and managers who in the last decades have been told to focus on the performance of the staff, agency, or department that they supervise (Christensen and Lægreid 2007). The efforts of public leaders and managers to enhance public innovation through multi-actor collaboration call for a new type of leadership and management that is more distributive, horizontal, collaborative, and integrative. In the 1980s many people thought that the public sector was in need of a strong, charismatic, and visionary leadership that was capable of redefining objectives, inspiring the workforce, and turning around the ossified and run-down public organizations overnight. In hindsight we can see that this kind of change in leadership was merely relevant for the executive managers who often failed both to connect with the rest of the organization and to generate sustainable and long-lasting transformations of public organizations.

Today we need to cultivate a new kind of *distributive leadership* that encourages public leaders and managers to direct others in ways that enable them to lead themselves (Pearce and Conger 2003; Parry and Bryman 2006). Leaders and managers at all levels of the organization should distribute and disperse leadership functions within their organizations by empowering their employees and creating self-managing projects, teams, and networks (Wart 2013). Innovation is created by people with a comprehensive understanding of problems and challenges and by people with the competences and knowledge required for developing and implementing new and bold solutions. These people need support from sponsors and champions at the executive level, but, first and foremost, they need decentered day-to-day leadership at their organizational level. They require project and team leaders and network managers who can help them focus their attention, search for new ideas, and facilitate the testing of the most promising ones in daily operations. The middle managers must find ways of recruiting, training, and empowering employees who can exercise innovation leadership even though they do not have a formal leadership role. In addition, they must support and coach those employees who take on the dispersed leadership functions and act as innovation managers. The ultimate goal of distributive leadership is to facilitate self-regulation. Hence, in a certain sense, leadership is most successful when it has made itself redundant.

When leading a group of people who share the same level of authority and experience as ourselves, we cannot pull rank and invoke a hierarchical authority; rather, we must adopt a management style known as *horizontal leadership*. In projects, teams, and networks, this approach enables group members to lead other members by asking the right questions, seeking and exploring answers through dialogue based on mutual respect, empowering the participants by involving them in discussions about what to do next, and encouraging them to lead each other in the course of action (Denis, Langley, and Sergi 2012). Horizontal leadership is particularly important in communities of practice in which professionals with different experiences, methods, and educational backgrounds collaborate to overcome obstacles and to improve performance by creating step change. This method can also facilitate collaboration with and between private actors such as service users, citizens, nongovernmental organizations, and private firms that can bring new ideas to the table.

To illustrate, some Danish municipalities have created new positions for public employees who serve as "playmakers" or "bridge builders" and are given the task of initiating and supporting collaboration between public and private actors to spur the development of new and better public solutions. Instead of organizing the collaborative process and steering it toward a certain goal, the playmakers bring together different actors around a particular agenda, problem, or ambition and empower and persuade them to share the task of leading the group so that the leadership emerges as a result of their interaction. Public facilitators dedicated to stimulating horizontal interaction between public and private actors are likely to play an important role in opening up the public sector to new ideas. Unfortunately, public authorities are not always committed to collaborating with private actors either because they think that it is too difficult and time consuming or because they do not think such collaboration will generate inputs that match the ideas of the highly competent professions in the public sector. The latter is confirmed in a large survey of public managers conducted by the Collaborative Innovation in the Public Sector project in Denmark. Here only 11 percent of the public managers claim that they regularly involve citizens in public innovation, and the involvement of private corporations is down to 6 percent. While the good news is that 53 percent of the public mangers say that they involve the local users of public services in innovation processes, only 28 percent of the public managers see the users as a source of innovation. Hence, the users are involved, but they do not really influence the innovative outcomes (FTF 2013).

Horizontal leadership is sometimes referred to as *collaborative leadership*. Its task is to design appropriate institutional arenas for collaborative governance and facilitate collaborative processes by emphasizing the mutual interdependence of the public and private actors, building trust, developing a shared understanding of the overall mission, and encouraging the production of intermediate outcomes (Ansell and Gash 2007; Archer and Cameron 2008). A crucial challenge for collaborative leadership is to drive the process onward from problem definition, direction setting, and policy development to decision making and implementation. Making bold decisions and implementing them in practice is the sine qua non for innovation, but the process often presents a challenge to leaders of collaboration as choosing one solution over another gives rise to conflicts and antagonism. Thus, conflict mediation becomes a key part of collaborative leadership (Gray 1989; Ansell and Gash 2007).

Integrative public leadership also focuses on collaboration in horizontal arenas. The key ambition of integrative public leadership is to bring diverse groups and organizations together in semipermanent ways, and typically across sector boundaries, and remedy complex problems by developing a new set of solutions that achieve the common good (Crosby and Bryson 2010, 211). According to Crosby and Bryson (2010), the research on integrative public leadership shows that leaders are most likely to have success with creating cross-sector collaboration in turbulent environments and when separate efforts by several actors from different sectors have failed. The research results indicate that successful leaders work to form an initial agreement about the problem and design the collaborative process in ways that involve creating boundary objects, boundary experiences, and boundary groups. They draw on the different competences of the collaborators, are responsive to key stakeholders, and pointedly avoid imposed solutions. Integrative leaders ensure that trust-building activities are continuous and that the structure of the collaboration is flexible and open to the incorporation of new actors as well as for leadership succession. In addition, these leaders are prepared to commit their time and energy to mitigate power imbalances and deal with shocks, and they usually manage to reframe conflicts and disputes in ways that have appeal across sectors. Finally, they insist on building accountability systems that track inputs, processes, and outcomes and on developing methods for gathering, interpreting, and using data in processes of creative problem solving. Although integrative leadership is important for enhancing boundary-spanning collaboration, Crosby and Bryson caution us not to exaggerate its impact by insisting that "the normal expectation ought to be that success will be very difficult to achieve in cross-sector collaborations, regardless of leadership effectiveness" (227).

METAGOVERNANCE OF COLLABORATIVE INNOVATION

Governance network theory makes a distinct contribution to understanding how collaborative innovation can be initiated, facilitated, and directed. Whereas theories of public leadership and management focus on what leaders and managers can do to influence actual processes of collaboration and innovation, governance network theory reflects on how it is possible to govern the complex governance processes and, in particular, how it is possible to govern relatively self-governing networks, partnerships, and collaborations (Kickert, Klijn, and Koppenjan 1997; Jessop 2002; Agranoff 2003, 2007; Milward and Provan 2006; Torfing et al. 2012). The key concept is metagovernance, which refers to reflexive governance practices aiming to govern more or less institutionalized governance arenas that produce concrete acts of governance. Thus, metagovernance is a particular kind of third-order governance that selects and combines suitable forms of governance and makes sure that they function properly and deliver the expected results (Kooiman 1993, 2003). Metagovernance involves developing hegemonic ideas about how to govern and be governed, as well as defining the normative foundation of public governance. In metagoverning, one makes a political, normative, and context-dependent choice between different modes of governance and perhaps even between different combinations of hierarchy, markets, and networks. Finally, it also includes the strategic structuring and managing of particular modes of governance to prevent dysfunctions and to advance particular processes and goals (Torfing et al. 2012, 131).

To illustrate, the attempt to fight unemployment in a neighborhood of immigrants and refugees (first-order governance) may rely on a combination of particular contracted training activities and sustained collaboration between trade unions and employers' organizations to encourage workplaces to hire new laborers with little labor-market experience (second-order governance). Both the relational contracts with the private providers of training courses and the collaborative arenas for joint decision making must be metagoverned to function properly and produce the expected results (third-order governance). The metagovernance of the particular modes of governance not only involves choosing a mode of governance but also invokes particular political goals and is informed by a public discourse that defines the norms and values for how to govern society and the economy.

Although metagovernance is generally relevant when analyzing the governance of different modes of governance (Meuleman 2008), it has a particularly important role in rethinking the role of the state and government vis-à-vis governance networks (Kooiman 1993, 2003). There has been an unfortunate tendency to view governance networks as a new mode of governance that contributes to the hollowing out of the state (Milward and Provan, 2000), and, thus, it goes on to portray the relationship between governance and government as a zero-sum game in which the former expands at the expense of the latter. This understanding is problematic because it downplays and obfuscates the state's role in relation to interactive and collaborative governance processes (Bell and Hindmoor 2009). To solve this problem, we shall insist that although governance networks are self-governing in that the political agenda, the rules of the game, and the final outputs are the results of negotiation, the autonomy of governance networks is always bounded given the constant attempts to influence the results of networked governance.

Government plays a crucial role in initiating, supporting, and giving direction to self-governing governance networks, and the concept of metagovernance helps us understand how public authorities can exercise power in subtle and indirect ways by regulating the self-regulated processes in collaborative network arenas. The ultimate challenge for governments in this regard is to find ways of influencing collaborative governance processes without reverting to traditional forms of command and control that will scare off the private actors or, at least, generate fierce opposition. In fact, metagoverning has its risks. Doing *too much* puts the interactive governance arena in a straitjacket; doing *too little* does not provide adequate support, direction, and conflict mediation. Both extremes jeopardize the collaborative innovation process.

The different theories of governance networks offer different insights into how metagovernance can and should be exercised (Sørensen and Torfing 2007). *Interdependency theorists* such as Rhodes (1997) and Kickert, Klijn, and Koppenjan (1997) focus on how networks can contribute to joint problem solving through a negotiated exchange of resources among interdependent but operationally autonomous actors from the public and private sector. In this perspective, metagovernance takes the form of network management, which seeks to stabilize and improve the interaction among network actors (Koppenjan and Klijn 2004). Network management involves a skillful combination of process management, which mobilizes actors, builds trust, and reduces the transaction costs of collaborating, and process design, which creates fruitful dialogue and encourages risk taking while reducing the role and impact of defensive and noncooperative strategies (Kickert, Klijn, and Koppenjan 1997).

Governability theorists such as Kooiman (2003), Mayntz (1993a, 1993b), and Scharpf (1994) also perceive the stakeholders as strategic actors with diverging interests, but they tend to downplay the role of conflict. They see governance networks as game-like structures and assume that under the right conditions it is possible to create cooperative games that lead to both negative and positive coordination. Hence, metagovernance involves game structuration through creating incentive structures that encourage participation and collaboration. It also clearly signals that collaborative governance takes place in "the shadow of hierarchy"; that is, the capacity for self-regulation is removed or, at least, significantly reduced if the governance network fails to provide an appropriate and feasible solution to joint problems.

Normative integration theorists such as DiMaggio and Powell (1983), March and Olsen (1989, 1995), Powell and DiMaggio (1991), and Scott (1995) agree that governance networks are formed because the actors are interdependent and need to exchange or pool their resources to solve joint problems, but they do not think that the social and political actors are driven by a rational calculation of the consequences of alternative actions. People are rule followers in that they tend to act in accordance with "the logic of appropriate action" that is defined by the institutional rules, norms, and values that dominate its context. Therefore, metagovernance is not a question of stabilizing interaction in the face of potential conflicts by manipulating the incentive structure. Rather, metagovernance is a question of (a) "developing the identities and capabilities" of the actors so they can negotiate their internal differences in a civilized manner and (b) "ensuring the accountability and adaptiveness" of the interactive governance arrangements to strengthen democracy and enhance innovation (March and Olsen 1995).

Governmentality theorists such as Foucault (1991), Rose (1999), and Dean (1999) recognize the decentered and networked organization of power in advanced liberal societies. The failure of neoliberalism to replace bureaucratic and hierarchical government with self-regulated market governance based on competition has transformed the overall idea about how to govern and be governed. The new governmentality, referred to as advance liberal governance, aims to mobilize public and private actors in interactive and self-regulated arenas so they can use their resources, energies, and free action to solve emerging problems in accordance with the overall goals of society. To achieve this, metagovernance combines technologies of agency with technologies of performance (Dean 1999; Triantafillou 2007). While the former attempts to mold citizens, civil society organizations, and business firms as empowered, entrepreneurial, and self-regulated subjectivities, the latter seeks to regulate the free and responsible actors' conduct by producing and disseminating a large array of norms, values, standards, benchmarks, and performance targets that help to ensure the results of interactive governance comply with the overall policy objectives. In short, metagovernance aims to regulate the self-regulated actions of free, energetic, and creative subjectivities to ensure their conformity with hegemonic power strategies.

While differing in their conception of governance networks and their perception of both the drivers of human action and the role of conflicts in public governance, the four theories of network governance all agree—more or less explicitly—that interactive governance calls for some kind of metagovernance. What the theories are not so clear about is the question of who the metagovernor is. We are offered only vague references to "the state," "the government," or "the public authorities." In an important exception to the rule, Provan and Kenis (2008) discuss the advantages of having a lead actor, a plenary assembly of participating actors, or a network administrative organization, which establishes a permanent leadership group appointed by the network as a whole, to metagovern a governance network. The lead actor will often be a public actor, but both the collective network management through joint discussion and decision making and the appointed leadership group in the network administrative organization open up the possibility that the exercise of metagovernance is shared by public or private actors or is delegated to a group of public and/or private actors. According to Jessop (2004), metagovernors might also be placed at different levels, and sometimes local networks are subject to multilevel metagovernance as regional authorities, national laws, and supranational funding schemes all partake in metagoverning the local arenas of networked interaction.

That there might be a choice between different metagovernors, and sometimes even a rivalry between metagovernors placed at different scales of governance, prompts the question of what it takes to become a metagovernor. In answering this question, a reference to Hood's (1986) so-called *NATO resources* appears to be helpful. Torfing et al. (2012) have argued that in order to serve as a metagovernor, an actor must have *nodality*, as a central actor with whom the other actors regularly interact; *authority*, as one whom other actors listen to and respect; *treasure*, or the material and immaterial resources that can help cover the transaction costs of collaboration, finance knowledge acquisition, and support small-scale experiments; and *organization*, in terms of an organizational backup that facilitates a reflexive monitoring of the interaction and innovation process. In principle both public and private actors may possess these NATO resources, but public agencies often have an advantage because of their legitimacy and their access to different kinds of resources (Klijn and Koppenjan 2000).

Having established the conditions for being able to exercise metagovernance, the next question concerns how metagovernance is exercised and which concrete tools can be used (Torfing et al. 2012). First of all, metagovernors may influence the form, functioning, and effect of the interactive governance arrangement by shaping the overall political, institutional, and socioeconomic structures of society that may support or constrain the use of governance networks. Hence, changes in the public discourse on governance, reforms of the organizational structure of local and regional government, and reorganization of the relationship between state and society can either hamper or facilitate collaborative governance.

In addition to these forms of metagovernance that involve the "mobilization of bias" (Schattschneider 1960, 71), metagovernors who are relatively close to the interactive governance arrangements can deploy different tools to influence the actual functioning of governance networks without reverting to hierarchical forms of imperative rule through imposition. In essence there are four different metagovernance tools. *Institutional design* uses the formation of rules, norms, and procedures to influence the scope, character, and composition of governance networks. *Goal and network steering* give purpose and direction to governance networks and facilitate evaluation by defining the overall political objectives, the legal framework, the fiscal basis, and the discursive story lines. *Process management* seeks to reduce tensions, resolve or mediate conflicts, selectively empower particular actors, reduce the transaction costs, and drive the decision-making process forward by reframing problems and solutions, providing material and immaterial resources, and creating a good and constructive environment for sustained interaction. Finally, *direct participation* enables the metagovernor to influence the policy agenda, the range of feasible options, the premises for decision making, and the final decisions and outcomes by using personal leadership, argumentation, rhetorical ploys, and coalition building.

Metagovernance of collaborative governance processes that aim to spur public innovation is a crucial condition for success, but public authorities confront a series of dilemmas when trying to metagovern governance networks. First, should the metagovernors rely on the self-governing capacity of the network to remove an obstacle to either collaboration or innovation while risking a period of stalemate given the presence of collective action problems, or should they intervene to solve the problem and risk hampering the internal learning processes and disempowering the governance network? Second, should the metagovernors rely on hands-off metagovernance—in terms of institutional design and goal and framework steering—that is exercised at a distance and leaves considerable room for self-governance, or should they embark on a more hands-on metagovernance based on process management and direct participation that involves a relatively close interaction with the network actors and might be more intrusive? Finally, should the metagovernors clearly signal that the network will be overruled by hierarchical authorities if a particular solution is chosen and will be forced to reconsider its decision in light of overall policy goals, or should they abstain from invoking references to the shadow of hierarchy because it will undermine the integrity of the governance network? These questions remind us that metagovernance cannot be reduced to a managerial task of getting things done by involving a plethora of public and private actors in public governance. Metagovernance involves making tough political decisions and should ideally be exercised in and through a close dialogue between administrative leaders and managers and elected politicians who possess democratic legitimacy.

CONCLUSION

This chapter has identified some specific drivers of collaborative innovation in the public sector that make it reasonable to expect that collaboration can become a prevalent method for enhancing innovation despite the long-lasting tradition for bureaucratic compartmentalization and the recent attempt to imitate the private sector by stimulating internal and external competition in public service production. The chapter has adopted a process perspective on collaborative innovation to track the barriers that may arise in different stages of the process. In attempting to overcome these barriers, public managers or other relevant actors must act as conveners, facilitators, and catalysts. These new roles for leaders and managers must be cultivated, expanded, and refined in the years to come. However, as noted, convening, facilitating, and catalyzing concrete processes of collaborative innovation are not enough. Hands-on innovation management must be combined with a hands-off management that aims to build a stronger innovation culture in the public sector. This argument is pursued in chapter 10 by linking the debate on how to enhance public innovation with the debate on changing governance paradigms in the public sector.

This chapter has drawn attention to the relevance of new trends in leadership research and governance network theory for studying the leadership and management of collaborative innovation processes. Theories of adaptive and pragmatic leadership and design thinking advance the knowledge of how to lead and manage innovation processes, while recently developed theories of distributive, horizontal, collaborative, and integrative leadership have much to offer for understanding the facilitation of collaboration across organizations, sectors, and levels. Whereas public leadership theory focuses on what leaders and managers do, governance network theory takes the interaction in networks involved in producing public governance, regulation, and service as the starting point for reflecting on how collaborative processes can be sustained. This perspective allows governance theorists to advance the notion of metagovernance, which leads us to appreciate how more or less self-regulating governance networks can be governed without undermining their capacity for self-regulation. Theories of metagovernance are not very specific about who exercises metagovernance, but they are helpful in seeing how public managers can lead and manage successfully without doing either too much or too little.

10

REFORMING PUBLIC GOVERNANCE, ENHANCING COLLABORATIVE INNOVATION

PRESSURE IS GROWING on public organizations to spur policy and service innovation so they can solve complex problems, break policy deadlocks, and satisfy unmet social needs. Public organizations are also encouraged to change their organizational designs, exploit new digital technologies, and rethink their relation to citizens and private stakeholders in order to enhance productivity and mobilize resources in times of shrinking budgets. As we have seen, public innovation can benefit tremendously from collaboration across organizations and sectors. The big question then becomes how to organize, govern, and manage public sector organizations to further accelerate public innovation in general and collaborative innovation in particular. Answering this pertinent question brings us into the realm of public administration policy in which dialogue between researchers and practitioners is essential both to identify the key challenges and to develop and test new institutional formats and modes of governance in response.

Fads and fashions come and go in public administration policy, and their role and impact depend on political sentiments, institutional conditions, and cultural traditions. However, looking at the so-called organizational megatrends, three public administration paradigms have played and continue to play a significant role for organizing, governing, and managing public organizations. The first, the Old Public Administration (OPA) paradigm, is based on the defining traits of Weberian and Wilsonian bureaucracy. The second is the NPM paradigm, which from the mid-1980s onward has introduced market logics and strategic performance management into the public sector. The last paradigm is New Public Governance, which favors the development of collaborative forms of governance and a more integrative and trust-based management. Rather than following neatly after each other, the three public administration paradigms and their associated practices coexist as they tend to have been layered on top of one another. Hence, just as New Public Management's arrival did not eliminate bureaucratic forms of governance associated with Old Public Administration, the surge of New Public Governance merely adds a new layer on top of the existing OPA and NPM layers. The more recently developed public administration paradigms might dominate the contemporary thinking and action of a broad range of opinion leaders, policy advisers, politicians, executive managers, researchers, and newly educated public administration students; however, despite the apparent hegemony of the new ideas and practices, the old and sedimented public administration paradigms will still heavily influence large parts of the public sector. Where the paradigms meet, elements from the different paradigms merge and mutually reinforce each other, producing unpredictable and unintended effects as hybrid forms of governance develop.

This chapter provides a critical assessment of the strengths and weaknesses of the three public administration paradigms in order to discover what an innovative public sector would look like. The assessment is biased toward New Public Governance because it recommends a stronger focus on public innovation and calls for developing crosscutting forms of collaboration. However, as we shall see, all three paradigms provide important drivers for innovation, and there are also limits to how well New Public Governance supports the enhancement of collaborative innovation.

The chapter first briefly assesses the problems and merits of the bureaucratic model that lies at the heart of Old Public Administration. It then considers the innovation-enhancing promise of New Public Management before scrutinizing its drawbacks. Next is an analysis of the factors behind the recent transition from the NPM paradigm to a growing interest in New Public Governance and the impact of its associated ideas. The drivers and barriers of New Public Governance are briefly assessed before, finally, the prospects for building a more innovative public sector are discussed.

WHAT IS SO WRONG ABOUT BUREAUCRACY?

Old Public Administration captures the way that a nonelected administration, which takes the form of a bureaucracy, prepares, implements, and adjusts the elected government's authoritative political decisions. Bureaucratic forms of rule-based administration have existed for many centuries, but they have played a special role in modern liberal democracies, where they provide a legal-rational foundation of democratic governance. They ensure that an impartial, professional, and efficient administration primes and executes political decisions based on written rules and rational decision making.

While Wilson (1887) demanded that the administration operate independently from the elected branches of government when implementing public policy, Weber (1922) sought to construct an ideal typical model of bureaucracy that pinpointed its core features as a legal-rational mode of governance. Apart from the separation of politics from administration that both Wilson and Weber emphasized, the Weberian-type bureaucracy has five defining characteristics: hierarchical levels of super- and subordination along the vertical axis of public organizations, specialization and organizational division of labor along the horizontal axis, centralized command and control with lower levels and specialized agencies, formalized and rational decision-making processes based on and leading to the formulation of written rules and fixed procedures, and administrative tasks solved by professional civil servants who are hired on a meritocratic basis, have a specialized knowledge, and are motivated by altruistic concerns for society at large. The empirical correlation between the defining characteristics of bureaucracy varies and is not always high (Walton 2005). Hence, some public organizations are extremely hierarchical but have a limited division of labor and a rather decentralized decision-making structure. However, the idea is that the closer public organizations are to possessing all the defining traits, the more bureaucratic they are. Whether a public organization is a bureaucracy is a matter of degree rather than a question of either-or.

Bureaucracy is often criticized for preventing, or at least limiting, public innovation (Burns and Stalker 1961; Damanpour 1996; O'Toole and Meier 2011). Thus, the defining traits of public bureaucracies impede the development and/or the implementation of innovative solutions. For instance, the presence of hierarchy combined with a high degree of centralization reduces the commitment and active engagement of frontline personnel in developing new ideas and innovative solutions (Thompson 1965). Multiple layers of leaders and managers at different hierarchical levels also increase the number of veto points in public organizations and thus jeopardize the implementation of bold ideas. In addition, formalized decision-making processes based on written rules and routinized behavior create rigidities that hamper innovation. Hence, asking employees to follow an authoritative set of predefined rules will discourage the search for new solutions (Zaltman, Duncan, and Holbek 1973), and the drive toward standardization in so-called mechanistic bureaucracies will stifle creative thinking and experimentation (Mintzberg 1983). Moreover, rule following often becomes a goal in itself in mechanistic bureaucracies, and it treats new ideas and innovative practices as unwelcome disturbances of the stable functioning of the organization (Jacobsen and Thorsvik 2008). When rule following is combined with hierarchical controls, we also see the development of a risk-averse culture in which failure and error is frowned upon and even penalized. This disapproval will tend to hinder innovation, which is always predicated on some degree of risk taking. Finally, a clear-cut departmental and agency-based division of labor combined with the recruitment of professional staff members who have different kinds of specialized knowledge might prevent innovation-enhancing collaboration and knowledge exchange, leading to a situation in which new ideas are trapped in the departments and agencies in which they are developed (Eggers and O'Leary 2009).

The critique of bureaucracy for hampering innovation sometimes overshadows the fact that bureaucracy may also trigger and enhance public innovation (Jakobsen 2013; Mazzucato 2013). As a result we become too negative toward bureaucratic forms of organization and perhaps also frustrated that bureaucracy is not easily bypassed by other forms of organization (Eggers and Singh 2009, 42). Bureaucracy might not be a strong driver of collaboration and innovation, but it does have positive aspects that counter the overly negative image painted in the innovation literature. For one, public hierarchies in which the power to make authoritative decisions is concentrated at the executive level are usually good at setting the agenda and allocating resources to new and innovative endeavors. Hence, if the executive leadership wants to enhance the organization's innovation of policies, organizational procedures, and services, then it will ensure both that middle managers and frontline personnel pay attention to the new plan and that sufficient money and time are devoted to pursuing it. For example, training managers and staff and creating special-purpose units (sometimes referred to as ad-hocracies) that can convene relevant actors may strengthen the development of new and innovative solutions. Visionary goal-setting by executive leaders might also stimulate idea generation. New ideas are not developed in organizations that lack purpose and concrete goals; instead, their development requires an explicitly formulated ambition and direction for the organization in question. The executive leadership can provide the clear vision and mission that calls for innovative initiatives. Their implementation may also be improved by centralized top-down control, which will support coordination and reduce uncertainty although not necessarily in a way that preserves or improves the integrity of arenas for multi-actor collaboration.

Another good aspect of bureaucracy is that its formal rules and procedures do not act merely as constraints on developing and realizing fresh ideas. The literature distinguishes between red tape, which prevents innovation, and "green tape," which might enable or spur innovation by establishing rules, norms, and procedures for jointly exploring new ideas and for testing the possibilities for exploiting them in practice (Bozeman 2000; DeHart-Davis 2009). Formalized routines concerning when and how to initiate search and learning processes and rules and procedures that support professional staff in their efforts to improve service quality and solve complex problems will enhance rather than hamper innovation.

A third point is that the meritocratic recruitment of specialized staff members with different competences and forms of knowledge ensures the existence of a plurality of ideas that may boost creativity and the development of new ideas. Moreover, organizational silos with a critical mass of professionally trained workers provide safe and stable environments for augmenting professional knowledge and stimulating experiences that can trigger innovation. On the contrary, a totally loose and fluid organization in which the professional employees constantly move around and have no regular interaction with people of their own professional background might result in the professionally trained employees becoming defensive, introverted, and incapable of advancing the professional knowledge that they have.

Last but not least, the size of public bureaucracies and their large budgets raise the ability of bureaucratic actors to take risks and make it possible for public bureaucracies to absorb the costs of failure that often will represent only a tiny fragment of the total budget. Mazzucato (2013) claims that the public sector often is prepared to take larger risks than the private sector can, and, as noted previously, she believes that this mind-set led to some of the most spectacular public innovations such as the Internet and GPS being developed.

Local circumstances determine whether the barriers or drivers inherent in bureaucracy will dominate; therefore, assessing the overall impact of bureaucracy is difficult. However, some have conducted meta-analyses of the impact that bureaucracy has on innovation by systematically selecting independent empirical studies on the basis of explicit quality criteria and assessing the results (Damanpour 1991, 1996; Zornoza, Navarro, and Ciprés 2007). The findings presented in these meta-analyses give us a hint of the general effect that various aspects of bureaucracy have on the ability to innovate. For one, although hierarchy in itself does not seem to have a negative impact, centralized control clearly does have a negative influence on the ability to innovate. Formalization has no significant impact as such, which suggests that perhaps the positive and negative effects of formal rules cancel each other out. Innovation appears to be enhanced by specialization that is supported by an organizational division of labor and the use of professional staff with particular forms of knowledge, competence, and experience. The latter effect seems to be contingent on what phase of the innovation process is under review. Specialization has a positive effect on implementation and a negative effect on initiation, which suggests that the professions and the public organizations must be disturbed by external inputs to foster new and bold ideas (see also Jacobsen and Thorsvik 2008).

While it is interesting that the effect of bureaucracy tends to be quite ambivalent, we should view these results skeptically for two reasons. First, the high level of aggregation might hide more than it reveals. Also, the units of analysis in the meta-analyses are private firms and nonprofit organizations (public and private) rather than more conventional public organizations, which are the key focus of this book. The bias toward private sector organizations might well reduce the negative effect of bureaucracy because the reliance on formalized rules and procedures tends to be much stronger in public bureaucracies, which are ruled by laws and other kinds of legal and bureaucratic regulations. The public sector has an unfortunate tendency to add more rules with a shovel and remove superfluous rules with a pair of tweezers.

THE INNOVATION-ENHANCING PROMISE OF NEW PUBLIC MANAGEMENT

In the beginning, the bureaucratization of the public sector contributed immensely to improving its efficiency. Clear command structures, coordinated efforts to reach common goals, the harvesting of gains from increased organizational and professional specialization, and increased routinization of daily operations so that middle managers and frontline staff did not have to reinvent procedures every time they faced a particular task or situation—all of these factors improved the performance of the public sector in terms of service delivery, regulatory capacity, and associated costs. However, gradually there was a decreasing return to scale. Hence, after a certain point, more bureaucratization no longer enhances but reduces efficiency. Large and complex organizations lose sight of their mission, long elaborated chains of command give rise to implementation deficits, further specialization fragments agencies and leads to coordination problems, and the ongoing production of detailed rules creates rigidities that prevent the development of flexible solutions based on professional knowledge and discretion. Increasingly the public sector has been described as an ossified, control-fixated, and compartmentalized apparatus with far too much red tape (Downs 1967).

Public choice theorists launched severe criticism of public bureaucracies for being inefficient and based their arguments on neoclassical free market theory and theories emphasizing the asymmetric distribution of information between principals and agents. Hence, they held responsible the monopoly status of the public sector in certain areas for producing services that were far too expensive and of poor quality. Because the public sector typically does not face the same competitive pressures as the private sector, the theorists assumed that the public sector had no incentive to improve its efficiency and innovate its services to meet the needs and demands of its users (Roessner 1977). Another argument against the traditional functioning of public bureaucracy was based on principal-agency theory (Rees 1985a, 1985b; Stiglitz 1987). As principals, elected politicians and executive public managers have insufficient knowledge of the costs and quality of the services that the local service-delivering agents provide, and they know way too little about the agents' real competences and actual efforts. Being rational and self-interested, the local agents exploit the information asymmetry to act opportunistically and thus tend to do less than they are expected to. The results, again, are that public service becomes too costly and substandard, and that innovations in public services and the organizational systems are few and far between.

According to New Public Management, the inherent inefficiency problems of the public sector can be cured through a combination of enhanced competition and more strategic leadership, and performance management will make public service production much more dynamic (Hood 1991; Osborne and Gaebler 1992). Competition can be promoted through privatization, contracting out, and the creation of internal markets in the public sector. To further imitate the free market economy in which the attempt to attract and satisfy an increasing number of customers allegedly drives quality up and prices down, the competition between public and private service providers for contracts to supply particular public services should be supplemented by offering public service users a free choice of service provider in order to stimulate competition on the demand side. Thus, marketization and customization should walk hand in hand.

To help executive public managers cope with the increasing pressures from enhanced competition, they should be given full responsibility for the strategic leadership of the public sector and for using their staff, their organizational resources, and their increasingly deregulated institutional environment in a flexible and efficient manner to improve performance and attract customers. To do so, strategic leaders and managers in the public sector must expand the managerial toolbox to include a variety of "sticks, carrots and sermons" (Bemelmans-Videc, Rist, and Vedung 2011). They should rigorously apply performance management techniques from the private sector to monitor inputs and outputs through developing standards and performance targets, measuring and benchmarking results, and deploying appropriate sanctions in relation to low-performing employees and agencies. In addition, positive incentives to enhance performance were introduced in the form of collective bonuses and individual performance-related pay systems. Finally, value-based management and transformational leadership aiming to inspire public employees, boost their morale, and mobilize their professional identity in the pursuit of organizational excellence were seen as a necessary supplement to the attempt to ensure an even exchange between performance and wages by means of transactional leadership.

New Public Management was primarily interested in finding new post-bureaucratic ways of enhancing efficiency while simultaneously responding to the neoliberal call for "less state and more market." The NPM reform program, however, was also instrumental in spurring the interest in innovation and public entrepreneurship (Paulsen 2006). Osborne and Gaebler (1992) sought to "reinvent government" by spurring organizational innovation, but they also wanted to create a public sector that puts a premium on entrepreneurship and is more capable of producing new and innovative service solutions. From this perspective, the key to enhancing innovation is to remove the traditional bureaucratic constraints on public managers and replace them with strong performance incentives (Ansell and Torfing 2014). Thus, the basic idea of New Public Management is captured in two well-known catchphrases: "Let the managers manage," and "make the mangers manage" (Verhoest, Verschuere, and Bouckaert 2007; Lægreid, Roness, and Verhoest 2011). To develop and test innovative ideas, not only will public managers require organizational autonomy and institutional flexibility, but also they need to be encouraged and pushed—by competition and performance management—to aggressively search for new and better ways of doing things. When managers both enjoy increasing autonomy and confront strong incentives from market pressures and performance measures, they will become more entrepreneurial and pursue radical efficiencies through innovation (Ansell and Torfing 2014).

The attempt to transform administrative managers into innovative entrepreneurs is propelled by structural reforms aiming to provide the twin conditions of more autonomy and stronger incentives. The reforms create a lean corporate leadership at the top of public organizations and enhance the strategic maneuverability of executive managers. At the same time, the role of elected politicians is transformed by recasting them as members of a corporate board that focuses on overall target setting and budget allocation while leaving the responsibility for policy implementation and service production with the administration. Separating the "steering" from the "rowing" strengthens the autonomy of public managers and prevents political interference in the dynamic and strategic development of public organizations. Whereas politicians should exercise political leadership by defining the overall objectives, setting ambitious targets, and allocating tight budget frames, public managers should exercise administrative leadership to drive the organizations and their employees toward greater efficiency and effectiveness.

These structural changes also involve corporatization and further disaggregation of agencies at the bottom of public organizations. New Public Management reforms recommend the creation of semi-autonomous, so-called arm's-length agencies that focus on delivering specialized services (Koch and Hauknes 2005; Osborne 2006). The hope is that the managers of such agencies, which are smaller in size and have a clearer mission and more degrees of freedom, will be able to use their entrepreneurial skills to enhance innovation.

The NPM reform program takes a managerial perspective on innovation. Its focus on managerial autonomy and motivation draws attention to the personal characteristics of public managers that might influence their decisions to develop and adopt innovation solutions (Damanpour and Schneider 2009). By viewing public managers as the main agents of change, New Public Management adopts a top-down focus on public innovation; however, the managerial incentive-based logic also extends downward from managers to employees and outward to private service providers. Performance-related wage systems and special award schemes are introduced to promote creativity and innovation among employees (Berman and Kim 2010), who are encouraged to focus on user satisfaction and to use inputs from the customers as a vehicle for service innovation and process improvement. Likewise, New Public Management sees private contractors and service providers as innovators driven by competition for contracts and clients (Coule and Patmore 2013).

The public sector can use public procurement as an instrument for enhancing public innovation given that private contractors are competing to meet the demands of the public agencies in new and innovative ways (Edquist and Zabala-Iturriagagoitia 2012). In addition, contracting out public services should spur innovation in service delivery because the private providers produce innovations that public service providers will eventually adopt.

Empirical evaluations of the effect of incentivized managerialism and enhanced competition are somewhat mixed (Ansell and Torfing 2014). In a study of public agencies in Belgium, Verhoest, Verschuere, and Bouckaert (2007) found that managerial autonomy over operations was an important factor in innovation but that competition and performance management supported innovation only in certain conditions. In a similar study comparing Flemish and Norwegian state agencies, Lægreid, Roness, and Verhoest (2011) found no evidence for the importance of managerial autonomy and only indirect support for the impact of performance management.

NEW PUBLIC MANAGEMENT: A STRAITJACKET FOR COLLABORATIVE INNOVATION?

While New Public Management can be credited for having given new impetus to the discussion of public innovation and for having fostered considerable organizational innovation aiming to clear away traditional bureaucratic constraints, the question is whether the innovation-enhancing impact of New Public Management has been oversold. For while the emphasis on managerial autonomy, results orientation, performance management, and public-private competition might stimulate public sector innovation under certain circumstances, several constraints inherent to New Public Management tend to hamper innovation in general and collaborative innovation in particular.

First, the attempt to remake public organizations so they work more like private firms—the basis of New Public Management—fails to appreciate and take into account the differences between the public and private sectors, particularly when it comes to the conditions for innovation (Koch and Hauknes 2005, 24–26). A key difference is that public organizations face a more complex, strict, and unforgiving "authorizing environment" than private organizations do (Bernier and Hafsi 2007). The clientele for innovation is often not very clear in public organizations, and recipients of public benefits and services often put a premium on stability and predictability rather than on change and innovation. Public managers refer to political leaders, who tend to be quite risk averse because they fear negative media coverage and voter reactions should the innovation fail and waste public money. Finally, public policies and services are embedded in thick layers of legal regulations, rights, and entitlements that reflect political compromises between government and opposition parties, as well as between public and private stakeholders, and this situation creates hard-to-change path dependences. Failing to recognize these sector-specific barriers to public innovation can be fatal.

The NPM reform program's persistent emphasis on creating external incentives through competitive pressures and performance management goes against the general observation that public innovation tends to be problem driven rather than incentive driven (Borins 2000). Admittedly problem-driven innovation is not antithetical to incentive-driven innovation, and incentives sometimes stimulate innovation (Zoghi, Mohr, and Meyer 2010). The implicit emphasis on the *extrinsic* motivation of public managers and employees to find new solutions to emerging problems and challenges, however, might crowd out the *intrinsic* motivation that is anchored in the professional identity of public sector workers, who tend to possess a high degree of public service motivation (Amabile, Hennessey, and Grossman 1986; Perry 1996). Telling public sector workers that they should innovate to stay in business, to avoid penalties, and to receive performance-related bonuses and rewards might undermine their motivation to improve processes and outcomes out of their compassion and their concern for the public interest, civic duty, and social justice.

The NPM perspective on innovation envisions it as an intentional activity based on a preformed agenda, idea, and strategy of public managers; however, this view has been criticized for missing the way that innovation emerges through interaction, mutual learning, and chance discoveries (Fuglsang 2010). Although Borins (2000) found strategic planning was a key driver of public sector innovation in the United States and Canada, "groping along" was also a significant way of producing public sector innovation. The managerial emphasis of New Public Management typically combines with a preference for radical, cost-saving innovations. Its preference for radical rather than incremental innovation thus raises the stakes for public managers who might end up becoming deeply frustrated and develop an "innovation-inferiority complex" when they search in vain for innovative ideas but fail to produce big, path-breaking innovations that lead to huge cost reductions while improving customer satisfaction.

Next, the emphasis on the operational autonomy of managers and administrative units favors in-house innovation and prevents external collaboration.

Managers are supposed to exploit their enhanced autonomy to create innovation and mobilize the ideas and resources of their departments or agencies in the pursuit of radical efficiencies. Managerial autonomy exists within well-defined fiscal and legal boundaries, and the managers are expected to deliver some clearly defined results. Striving to meet a specific set of performance targets with a limited budget, though, will discourage managers from spending valuable resources on collaboration with other agencies and private stakeholders. Moreover, if managers fear that other agencies and actors will not really want to help them meet their performance targets, they will see the costs of collaborating as exceeding the gains. This is problematic in light of a major European research project that found "the *engagement of stakeholders* and extensive and ongoing *consultative and participatory processes* were key factors in initiating, sustaining and implementing innovation" (Koch and Hauknes 2005, 54, emphasis in original).

While creating quasi-markets with cutthroat competition between public and private service providers may encourage them to develop new and innovative services and methods for service delivery (Lubienski and Linick 2011), this competitive environment may prevent collaboration in the development phase and hamper innovation diffusion. In addition, the contracts regulating the service production of private contractors often fail to reward innovation. Rather, private contractors are paid to deliver a well-defined service that is described in great detail. The idea that innovative solutions developed by private contractors will spill over into the public sector may be more likely in theory than in practice.

Performance management creates a constant focus on results and improvements that might help spur innovation in public service organizations. However, it is no secret that performance management systems consume much time and energy that could be used in designing, testing, and implementing innovative ideas. Moreover, a rigorous implementation of performance management that links fulfilling performance targets with positive and negative sanctions may also create a risk-averse culture that prevents experimentation. Finally, the measurement of inputs and outputs of public service production will lead to a standardization of public services that, in turn, creates a disincentive to innovate for there is no guarantee that the performance measurement system will pick up and recognize the innovative features of a particular service (Moynihan 2013).

The recasting of citizens and public service users as customers operating in a service market where they can freely choose their service provider puts pressure on public organizations to maintain or increase their number of customers, especially if the money follows the customers. However, when users become customers, they also tend to behave as such in that they perceive public service as a good that others are supposed to deliver to them. As customers they do not feel they have responsibility either for its provision or for its quality and impact. This lack of responsibility makes it virtually impossible to involve the users in processes of coproduction and cocreation that could stimulate innovation.

Finally, the drive for efficiency inherent to the logic of New Public Management may undermine rather than spur innovation, because the experimentation necessary for innovation always entails a risk of waste (Potts 2009). The desire to improve efficiency can certainly drive innovation, but it requires slack, or excess, resources and a willingness to spend them in iterative rounds of design and experimentation (Bingham 1978; Fernández and Wise 2010). Public organizations that persistently have used lean techniques to eliminate slack might not have many resources left for designing and testing new solutions, and the general sentiment in lean-based organizations might run against the idea of spending money on risky projects with uncertain outcomes.

FROM NEW PUBLIC MANAGEMENT TO NEW PUBLIC GOVERNANCE

The global spread of public sector reforms inspired by NPM ideas attests to their immense popularity among politicians and executive managers (Pollitt and Bouckaert 2004). In the 1980s governments at all levels and in many countries sought alternatives to traditional forms of bureaucracy. The quest for greater efficiency through marketization and strategic performance management had considerable appeal in times of dire fiscal constraints and strong neoliberal currents. Thus, New Public Management gradually became a new fad and disseminated through recommendations from the Organization for Economic Cooperation and Development and the World Bank. The NPM paradigm fed the need of governments to gain legitimacy by doing what was considered the right thing to do (DiMaggio and Powell 1983). Not all countries fully embraced New Public Management, but most countries adopted reforms inspired by its core ideas.

The NPM reform program was sold not on its ability to spur innovation but on its promise to reduce public expenditure, to enhance the role of competition and private providers in public service production, and to modernize government by cutting red tape and stimulating strategic management, entrepreneurial leadership, and performance measurement. After more than two decades of reforms carried out under the NPM banner, we can see that the results are mixed. New Public Management reforms succeeded in enlisting a range of private contractors to produce public service in ways that contribute to cost savings and quality improvement in the more technical areas of service provision (Petersen, Houlberg, and Christensen 2015). The reforms have also improved the steering of public budgets, enhanced the responsibility and leadership competences of public managers, strengthened the organizational focus on objectives and results, created a new evaluation culture that encourages public employees to measure and do what works best in terms of programs and service, and shifted our attention more toward the needs and satisfaction of the users of public regulations and services. However, most of these good and positive achievements have now become a part of everyday life in most public organizations, and they therefore cannot function as signposts or guiding stars for the future development of the public sector.

At the same time, the focus on the unfulfilled promises of New Public Management has been increasing, with considerable disappointment found both in the public sector and among public administration researchers (Hood and Dixon 2015). Very limited evidence suggests that New Public Management has managed to strengthen organizational autonomy, to reduce the numbers of bureaucratic rules and procedures, to produce both cheaper and better public services by means of contracting out, and to improve the conditions for innovation and entrepreneurship. Moreover, the quest for higher efficiency through performance management tends to strengthen top-down control as the measurement of results becomes self-accelerating and extends to include the measurement of processes and the use of particular methods. When the measurement of results reveals poor or failing outcomes, politicians and executive managers often react by issuing new rules and regulations specifying how the service-producing agencies should produce and deliver services. Consequently, the number of bureaucratic rules increases rather than decreases (Danish Productivity Commission 2013).

Meanwhile, the evidence that contracting out leads to economic gains and service improvement is inconclusive and depends to a large extent on the nature and character of the service in question. Hence, standardized services with low asset specificity—typically found in the technical area (water supply, garbage collection, transportation, etc.)—seem to be most amenable to contracting out, whereas privatization of complex services that are difficult to define and measure often fails to improve economic efficiency without the erosion of quality (Petersen, Houlberg, and Christensen 2015). Further, the economic gains associated with outsourcing are typically a result of political decisions to reduce costs rather than a result of market competition. Finally, as we have seen, there are many explanations why New Public Management has failed to enhance the innovative capacity of the public sector despite its strong rhetoric about entrepreneurship, user focus, results orientation, and high-powered incentives.

Along with the failure of New Public Management to fulfill its initial ambitions, a growing amount of research literature has pointed out the presumably unintended but negative effects of NPM reforms (Christensen and Lægreid 2007). For one, the increased use of performance measurement generates considerable mistrust between those who measure and those whose performance is measured and tends to undermine the public service motivation of public employees when the auditing is perceived as controlling rather than supportive (Jacobsen, Hvidtved, and Andersen 2014). Arm's-length steering of specialized agencies and an increasing number of private contractors enhance organizational fragmentation and prevent adequate coordination (Rhodes 1997). Contracting out public services creates perverse effects when public employees with special skills and competences leave the public sector to work for private contractors who offer higher wages than they could get as public employees, when creaming and parking effects rise so private contractors can turn a profit in markets that are often far from lucrative, and when the costs of competitive tendering, setting up and monitoring contracts, and regulating the new quasi-markets eat up the gains incurred from enhanced competition (Le Grand 2003; Bozeman 2000; Hartman 2011; Vrangbæk, Petersen, and Hjelmar 2014). Turning citizens and users into customers who can choose between public and private providers tends to make them more demanding and less likely to see themselves as a part of the solution. Finally, placing elected politicians in the role of pilots who do the steering rather than the rowing seems to cause considerable frustration when their detachment from daily management and service provision reduces their role in developing public policy and in legitimizing the control systems (Boin, James, and Lodge 2006).

For all these reasons, and many more, people have started to ask themselves whether there is a life after New Public Management. What will the response to the problems of New Public Management and the challenges of modern governance look like? What will take the place of New Public Management as the predominant public administration paradigm? Whereas some researchers merely talk about "post–New Public Management" (Christensen and Lægreid 2011; Christensen 2012), others dream of a "neo-Weberian state" based on the reign of public bureaucracy, the praise of public values, an enhanced civic responsiveness, and a reinvigorated public leadership (Pollitt and Bouckaert 2004; Lynn 2008). Osborne offers a more comprehensive NPM alternative when he outlines the main features of New Public Governance (Osborne 2006, 2010). The differences between New Public Management and New Public Governance are shown in table 10.1.

TABLE 10.1. Comparing new public management and new public governance

	New Public Management	New Public Governance
Foundational view	Opportunistic behavior founded on information asymmetry must be reduced through control-based performance management	Self-interest is supplemented by a high degree of public service motivation that must be enhanced through trust-based management
Problem	Public monopoly makes service too poor and too expensive	Growing number of wicked and unruly problems
Solution	Enhance market-based competition and high-powered incentives	Public-private collaboration through governance networks, partnerships, and relational contracting
Overall goal	Increase effectiveness through persistent efforts to rationalize and cut slack	Increase effectiveness, quality, and public problem solving through innovation
Role of politicians	Provide an overall steering of the administration by defining targets and allocating budget	Act as leaders of the political community by defining problems and goals and developing new policy solutions
Role of managers	Strategic management of their department or agency while focusing on input and output	Manage intraorganizational teams and interorganizational interactions while focusing on process and results
Role of employees	Function as service-minded providers who aim to understand and satisfy the needs of the customers and who are predominantly driven by extrinsic motivation	Operate as enablers and facilitators who work to discover and mobilize the citizens' resources and who are predominantly driven by intrinsic motivation
Conception of citizens	Customers making rational choices between service providers	Active citizens engaged in coproducing public services

While New Public Management perceives increased control and positive and negative incentives as necessary to curtail the opportunistic behavior of self-interested social and political actors, New Public Governance assumes that public sector actors have mixed motives. In the public sector, the actors' self-interest is combined with a high degree of public service motivation. The latter is undermined by the enhancement of control-based performance management. However, it can be augmented by the creation of a trust-based management and leadership that involves a low degree of ruled-based work structuration, limits performance measurement to a handful of shared objectives, includes staff in a broad range of management decisions, establishes the mechanisms for providing mutual feedback between managers and employees, and makes persistent efforts to empower staff members (Nyhan 2000).

The perception of the main challenges facing the public sector and of how they are going to be addressed also radically changes when seen from the perspective of New Public Governance. The problem is not the public monopoly on service production as that monopoly has already been broken, and the solution is not more market-based competition. Rather, the problem is the growing number of intractable problems that can only be solved by bringing together the relevant and affected stakeholders from the public and private sectors in fruitful exchange and constructive collaboration. Further, the goal is to make the public sector more effective not by deploying different rationalization techniques but by enhancing its efficacy, quality, and general capacity for public problem solving through innovation.

The roles of politicians, public managers, and public employees are also different in New Public Governance as compared to New Public Management. Politicians should act as political leaders of the political community and engage in collaborative policy innovation rather than being reduced to a goal-setting appendix to the executive administrative leadership that is in charge of strategically developing the public sector. Public managers should focus on creating constructive processes of collaboration between agencies, departments, and the private sector and on ensuring desirable outcomes of interactive governance processes rather than merely being preoccupied with the performance of their own agency, department, or silo and how it utilizes resources. Finally, the role of public employees is transformed from being providers of public services who fulfill the needs of the citizens to being facilitators of coproduced services who presuppose the active involvement of users and volunteers. These role transformations are all induced by the collaborative aspect of New Public Governance that aims to bring all relevant resources and ideas into play.

Last but not least, New Public Governance seeks to change the understanding of citizens as customers acting as informed, rational, and sovereign choosers in the public-private marketplace to instead active citizens who are expected and encouraged to contribute to public governance and service production. In this perspective, setting up user boards, digital self-service, and remote rehabilitation of elderly people, for instance, are merely the first steps in developing the cocreating citizen. The ambition is to ensure that citizens will use the resources and competences they have to coproduce not only their own welfare services but also services that can benefit other citizens and solutions that can improve society at large. The ultimate goal is to cultivate an active citizenry that co-initiates, co-designs, and co-implements public policies and services.

Adding a third governance paradigm to the existing governance paradigms and having them coexist in messy and contradictory ways will undoubtedly increase the complexity of public governance. The result will be extremely demanding. Public and private actors will not only be expected to move in and out of competing paradigmatic logics but also will be forced to deal with hybrid forms of governance that are elements from different governance paradigms fused into an institutional mechanism with unintended and erratic effects (Christensen and Lægreid 2011). To illustrate, as local governments begin to measure the activity and contribution of a growing number of volunteers engaged in public-private coproduction, the volunteers lose their motivation when they feel that they are subjected to a systemic control regime that is foreign to the voluntary sector.

NEW PUBLIC GOVERNANCE AS A TRIGGER FOR COLLABORATIVE INNOVATION

While both classical forms of bureaucracy and NPM reforms can enhance public innovation, expectations are high that New Public Governance can further accelerate public innovation in general and collaborative innovation in particular (Hartley, Sørensen, and Torfing 2013). Not only has New Public Governance put innovation high on the public sector agenda but also its new thinking about how to organize, govern, and manage the public sectors provides key drivers of collaborative innovation. Let us briefly highlight five of the key drivers of collaborative innovation that will most likely be triggered by public sector reforms under New Public Governance.

Trust-Based Leadership and Management

The commitment and active engagement of public employees will increase if the intensive and costly control and monitoring system in the public sector is toned down and if public leadership and management are founded on a general but calculated trust in the professional knowledge, competences, and intrinsic motivation of the public employees (Nyhan 2000; Covey 2006; Covey and Link 2012). Further, if public managers reduce the number of performance targets to a minimum, eliminate unnecessary bureaucratic rules, and empower the professionally trained staff through a combination of delegation, training, and recognition, then they will greatly enhance the space for creative problem solving and crosscutting collaboration. Such a development will unleash the innovative potential of frontline personnel. These moves will allow public employees not only to build their public service motivation but also to use the widened room for empowered action to work with each other and with external actors to create new and better services to the benefit of the citizens and the public sector as a whole. It will be especially effective if the public leaders and managers work closely together to put innovation high on their agenda and support it with a strong innovation culture in which innovation is encouraged, appreciated, and rewarded.

Vertical and Horizontal Integration

The prospect for collaborative innovation will increase if the vertical, control-fixated, arm's-length governance of public agencies is replaced with a more integrated and trust-based governance that brings together principals and agents in a continued dialogue based on jointly formulated objectives (Schillemans 2013). In this scenario, public leaders with their policy ambitions and resource management and frontline personnel with their professional aspirations and experiences will work in tandem to create new ways of doing things. At the same time, the flow of knowledge, ideas, and resources between public organizations as well as between public and private actors will improve if they reduce the horizontal fragmentation of public bureaucracies. Such fragmentation is caused by the ongoing recruitment of private contractors and the proliferation of special-purpose agencies. The actors can lessen its impact by creating new arenas for exchange and coordination between public and private contractors and by introducing new forms of joined-up government that link government agencies across administrative silos (Eggers and Singh 2009; Fenger and Bekkers 2012). In turn, the horizontal flow of dialogue between public and private actors facing the same problems and challenges will stimulate the development and realization of innovative solutions. In sum, reforms aiming to improve vertical and horizontal integration will enhance the public sector's connective capacity, which is a key driver of innovation (Christensen and Lægreid 2011). An important condition for the connective capacity to spur innovation, however, is that there must be a strong focus on mutual, expansive, and transformative learning in the dialogue between the public and private actors.

Collaboration in Partnerships and Networks

As persistently argued throughout this book, a problem-focused collaboration between public and private stakeholders in partnerships and networks will improve the understanding of problems and challenges and enhance the richness and quality of the ideas for new solutions. Such collaboration will also foster a joint ownership of public innovations that, in turn, will increase the chance of smoothly and successfully implementing step changes (Eggers and Singh 2009; Sørensen and Torfing 2011). Networks and partnerships are often formed merely to promote information exchange and facilitate pluricentric coordination, but they can also play a crucial role in creating and diffusing innovation. Whereas the former is conditioned by the exercise of innovation management, the latter is conditioned by the actors' willingness and opportunity to circulate and discuss innovative ideas in and through face-to-face meetings that bring together public employees within and across different sectors.

Active Citizenship

If the customerization of citizens and users is halted and replaced with an active citizenship that aims to empower and encourage people to contribute to the production and delivery of service to themselves as well as to other citizens and users through voluntarism, then coproduction and cocreation will go hand in hand. The citizens' needs, experiences, and ideas will thus drive service innovation and change the organizational systems for service delivery, as well as the role of the public sector vis-à-vis the private sector (Bovaird and

Loeffler 2012). Hence, the active participation of empowered citizens in coproducing public welfare will enable them to initiate innovation processes and facilitate collaboration with public employees in designing and implementing innovative solutions (Bekkers, Tummers, and Voorberg 2013). The chief conditions for a happy marriage between coproduction and cocreation are that the public sector—that is, public employees, public managers, and elected officials—must be open to the citizens' input and must develop a systematic way of harvesting and assessing the ideas advanced by collaborating citizens and voluntary organizations that are contributing to the production of public value (Lees-Marshment 2015; Nabatchi and Leighninger 2015).

Strengthening the Political Leadership Role of Politicians

If elected politicians stop acting either as goal setters and controllers of executive managers or as ideologically pure media stars and instead assume the difficult task of working as political leaders who define problems, give direction to and participate in formulating new solutions, and generate support for new, bold solutions (Tucker 1995), then they will enhance policy innovation and spur innovations both in public services and in the processes and organizations through which these services are produced and delivered. Engaging elected politicians in formulating and realizing innovative solutions to the burning issues of our time will strengthen their role as political leaders. Further, it will also turn them into drivers of policy innovation who reformulate problem definitions, redefine the objectives, design new policy instruments, and transform the way that policies are implemented. However, because politicians need input from the administration, scientific experts, organized interests, and citizens to develop and implement new and innovative policy solutions, political leadership will only spur innovation if public managers also help construct institutional arenas for collaborative policy innovation (Sørensen and Torfing 2016; Ansell and Torfing 2016).

Some evidence reveals that politicians at the local level are attempting to bolster the political leadership by engaging in processes of collaborative policy innovation. In Denmark more than half of the local municipalities have created collaborative policy arenas in which elected politicians work with local stakeholders to develop new policies (Sørensen and Torfing 2013). At the national level, collaborative policy innovation may sometimes take place in public hearings and public commissions that are involved in preparing new policies. However, the lack of administrative support to elected politicians, the absence of forums for dialogue with relevant and affected actors, and the short-termism imposed by the mass media and the election cycle make it difficult for national politicians to engage in collaborative policy innovation. Thus, the working conditions for national politicians must be reformed before they can become more actively involved in cocreating public policies with citizens and private stakeholders.

On the one hand, while these five drivers of collaboration require a careful empirical evaluation and thus call for further research, they clearly demonstrate the potential of New Public Governance for spurring collaborative innovation. Thus, it appears that we will have to transform governance in order to enhance innovation. On the other hand, however, New Public Governance does have some drawbacks that we should not gloss over. Many barriers to innovation that are associated with New Public Governance also confront collaborative innovation and need no further explanation. Here we will briefly review three important barriers to innovation in a public sector dominated solely by ideas and practices associated with New Public Governance.

First of all, collaborators will lack incentives to innovate if all forms of competition are eliminated. Competition between different networks and partnerships seems to be an important driver of collaborative innovation (Powell and Grodal 2004). Second, without hierarchical control and steering, the risk is that public and private actors will spend all their energy and resources in seemingly endless processes of brainstorming, deliberation, and consultation without producing a clear and tangible result. Thus, failing to give directions, set overall goals, and monitor results is fatal to the attempt to jump-start collaborative innovation. Finally, implementing new solutions might suffer from the lack of funding, the dispersion of responsibility, and the absence of rule-based coordination in multi-actor settings. Hence, dismissing the virtues of bureaucracy may result in the accumulation of innovative ideas and solutions that never are properly implemented.

While these typical barriers to innovation in collaborative environments are sustained by New Public Governance, the attempt to avoid them calls for preserving, and perhaps rearticulating, key elements of Old Public Administration and New Public Management. Whereas New Public Management may infuse collaborative innovation processes with varying degrees of competition and results orientation, bureaucracy provides the tools for securing the implementation of innovative solutions in multi-actor settings. In sum, a certain mix of governance paradigms seems to be helpful in optimizing the processes, outputs, and outcomes of collaborative innovation.

CAN WE TRANSFORM THE PUBLIC SECTOR TO ENHANCE COLLABORATIVE INNOVATION?

Ideas and practices associated with Old Public Administration and New Public Management have proved their value in producing public governance, and they will probably continue to exist as fundamental layers of the public sector. However, as hinted earlier, adding a new layer of New Public Governance to the existing layers of governance is likely to stimulate collaborative innovation on public policies, organizational designs, and public services. Because changing the basic conception of how to organize, govern, and manage the public sector is notoriously difficult, the question becomes whether we can shift the balance from New Public Management to New Public Governance in order to improve the conditions for public sector innovation.

Pollitt and Bouckaert (2004) have developed a general model for analyzing public administration reforms, and the two basic conditions for triggering these reforms—socioeconomic forces and new ideas and developments in the political-administrative system—seem to be fulfilled. Current socioeconomic conditions—for example, economic recession, demographic pressures, climate change, new migration patterns, and social exclusion of citizens with poor education, lack of employment, and low income—require new, better, and more efficient solutions. This situation calls for public administration reform, for it is hard to believe that New Public Management can continue to deliver the same level of improvements that it produced in the 1980s and 1990s. Hence, the effect of NPM reforms such as contracting out, which initially produced considerable effectivity gains, seems to be waning (Petersen, Hjelmar, and Vrangbæk 2015). According to the public administration reform model, the socioeconomic pressures for change must be matched by new political and administrative ideas that can inspire creative reform initiatives. This condition also appears to be fulfilled since New Public Governance has received growing attention both in international research and among public sector practitioners (Salamon 2002; Osborne 2006, 2010 Koppenjan 2012; Torfing and Triantafillou 2013; Ansell and Torfing 2014; Morgan and Cook 2014).

In much the same way that New Public Management succeeded in identifying some new and important empirical trends in the public sector and giving them a name (Hood 1991), New Public Governance aims to provide a label for the current trends in terms of organizational integration, networks, collaboration, and active citizenship. A clear and consistent definition of New Public Governance is not important in the present situation; rather, the name itself makes it possible for people to imagine and talk about an alternative to New Public Management and ascribe to it a variety of qualities and promises.

Public management reforms are accomplished by the political and administrative elites who balance what they consider as desirable changes with those that they think are possible to make (Pollitt and Bouckaert 2004). Relatively few obstacles impede reforms that try to bring the public sector closer to the ideas inherent to New Public Governance. Indeed, its elements of organizational integration, networking, collaboration, and more active citizen participation have already spread rapidly. At the local level especially, public administrators have been eager to find ways of mobilizing the competences, resources, and ideas of private actors in a joint effort to solve the growing number of complex problems in new and better ways (Warren 2009). The big question is, therefore, whether the national political and administrative elites consider the reforms inspired by New Public Governance as desirable. Although they may be under pressure from below to move in this direction, undoubtedly the NPM paradigm, with its tight budget control and strict performance management, gives the executive political and administrative leaders considerable power, and they might lose it should New Public Governance inspire reform initiatives.

A certain path dependency also works against governance reforms because the executive level is familiar with the current couplet of classical bureaucracy and New Public Management and tends to believe that this system is the only way to pursue radical efficiencies. However, Tony Blair's government in the United Kingdom and the Obama administration took a number of public management reform initiatives that are akin to New Public Governance, and the Netherlands, Norway, and Denmark have long corporatist traditions that seem to be moving more and more in the direction of New Public Governance. Exactly how the interaction between different political and administrative elites and the institutional and cultural traditions plays out in different countries requires a much more detailed study than it is possible to offer here. Some signs, at least, indicate that the public sector is being transformed yet again, and it might well move in a direction that will make collaborative innovation a part of its DNA.

CONCLUSION

This chapter has linked the demand for public innovation with the much larger question of public administration policy and the need for public sector reforms. Instead of writing off classical bureaucracy and New Public Management as the ultimate barriers to collaborative innovation and calling for a complete removal of these well-established forms of public governance, the chapter has shown how bureaucratic forms of governance and market-based forms of governance associated with New Public Management contain both drivers of and barriers to the enhancement of public innovation. Further, the analysis has also revealed how public sector reforms inspired by New Public Governance can help boost public innovation in general and collaborative innovation in particular. However, the limitations of New Public Governance seem to suggest that both Old Public Administration and New Public Management have an important role to play in the future as they can facilitate and support collaborative innovation in the public sector. Thus, the construction of a mixed governance regime that combines different public administration paradigms is preferable to a complete shift to New Public Governance that prevents us from reaping the fruits of the former paradigms.

CONCLUSION

Summary Propositions about Collaborative Innovation

THIS BOOK has sought to open a new avenue for cross-disciplinary social science research by making two major claims: A persistent and systematic endeavor to enhance innovation may help the public sector do more and better with less, and collaboration between multiple actors inside and outside of government constitutes a key driver of public innovation. The hope is that academic scholars, postgraduate students, and practitioners in and around the public sector will take on the challenge of exploring further the ways that collaboration can be spurred and harnessed to create new and innovative solutions that can improve public services, break policy deadlocks, and make organizations and delivery systems more efficient. Perhaps they can even rethink the role of the public sector so that it can develop new and better solutions that are delivered in new and better ways (Eggers and Macmillan 2013). The goal, however, is not to have more or less government but to improve the functioning and impact of government to the benefit of citizens, voluntary organizations, private firms, and others who depend on government being smart, effective, and responsive.

The book has drawn on a wide variety of theoretical and intellectual sources to make the strongest possible case for collaborative innovation in the public sector and to show how each of the constitutive phases of public innovation processes can be strengthened through collaborative interaction that brings together relevant and affected actors. Theoretical arguments have been advanced, scrutinized, improved, and integrated; analytical distinctions have been drawn; empirical insights have been invoked; and examples of collaborative innovations from around the world have been used to illustrate key points. Now it is time to take stock and briefly revisit the arguments that have been made. This is done by presenting a number of propositions that summarize and sharpen the main findings.

Chapter 1 aimed to define and contextualize the notion of innovation. The recent focus on public innovation is part of a new discourse on constant reform and transformation that, allegedly, intends to enhance efficiency in the public sector. In its most exaggerated and perverse forms, the pursuit of organizational and managerial change becomes a goal in itself rather than a means to an end. Nevertheless, the successful problematization of the traditional bureaucratic virtues of stability, order, and predictability creates a new and welcome opportunity to talk about public innovation and to use innovation as a tool for improving public policies, organizations, and services to the benefit of citizens, society, and the public and private economy.

Innovation is defined as the development and realization, and frequently also the spread, of new and creative ideas. On the one hand, innovation is more than a continuous improvement that merely adjusts existing practices, and on the other hand, it is less than a radical transformation that replaces one fully integrated action system with another one. Innovation involves a step change that breaks with the common wisdom and established practices in a certain context by combining old and new elements in original and creative ways. It is a contingent and combined process driven by the ambition to do new things in new ways. Thus, it is proposed:

> Innovation is a multidimensional, complex, and potentially chaotic process that analytically can be divided into five constitutive phases: defining problems, generating ideas, selecting ideas, implementing new solutions, and diffusing new ideas and practices.

In the public sector, innovation processes will produce public rather than private value. Hence, public innovations will yield innovative public goods or services; more efficient, effective, and democratic organizations, processes, and forms of governance; or innovative policies and discourses that transform our problem-solving strategies and the way that we think about society and the role of government. There are plenty of empirical examples of public innovation, and more are generated by the day. Indeed, the public sector appears to be much more dynamic and innovative than its reputation would suggest. The problem is that public innovation tends to be episodic and linked to accidental events, and, as a consequence, we fail to enhance the innovative capacity of the public sector. Thus, it is proposed:

> We need a new innovation agenda in the public sector that aims to turn innovation into a permanent and systematic activity that pervades the entire public sector from top to bottom and inside out. At the same time, we should be careful not to see public innovation as a goal in itself; rather, it is merely a tool for improving the functioning and impact of government.

The standard references when explaining the limits to public innovation are the presence of hierarchy, administrative silos, and red tape and the absence of competition and economic incentives. However, listing the many barriers to public innovation cannot hide the fact that there are also numerous drivers of public innovation: new and changing demands, high political and professional ambitions, systematic performance reviews, a large budget that can absorb the cost of failure, and so forth. Indeed, there are many reasons to think that a conscious and strategic effort to enhance public innovation will have a good chance of becoming successful.

To avoid being carried away by overoptimistic expectations about the prospect and impact of public innovation, it is important to elude the pro-innovation bias that too readily asserts that public innovation is always called for, always successful, and always leads to improvement (Hartley 2006). Hence, it is proposed:

> First, the decision to search for innovative solutions in the public sector should always rest on a careful analysis of what works and what does not work, as well as on a thorough assessment of the uncertainty and risks of innovating. Second, it normally takes several failures to produce a successful innovation with discernible and desirable effects. Third, innovation does not always lead to improvements, and improvements are not always a result of innovation.

Chapter 2 sought to explain why and how collaborative interaction can drive innovation. In the last decades, there has been growing interest in interactive forms of governance that seem to offer an alternative to the traditional notion of government. That notion focuses on formal political institutions and fails to capture the multifarious, messy, and potentially chaotic processes through which public and private actors interact to govern society and the economy. Interactive governance covers a large array of governance arrangements including quasi-markets based on relational contracts, public-private partnerships, and governance networks that may comprise many different kinds of actors such as private firms, civil society actors, and citizens.

Since the discovery of network-type governance in the early 1970s, the study of governance across a broad variety of social science disciplines has grown exponentially. Gradually the initial attempts to explain the emergence of networked governance and the composition and internal dynamics of networks gave way to new research focusing on the potential and actual impact of governance networks and how desirable outcomes can be ensured through metagovernance of more or less self-governing networks. Most scholars were mainly concerned with how governance networks could contribute to making public policy and governance more effective by enhancing knowledge sharing and coordination, but others have expressed interest in how interactive forms of governance contribute to democratizing society by promoting political empowerment, participation, and deliberation. More recently, researchers have explored how interactive governance can spur innovation in ways that may enhance effective and democratic governance or help realize other important public sector goals such as equity, transparency, and environmental sustainability. Thus, it is proposed:

> Interactive forms of governance in networks, partnerships, and other arenas of multilateral action provide an important tool for spurring public innovation, which in turn may lead to more effective and democratic governance and help to achieve other important goals of the public sector.

Governance networks are complex structures that consist of a large set of relations and non-relations between social and political actors who need to exchange or pool knowledge, resources, and ideas to solve common problems or achieve particular goals. The networked interaction between relevant and affected actors in a certain area provides the conditions for the emergence of multi-actor collaboration. Social and political actors may share information and coordinate their actions to avoid overlaps and create synergies, but they may also aspire to collaborate in order to define common problems and search for joint solutions through a process of negotiation that may span the whole register from open-ended deliberation to hard-nosed bargaining. The problem with collaboration is that it is often associated with a cumbersome search for unanimous consent. Total consensus is hard to achieve and will often be founded in the least common denominator, which seldom fosters ambitious and innovative solutions. Indeed, the tensions and conflicts between different actors often drive the processes of creative problem solving. Therefore, what is important in collaboration is not to eliminate conflicts but to harness them by finding constructive ways of managing differences. Thus, it is proposed:

> Collaboration should be defined as a process through which two or more actors exchange views, ideas, and resources to define and work on a common object. When working together to transform their common object, the actors manage cognitive and ideational differences and social and political conflicts in ways that facilitate a provisional agreement on joint goals and solutions that may coexist with varying degrees of dissent.

Governance networks may be sites of destructive conflicts and antagonistic struggles between self-interested actors trying to get their way, but they may also enable collaboration through which different actors can find a common ground for creative problem solving. The collaborative aspect of interactive governance arenas is important as it provides a potent lever for spurring public innovation. Thus, it is proposed:

> Each of the constitutive phases in the complex and contingent innovation cycle can be strengthened in and through processes of multi-actor collaboration. As such, it enhances the understanding of the problems and challenges at hand, the generation of new ideas, the selection and testing of the most promising solutions, the implementation of new and bold ideas, and the dissemination of innovative practices within and across public organizations.

Empirically we are witnessing the development of different strategies, forums, and arenas for collaborative innovation. Underlying this development is the recognition that public innovation is a team sport rather than an individual achievement. However, the causal relationship between collaboration and innovation in the different parts of the innovation cycle may be interrupted by contingent factors that prevent us from reaping the fruits of collaborative innovation.

Fortunately collaboration is not the only way of enhancing public innovation. Public bureaucracies may deploy their strong leadership, huge resources, and rule-based routines in the search for innovative solutions to old, new, and emerging problems. Their authoritative decision making will help swiftly determine the nature and character of the problems and weigh the costs and benefits of alternative solutions. Mutual rivalry will encourage market-based actors to think outside the box, and the competitive logic will prevent established authorities from controlling and putting a lid on the creative processes. However, the innovative potential of hierarchies and markets has inherent limits, which are evidenced by the fact that both public agencies and private firms rely too much on in-house innovation. In recognizing these limits, chapter 2 proposes:

> Collaboration holds a major advantage vis-à-vis hierarchy and markets when it comes to fostering innovation. Collaboration allows multiple actors to share, scrutinize, and build on each other's ideas and work across established organizational and sectorial boundaries that tend to prevent both public hierarchies and private firms from tapping into the ideas and competences of external actors.

In advancing a theory of collaborative innovation, chapter 3 helps us conceptualize and understand the conditions, forms, functioning, and impact of collaborative innovation. The initial formation of this new field of research drew on hitherto unrelated theories of collaborative governance and public innovation. However, in the attempt to avoid a purely descriptive, anecdotal, and impressionistic account of instances of collaborative innovation by advancing a purpose-built theoretical framework, we should not go to the polar extreme of developing a general theory that subsumes empirical cases of collaborative innovation under a few law-like hypotheses grounded in abstract and reductive assumptions about the nature of politics, society, and human behavior. Instead, it is proposed:

> We should develop a problem-driven study of collaborative innovation that uses theory as a pragmatic tool for advancing our understanding of puzzles and problems while at the same time allowing theoretical concepts and stipulations to be challenged and revised in light of new empirical observations and insights.

The problems to be addressed through a constant oscillation between theoretical and empirical insights are set out in chapter 3 and structure the rest of the book. In the initial search for a theoretical point of departure to help us better understand the conditions and dynamic of collaborative innovation, the traditional theories of public administration are scrutinized, and the result is disappointing. Hence, despite a few positive exceptions, traditional public administration theory holds a rather pessimistic view of the prospect of public innovation. A more encouraging theoretical starting point is found in theories of collaborative planning, research on innovation systems, participatory science, technology and society studies, and the new design thinking. Thus, it is suggested:

> Whereas mainstream public administration theory has little to offer in terms of advancing a theory of collaborative innovation, interdisciplinary theories at the borders between public governance studies and sociology, institutional economics and organization studies, and business economics and design theory provide valuable insights into how collaboration can spur public innovation.

To build a robust theoretical framework for studying the many different aspects of collaborative innovation in the public sector, the insights from the four precursors to a theory of collaborative innovation are combined with central insights from other theories that can shed light on the puzzles and problems of collaborative innovations addressed in this book. Hence, theoretical building blocks from innovation theory, discourse theory, institutional theory, theories of learning and systems, and complexity theory are invoked to capture the intricacies of collaborative innovation. They all seem to be compatible with the theory of collaborative network governance, which offers a good starting point for theory building in this area.

Further, the recently developed models of collaborative governance inspired by Ostrom, Gardner, and Walker's (1994) institutional analysis and development framework can be used to sketch a simple analytical model that allows us to understand the conditions, dynamics, and outcomes of collaborative innovation. The model assumes that collaborative processes intended to spur innovation are imbedded in institutional arenas of networked interaction. A number of initial conditions affect the institutional arenas and the processes of collaborative innovation they facilitate, and the institutional arenas themselves provide drivers and barriers for collaborative innovation. They call for innovation leadership and management that can be seen as a form of metagovernance. Under the right conditions, the processes of collaborative innovation will produce different forms of public innovation, the outcomes of which are evaluated on the basis of different values, standards, and methods. Therefore, it is proposed:

> Contingent historical contexts, institutional arenas, collaborative interaction, specific drivers and barriers, and particular forms of leadership and management interact in the production of public innovation.

Chapter 4 analyzed the triggers of innovation and the collaborative efforts to foster innovation. Given that change and innovation are painful and disrupt our identities, roles, and habits, the initiation of an innovation process requires more than positive stimuli in terms of good ideas about how to improve performance by doing things in a new and smarter way. Crises caused by internal or external developments may force public organizations to adopt new and innovative solutions, but stable procedures for evaluating performance, exploring new ideas, and exploiting the most promising ones may also prove effective in spurring innovation. The difficulty with determining a priori whether uncertain crises or stable routines will trigger public innovation calls for a different approach to analyzing the initiation of innovation. Therefore, it is proposed:

> When looking for the triggers of public innovation, we should hunt for the serious and threatening problems that tend to push public organizations down the road to innovation and the stimulating challenges and new opportunities that pull public organizations toward an open-ended search for innovative solutions.

Both crisis situations and the routinized search for innovative solutions feed on problems, challenges, and new opportunities that seem to be the real triggers of innovation. However, given that not all problems, challenges, and opportunities spur innovation processes, we need to look for the special conditions that turn them into innovation drivers. The analysis proposes that three conditions are particularly important:

> The discursive construction of a sense of urgency; the contextual factors that make certain events, problems, challenges, and opportunities stand out; and the presence of social and political actors with enough curiosity, vision, skills, and courage to initiate and drive innovation.

Some actors might consider themselves as strong and resourceful enough to pursue a go-it-alone strategy and create their own innovation solution, which they can then try to impose on the other actors in the field. Such go-it-alone strategies are likely to spur conflict and antagonism and produce externalities that might give rise to expensive legal disputes. Multi-actor collaboration provides a welcome alternative. Undoubtedly not only the creativeness, capacity, and scope of public innovations but also the prospect for their realization, consolidation, and spread will benefit tremendously from the involvement of and mutual exchange between the relevant and affected actors. However, there is no guarantee that the institutionally situated social and political actors will choose a collaborative strategy when pursuing public innovation. The analysis proposes that six conditions are crucial for the emergence of collaborative innovation:

> Structural conditions in terms of social, political, and economic turbulence that call for a collective response; the tradition and past experience with collaboration that may vary between countries, levels, and policy areas; the existence of social capital in terms of a web of social contacts and relationships based on generalized and specific trust; the interest and identity-based calculations of the potential collaborators; the extent to which actors are unified by discursively constructed story lines and metaphors; and the dramaturgical effects created through the setting, staging, and scripting of the interaction between relevant and affected actors.

Depending on these crucial factors, collaborative innovation offers a promising strategy for enhancing innovation in the public sector.

Today the call for improving crosscutting collaboration is particularly important as there is an urgent need to counter the increasing horizontal and vertical fragmentation of the public sector caused by the recent experiences with New Public Management. This management system has recommended increasing contracting out of public services, creating special-purpose agencies, formally splitting political steering and administrative service production, and expanding the arm's-length governance of public agencies. In contrast, collaboration is helpful in bringing together public and private actors and facilitating their exchange and pooling of resources, competences, and ideas to get things done. However, in the midst of the pragmatic and managerial appraisal of interagency and cross-sector collaboration, we should not forget two points: There is always a limit to the inclusion of relevant and affected actors, and the process of including and excluding actors involves the exercise of power—namely, political power. Thus, the following is proposed:

> Because the actors who are included in processes of collaborative innovation will be able to influence the outputs and outcomes that other groups of actors will often evaluate differently, the important decisions about who should be included and excluded in the collaborative arenas and about how much influence the participating actors should have are strictly political. They involve the exercise of power and, therefore, require the involvement of elected politicians, or other actors, with democratic legitimacy.

Thus, two factors influence the external exclusion and internal sidelining of participants in collaborative arenas—the actual decisions of the (democratically) authorized power holders and the discursive framing of the problems, challenges, and opportunities that trigger and drive public innovation. The framing enables some actors, and not others, to justify and validate their claims to be represented; consequently, it creates asymmetric opportunities for the actors to voice their opinions and influence the process of collaborative innovation. Therefore, it is proposed:

> We need to analyze the structural and discursive forms of power that pervade collaborative arenas and determine the scope for social and political actors to use their free, responsible, and empowered actions in the pursuit of public innovation.

Chapter 5 reviewed the conditions and strategies for mobilizing and empowering actors and institutionalizing their interaction to facilitate collaborative innovation. Three types of actors are important to engage in collaborative innovation processes: the affected actors who have experience with the problems or are impacted by the new and innovative solutions; the relevant actors who possess knowledge, competences, and ideas; and intermediaries and boundary spanners who can facilitate the dialogue and constructive exchange between actors with different vocabularies, views, and visions. Getting all these actors on board can be difficult due to negative past experiences and the lack of tradition and incentives. Not only must the conveners then have the sufficient social capital to draw on a large network of contacts but they must also play an active role in convincing the relevant, affected actors of the urgency of the problem and the desirability of an innovative solution and help persuade them that the benefits of collaborating far exceed the efforts in terms of time and energy.

Now since the context-bound calculations of social and political actors are based on their particular identities, it appears that their active involvement in processes of collaborative innovation hinges on the particular way they are addressed. Thus, the analysis suggests:

> The promotion of collaborative innovation calls for recasting the identity of politicians as *organic political leaders*, public managers and employees as *network entrepreneurs*, citizens as *cocreators*, interest organizations and nongovernmental organizations as *social partners*, and private firms as *stakeholders* with a strong corporate social responsibility.

Cultivating these or similar identities will help mobilize the relevant and affected actors in collaborative innovation, but to facilitate their interaction—that is, to get them to share their different experiences and exchange their knowledge and ideas—a bond between the actors must be constructed. In sum, it is proposed:

> The clarification, reinforcement, or creation of relationships of mutual resource dependence and the discursive construction of a community of destiny are crucial conditions for facilitating collaborative interaction among the relevant and affected actors.

What the participating actors bring to the table and how they contribute to the collective processes of creative problem solving depend on the empowerment and disempowerment of the actors. Empowerment involves enhancing the rights, resources, competences, knowledge, organizational capacities, and political know-how of the actors. Conscious efforts and long-term strategies for empowering citizens and private actors are important for collaborative processes to have a real impact on the public sector's innovative capacity. Therefore, as collaboration tends to thrive in settings where power resources are relatively evenly distributed, it is sometimes necessary to disempower strong and self-interested actors who resist engaging in a proper dialogue with other actors and instead want to dictate the content of the innovative solution and impose it on the other actors. Thus, the following is proposed:

> We want not only to empower particular actors so that they can participate in collaborative processes and engage in a constructive exchange of ideas but also to disempower actors who are so strong and mighty that they are tempted to act independently and threaten to obstruct the

collaborative interaction between the actors. While the goal is not to make all actors equal in terms of their power resources and position in the network of actors, it is important to ensure that the power asymmetries are not so large that they prevent collaboration.

To ensure sustained interaction between the empowered actors and thus facilitate collaborative innovation in the face of different interests, power games, and conflicts, some degree of institutionalization is necessary. Institutionalization implies the formation of rules, norms, values, and procedures, as well as the distribution and control over legitimate resources. Institutionalizing interactive governance processes is important because it lowers the transaction costs, reduces uncertainty, and prevents destructive conflicts by defining some commonly agreed rules of the game and promoting normative integration. However, too much institutionalization can create rigidity and thus undermine the flexibility and innovation gains associated with interactive governance. Therefore, it is proposed:

> Public managers and other actors who are capable of governing interactive arenas and aim to foster collaborative innovation should strive to balance processes of institutionalization with processes of de-institutionalization in order to get the right mix between stable and sustained interaction, on the one hand, and flexibility and innovation, on the other hand.

Since there is no guarantee that sustained interaction between empowered actors in relatively institutionalized arenas will foster collaboration rather than competition, rivalry, and conflict, we need to explore how proactive measures such as trust building, game structuration, and process management can spur collaboration. Trust-building exercises among the actors involve recalling positive past experiences, interacting socially to develop personal bonds, jointly calculating how collaboration will make everyone better off, and establishing procedures for punishing opportunistic behaviors. Trust building can be supplemented with game-like structures that reward cooperative behavior and with process management techniques that aim to constructively manage differences through resolution or mediation of emerging conflicts.

Although trust building, game structuration, and process management involve the institutionalization of particular conditions for collaborative interaction, they all presuppose the presence of a strategic agency that seeks to enhance collaboration by manipulating the conditions for collaborative interaction. Facilitating collaborative interaction involves continuously shaping and reshaping the institutional conditions for cooperative behavior in response to interpretations of actual performance. In the beginning proactive efforts to encourage collaboration are often urgently required, but after a while collaborative processes tend to become self-sustaining as a virtuous circle between mutual trust and mutual benefits from collaboration emerges and becomes institutionalized. However, when the trust-benefit spiral breaks down, proactive measures are needed again. Thus, we can conclude:

> Collaboration between empowered actors in interactive arenas hinges on a complex interaction between processes of institutionalization and proactive strategic measures.

Chapter 6 explored how collaboration spurs innovation by means of stimulating mutual, expansive, and transformative learning. Collaboration stimulates learning, which enables the development of new and creative ways of understanding and solving complex problems, dealing with emerging challenges, and exploiting new opportunities. Circulating new and relevant information to the right actors at the right time produces a learning effect because it allows the recipients to do new things that break with the past. Such information is often shared in networks of public, private, and non-profit actors. Whereas some information networks consist of weak ties between relatively anonymous actors, other networks create strong collaborative ties as information is sent back and forth and triggers discussions of how to solve problems and challenges in new ways. The learning effect produced by information circulation remains captured in a simple stimuli-response model, according to which new information is supposed to promote behavioral changes. Thus, it is proposed:

> While the circulation of information may inspire actors to imitate solutions developed elsewhere, it does not produce learning in the strict sense of revising prior beliefs, ideas, and understandings that are results of critical reflection upon empirical and theoretical experiences.

Collective learning is interactive because it compares, juxtaposes, and aligns the reflections of different actors to accommodate their different and changing experiences. In the public sector, mutual learning may involve users and private stakeholders. Learning about, from, and with users and other stakeholders is crucial, for they might provide important inputs that challenge the views and ideas of the public actors and qualify the assessment of new and bold solutions. The typical form of mutual learning, however, takes place in communities of practice that are formed by public employees, often with different professional backgrounds, who work together and create situated learning to overcome the obstacles that they encounter in their daily working lives. While communities of practice may produce incremental innovations by using jointly developed repertoires, discourses, and styles to accomplish tasks in new and better ways, the production of more radical innovations requires an external disturbance of the logic of appropriate action dominating a particular community of practice. Therefore, it is proposed:

> Interorganizational, or cross-sectorial, communities of practice based on multidisciplinarity, mutual recognition, and problem-focused communication may have a larger innovative potential than intraorganizational communities of practice.

Learning can be factual as well as normative and facilitate the socialization of newcomers to a particular community of practice. Learning can also be instrumental and take the form of reflexive problem solving, which aims either to match well-known solutions to emerging problems through trial and error or to experiment and adapt existing solutions to meet new challenges. In addition, learning may be expansive in that it broadens the repertoire of solutions through a coherent understanding of contexts, problems, and new possibilities that are revealed during a communicative search for new ways of thinking that give meaning to the unknown. While expansive learning creates innovative solutions by generating and interpreting new insights in continuation with established insights, transformative learning uses critical reflection to problematize accepted knowledge and thus changes both the subject of learning and the conditions for interpreting and acting in the world. Therefore, it is proposed:

> The ability of collaborative processes to foster new, creative, and potentially disruptive solutions depends on the development of expansive and transformative learning processes based on an open-minded search for new insights and ideas and a problematization of sedimented forms of knowledge and the discourse through which they are formulated.

The problematization of tacit assumptions and the reframing of established ideas are often associated with creativity. In the research on creative problem solving, there has been a growing interest in collective creativity either through open sources or through collaborative interaction. Creativity involves not only the recombination of existing ideas but also the discovery and integration of new ones. The tricky part is that discovery and integration require sustained and trust-based interaction among actors with different experiences, views, and ideas. Thus, both disruptive learning and creativity are enhanced through collaboration. However, there is no guarantee that collaboration promotes learning and innovation. Fortunately, learning from past failures, followed with proactive attempts to build future capacities, may increase the success rate of collaborative innovation. Therefore, it is proposed:

> Practical and situational learning in collaborative arenas need to be supplemented with ex post learning to forge and reinforce the link between collaboration, learning, and innovation.

Chapter 7 showed how collaboration can help overcome the problems arising in the selection and implementation of new, bold, and creative ideas. In the process of innovation, the euphoric revelation of new and promising ideas and visions is quickly replaced by a more realistic view of the troubles facing innovators when selecting and implementing innovative designs—a process that is associated with uncertainty, risk, complexity, collective action problems, power struggles, and potential conflicts. However, as it was demonstrated in the chapter, collaboration can help social and political actors overcome or at least mitigate these obstacles. Thus, the following is proposed:

> Multi-actor collaboration facilitates the sharing of information, knowledge, and assessments. It reveals the hidden and unforeseen effects of innovative solutions; spurs the development of generalized trust, which enables social and political actors to take and share risks; fosters pluricentric coordination between different arenas, actors, and strategies; motivates actors to act together by producing a common discourse and story line; and prevents the emergence of destructive conflicts by involving skeptical actors in the decision-making process and in building joint ownership.

Collaborative processes intending to select the most promising innovative solutions for further design and testing tend to rely either on a cost-benefit analysis based on an instrumental means-ends rationality or on a deliberative process based on reason giving and the willingness to change one's standpoint. The limitations of cost-benefit analysis in the face of deficient cognitive capacities, intangibles, uncertainties, and risk have stimulated the interest in deliberation as a tool for decision making in collaborative innovation processes. However, the literature has pointed to several weaknesses of deliberative processes based on communicative reason. Thus, the following is suggested:

> A dispassionate production and evaluation of reasons in a power-free environment may not be sufficient to create the momentum for change that is required when deciding to realize a particular innovative solution. Deliberation needs to be supplemented with more engaging and passionate attempts to build a political as well as moral-intellectual leadership that captures the hearts and minds of the relevant stakeholders and encourages them to adopt new and untried solutions despite the lack of apodictic knowledge of their superiority.

When implementing new innovative designs, another set of obstacles emerges in the form of few resources, competences, capacities, support, incentives, and proper mechanisms of coordination. While the rational response is either to eliminate these obstacles or to give up if the obstacles cannot be removed, a third option is to explore the possibilities of using them as triggers of innovation. Hence, it is proposed:

> Obstacles to the implementation of innovative ideas can lead to a reinvention that improves the function and feasibility of the innovative solution that is sought. However, reinventing innovative ideas in the face of unforeseen barriers requires mental agility, experimentation, and flexible governance structures that can help turn seemingly insurmountable obstacles into creative constraints that inspire innovators to rethink and improve their original ideas and to revise their strategy for implementing them in practice.

Turning obstacles into innovation drivers is not always possible, and a tension persists between the stability, predictability, and inertia of the daily operations of public service organizations and their efforts to create innovative step changes. However, the paradoxical relationship between the bureaucratic operation of public agencies and the disruptive processes of innovation can be made less convoluted by creating spaces for innovation close to but outside of operational processes, by establishing a cloud of competent and mobile facilitators who can be called upon to support the search for innovative designs, and by developing an innovation culture that recommends the pragmatic use of bureaucratic tools so that they are only deployed when they enhance the implementation of innovative solutions and not when they block the development and design of new ideas. Thus, it is proposed:

> It is important to avoid divorcing the development of an innovative solution from the daily operation of public organizations because both the implementation of the innovative designs and their ability to solve the problems being addressed hinge on the proximity, integration, and dialogue between those responsible for the daily running of public bureaucracy and those in charge of creating new and better solutions.

Chapter 8 analyzed how public innovation is diffused through networks and multi-actor collaboration. Although some organizations remain skeptical about new ideas from the outside, most public organizations are happy to broadcast their most successful innovations, and many organizations will benefit from becoming second movers who readily adopt innovative solutions that are invented elsewhere. Such innovation diffusion connects suppliers of new ideas with potential adopters and facilitates a two-way communication that is often mediated by change agents and opinion leaders. The decision to adopt an innovative solution from elsewhere depends not only on a series of actions and inactions on the part of the potential adopter but also on the innovation itself, the organizational context, and the external environment of the adopter. Thus, it is proposed:

> Innovation diffusion is a complex process through which an agency situated in a particular organizational, institutional, and discursive environment becomes aware of an innovative solution, forms an opinion about it, and perhaps decides to adopt, implement, and consolidate it.

Potential adopters are a part of wide-ranging diffusion networks in and through which different adopters, suppliers, and mediators interact and collaborate with each other to find and spread innovative solutions. Networks facilitate intra- and interorganizational learning between different kinds of public and private actors and between different countries and jurisdictions. Compared to alternative drivers of innovation diffusion such as coercion, competition, and the formation of hegemonic norms, the organizational learning perspective appears to have a major advantage. As such, it is proposed:

> The advantage of the collaborative learning approach to innovation diffusion is that it pays attention both to the internal search for innovative designs and the external contacts and relations that provide access to new knowledge and ideas. Thus, internal needs are combined with external opportunities.

The functioning and effects of innovation diffusion networks depend on their composition, exchange relations, and structure, but change agents and opinion leaders also play a crucial role in bringing people together and creating a fertile environment for interorganizational and cross-sector learning. In addition, role models may function as beacons for broadcasting new ideas to relevant audiences. However, innovative solutions that find their way into public organizations seldom provide a perfect match for the problem at hand and the context of implementation. For this reason, the adoption of innovative solutions is premised on their adaptation to the new context. Thus, it is asserted:

> We need a fundamental shift from the linear model, which runs from copy and paste through the dissemination of best practices and the launch of pilots, to a collaborative and experimental graft-and-grow model based on developing next practices through pathfinders who seek new ways of realizing particular goals based on some new and promising ideas rather than rolling out new innovative designs based on a fixed manual.

However, despite the pro-diffusion bias in much of the innovation diffusion literature, we cannot assume that innovation diffusion is always a good thing. Nor can we presume that public organizations are free to adopt innovative solutions and will do so whenever they seem to enhance efficiency. Thus, it is proposed:

> Unclear organizational goals and uncertain outcomes of innovation tend to prevent innovation diffusion based on strict efficiency calculations, and the result is that diffusion is often determined by shifting administrative fads and fashions that spread through isomorphic pressures and

produce more or less unpredictable effects when they are passed to and reinvented in new organizational contexts.

Efficiency is an important goal when measuring the outcomes of collaborative innovation, but the goals are multiple and changing, the measurement of goal attainment is complicated, and the results are difficult to handle. Negative outcomes might call either for iterative rounds of redesign and testing or for a complete termination of the innovative solution.

Chapter 9 studied the role of leadership and management in enhancing collaboration and stimulating innovation and thus offered more depth to a recurrent theme of the book. To begin, the chapter identified a number of drivers and barriers to collaborative innovation. The drivers—in terms of public agenda setting, the shared commitment to public value production, the favorable conditions for coproduction in public service delivery, and the democratic norms for collaborative involvement of intensely affected actors—show that collaboration is by no means foreign to the public sector.

In analyzing the barriers from a process perspective, the survey discovered crucial obstacles in attempting to establish interaction between relevant and affected actors, in getting them to collaborate, and in ensuring that collaboration fosters innovation. The barriers reveal the contingency of collaborative innovation in the public sector. Thus, it is asserted:

> A readiness to collaborate and a willingness to explore and exploit new and bold solutions are not enough to ensure a successful outcome of the attempt to spur collaborative innovation since many things can go wrong in the process.

However, developing a new form of leadership and management that is tailored to enhancing the drivers and overcoming the barriers might help to significantly improve the success rate. Hence, it is proposed:

> Public (and private) leaders and managers should act as conveners, facilitators, and catalysts in order to spur collaborative innovation in the public sector.

Each of these three roles comes with a special toolbox, but leading and managing collaborative innovation also requires a great deal of reflexivity, intuition, improvization, and creativity, as well as a flexible combination and integration of the three roles. While the three roles prescribed for leaders and managers of collaborative innovation focus on hands-on management, there is also a huge need for creating a stronger innovation culture in the public sector through hands-off leadership and management efforts. As such, it is proposed:

> Hands-on innovation management focusing on massaging relational and creative processes through a series of discrete interventions must be combined with a continuous hands-off effort of innovation leadership that means to build a stronger innovation culture in public organizations.

Innovation culture is a multidimensional phenomenon. It calls upon the strategic and operational commitments to innovation at different levels of the organization; the skills, knowledge, motivation, and courage of managers and employees who can support the effort to innovate; and the ability of the organization to engage relevant actors inside and outside the organization when developing and implementing innovative solutions. When aiming to build a strong innovation culture, it can be difficult to determine where to begin, but a flow perspective targeting bottlenecks is often helpful.

The role of leaders and managers in supporting innovation processes finds support in recently developed theories of adaptive leadership, pragmatic leadership, and design thinking, and their role in fostering collaboration finds support in theories of distributive, horizontal, collaborative, and integrative leadership. These theories constitute an important turn in the research on leadership and management. Thus, the following is proposed:

> The aforementioned leadership theories break with the traditional assumption that public leaders and managers should first and foremost focus on minimizing the resources and maximizing the performance of their own organizations through a combination of transactional and transformational leadership. Instead, public leaders and managers are urged to focus on intra- and interorganizational processes and on how they can facilitate the emergence of the otherwise possible by realizing the innovative potential that arises in the meeting between actors with different experiences, ideas, and resources.

The attempt to rethink leadership and management theory from the perspective of collaborative innovation may benefit from a further development of the concept of metagovernance. Various network theorists established the concept to understand how self-governing arenas are governed so that they produce desirable outcomes such as policy, governance, or service innovation. Therefore, it is proposed:

> Metagovernance provides a toolbox for managing collaborative interaction and stimulating creative problem solving through a combination of institutional design, goal and framework steering, process management, and direct participation.

Chapter 10 answered the key question of how to build a public sector that is more capable of advancing innovation in general and collaborative innovation in particular. Public bureaucracies, for good reasons, are criticized for impeding innovation. Centralized decision making, long implementation chains, rule following, and a general preference for stability—all tend to hamper innovation. Further, formal decision-making procedures, administrative silos, and organizational insulation from the external environment also prevent the creation of arenas for horizontal collaboration within and across organizations. However, such "bureaucracy bashing" overlooks the fact that centralized leadership can enhance innovation by setting the agenda, developing clear goals and visions, committing resources, and ensuring the implementation of innovative solutions. Rules and procedures may also support the exploration and exploitation of new ideas and the specialized staff members who develop their professional knowledge and expertise in close interaction with their colleagues in their administrative unit. Thus, it is asserted:

> While little in the classical bureaucracy model supports multi-actor collaboration, the effects on public innovation are ambiguous because both the search for and implementation of innovative solutions are enhanced by bureaucracy while the generation of new and creative ideas is not.

The drawbacks of bureaucracy explain the widespread embrace of New Public Management, which promised both to stimulate innovation by increasing the reliance on market-based competition and to enhance efficiency by incentivizing public managers to use their managerial tools in response to external pressures from intensified performance measurement, the users' free choice of services, and the threat of being privatized or contracted out. While the focus on efficiency, performance management, and marketization tends to reduce the public sector to a corporate enterprise (see Morgan and Cook 2014), New Public Management provided a convincing narrative that emphasized how an incentive-driven results orientation could breathe new life into slumbering public bureaucracies. However, we seem to have paid a high price for the innovation-enhancing features of New Public Management. As such, it is proposed:

> New Public Management has been oversold as a driver of public innovation since it experiences several inherent constraints that hamper innovation in general and collaborative innovation in particular.

Public administration researchers and practitioners have asked themselves whether there is a life after New Public Management, which despite mounting criticisms tends to maintain its hegemony, at least in top-level government offices. The debate has been vigorous. While some advocate a return to cherished bureaucratic values, others point to the content and potential impact of New Public Governance, which not only aims to enhance innovation but also perceives multi-actor collaboration as a key driver of innovation. Hence, it is proposed:

> The turn to factors associated with New Public Governance—for example, trust-based leadership, vertical and horizontal integration, networked collaboration, active citizenship, and strengthened political leadership—will spur cocreated service and policy innovation.

The link between New Public Governance and collaborative innovation is obvious, although it has not yet been brought out fully in the literature. Nevertheless, there is no reason to believe that all problems and tasks can be effectively solved by relying on one particular public administration paradigm. Nor is it likely that embracing New Public Governance will eliminate the former public administration paradigms. Rather, it is proposed:

> In the future we will see not only the coexistence of governance practices associated with competing public administration paradigms but also the fusion of different practices into hybrids with unpredictable consequences. Therefore, we will need both a contingency theory that enables us to understand the comparative advantages of the different public administration paradigms and empirical studies of the impact of the paradigms' interaction and articulation.

Bureaucracy might continue to be the preferred paradigm for public regulation and service provision that involves exercising public authority, and New

Public Management's recommendation to contract out the delivery of highly standardized services has been heeded. However, the current demand for innovative solutions that cut public expenditure, improve service quality, break policy logjams, and meet hitherto unmet social needs and the growing impetus to mobilize the hidden wealth of citizens, civil society, and private firms are likely to shift the balance in the direction of New Public Governance. Therefore, it is proposed:

> The path dependencies working against public administration reforms are challenged both by the on-going reinterpretation and rearticulation of the existing public administration paradigms and by the scale of the current political, economic, and social crisis, which provides a window of opportunity for rethinking public administration and governance and reforming its infrastructure and modus operandi.

It is my hope that the propositions set out here will stimulate and guide further research on collaborative innovation and thus help forge a closer link between theories of collaborative governance and theories of public innovation. However, as this book has demonstrated, the study of the conditions, mechanisms, and impact of collaborative innovation in the public sector is truly an interdisciplinary effort, one that hopefully will engage academic scholars and public sector practitioners in an interactive research endeavor.

These propositions call for further development, modification, and empirical testing. Future research will generate new propositions, broaden the range of relevant theories, and perhaps develop new methodological strategies for assessing the empirical purchasing power of the propositions. The tasks ahead are many. However, the goal is not to develop a comprehensive theory of collaborative innovation but merely to advance our theoretical and empirical understanding of how multiple actors can interact and collaborate to foster new and innovative solutions to the growing number of wicked and unruly problems that we currently face.

REFERENCES

Abrahamson, E. 1991. "Managerial Fads and Fashions: The Diffusion and Rejection of Innovations." *Academy of Management Review* 16 (3): 586–612.

Adler, P. S., and C. Hecksher. 2006. *The Firm as a Collaborative Community: Reconstructing Trust in the Knowledge Economy*. New York: Oxford University Press.

Agranoff, R. 2003. *Leveraging Networks: A Guide for Public Managers Working across Organizations*. Washington DC: IBM Endowment for the Business of Government.

———. 2007. *Managing within Networks: Adding Value to Public Organizations*. Washington DC: Georgetown University Press.

Albury, D. 2005. "Fostering Innovation in Public Services." *Public Money & Management* 25 (1): 51–56.

Aldrich, H. E. 1979. *Organizations and Environments*. Englewood Cliffs NJ: Prentice Hall.

Amabile, T. M. 1983. "The Social Psychology of Creativity: A Componential Conceptualization." *Journal of Personality and Social Psychology* 45 (2): 357–76. http://dx.doi.org/10.1037/0022-3514.45.2.357.

———. 1998. "How to Kill Creativity." *Harvard Business Review* 76 (5): 76–87.

Amabile, T. M., B. A. Hennessey, and B. S. Grossman. 1986. "Social Influences on Creativity: The Effects of Contracted-for Reward." *Journal of Personality and Social Psychology* 50 (1): 14–23. http://dx.doi.org/10.1037/0022-3514.50.1.14.

Ansell, C. 2016, forthcoming. "Pragmatism." In *Handbook on Theories of Governance*, edited by J. Torfing and C. Ansell. Cheltenham UK: Edward Elgar.

Ansell, C., and A. Gash. 2007. "Collaborative Governance in Theory and Practice." *Journal of Public Administration: Research and Theory* 18 (4): 543–71. http://dx.doi.org/10.1093/jopart/mum032.

———. 2012. "Stewards, Mediators, and Catalysts: Towards a Model of Collaborative Leadership." *The Innovation Journal* 17 (1): article 7.

Ansell, C., and J. Torfing, eds. 2014. *Public Innovation through Collaboration and Design*. London: Routledge.

———. 2016. "Strengthening Political Leadership and Policy Innovation through the Expansion of Collaborative Forms of Governance." *Public Management Review*, in press.

Archer, D., and A. Cameron. 2008. *Collaborative Leadership: How to Succeed in an Interconnected World*. Abingdon UK: Routledge.

Argyris, C., and D. A. Schön. 1978. *Organizational Learning: A Theory of Action Perspective*. Reading MA: Addison-Wesley.

Arthur, W. B. 1994. *Increasing Returns and Path Dependence in the Economy*. Ann Arbor MI: University of Michigan Press.

Arundel, A., and K. H. Smith. 2013. "History of the Community Innovation Survey." In *Handbook of Innovation Indicators and Measurement*, edited by F. Gault, 60–87. Cheltenham UK: Edward Elgar.

Asheim, B., and M. S. Gertler. 2004. "The Geography of Innovation: Regional Innovation Systems." In *The Oxford Handbook of Innovation*, edited by J. Fagerberg, D. C. Mowery, and R. R. Nelson, 291–317. Oxford: Oxford University Press.

Axelrod, R., and M. Cohen. 1999. *Harnessing Complexity: Organizational Implications of a Scientific Frontier*. New York: Free Press.

Bache, I., and M. Flinders, eds. 2004. *Multi-level Governance*. Oxford: Oxford University Press. http://dx.doi.org/10.1093/0199259259.001.0001.

Banerjee, B. 2010. "Designer as Agent of Change: A Vision for Catalyzing Rapid Change." https://changelabs.stanford.edu/sites/default/files/Banny%20Banerjee-Designer%20as%20Agent%20of%20Change.pdf.

Banfield, E. C. 1973. "Ends and Means in Planning." In *A Reader in Planning Theory*, edited by A. Faludi, 139–49. Oxford: Pergamon Press. http://dx.doi.org/10.1016/B978-0-08-017066-4.50014-X.

Baños, R. A., J. Borge-Holthoefer, N. Wang, Y. Moreno, and S. Ganzález-Bailón. 2013. "Diffusion Dynamics with Changing Network Composition." *Entropy* (Basel, Switzerland) 15 (11): 4553–68. http://dx.doi.org/10.3390/e15114553.

Banthien, H., M. Jaspers, and A. Renner. 2003. *Governance of the European Research Area: The Role of Civil Society*. Brussels: EU Commission.

Bartels, K. P. R., G. Cozzi, and N. Mantovan. 2013. "'The Big Society,' Public Expenditure, and Volunteering." *Public Administration Review* 73 (2): 340–51. http://dx.doi.org/10.1111/puar.12012.

Barthes, R. 1987. *Mythologies*. London: Paladin Grafton Books.

Bason, C. 2007. *Velfærdsinnovation: Ledelse af nytænkning i den offentlige sector* [Welfare innovation: Management of innovation in the public sector]. Copenhagen: Børsens Forlag.

———. 2010. *Leading Public Sector Innovation: Co-creating for a Better Society*. Bristol: Policy Press.

———. 2014. "Design Attitude as an Innovation Catalyst." In *Public Innovation through Collaboration and Design*, edited by C. Ansell and J. Torfing, 209–28. London: Routledge.

Bateson, G. 1972. *Steps to an Ecology of Mind: Collected Essays in Anthropology, Psychiatry, Evolution, and Epistemology*. Chicago: University of Chicago Press.

Baumol, W. J. 2002. *The Free-Market Innovation Machine: Analyzing the Growth Miracle of Capitalism*. Princeton NJ: Princeton University Press. http://dx.doi.org/10.1515/9781400851638.

Bekkers, V., J. Edelenbos, and B. Steijn, eds. 2011. *Innovation in the Public Sector: Linking Capacity and Leadership*. Basingstoke UK: Palgrave-Macmillan. http://dx.doi.org/10.1057/9780230307520.

Bekkers, V., L. Tummers, and W. Voorberg. 2013. "From Public Innovation to Social Innovation in the Public Sector: A Literature Review of Relevant Drivers and Barriers." Paper presented at the IRSPM Conference, Prague, April 10–12.

Bell, S., and A. Hindmoor. 2009. *Rethinking Governance: The Centrality of the State in Modern Society*. New York: Cambridge University Press. http://dx.doi.org/10.1017/CBO9780511814617.

Bemelmans-Videc, M.-L., R. C. Rist, and E. Vedung. 2011. *Carrots, Sticks & Sermons: Policy Instruments and Their Evaluation*. Copenhagen: Nota.

Benson, J. K. 1978. "The Interorganizational Network as a Political Economy." In *Organization and Environment*, edited by L. Karpik, 69–102. London: Sage.

Bentley, A. F. 1967. *The Process of Government: A Study of Social Pressure*. Edited by P. H. Odegard. Cambridge MA: Harvard University Press. http://dx.doi.org/10.4159/harvard.9780674733657.

Benz, A., and Y. Papadopoulos, eds. 2006. *Governance and Democracy*. London: Routledge.

Berman, E. M., and C.-G. Kim. 2010. "Creativity Management in Public Organizations: Jump-Starting Innovation (in Seoul)." *Public Performance & Management Review* 33 (4): 619–52. http://dx.doi.org/10.2753/PMR1530-9576330405.

Bernier, L., and T. Hafsi. 2007. "The Changing Nature of Public Entrepreneurship." *Public Administration Review* 67 (3): 488–503. http://dx.doi.org/10.1111/j.1540-6210.2007.00731.x.

Bevir, M. 2010. *Democratic Governance*. Princeton NJ: Princeton University Press. http://dx.doi.org/10.1515/9781400836857.

Bevir, M., and Q. Bowman. 2011. "Innovations in Democratic Governance." In *Innovation in Public Governance*, edited by A. Anttiroiko, S. Bailey, and P. Valkama, 174–93. Amsterdam: ISO Press.

Bevir, M., and R. A. W. Rhodes. 2006. *Governance Stories*. London: Routledge.

Bevir, M., and D. Richards. 2009. "Decentering Policy Networks: A Theoretical Agenda." *Public Administration* 87 (1): 3–14. http://dx.doi.org/10.1111/j.1467-9299.2008.01736.x.

Biggs, J. B. 1985. "The Role of Metalearning in Study Processes." *British Journal of Educational Psychology* 55 (3): 185–212. http://dx.doi.org/10.1111/j.2044-8279.1985.tb02625.x.

Bijker, W. E. 1995. *Of Bicycles, Bakelites, and Bulbs: Toward a Theory of Sociotechnical Change*. Cambridge MA: MIT Press.

———. 2010. "How Is Technology Made?—That Is the Question!" *Cambridge Journal of Economics* 34 (1): 63–76. http://dx.doi.org/10.1093/cje/bep068.

Bingham, R. D. 1978. "Innovation, Bureaucracy, and Public Policy: A Study of Innovation Adoption by Local Government." *Western Political Quarterly* 31 (2): 178–205. http://dx.doi.org/10.2307/447811.

Boardman, A., D. Greenberg, A. Vining, and D. Weimer. 2006. *Cost-Benefit Analysis*. Upper Saddle River NJ: Prentice Hall.

Boin, A., O. James, and M. Lodge. 2006. "The New Public Management 'Revolution' in Political Control of the Public Sector: Promises and Outcomes in Three European Prison Systems." *Public Policy and Administration* 21 (2): 81–100. http://dx.doi.org/10.1177/095207670602100207.

Boland, R., and F. Collopy, eds. 2004. *Managing as Designing*. Stanford CA: Stanford University Press.

Bommert, B. 2010. "Collaborative Innovation in the Public Sector." *International Public Management Review* 11 (1): 15–33.

Booher, D. E., and J. E. Innes. 2010. *Planning with Complexity: An Introduction to Collaborative Rationality for Public Policy*. London: Routledge.

Borins, S. F. 1998. *Innovating with Integrity*. Washington DC: Georgetown University Press.

———. 2000. "What Border? Public Management Innovation in the United States and Canada." *Journal of Policy Analysis and Management* 19 (1): 46–74. http://dx.doi.org/10.1002/(SICI)1520-6688(200024)19:1<46::AID-PAM4>3.0.CO;2-Z.

———. 2001a. *The Challenge of Innovating in Government*. Washington DC: IBM Center for the Business of Government.

———. 2001b. "Encouraging Innovation in the Public Sector." *Journal of Intellectual Capital* 2 (3): 310–9. http://dx.doi.org/10.1108/14691930110400128.

———. 2008. *Innovations in Government: Research, Recognition, and Replication*. Washington DC: Brookings Institution Press.

———. 2014. *The Persistence of Innovation in Government: A Guide for Public Servants*. Washington DC: IBM Center for the Business of Government.

Bovaird, T. 2007. "Beyond Engagement and Participation: User and Community Coproduction of Public Services." *Public Administration Review* 67 (5): 846–60. http://dx.doi.org/10.1111/j.1540-6210.2007.00773.x.

Bovaird, T., and E. Loeffler. 2012. "From Engagement to Co-production: The Contribution of Users and Communities to Outcomes and Public Value." *Voluntas* 23 (4): 1119–38. http://dx.doi.org/10.1007/s11266-012-9309-6.

Bowden, A. 2005. "Knowledge for Free? Distributed Innovation as a Source of Learning." *Public Policy and Administration* 20 (3): 56–68. http://dx.doi.org/10.1177/095207670502000306.

Boyne, G. A. 2003. "Sources of Public Service Improvement: A Critical Review and Research Agenda." *Journal of Public Administration: Research and Theory* 13 (3): 367–94. http://dx.doi.org/10.1093/jopart/mug027.

Bozeman, B. 2000. *Bureaucracy and Red Tape*. Upper Saddle River NJ: Prentice Hall.

Brand, R., and F. Gaffikin. 2007. "Collaborative Planning in an Uncollaborative World." *Planning Theory* 6 (3): 282–313. http://dx.doi.org/10.1177/1473095207082036.

Bressers, N. 2014. "The Impact of Collaboration on Innovative Projects: A Study of Dutch Water Management." In *Public Innovation through Collaboration and Design*, edited by C. Ansell and J. Torfing, 89–105. London: Routledge.

Brown, J., and P. Duguid. 1991. "Organizational Learning and Communities-of-Practice: Toward a Unified View of Working, Learning, and Innovation." *Organization Science* 2 (1): 40–57. http://dx.doi.org/10.1287/orsc.2.1.40.

Brown, L., and S. Osborne. 2013. "Risk and Innovation: Towards a Framework for Risk Governance in Public Services." *Public Management Review* 15 (2): 186–208. http://dx.doi.org/10.1080/14719037.2012.707681.

Bruner, J. 1990. *Acts of Meaning*. Cambridge MA: Harvard University Press.

———. 1996. "Frames for Thinking: Ways of Making Meaning." In *Modes of Thought*, edited by D. Olson and N. Torrance, 93–105. New York: Cambridge University Press.

Bryson, J. M., and W. D. Roering. 1988. "Initiation of Strategic Planning by Governments." *Public Administration Review* 48 (6): 995–1004. http://dx.doi.org/10.2307/976996.

Bugge, M. M., J. Hauknes, C. Bloch, and S. Slipersæter. 2010. "The Public Sector in Innovation Systems." Working paper from the joint Nordic research project Measuring Public Innovation in Nordic Countries: Toward a Common Statistical Approach of the Norwegian Institute for Studies in Innovation, Research and Education and the Danish Centre for Studies in Research and Research Policy. http://www.innovation.fo/wp-content/uploads/2013/09/The_public_sector_in_innovation_systems.pdf.

Bulkeley, H., and M. M. Betsill. 2003. *Cities and Climate Change: Urban Sustainability and Global Environmental Governance*. New York: Routledge. http://dx.doi.org/10.4324/9780203219256.

Burns, T., and G. M. Stalker. 1961. *The Management of Innovation*. London: Tavistock Books.

Burt, R. S. 1992. *Structural Holes*. Cambridge MA: Harvard University Press.

Callon, M., P. Lascoumes, and Y. Barthe. 2001. *Agir dans un monde incertain*. Paris: Le Seuil.

Carter, L., and F. Bélanger. 2005. "The Utilization of e-Government Services: Citizen Trust, Innovation and Acceptance Factors." *Information Systems Journal* 15 (1): 5–25. http://dx.doi.org/10.1111/j.1365-2575.2005.00183.x.

Chesbrough, H. W. 2003. *Open Innovation*. Boston: Harvard Business School Press.

Chhotray, V., and G., Stoker. 2010. *Governance Theory and Practice: A Cross-Disciplinary Approach*. Basingstoke UK: Palgrave Macmillan.

Christensen, T. 2012. "Post-NPM and Changing Public Governance." *Meiji Journal of Political Science and Economics* 1 (1): 1–11.

Christensen, T., and P. Lægreid. 2007. *Transcending New Public Management: The Transformation of Public Sector Reforms*. Hampshire UK: Ashgate.

———. 2011. "Complexity and Hybrid Administration—Theoretical and Empirical Challenges." *Public Organization Review* 11 (4): 407–23. http://dx.doi.org/10.1007/s11115-010-0141-4.

Cohen, M., J. G. March, and J. P. Olsen. 1972. "A Garbage Can Model of Organizational Choice." *Administrative Science Quarterly* 17 (1): 1–25. http://dx.doi.org/10.2307/2392088.

Collier, R. B., and D. Collier. 1991. *Shaping the Political Arena*. Princeton NJ: Princeton University Press.

Considine, M. 2009. "Network Governance: Towards a Theory of Transformation." Paper presented at 5th ECPR General Conference, Potsdam, September 10–12.

Considine, M., and A. Hart. 2008. "Integrating Young Homeless People into Housing and Employment." In *The Theory and Practice of Local Governance and Economic Development*, edited by M. Considine and S. Giguère, 161–84. Basingstoke UK: Palgrave Macmillan. http://dx.doi.org/10.1057/9780230582682.

Considine, M., J. Lewis, and D. Alexander. 2009. *Networks, Innovation and Public Policy*. Basingstoke UK: Palgrave Macmillan. http://dx.doi.org/10.1057/9780230595040.

Coule, T., and B. Patmore. 2013. "Institutional Logics, Institutional Work, and Service Innovation in Non-profit Organizations." *Public Administration* 91 (4): 980–97. http://dx.doi.org/10.1111/padm.12005.

Covey, S. M. R. 2006. *The Speed of Trust: The One Thing That Changes Everything*. New York: Free Press.

Covey, S. M. R., and G. Link. 2012. *Smart Trust: Creating Prosperity, Energy, and Joy in a Low-Trust World*. New York: Free Press.

Crosby, B. C., and J. M. Bryson. 2010. "Integrative Leadership and the Creation and Maintenance of Cross-sector Collaboration." *Leadership Quarterly* 21 (2): 211–30. http://dx.doi.org/10.1016/j.leaqua.2010.01.003.

Crozier, M. 1964. *The Bureaucratic Phenomenon*. Chicago: University of Chicago Press.

Crozier, M., S. P. Huntington, and J. Watanuki. 1975. *The Crisis of Democracy*. New York: New York University Press.

Cruikshank, B. 1999. *The Will to Empower: Democratic Citizens and Other Subjects*. Cornell NY: Cornell University Press.

Csikszentmihalyi, M. 1996. *Creativity: Flow and the Psychology of Discovery and Invention*. New York: HarperCollins.

Dahl, R. A. 1961. *Who Governs: Democracy and Power in an American City*. New Haven CT: Yale University Press.

Damanpour, F. 1991. "Organizational Innovation: A Meta-Analysis of Effects of Determinants and Moderators." *Academy of Management Journal* 34 (3): 555–90. http://dx.doi.org/10.2307/256406.

———. 1996. "Bureaucracy and Innovation Revisited: Effects of Contingency Factors, Industrial Sectors, and Innovation Characteristics." *Journal of High Technology Management Research* 7 (2): 149–73. http://dx.doi.org/10.1016/S1047-8310(96)90002-4.

Damanpour, F., and M. Schneider. 2009. "Characteristics of Innovation and Innovation Adoption in Public Organizations: Assessing the Role of Managers." *Journal of*

Public Administration: Research and Theory 19 (3): 495–522. http://dx.doi.org/10.1093/jopart/mun021.

Damgaard, B., and J., Torfing. 2010. "Network Governance of Active Employment Policy: The Danish Experience." *Journal of European Social Policy* 20 (3): 248–62. http://dx.doi.org/10.1177/0958928710364435.

Danish Productivity Commission. 2013. *Styring, ledelse og motivation i den offentlige sektor*, Report 3. Copenhagen: Danish Productivity Commission. http://produktivitetskommissionen.dk/media/151231/Analyserapport%20til%20web.pdf.

Darr, E., and T. Kurtzberg. 2000. "An Investigation of Partner Similarity Dimensions on Knowledge Transfer." *Organizational Behavior and Human Decision Processes* 82 (1): 28–44. http://dx.doi.org/10.1006/obhd.2000.2885.

David, P. A. 1985. "Clio and the Economics of QWERTY." *American Economic Review* 74 (2): 332–37.

Dean, M. 1999. *Governmentality: Power and Rule in Modern Society*. London: Sage.

DeHart-Davis, L. 2009. "Green Tape and Public Employee Rule Abidance: Why Organizational Rule Attributes Matter." *Public Administration Review* 69 (5): 901–10. http://dx.doi.org/10.1111/j.1540-6210.2009.02039.x.

Denis, J. L., Y. Hérbert, A. Langley, D. Lozeau, and L. H. Trottier. 2002. "Explaining Diffusion Patterns for Complex Health Care Innovations." *Health Care Management Review* 27 (3): 60–73. http://dx.doi.org/10.1097/00004010-200207000-00007.

Denis, J.-L., A. Langley, and V. Sergi. 2012. "Leadership in the Plural." *Academy of Management Annals* 6 (1): 211–83. http://dx.doi.org/10.1080/19416520.2012.667612.

Dente, B., L. Bobbio, and A. Spada. 2005. "Government or Governance of Urban Innovation?" *DIPS* 162:1–22.

Dewey, J. 1916. *Democracy and Education: An Introduction to the Philosophy of Education*. Basingstoke UK: Macmillan.

———. 1922. *Human Nature and Conduct*. New York: Henry Holt.

———. 1938. *Experience and Education*. New York: Macmillan.

DiMaggio, J., and W. W. Powell. 1983. "The Iron Cage Revisited: Institutional Isomorphism and Collective Rationality in Organizational Fields." *American Sociological Review* 48 (2): 147–60. http://dx.doi.org/10.2307/2095101.

Djelic, M.-L., and K. Sahlin-Andersson, eds. 2006. *Transnational Governance: Institutional Dynamics of Regulation*. Cambridge: Cambridge University Press. http://dx.doi.org/10.1017/CBO9780511488665.

Dobbin, F., B. Simmons, and G. Garrett. 2007. "The Global Diffusion of Public Policies: Social Construction, Coercion, Competition, or Learning?" *Annual Review of Sociology* 33 (1): 449–72. http://dx.doi.org/10.1146/annurev.soc.33.090106.142507.

Dobni, C. B. 2008. "Measuring Innovation Culture in Organizations." *European Journal of Innovation Management* 11 (4): 539–59. http://dx.doi.org/10.1108/14601060810911156.

Doig, J. W., and E. C. Hargrove. 1990. *Leadership in Innovation: Entrepreneurs in Government*. Baltimore: John Hopkins University Press.

Downs, A. 1967. *Inside Bureaucracy*. Boston: Little, Brown.

Dreyfus, H., and S. Dreyfus. 1986. *Mind over Machine: The Power of Human Intuition and Expertise in the Era of the Computer*. New York: Free Press.

Dryzek, J. S. 1990. *Discursive Democracy: Politics, Policy, and Political Science*. Cambridge: Cambridge University Press.

———. 2000. *Deliberative Democracy and Beyond: Liberals, Critics, Contestations*. Oxford: Oxford University Press.

Dunne, D., and R. Martin. 2006. "Design Thinking and How It Will Change Management Education." *Academy of Management Learning & Education* 5 (4): 512–23. http://dx.doi.org/10.5465/AMLE.2006.23473212.

Edelenbos, J., B. Steijn, and E.-H. Klijn. 2010. "Does Democratic Anchorage Matter? An Inquiry into the Relation between Democratic Anchorage and Outcome of Dutch Environmental Projects." *American Review of Public Administration* 40 (1): 46–63. http://dx.doi.org/10.1177/0275074009332064.

Edquist, C. 2004. "Systems of Innovation: Perspectives and Challenges." In *The Oxford Handbook of Innovation*, edited by J. Fagerberg, D. C. Mowery, and R. R. Nelson, 181–208. Oxford: Oxford University Press.

Edquist, C., and L. Hommen. 1999. "Systems of Innovation: Theory and Policy for the Demand Side." *Technology in Society* 21 (1): 63–79. http://dx.doi.org/10.1016/S0160-791X(98)00037-2.

Edquist, C., and J. M. Zabala-Iturriagagoitia. 2012. "Public Procurement for Innovation as Mission-Oriented Innovation Policy." *Research Policy* 41 (10): 1757–69. http://dx.doi.org/10.1016/j.respol.2012.04.022.

Eggers, W. D. 2003. "Overcoming Obstacles to Technology-Enabled Transformation." Occasional Papers series. Cambridge MA: John F. Kennedy School of Government, Harvard University.

Eggers, W. D., and P. Macmillan. 2013. *The Solution Revolution: How Business, Government, and Social Enterprises Are Teaming Up to Solve Society's Toughest Problems*. Boston: Harvard Business Review Press.

Eggers, W. D., and J. O'Leary. 2009. *If We Can Put a Man on the Moon: Getting Big Things Done in Government*. Boston: Harvard Business Press.

Eggers, W. D., and S. Singh. 2009. *The Public Innovator's Playbook: Nurturing Bold Ideas in Government*. Cambridge MA: Ash Institute, Harvard Kennedy School of Government.

Engeström, Y. 1987. *Learning by Expanding: An Activity-Theoretical Approach to Developmental Research*. Helsinki: Orienta-Konsultit.

———. 2008. *From Teams to Knots: Activity-Theoretical Studies of Collaboration and Learning at Work*. New York: Cambridge University Press. http://dx.doi.org/10.1017/CBO9780511619847.

Etzioni, A. 1967. "Mixed-Scanning: A 'Third' Approach to Decision-Making." *Public Administration Review* 27 (5): 385–92. http://dx.doi.org/10.2307/973394.

Etzkowitz, H., and L. Leydesdorff. 2000. "The Dynamics of Innovation: From National Systems and 'Mode 2' to a Triple Helix of University-Industry-Government Relations."" *Research Policy* 29 (2): 109–23. http://dx.doi.org/10.1016/S0048-7333(99)00055-4.

European Commission. 2013. *European Public Sector Innovation Scoreboard, 2013.* Brussels: EU.

Fagerberg, J. 2004. "Innovation: A Guide to the Literature." In *The Oxford Handbook of Innovation*, edited by J. Fagerberg, D. C. Mowery, and R. R. Nelson, 1–26. Oxford: Oxford University Press.

Faludi, A. 1973. *A Reader in Planning Theory.* Oxford: Pergamon Press.

Faludi, A., and A. Van der Valk. 1994. *Rule and Order: Dutch Planning Doctrine in the Twentieth Century.* Dordrecht: Kluwer Academic Publishers. http://dx.doi.org/10.1007/978-94-017-2927-7.

Fay, D., C. Borrill, Z. Amir, R. Haward, and M. West. 2006. "Getting the Most out of Multidisciplinary Teams: A Multi-sample Study of Team Innovation in Health Care." *Journal of Occupational and Organizational Psychology* 79 (4): 553–67. http://dx.doi.org/10.1348/096317905X72128.

Fenger, M., and V. J. J. M. Bekkers, eds. 2012. *Beyond Fragmentation in Public Governance: Challenges and Contributions.* Amsterdam: IOS Press.

Fernández, S., and L. R. Wise. 2010. "An Exploration of Why Public Organizations 'Ingest' Innovations." *Public Administration* 88 (4): 979–98. http://dx.doi.org/10.1111/j.1467-9299.2010.01857.x.

Ferreira, M., S. Farah, and P. Spink. 2008. "Subnational Innovation in a Comparative Perspective: Brazil." In *Innovations in Government*, edited by S. Borins, 71–92. Washington DC: Brookings Institution Press.

Fischer, F., and J. Forester, eds. 1993. *The Argumentative Turn in Policy Analysis and Planning.* Durham NC: Duke University Press. http://dx.doi.org/10.1215/9780822381815.

Forester, J. F. 1989. *Planning in the Face of Power.* Berkeley: University of California Press.

Forester, J. 1999. *The Deliberative Practitioner: Encouraging Participatory Planning Processes.* Cambridge MA: MIT Press.

Foucault, M. 1980. *Power/Knowledge: Selected Interviews and Other Writings, 1972–1997.* Brighton, Sussex: Harvester Press.

———. 1990. *The History of Sexuality.* Harmondsworth UK: Pelican.

———. 1991. "Governmentality." In *The Foucault Effect*, edited by G. Burchell, C. Gordon, and P. Miller, 87–104. Hertfordshire UK: Harvester Wheatsheaf.

Freeman, C. 1974. *The Economics of Industrial Innovation.* Harmondsworth UK: Penguin.

———. 1991. "Networks of Innovators: A Synthesis of Research Issues." *Research Policy* 20 (5): 499–514. http://dx.doi.org/10.1016/0048-7333(91)90072-X.

FTF. 2010. *Lederpejling, nr. 7.* Copenhagen: FTF Documentation.

———. 2013. *Lederpejling, nr. 8: Udviklingen i FTF-lederes erfaring med innovation.* Copenhagen: FTF Documentation. http://www.ftf.dk/aktuelt/ftf-dokumentation/artikel/lederpejling-nr-8-udviklingen-i-ftf-lederes-erfaring-med-innovation/.

Fuglsang, L. 2010. "Bricolage and Invisible Innovation in Public Service Innovation." *Journal of Innovation Economics* 1 (5): 67–87. http://dx.doi.org/10.3917/jie.005.0067.

Fung, A. 2008. "Civic Participation in Government Innovations." In *Innovations in Government: Research, Recognition, and Replication*, edited by S. Borins, 52–70. Washington DC: Brookings Institution Press.

Fung, A., and E. O. Wright, eds. 2003. *Deepening Democracy: Institutional Innovations in Empowered Participatory Governance*. London: Verso.

Gaventa, J. 2002. "Introduction: Exploring Citizenship, Participation and Accountability." *IDS Bulletin* 33 (2): 1–14. http://dx.doi.org/10.1111/j.1759-5436.2002.tb00020.x.

Geertman, S. 2006. "Potentials for Planning Support: A Planning-Conceptual Approach." *Environment and Planning B: Planning & Design* 33 (6): 863–80. http://dx.doi.org/10.1068/b31129.

Gloor, P. A. 2005. *Swarm Creativity: Competitive Advantage through Collaborative Innovation Networks*. Oxford: Oxford University Press.

Goodin, R. 2008. *Innovating Democracy: Democratic Theory and Practice after the Deliberative Turn*. Oxford: Oxford University Press. http://dx.doi.org/10.1093/acprof:oso/9780199547944.001.0001.

Gramsci, A. 1971. *Selections from Prison Notebooks*. London: Lawrence and Wishart.

Granlien, M. S. 2010. *Participation and Evaluation in the Design of Healthcare Work Systems*. Roskilde, Denmark: Roskilde University Press.

Granovetter, M. 1973. "The Strength of Weak Ties." *American Journal of Sociology* 78 (6): 1360–80. http://dx.doi.org/10.1086/225469.

Gray, B. 1989. *Collaborating: Finding Common Ground for Multiparty Problems*. San Francisco: Jossey-Bass.

Gray, B., and H. Ren. 2014. "The Importance of Joint Schemas and Brokers in Promoting Collaboration for Innovation." In *Public Innovation through Collaboration and Design*, edited by C. Ansell and J. Torfing, 125–47. London: Routledge.

Greenhalgh, T., G. Robert, F. Macfarlane, P. Bate, and O. Kyriakidou. 2004. "Diffusion of Innovations in Service Organizations: Systematic Review and Recommendations." *Milbank Quarterly* 82 (4): 581–629. http://dx.doi.org/10.1111/j.0887-378X.2004.00325.x.

Griggs, S., and H. Sullivan. 2014. "Necessity as the Mother of Reinvention: Discourses of Innovation in Local Government." In *Public Innovation through Collaboration and Design*, edited by C. Ansell and J. Torfing, 19–40. London: Routledge.

Grote, J. R., and B. Gbikpi, eds. 2002. *Participatory Governance: Political and Societal Implications*. Opladen, Germany: Leske and Budrich.

Haas, P. M. 1992. "Epistemic Communities and International Policy Coordination." *International Organization* 46 (1): 1–35. http://dx.doi.org/10.1017/S0020818300001442.

Habermas, J. 1981. *The Theory of Communicative Action*. Boston: Beacon Press.

Hagedoorn, J. 1996. "Innovation and Entrepreneurship: Schumpeter Revisited." *Industrial and Corporate Change* 5 (3): 883–96. http://dx.doi.org/10.1093/icc/5.3.883.

Hajer, M. 2009. *Authoritative Governance: Policy Making in the Age of Mediatization*. Oxford: Oxford University Press. http://dx.doi.org/10.1093/acprof:oso/9780199281671.001.0001.

Hajer, M., and W. Versteeg. 2005. "Performing Governance through Networks." *European Political Studies* 4 (3): 340–47. http://dx.doi.org/10.1057/palgrave.eps.2210034.

Hajer, M., and H. Wagenaar, eds. 2003. *Deliberative Policy Analysis: Understanding in the Network Society*. Cambridge: Cambridge University Press. http://dx.doi.org/10.1017/CBO9780511490934.

Hale, K. 2011. *How Networks Matters: Networks and Public Policy Innovation*. Washington DC: Georgetown University Press.

Hall, P. 1993. "Policy Paradigms, Social Learning and the State: The Case of Economic Policymaking in Britain." *Comparative Politics* 25 (3): 275–96. http://dx.doi.org/10.2307/422246.

Halvorsen, T., J. Hauknes, I. Miles, and R. Røste. 2005. "On the Differences between Public and Private Sector Innovation." PUBLIN Report no. D9. Oslo: NIFU STEP.

Hargadon, A., and B. Bechky. 2006. "When Collections of Creatives Become Creative Collectives: A Field Study of Problem Solving at Work." *Organization Science* 17 (4): 484–500. http://dx.doi.org/10.1287/orsc.1060.0200.

Hartley, J. 2005. "Innovation in Governance and Public Service: Past and Present." *Public Money & Management* 25 (1): 27–34.

———. 2006. *Innovation and Its Contribution to Improvement*. London: Department for Communities and Local Government.

———. 2008. "Does Innovation Lead to Improvement in Public Services? Lessons from the Beacon Scheme in the United Kingdom." In *Innovations in Government: Research, Recognition, and Replication*, edited by S. Borins, 159–87. Washington DC: Brookings Institution Press.

Hartley, J., and J. Benington. 2006. "Copy and Paste, or Graft and Transplant? Knowledge Sharing through Inter-Organizational Networks." *Public Money & Management* 26 (2): 101–8. http://dx.doi.org/10.1111/j.1467-9302.2006.00508.x.

Hartley, J., and J. Downe. 2007. "The Shining Lights? Public Service Awards as an Approach to Service Improvement." *Public Administration* 85 (2): 329–53. http://dx.doi.org/10.1111/j.1467-9299.2007.00652.x.

Hartley, J., and L. Rashman. 2014. "Population-Level Learning and Innovation." Paper presented at the International Research Society on Public Management, Ottawa, April.

Hartley, J., E. Sørensen, and J. Torfing. 2013. "Collaborative Innovation: A Viable Alternative to Market Competition and Organizational Entrepreneurship." *Public Administration Review* 73 (6): 821–30. http://dx.doi.org/10.1111/puar.12136.

Hartman, L. 2011. *Konkurrensens konsekvenser*. Stockholm: SNS Förlag.

Healey, P. 1992. "Planning through Debate: The Communicative Turn in Planning Theory." *Town Planning Review* 63 (2): 143–62. http://dx.doi.org/10.3828/tpr.63.2.422x602303814821.

———. 1997. *Collaborative Planning*. Basingstoke UK: Macmillan. http://dx.doi.org/10.1007/978-1-349-25538-2.

———. 2007. *Urban Complexity and Spatial Strategies: Towards a Relational Planning for Our Time*. London: Routledge.

Heclo, H. 1978. "Issue Networks and the Executive Establishment." In *The New American Political System*, edited by A. King, 87–124. Washington DC: American Enterprise Institute.

Heffen, O. V., W. J. M. Kickert, and J. A. Thomassen, eds. 2000. *Governance in Modern Society: Effects, Change and Formation of Government Institutions*. Dordrecht, the Netherlands: Kluwer Academic Publishers. http://dx.doi.org/10.1007/978-94-015-9486-8.

Heifetz, R. A., M. Linsky, and A. Grashow. 2009. *The Practice of Adaptive Leadership: Tools and Tactics for Changing Your Organization and the World*. Cambridge MA: Harvard Business Press.

Heinrich, C. L., L. E. Lynn, and H. B. Milward. 2010. "A State of Agents? Sharpening the Debate and Evidence over the Extent and Impact of the Transformation of Governance." *Journal of Public Administration: Research and Theory* 20 (suppl. 1): 3–19. http://dx.doi.org/10.1093/jopart/mup032.

Hertting, N. 2007. "Mechanisms of Governance Network Formation: A Contextual Rational Choice Perspective." In *Theories of Democratic Network Governance*, edited by E. Sørensen and J. Torfing, 43–60. Basingstoke UK: Palgrave Macmillan.

Hippel, E. V. 1986. "Lead Users: A Source of Novel Product Concepts." *Journal of Management Science* 32 (7): 791–805. http://dx.doi.org/10.1287/mnsc.32.7.791.

———. 1988. *The Sources of Innovation*. Oxford: Oxford University Press.

———. 2005. *Democratizing Innovation*. Cambridge MA: MIT Press.

Hippel, E. V., and G. N. Krogh. 2003. "Open Source Software and the 'Private-Collective' Innovation Model: Issues for Organization Science." *Organization Science* 14 (2): 209–23. http://dx.doi.org/10.1287/orsc.14.2.209.14992.

Hjern, B., and D. O. Porter. 1981. "Implementation Structures: A New Unit of Administrative Analysis." *Organization Studies* 2 (3): 211–27. http://dx.doi.org/10.1177/017084068100200301.

Hood, C. 1986. *The Tools of Government*. Chatham UK: Chatham House.

———. 1991. "A Public Administration for All Seasons?" *Public Administration* 69 (1): 3–19. http://dx.doi.org/10.1111/j.1467-9299.1991.tb00779.x.

Hood, C., and R. Dixon. 2015. *A Government That Worked Better and Cost Less? Evaluating Three Decades of Reform and Change in UK Central Government*. Oxford: Oxford University Press.

Howarth, D., and J. Glynos. 2007. *Logics of Critical Explanation in Social and Political Theory*. London: Routledge.

Howe, J. 2006. "Crowdsourcing: A Definition." *Crowdsourcing: Why the Power of the Crowd Is Driving the Future of Business*. June 2. http://crowdsourcing.typepad.com/cs/2006/06/crowdsourcing_a.html.

Hull, C. J., and B. Hjern. 1987. *Helping Small Firms Grow: An Implementation Approach*. London: Croom Helm.

Ibbotson, P. 2008. *The Illusion of Leadership: Directing Creativity in Business and the Arts*. Basingstoke UK: Palgrave Macmillan. http://dx.doi.org/10.1057/9780230202009.

IMF (International Monetary Fund). 1997. *Good Governance: The IMF's Role*. Washington DC: IMF.

Innes, J. E. 1995. "Planning Theory's Emerging Paradigm: Communicative Action and Interactive Practice." *Journal of Planning Education and Research* 14 (3): 183–89. http://dx.doi.org/10.1177/0739456X9501400307.

Jacobs, W. B., L. Cohen, L. Kostakidis-Lianos, and S. Rundell. 2009. "Proposed Roadmap for Overcoming Legal and Financial Obstacles to Carbon Capture and Sequestration." Discussion Paper 2009-04. Cambridge MA: Belfer Center for Science and International Affairs.

Jacobsen, C. B., J. Hvidtved, and L. B. Andersen. 2014. "Command and Motivation: How the Perception of External Interventions Relates to Intrinsic Motivation and Public Service Motivation." *Public Administration* 92 (4): 790–806. http://dx.doi.org/10.1111/padm.12024.

Jacobsen, D. I., and J. Thorsvik. 2008. *Hvordan organisationer fungerer: Indføring i organisation og ledelse*. Copenhagen: Hans Reitzels Forlag.

Jakobsen, M. L. F. 2013. "Bureaukrati: Ven eller fjende af (offentlig sektor) innovation?" *Politica* 45 (3): 250–66.

Jehn, K. A., G. B. Northcraft, and M. Neale. 1999. "Why Differences Make a Difference: A Field Study of Diversity, Conflict, and Performance in Work Groups." *Administrative Science Quarterly* 44 (4): 741–63. http://dx.doi.org/10.2307/2667054.

Jessop, B. 2002. *The Future of the Capitalist State*. Cambridge UK: Polity Press.

———. 2004. "Multi-level Governance and Multi-level Metagovernance." In *Multi-level Governance*, edited by I. Bache and M. Flinders, 49–74. Oxford: Oxford University Press. http://dx.doi.org/10.1093/0199259259.003.0004.

Jessop, B., K. Nielsen, and O. K. Pedersen, eds. 1991. *Markets, Politics and the Negotiated Economy: Scandinavian and Post-Socialist Perspectives*. Cracow: Cracow Academy of Economics.

Jones, C., W. S. Hesterly, and S. P. Borgatti. 1997. "A General Theory of Network Governance: Exchange Conditions and Social Mechanisms." *Academy of Management Review* 22 (4): 911–45.

Jæger, B. 2011. "Teorier om teknologisk innovation: Veje til samarbejdsdrevet innovation." In *Samarbejdsdrevet innovation i den offentlige sektor*, edited by E. Sørensen and J. Torfing, 85–100. Copenhagen: DJØF Publishers.

Kattel, R., A. Cepilovs, W. Drechsler, T. Kalvet, V. Lember, and P. Tõnurist. 2014. "Can We Measure Public Sector Innovation? A Literature Review." Learning from Innovation in Public Sector Environments (LIPSE) Working Paper series, no. 2. Rotterdam: University of Rotterdam.

Katz, D., and D. R. Kahn. 1978. *The Social Psychology of Organizations*. New York: Wiley.

Kaufman, J. L., and H. M. Jacobs. 1996. "A Public Planning Perspective on Strategic Planning." In *Readings in Planning Theory*, edited by S. Campbell and S. S. Fainstein, 323–43. Oxford: Blackwell.

Keast, R., K. Brown, and M. Mandell. 2007. "Getting the Right Mix: Unpacking Integration, Meanings and Strategies." *International Public Management Journal* 10 (1): 9–33. http://dx.doi.org/10.1080/10967490601185716.

Kelman, S. 2005. *Unleashing Change: A Study of Organizational Renewal in Government.* Washington DC: Brookings Institution Press.

Kenis, P., and V. Schneider. 1991. "Policy Networks and Policy Analysis: Scrutinizing a New Analytical Toolbox." In *Policy Networks: Empirical Evidence and Theoretical Considerations*, edited by B. Marin and R. Mayntz, 25–59. Frankfurt-am-Main: Campus Verlag.

Kensing, F. 2003. *Methods and Practices in Participatory Design.* Copenhagen: ITU Press.

Kersbergen, K. V., and F. V. Waarden. 2004. "'Governance' as a Bridge between Disciplines: Cross-disciplinary Inspiration regarding Shifts in Governance and Problems of Governability, Accountability and Legitimacy." *European Journal of Political Research* 43 (2): 143–71. http://dx.doi.org/10.1111/j.1475-6765.2004.00149.x.

Kesting, P., and J. P. Ulhøi. 2010. "Employee-Driven Innovation: Extending the License to Foster Innovation." *Management Decision* 48 (1): 65–84. http://dx.doi.org/10.1108/00251741011014463.

Kettl, D. F. 2002. *The Transformation of Governance: Globalization, Devolution, and the Role of Government.* Baltimore: Johns Hopkins University Press.

Kickert, W. J. M., E.-H. Klijn, and J. F. M. Koppenjan, eds. 1997. *Managing Complex Networks.* London: Sage.

Kim, L. 1998. "Crisis Construction and Organizational Learning: Capability Building in Catching-up at Hyundai Motor." *Organization Science* 9 (4): 506–21. http://dx.doi.org/10.1287/orsc.9.4.506.

Kingdon, J. W. 1984. *Agendas, Alternatives, and Public Policies.* Boston: Little, Brown.

Klausen, K. K., and K. Ståhlberg, eds. 1998. *New Public Management i Norden.* Odense: Odense University Press.

Klein, K. J., and A. P. Knight. 2005. "Innovation Implementation: Overcoming the Challenge." *Current Directions in Psychological Science* 14 (5): 243–46. http://dx.doi.org/10.1111/j.0963-7214.2005.00373.x.

Klein, K. J., and J. S. Sorra. 1996. "The Challenge of Innovation Implementation." *Academy of Management Review* 21 (4): 1055–80.

Klijn, E.-H., and J. Edelenbos. 2007. "Metagovernance as Network Management." In *Theories of Democratic Network Governance*, edited by E. Sørensen and J. Torfing, 199–214. Basingstoke UK: Palgrave Macmillan.

Klijn, E. H., and J. F. M. Koppenjan. 2000. "Public Management and Policy Networks: Foundations of a Network Approach to Governance." *Public Management* 2 (2): 135–58. http://dx.doi.org/10.1080/146166700411201.

Klijn, E.-H., and C. Skelcher. 2007. "Democracy and Governance Networks: Compatible or Not?" *Public Administration* 85 (3): 587–608. http://dx.doi.org/10.1111/j.1467-9299.2007.00662.x.

Knoepfel, P., and I. Kissling-Näf. 1998. "Social Learning in Policy Networks." *Policy and Politics* 26 (3): 343–67. http://dx.doi.org/10.1332/030557398782213638.

Koch, P., and J. Hauknes. 2005. *On Innovation in the Public Sector*. PUBLIN Report no. D20. Oslo: NIFU STEP.

Koliba, C., J. W. Meek, and A. Zia. 2011. *Governance Networks in Public Administration and Public Policy*. Boca Ranto FL: CRC Press.

Kooiman, J., ed. 1993. *Modern Governance: New Government-Society Interactions*. London: Sage.

———. 2003. *Governing as Governance*. London: Sage.

Koppenjan, J. F. M. 2012. *The New Public Governance in Public Service Delivery*. The Hague: Eleven International Publishing.

Koppenjan, J., and E.-H. Klijn. 2004. *Managing Uncertainties in Networks*. London: Routledge.

Kraemer, K. L., and J. L. Perry. 1979. "The Federal Push to Bring Computer Applications to Local Governments." *Public Administration Review* 39 (3): 260–70. http://dx.doi.org/10.2307/975951.

———. 1980. "Chief Executive Support and Innovation Adoption." *Administration & Society* 12 (2): 158–77. http://dx.doi.org/10.1177/009539978001200203.

———. 1989. "Innovation and Computing in the Public Sector: A Review of Research." *Knowledge in Society* 2 (1): 72–87. http://dx.doi.org/10.1007/BF02737076.

Laclau, E. 1990. *New Reflections on the Revolution of Our Time*. London: Verso.

Laclau, E., and C. Mouffe. 1985. *Hegemony and Socialist Strategy*. London: Verso.

Lake, D. A., and W. H. Wong. 2009. "The Politics of Networks: Interest, Power and Human Rights Norms." In *Networked Politics: Agency, Power and Governance*, edited by M. Kahler, 127–50. Ithaca NY: Cornell University Press.

Langton, H., M. Barnes, S. Haslehurst, J. Rimmer, and P. Turton. 2003. "Collaboration, User Involvement and Education: A Systematic Review of the Literature and Report of an Educational Initiative." *European Journal of Oncology Nursing* 7 (4): 242–52. http://dx.doi.org/10.1016/S1462-3889(03)00033-4.

Latour, B. 1987. *Science in Action: How to Follow Scientists and Engineers through Society?* Cambridge MA: Harvard University Press.

Lave, J., and E. Wenger. 1991. *Situated Learning: Legitimate Peripheral Participation*. Cambridge: Cambridge University Press. http://dx.doi.org/10.1017/CBO9780511815355.

Le Grand, J. 2003. *Motivation, Agency, and Public Policy: Of Knights and Knaves, Pawns and Queens*. Oxford: Oxford University Press. http://dx.doi.org/10.1093/0199266999.001.0001.

Le Grand, J., and W. Bartlett, eds. 1993. *Quasi-Markets and Social Policy*. Basingstoke UK: Macmillan. http://dx.doi.org/10.1007/978-1-349-22873-7.

Lees-Marshment, J. 2015. *The Ministry of Public Input: Integrating Citizen Views into Public Leadership*. Basingstoke UK: Palgrave Macmillan.

Lesser, E., and K. Everest. 2001. "Using Communities of Practice to Manage Intellectual Capital." *Ivey Business Journal*, March/April, 37–41.

Levin, M., and B. Sanger. 1994. *Making Government Work: How Entrepreneurial Executives Turn Bright Ideas into Real Results*. San Francisco: Jossey-Bass.

Lin, N. 2001. *Social Capital: A Theory of Social Structure and Action*. Cambridge: Cambridge University Press. http://dx.doi.org/10.1017/CBO9780511815447.

Lindblom, C. E. 1959. "The Science of 'Muddling Through.'" *Public Management Review* 19 (2): 79–88.

———. 1979. "Still Muddling, Not yet Through." *Public Administration Review* 39 (6): 517–26.

Lipsky, M. 1980. *Street-Level Bureaucracy: Dilemmas of the Individual in Public Services*. New York: Russell Sage Foundation.

Lubienski, C. 2009. "Do Quasi-markets Foster Innovation in Education? A Comparative Perspective." Organization for Economic Cooperation and Development (OECD) Education Working Papers no. 25. Paris: OECD Publishing.

Lubienski, C., and M. Linick. 2011. "Quasi-markets and Innovation in Education." *Die Deutsche Schule* 103 (2): 139–57.

Luhman, N. 1995. *Social Systems*. Stanford CA: Stanford University Press.

Lukes, S. 1974. *Power: A Radical View*. Basingstoke UK: Macmillan. http://dx.doi.org/10.1007/978-1-349-02248-9.

———. 2005. *Power: A Radical View*. Basingstoke UK: Palgrave Macmillan.

Lund, B., and J. B. Jensen. 2011. "Læringsteori: Hvordan skabes kreative samarbejdsprocesser?" In *Samarbejdsdrevet innovation i den offentlige sektor*, edited by E. Sørensen and J. Torfing, 157–76. Copenhagen: DJØF Publishers.

Lundvall, B.-Å. 1985. *Product Innovation and User-producer Interaction*. Aalborg: Aalborg University Press.

———., ed. 1992. *National Systems of Innovation: Towards a Theory of Innovation and Interactive Learning*. London: Pinter Publishers.

———. 2011. "Økonomisk innovationsteori: Fra iværksættere til innovationssystemer." In *Samarbejdsdrevet innovation i den offentlige sektor*, edited by E. Sørensen and J. Torfing. Copenhagen: DJØF Publishers.

Lundvall, B.-Å., and S. Borras. 2004. "Science, Technology, and Innovation Policy." In *The Oxford Handbook of Innovation*, edited by J. Fagerberg, D. C. Mowery, and R. R. Nelson, 599–631. Oxford: Oxford University Press.

Lynn, L. E. 2008. "What Is a Neo-Weberian State? Reflections on a Concept and Its Implications." *NISPAcee Journal of Public Administration and Policy* 1 (2): 31–54.

Lyotard, F. 1984. *The Postmodern Condition*. Manchester: Manchester University Press.

Lægreid, P., P. G. Roness, and K. Verhoest. 2011. "Explaining the Innovative Culture and Activities of State Agencies." *Organization Studies* 32 (10): 1321–47. http://dx.doi.org/10.1177/0170840611416744.

Lødemel, I., and H. Trickey, eds. 2001. *An Offer You Can't Refuse: Workfare in International Perspective*. Bristol: Policy Press. http://dx.doi.org/10.1332/policypress/9781861341952.001.0001.

Mackintosh, M. 1997. "Economic Culture and Quasi-markets in Local Government: The Case of Contracting for Social Care." *Local Government Studies* 23 (2): 80–102. http://dx.doi.org/10.1080/03003939708433866.

Mahoney, J., and K. Thelen, eds. 2009. *Explaining Institutional Change: Ambiguity, Agency, and Power*. Cambridge: Cambridge University Press. http://dx.doi.org/10.1017/CBO9780511806414.

Malerba, F. 2004. “How and Why Innovation Differ across Sectors.” In *The Oxford Handbook of Innovation*, edited by J. Fagerberg, D. C. Mowery, and R. R. Nelson, 380–406. Oxford: Oxford University Press.

March, J. G. 1991. “Exploration and Exploitation in Organizational Learning.” *Organization Science* 2 (1): 71–87. http://dx.doi.org/10.1287/orsc.2.1.71.

March, J. G., and J. P. Olsen. 1989. *Rediscovering Institutions*. New York: Free Press.

———. 1995. *Democratic Governance*. New York: Free Press.

Marcussen, M., and J. Torfing, eds. 2007. *Democratic Network Governance in Europe*. Basingstoke UK: Palgrave Macmillan.

Marin, B., and R. Mayntz, eds. 1991. *Policy Networks: Empirical Evidence and Theoretical Considerations*. Frankfurt-am-Main: Campus Verlag.

Marsh, D., ed. 1998. *Comparing Policy Networks*. Buckingham: Open University Press.

Marsh, D., and R. A. W. Rhodes, eds. 1992. *Policy Networks in British Government*. Oxford: Oxford University Press. http://dx.doi.org/10.1093/acprof:oso/9780198278528.001.0001.

Mayntz, R. 1993a. “Modernization and the Logic of Interorganizational Networks.” In *Societal Change between Markets and Organization*, edited by J. Child, M. Crozier, and R. Mayntz, 3–16. Aldershot UK: Avebury. http://dx.doi.org/10.1007/BF02692798.

———. 1993b. “Governing Failure and the Problem of Governability: Some Comments on a Theoretical Paradigm.” In *Modern Governance: New Government-Society Interactions*, edited J. Kooiman, 9–20. London: Sage.

Mazmanian, D. A., and P. A. Sabatier. 1981. *Effective Policy Implementation*. Lexington MA: Lexington Books.

———. 1983. *Implementation and Public Policy*. Dallas: Scott, Foresman.

Mazzucato, M. 2013. *The Entrepreneurial State: Debunking Public vs. Private Sector Myths*. London: Anthem Press.

McKeown, M. 2008. *The Truth about Innovation*. London: Prentice Hall.

Meadows, D. H. 2008. *Thinking in Systems: A Primer*. Edited by Diana Wright. White River Junction VT: Chelsea Green Publishing.

Meier, K. J., and L. J. O'Toole. 2001. “Managerial Strategies and Behavior in Networks.” *Journal of Public Administration: Research and Theory* 11 (3): 271–94. http://dx.doi.org/10.1093/oxfordjournals.jpart.a003503.

———. 2003. “Public Management and Educational Performance: The Impact of Managerial Networking.” *Public Administration Review* 63 (6): 68975–9985. http://dx.doi.org/10.1111/1540-6210.00332.

Metze, T. 2010. *Innovation Ltd*. Delft, the Netherlands: Eburon Academic Publishers.

Meuleman, L. 2008. *Public Management and the Metagovernance of Hierarchies, Networks and Markets*. The Hague: Physica-Verlag.

Meyers, P. W., K. Sivakumar, and C. Nakata. 1999. “Implementation of Industrial Process Innovations: Factors, Effects, and Marketing Implications.” *Journal of Product Innovation Management* 16 (3): 295–311. http://onlinelibrary.wiley.com/doi/10.1111/1540-5885.1630295/abstract.

Mezirow, J., ed. 2000. *Learning as Transformation: Critical Perspectives on a Theory in Progress*. San Francisco: Jossey-Bass.

Michlewski, K. 2008. "Uncovering Design Attitude: Inside the Culture of Designers." *Organization Studies* 29 (3): 373–92. http://dx.doi.org/10.1177/0170840607088019.

Miller, G. J. 2005. "The Political Evolution of Principal-Agent Models." *Annual Review of Political Science* 8 (1): 203–25. http://dx.doi.org/10.1146/annurev.polisci.8.082103.104840.

Milward, H. B., and K. G. Provan. 2000. "Governing the Hollow State." *Journal of Public Administration: Research and Theory* 10 (2): 359–80. http://dx.doi.org/10.1093/oxfordjournals.jpart.a024273.

———. 2006. *A Manager's Guide to Choosing and Using Collaborative Networks*. Washington DC: IBM Endowment for the Business of Government.

Mintrom, M., and S. Vergari. 1998. "Policy Networks and Innovation Diffusion." *Journal of Politics* 60 (1): 126–48. http://dx.doi.org/10.2307/2648004.

Mintzberg, H. 1983. *The Nature of Managerial Work*. Upper Saddle River NJ: Prentice Hall.

Mitchell, R., V. Parker, M. Giles, and N. White. 2010. "Review: Toward Realizing the Potential of Diversity in Composition of Interprofessional Health Care Teams." *Medical Care Research and Review* 67 (1): 3–26. http://dx.doi.org/10.1177/1077558709338478.

Moore, M. H. 1995. *Creating Public Value: Strategic Management in Government*. Cambridge MA: Harvard University Press.

Morçöl, G., and A. Wachhaus. 2009. "Network and Complexity Theory: A Comparison and Prospects for a Synthesis." *Administrative Theory and Praxis* 31 (1): 44–58. http://dx.doi.org/10.2753/ATP1084-1806310103.

Morgan, D. F., and B. J. Cook, eds. 2014. *New Public Governance: A Regime-Centered Perspective*. New York: Routledge.

Morse, R. S. 2010. "Integrative Public Leadership: Catalyzing Collaboration to Create Public Value." *Leadership Quarterly* 21 (2): 231–45. http://dx.doi.org/10.1016/j.leaqua.2010.01.004.

Mosley, P., J. Harrigan, and J. Toye. 1995. *Aid and Power: The World Bank and Policy-Based Lending*. New York: Routledge.

Mouffe, C., ed. 1992. *Dimensions of Radical Democracy*. London: Verso.

———. 1993. *The Return of the Political*. London: Verso.

Moynihan, D. P. 2013. "Advancing the Empirical Study of Performance Management: What We Learned from the Program Assessment Rating Tool." *American Review of Public Administration* 43 (5): 499–517. http://dx.doi.org/10.1177/0275074013487023.

Mulgan, G. 2007. *Ready or Not? Taking Innovation in the Public Sector Seriously*. London: NESTA.

Mulgan, G., and D. Albury. 2003. "Innovation in the Public Sector." Working Paper, Version 1.9. London: Strategy Unit, UK Cabinet Office, October.

Nabatchi, T., and M. Leighninger. 2015. *Public Participation for 21st Century Democracy*. San Francisco: Jossey-Bass.

National Centre for Public Sector Innovation. 2015. "Innovationsbarometer." http://innovationsbarometer.coi.dk/main-results-in-english/.

Nelson, R. R., and S. G. Winter. 1982. *An Evolutionary Theory of Economic Change*. Cambridge MA: Harvard University Press.

Newman, J., J. Raine, and C. Skelcher. 2001. "Transforming Local Government: Innovation and Modernization." *Public Money & Management* 21 (2): 61–68. http://dx.doi.org/10.1111/1467-9302.00262.

Nonaka, I., and H. Takeuchi. 1995. *The Knowledge Creating Company*. Oxford: Oxford University Press.

Nooteboom, B. 2002. *Trust: Forms, Foundations, Functions, Failures and Figures*. Cheltenham UK: Edward Elgar.

Nyhan, R. C. 2000. "Changing the Paradigm: Trust and Its Role in Public Sector Organizations." *American Review of Public Administration* 30 (1): 87–109. http://dx.doi.org/10.1177/02750740022064560.

OECD (Organization for Economic Cooperation and Development). 2010. *The OECD Innovation Strategy: Getting a Head Start on Tomorrow*. Paris: OECD Publishing.

Olsen, J. P. 2009. "EU Governance: Where Do We Go from Here?" In *European Multilevel Governance*, edited by B. Kohler-Koch and F. Larat, 191–209. Cheltenham UK: Edward Elgar.

———. 2010. *Governing through Institution Building: Institutional Theory and Recent European Experiments in Democratic Organization*. Oxford: Oxford University Press. http://dx.doi.org/10.1093/acprof:oso/9780199593934.001.0001.

Olson, M. 1971. *The Logic of Collective Action: Public Goods and the Theory of Groups*. Cambridge MA: Harvard University Press.

Osborne, D., and T. Gaebler. 1992. *Reinventing Government: How the Entrepreneurial Spirit Is Transforming the Public Sector*. Reading MA: Addison-Wesley.

Osborne, S. 2006. "The New Public Governance?" *Public Management Review* 8 (3): 377–87. http://dx.doi.org/10.1080/14719030600853022.

———, ed. 2009. The *New Public Governance: Emerging Perspectives on the Theory and Practice of Public Governance*. London: Routledge.

———. 2010. *The New Public Governance? Emerging Perspectives on the Theory and Practice of Public Governance*. New York: Routledge.

Osborne, S. P., and L. Brown. 2011. "Innovation in Public Services: Engaging with Risk." *Public Money & Management* 31 (1): 4–6. http://dx.doi.org/10.1080/09540962.2011.545532.

Osborne, S. P., Z. Radnor, and G. Nasi. 2013. "A New Theory for Public Service Management? Toward a (Public) Service-Dominant Approach." *American Review of Public Administration* 43 (2): 135–58. http://dx.doi.org/10.1177/0275074012466935.

Ostrom, E. 1990. *Governing the Commons: The Evolution of Institutions for Collective Action*. Cambridge: Cambridge University Press. http://dx.doi.org/10.1017/CBO9780511807763.

Ostrom, E., R. Gardner, and J. Walker. 1994. *Rules, Games, and Common Pool Resources*. Ann Arbor MI: University of Michigan Press.

O'Toole, L .J. 1997. "Implementing Public Innovations in Network Settings." *Administration & Society* 29 (2): 115–38. http://dx.doi.org/10.1177/009539979702900201.

O'Toole, L. J., and K. J. Meier. 2011. *Public Management: Organizations, Governance, and Performance*. New York: Cambridge University Press. http://dx.doi.org/10.1017/CBO9780511784040.

Owen, J. M., IV. 2002. "The Foreign Imposition of Domestic Institutions." *International Organization* 56 (2): 375–409. http://dx.doi.org/10.1162/002081802320005513.

Page, S. 2010. "Integrative Leadership for Collaborative Governance: Civic Engagement in Seattle." *Leadership Quarterly* 21 (2): 246–63. http://dx.doi.org/10.1016/j.leaqua.2010.01.005.

Parjanen, S., V. Harmaakorpi, and T. Frantsi. 2010. "Collective Creativity and Brokerage Functions in Heavily Cross-disciplined Innovation Processes." *Interdisciplinary Journal of Information, Knowledge, and Management* 5:1–21.

Park, S., and F. Berry. 2014. "Successful Diffusion of a Failed Policy: The Case of Pay-for-Performance in the US Federal Government." *Public Management Review* 16 (6): 763–81. http://dx.doi.org/10.1080/14719037.2012.750835.

Parry, K. W., and A. Bryman. 2006. "Leadership in Organizations." In *The Sage Handbook of Organization Studies*, edited by S. Clegg, C. Hardy, T. Lawrence, and W. Nord, 446–68. London: Sage Publications. http://dx.doi.org/10.4135/9781848608030.n15.

Pattberg, P. 2010. "Public-Private Partnerships in Global Climate Governance." *Climatic Change* 1 (2): 279–87.

Paulsen, N. 2006. "New Public Management, Innovation, and the Non-profit Domain: New Forms of Organizing and Professional Identity." In *Organizing Innovation: New Approaches to Cultural Change and Intervention in Public Sector Organizations*, edited by M. Veenswijk, 15–28. Amsterdam: IOS Press.

Pearce, C. L., and J. A. Conger. 2003. *Shared Leadership: Reframing the Hows and Whys of Leadership*. London: Sage Publications.

Pedersen, A. R., K. Sehested, and E. Sørensen. 2011. "Emerging Theoretical Understandings of Pluricentric Coordination in Public Governance." *American Review of Public Administration* 41 (4): 375–94. http://dx.doi.org/10.1177/0275074010378159.

Perry, J. L. 1996. "Measuring Public Service Motivation: An Assessment of Construct Reliability and Validity." *Journal of Public Administration: Research and Theory* 6 (1): 5–22. http://dx.doi.org/10.1093/oxfordjournals.jpart.a024303.

Perry, J. L., and J. N. Danziger. 1980. "The Adoptability of Innovations: An Empirical Assessment of Computer Applications in Local Governments." *Administration & Society* 11 (4): 461–92. http://dx.doi.org/10.1177/009539978001100405.

Perry, J. L., and K. L. Kraemer. 1978. "Innovation Attributes, Policy Interventions, and the Diffusion of Computer Applications among Local Governments." *Policy Sciences* 9 (2): 179–205. http://dx.doi.org/10.1007/BF00143741.

Peters, B. G. 2012. *Institutional Theory in Political Science*. 3rd ed. New York: Continuum.

Petersen, O. H., U. Hjelmar, and K. Vrangbæk. 2015. "Is Contracting Out of Public Services Still the Great Panacea?" Working paper, ICPP Conference, Milan, July 1–4.

Petersen, O. H., K. Houlberg, and L. R. Christensen. 2015. "Contracting Out Local Services: A Tale of Technical and Social Services." *Public Administration Review* 75 (4): 560–70. http://dx.doi.org/10.1111/puar.12367.

Piaget, J. 1954. *The Construction of Reality in the Child*. New York: Basic Books. http://dx.doi.org/10.1037/11168-000.

Pierre, J., ed. 2000. *Debating Governance*. Oxford: Oxford University Press.

Pierson, P. 1994. *Dismantling the Welfare State? Reagan, Thatcher, and the Politics of Retrenchment*. New York: Cambridge University Press. http://dx.doi.org/10.1017/CBO9780511805288.

———. 1997. "Increasing Returns, Path-Dependency and the Study of Politics." Jean Monnet Chair Papers, 44. Florence: Robert Schuman Centre at the European University Institute.

Pinch, T. J., and W. E. Bijker. 1987. "The Social Construction of Facts and Artifacts." In *The Social Construction of Technological Systems: New Directions in the Sociology and History of Technology*, edited by W. E. Bijker, T. P. Hughes, and J. Pinch, 17–50. Cambridge MA: MIT Press.

Pløger, J. 2002. "Kommunikativ planlegging og demokrati—nye perspektiver i planforskningen." In *NIBR-report, 17*. Oslo: Norsk Institut for By- og Regionforskning.

Pollitt, C., and G. Bouckaert. 2004. *Public Management Reform: A Comparative Analysis*. Oxford: Oxford University Press.

Pollitt, C., and P. Hupe. 2011. "Talking about Government: The Role of Magic Concepts." *Public Management Review* 13 (5): 641–58. http://dx.doi.org/10.1080/14719037.2010.532963.

Polsby, N. W. 1984. *Political Innovation in America: The Politics of Policy Initiation*. New Haven CT: Yale University Press.

Porter, M. 1985. *Competitive Advantage: Creating and Sustaining Superior Performance*. New York: Free Press.

Potts, J. 2009. "The Innovation Deficit in Public Services: The Curious Problem of Too Much Efficiency and Not Enough Waste and Failure." *Innovation: Management, Policy & Practice* 11 (1): 34–43.

Poundstone, W. 1992. *Prisoner's Dilemma*. New York: Anchor Books.

Powell, W. W. 1991. "Neither Market nor Hierarchy: Network Forms of Organization." *Research in Organizational Behavior* 12:295–336.

Powell, W. W., and P. J. DiMaggio, eds. 1991. *The New Institutionalism in Organizational Analysis*. Chicago: University of Chicago Press.

Powell, W. W., and S. Grodal. 2004. "Networks of Innovators." In *The Oxford Handbook of Innovation*, edited by J. Fagerberg, D. C. Mowery, and R. R. Nelson, 56–58. Oxford: Oxford University Press.

Power, M. 1999. *The Audit Society: Rituals of Verification*. Oxford: Oxford University Press. http://dx.doi.org/10.1093/acprof:oso/9780198296034.001.0001.

Pressman, J. L., and A. Wildavsky. 1973. *Implementation: How Great Expectations in Washington Are Dashed in Oakland*. Berkeley: University of California Press Books.

Provan, K. G., and P. Kenis. 2005. "Modes of Network Governance and Implications for Network Management and Effectiveness." Paper presented at the Eighth Public Management Research Association Conference, University of Southern California–Los Angeles, September 29–October 1.

———. 2008. "Modes of Network Governance: Structure, Management, and Effectiveness." *Journal of Public Administration: Research and Theory* 18 (2): 229–52. http://dx.doi.org/10.1093/jopart/mum015.

Provan, K. G., and B. H. Milward. 1995. "A Preliminary Theory of Interorganizational Effectiveness: A Comparative Study of Four Community Mental Health Systems." *Administrative Science Quarterly* 40 (1): 1–33. http://dx.doi.org/10.2307/2393698.

———. 2001. "Do Networks Really Work? A Framework for Evaluating Public-Sector Organizational Networks." *Public Administration Review* 61 (4): 414–23. http://dx.doi.org/10.1111/0033-3352.00045.

Putnam, R. D. 2000. *Bowling Alone: The Collapse and Revival of American Community*. New York: Simon & Schuster. http://dx.doi.org/10.1145/358916.361990.

Putnam, R. D., L. Feldstein, and D. Cohen. 2003. *Better Together: Restoring the American Community*. New York: Simon & Schuster.

Ranerup, A. 1996. *Användarmedverkan med representanter*. Gothenburg, Sweden: Gothenburg University Press.

Rashman, L., J. Downe, and J. Hartley. 2005. "Knowledge Creation and Transfer in the Beacon Scheme: Improving Services through Sharing Good Practice." *Local Government Studies* 31 (5): 683–700. http://dx.doi.org/10.1080/03003930500293732.

Rashman, L., and J. Hartley. 2008. "Knowledge Transfer: Sharing Learning in Public Service Organizations." *RENEW Northwest Intelligence Report*, April. London: Warwick Business School. http://urbanpollinators.co.uk/wp-content/plugins/downloads-manager/upload/knowledge%20transfer.pdf.

Rashman, L., E. Withers, and J. Hartley. 2009. "Organizational Learning and Knowledge in Public Service Organizations: A Systematic Review of the Literature." *International Journal of Management Reviews* 11 (4): 463–94. http://dx.doi.org/10.1111/j.1468-2370.2009.00257.x.

Rawls, J. 1971. *A Theory of Justice*. Cambridge MA: Belknap Press of Harvard University Press.

Reagans, R., and B. McEvily. 2003. "Network Structure and Knowledge Transfer: The Effects of Cohesion and Range." *Administrative Science Quarterly* 48 (2): 240–67. http://dx.doi.org/10.2307/3556658.

Rees, R. 1985a. "The Theory of Principal and Agent, Part I." *Bulletin of Economic Research* 37 (1): 3–26. http://dx.doi.org/10.1111/j.1467-8586.1985.tb00179.x.

———. 1985b. "The Theory of Principal and Agent, Part II." *Bulletin of Economic Research* 37 (2): 75–97. http://dx.doi.org/10.1111/j.1467-8586.1985.tb00185.x.

Renn, O. 2008. *Risk Governance: Coping with Uncertainty in a Complex World*. London: Earthscan.

Rhodes, R. A. W. 1995. "The Institutionalist Approach." In *Theories and Methods in Political Science*, edited by D. Marsh and G. Stoker, 42–57. London: Macmillan. http://dx.doi.org/10.1007/978-1-349-24106-4_3.

———. 1997. *Understanding Governance: Policy Networks, Governance, Reflexivity and Accountability*. Buckingham UK: Open University Press.

Roberts, N. C. 2000. "Wicked Problems and Network Approaches to Resolution." *International Public Management Review* 1 (1): 1–19.

Roberts, N. C., and R. T. Bradley. 1991. "Stakeholder Collaboration and Innovation." *Journal of Applied Behavioral Science* 27 (2): 209–27. http://dx.doi.org/10.1177/0021886391272004.

Roberts, N. C., and P. J. King. 1996. *Transforming Public Policy: Dynamics of Policy Entrepreneurship and Innovation*. San Francisco: Jossey-Bass.

Roepstorff, L. 2001. *Læring og implementering* [Learning and implementation]. Phd diss., Research School of Life-long Education, Roskilde University.

Roessner, J. D. 1977. "Incentives to Innovate in Public and Private Organizations." *Administration & Society* 9 (3): 341–65. http://dx.doi.org/10.1177/009539977700900304.

Rogers, E. M. 1995. *Diffusion of Innovations*. 4th ed. New York: Free Press.

Rogers, E. M., U. E. Medina, M. A. Rivera, and C. J. Wiley. 2005. "Complex Adaptive Systems and the Diffusion of Innovations." *Innovation Journal* 10 (3): 579–84.

Rokkan, S. 1969. "Norway: Numerical Democracy and Corporate Pluralism." In *Political Oppositions in Western Democracies*, edited by R. A. Dahl, 70–115. New Haven CT: Yale University Press.

Rose, N. 1999. *Powers of Freedom: Reframing Political Thought*. Cambridge: Cambridge University Press. http://dx.doi.org/10.1017/CBO9780511488856.

Rosenberg, N. 1982. *Inside the Black Box: Technology and Economics*. Cambridge: Cambridge University Press.

Rutter, D., C. Manley, T. Weaver, M. Crawford, and N. Fulop. 2004. "Patients or Partners? Case Studies of User Involvement in the Planning and Delivery of Adult Mental Health Services in London." *Social Science & Medicine* 58 (10): 1973–84. http://dx.doi.org/10.1016/S0277-9536(03)00401-5.

Røste, R. 2005. "Studies of Innovation in the Public Sector: A Theoretical Framework." PUBLIN Report no. D16. Oslo: NIFU STEP.

Røtnes, R., and P. D. Staalesen. 2009. *New Methods in User-Driven Innovation in the Health Care Sector*. Oslo: Nordic Innovation Center.

Røvik, Kjell A. 1992. "Institutionaliserede standarder og multistandardorganisasjoner." *Statsvetenskapelig Tidsskrift* 8 (4): 261–84.

Sabatier, P. A., and H. C. Jenkins-Smith. 1993. *Policy Change and Learning: An Advocacy Coalition Approach*. Boulder CO: Westview Press.

Sager, T. 1999. "The Rationality Issue in Land-Use Planning." *Journal of Management History* 5 (2): 87–107. http://dx.doi.org/10.1108/13552529910249869.

Salamon, L. M., ed. 2002. *The Tools of Government: A Guide to the New Governance.* New York: Oxford University Press.

Saussure, F. 1981. *Course in General Linguistics.* Suffolk: Fontana.

Saward, M. 2000. *Democratic Innovation: Deliberation, Representation and Association.* London: Routledge. http://dx.doi.org/10.4324/9780203165485.

———. 2006. "The Representative Claim." *Contemporary Political Theory* 5 (3): 297–318. http://dx.doi.org/10.1057/palgrave.cpt.9300234.

Scharpf, F. W. 1988. "The Joint-Decision Trap: Lessons from German Federalism and European Integration." *Public Administration* 66 (3): 239–78. http://dx.doi.org/10.1111/j.1467-9299.1988.tb00694.x.

———. 1994. "Games Real Actors Could Play: Positive and Negative Coordination in Embedded Negotiations." *Journal of Theoretical Politics* 6 (1): 27–53. http://dx.doi.org/10.1177/0951692894006001002.

———. 1998. *Games Real Actors Play: Actor Centered Institutionalism in Policy Research.* Boulder CO: Westview Press.

———. 1999. *Governing in Europe: Effective and Democratic?* Oxford: Oxford University Press. http://dx.doi.org/10.1093/acprof:oso/9780198295457.001.0001.

———. 2001. "Notes toward a Theory of Multi-level Governing in Europe." *Scandinavian Political Studies* 24 (1): 1–26. http://dx.doi.org/10.1111/1467-9477.00044.

Schattschneider, E. E. 1960. *The Semi-sovereign People: A Realist's View of Democracy in America.* New York: Holt, Rinehart and Winston.

Scherer, A. G., and G. Palazzo. 2011. "The New Role of Business in a Globalized World: A Review of a New Perspective on CSR and Its Implications for the Firm, Governance and Democracy." *Journal of Management Studies* 48 (4): 899–931. http://dx.doi.org/10.1111/j.1467-6486.2010.00950.x.

Schillemans, T. 2013. "Moving beyond the Clash of Interests: On a Stewardship Theory and the Relationships between Central Government Departments and Public Agencies." *Public Management Review* 15 (4): 541–62. http://dx.doi.org/10.1080/14719037.2012.691008.

Schmitter, P. C., and G. Lehmbruch, eds. 1979. *Trends towards Corporatist Intermediation.* London: Sage.

Schön, D., and M. Rein. 1995. *Frame Reflection: Toward the Resolution of Intractable Policy Controversies.* New York: Basic Books.

Schumpeter, J. 1934. *The Theory of Economic Development.* Cambridge: Harvard University Press.

Scott, R.W. 1995. *Institutions and Organizations: Ideas and Interests.* London: Sage Publications.

Serrat, O. 2010. "Design Thinking." Knowledge Solutions. Manila: Asian Development Bank. http://www.adb.org/sites/default/files/publication/27579/design-thinking.pdf

Simon, H. 1957. *Models of Man.* New York: Wiley.

———. 1969. *The Sciences of the Artificial.* Cambridge MA: MIT Press.

———. 1991. "Bounded Rationality and Organizational Learning." *Organization Science* 2 (1): 125–34. http://dx.doi.org/10.1287/orsc.2.1.125.

Skelcher, C., and J. Torfing. 2010. "Improving Democratic Governance through Institutional Design: Civic Participation and Democratic Ownership in Europe." *Regulation & Governance* 4 (1): 71–91. http://dx.doi.org/10.1111/j.1748-5991.2010.01072.x.

Skilton, P. F., and K. Dooley. 2010. "The Effects of Repeat Collaboration on Creative Abrasion." *Academy of Management Review* 35 (1): 118–34. http://dx.doi.org/10.5465/AMR.2010.45577886.

Slappendel, C. 1996. "Perspectives on Innovation in Organizations." *Organization Studies* 17 (1): 107–29. http://dx.doi.org/10.1177/017084069601700105.

Smith, G. 2009. *Democratic Innovations: Designing Institutions for Citizen Participation*. Cambridge: Cambridge University Press. http://dx.doi.org/10.1017/CBO9780511609848.

Spinosa, C., F. Flores, and H. L. Dreyfus. 1997. *Disclosing New Worlds: Entrepreneurship, Democratic Action, and the Cultivation of Solidarity*. Cambridge MA: MIT Press.

Stacey, R. 2012. *Tools and Techniques of Leadership Management: Meeting the Challenge of Complexity*. New York: Routledge.

Star, S., and J. Griesemer. 1989. "Institutional Ecology, 'Translations' and Boundary Objects: Amateurs and Professionals in Berkeley's Museum of Vertebrate Zoology, 1907–39." *Social Studies of Science* 19 (3): 387–420. http://dx.doi.org/10.1177/030631289019003001.

Steelman, T. A. 2010. *Implementing Innovation*. Washington DC: Georgetown University Press.

Stickdorn, M., and J. Schneider, eds. 2011. *This Is Service Design Thinking*. New York: Wiley.

Stiglitz, J. E. 1987. "Principal and Agent." In *The New Palgrave: A Dictionary of Economics*, 3:966–71. Basingstoke UK: Palgrave Macmillan.

Stoker, G., and P. John. 2009. "Design Experiments: Engaging Policy Makers in the Search for Evidence about What Works." *Political Studies Association* 57 (2): 356–73. http://dx.doi.org/10.1111/j.1467-9248.2008.00756.x.

Stoltz, P. G. 1997. *Adversity Quotient: Turning Obstacles into Opportunities*. New York: John Wiley.

Straus, D. 2002. *How to Make Collaboration Work: Powerful Ways to Build Consensus, Solve Problems, and Make Decisions*. San Francisco: Berrett Koehler Publishers.

Suter, E., J. Arndt, N. Arthur, J. Parboosingh, E. Taylor, and S. Deutschlander. 2009. "Role Understanding and Effective Communication as Core Competencies for Collaborative Practice." *Journal of Interprofessional Care* 23 (1): 41–51. http://dx.doi.org/10.1080/13561820802338579.

Swan, J., H. Scarbrough, and M. Robertson. 2002. "The Construction of Communities of Practice in the Management of Innovations." *Management Learning* 33 (4): 477–96. http://dx.doi.org/10.1177/1350507602334005.

Sørensen, E., and J. Torfing, eds. 2007. *Theories of Democratic Network Governance*. Basingstoke UK: Palgrave Macmillan.

———. 2009. "Making Governance Networks Effective and Democratic through Metagovernance." *Public Administration* 87 (2): 234–58. http://dx.doi.org/10.1111/j.1467-9299.2009.01753.x.

———. 2011. "Enhancing Collaborative Innovation in the Public Sector." *Administration & Society* 43 (8): 842–68. http://dx.doi.org/10.1177/0095399711418768.

———. 2013. "Kommunalpolitikere som ledere af politikinnovation [Local politicians as leaders of policy innovation]." *Økonomi og Politik* 86 (4): 18–32.

———. 2016, forthcoming. "Political Leadership in the Age of Interactive Governance: Reflections on the Political Aspects of Metagovernance." In *Critical Reflections on Interactive Governance*, edited by J. Edelenbos and I. F. Meerkerk. Cheltenham: Edward Elgar.

Sørensen, E., and P. Triantafillou, eds. 2009. *The Politics of Self-governance*. London: Ashgate.

Tait, L., and H. Lester. 2005. "Encouraging User-Involvement in Mental Health Services." *Advances in Psychiatric Treatment* 11 (3): 168–75. http://dx.doi.org/10.1192/apt.11.3.168.

Teece, D. J. 1992. "Competition, Cooperation, and Innovation." *Journal of Economic Behavior & Organization* 18 (1): 1–25. http://dx.doi.org/10.1016/0167-2681(92)90050-L.

Thelen, K. 1999. "Historical Institutionalism in Comparative Politics." *Annual Review of Political Science* 2 (1): 369–404. http://dx.doi.org/10.1146/annurev.polisci.2.1.369.

———. 2003. "How Institutions Evolve: Insights from Comparative Historical Analysis." In *Comparative Historical Analysis in the Social Science*, edited by J. Mahoney and D. Rueschemeyer, 208–40. Cambridge: Cambridge University Press. http://dx.doi.org/10.1017/CBO9780511803963.007.

Thelen, K., and S. Steinmo. 1992. "Historical Institutionalism in Comparative Politics." In *Structuring Politics: Historical Institutionalism in Comparative Analysis*, edited by S. Steinmo, K. Thelen, and F. Longstreth, 1–32. New York: Cambridge University Press. http://dx.doi.org/10.1017/CBO9780511528125.002.

Thompson, V. A. 1965. "Bureaucracy and Innovation." *Administrative Science Quarterly* 10 (1): 1–20. http://dx.doi.org/10.2307/2391646.

Tierney, C., S. Cottle, and K. Jorgensen. 2012. *GovCloud: The Future of Government Work*. Westlake TX: Deloitte University Press. http://dupress.com/articles/the-future-of-the-federal-workforce/.

Torfing, J. 1999a. *New Theories of Discourse*. Oxford: Blackwell.

———. 1999b. "Workfare with Welfare: Recent Reforms of the Danish Welfare State." *Journal of European Social Policy* 9 (1): 5–28. http://dx.doi.org/10.1177/095892879900900101.

———. 2007. "Discursive Governance Networks in Danish Activation Policies." In *Democratic Network Governance in Europe*, edited by M. Marcussen and J. Torfing, 111–29. Basingstoke UK: Palgrave Macmillan.

———. 2009. "Rethinking Path-dependence in Public Policy Research." *Critical Policy Studies* 3 (1): 70–83. http://dx.doi.org/10.1080/19460170903158149.

Torfing, J., B. G. Peters, J. Pierre, and E. Sørensen. 2012. *Interactive Governance: Advancing the Paradigm*. Oxford: Oxford University Press. http://dx.doi.org/10.1093/acprof:oso/9780199596751.001.0001.

Torfing, J., and P. Triantafillou, eds. 2011. *Interactive Policy Making, Metagovernance and Democracy*. Colchester UK: ECPR Press.

———. 2013. "What's in a Name? Grasping New Public Governance as a Political-Administrative System." *International Review of Public Administration* 18 (2): 9–25. http://dx.doi.org/10.1080/12294659.2013.10805250.

Triantafillou, P. 2007. "Governing the Formation and Mobilization of Governance Networks." In *Theories of Democratic Network Governance*, edited by E. Sørensen and J. Torfing, 183–98. Basingstoke UK: Palgrave-Macmillan.

Trist, E. L. 1983. "Referent Organizations and the Development of Interorganizational Domains." *Human Relations* 36 (3): 269–84. http://dx.doi.org/10.1177/001872678303600304.

Tucker, R. C. 1995. *Politics as Leadership*. Columbia: University of Missouri.

United Nations. 2009. *Good Practices and Innovations in Public Governance*. New York: United Nations.

Valente, T. W. 1995. *Network Models of the Diffusion of Innovations*. Cresskill NJ: Hampton Press.

———. 1996. "Social Network Thresholds in the Diffusion of Innovations." *Social Networks* 18 (1): 69–89. http://dx.doi.org/10.1016/0378-8733(95)00256-1.

Valkama, P., S. J. Bailey, and A. V. Anttiroiko, eds. 2013. *Organizational Innovation in Public Services*. Basingstoke UK: Palgrave Macmillan. http://dx.doi.org/10.1057/9781137011848.

Van de Ven, A., D. Polley, R. Garud, and S. Venkataraman. 2008. *The Innovation Journey*. New York: Oxford University Press.

Verhoest, K., B. Verschuere, and G. Bouckaert. 2007. "Pressure, Legitimacy, and Innovative Behavior by Public Organizations." *Governance: An International Journal of Policy and Administration* 20 (3): 469–97. http://dx.doi.org/10.1111/j.1468-0491.2007.00367.x.

Vigoda-Gadot, E. 2002. "From Responsiveness to Collaboration: Governance, Citizens, and the Next Generation of Public Administration." *Public Administration Review* 62 (5): 527–40. http://dx.doi.org/10.1111/1540-6210.00235.

Vigoda-Gadot, E., A. Shoham, N. Schwabsky, and A. Ruvio. 2008. "Public Sector Innovation for Europe: A Multinational Eight-Country Exploration of Citizens' Perspectives." *Public Administration* 86 (2): 307–29. http://dx.doi.org/10.1111/j.1467-9299.2008.00731.x.

Voorberg, W. H., V. J. J. M. Bekkers, and L. G. Tummers 2013. *Co-creation and Co-production in Social Innovation: A Systematic Review*. Research Report from the LIPSE Project, Ramon Llull University.

Vrangbæk, K., O. H. Petersen, and U. Hjelmar. 2014. "Is Contracting Out Good or Bad for Employees? A Systematic Review of International Experience." *Review of Public Personnel Administration* 35 (1): 3–23. http://dx.doi.org/10.1177/0734371X13511087.

Wakefield, J. F. 2003. "The Development of Creative Thinking and Critical Reflection: Lessons from Everyday Problem Finding." In *Critical Creative Processes*, edited by M. Runco, 253–74. Cresskill NJ: Hampton Press.

Walker, J. L. 1969. "The Diffusion of Innovations among the American States." *American Political Science Review* 63 (3): 880–99. http://dx.doi.org/10.2307/1954434.

Walton, E. J. 2005. "'The Persistence of Bureaucracy: A Meta-analysis of Weber's Model of Bureaucratic Control." *Organization Studies* 26 (4): 569–600. http://dx.doi.org/10.1177/0170840605051481.

Wang, C. L., and P. K. Ahmed. 2004. "The Development and Validation of the Organizational Innovativeness Construct Using Confirmatory Factor Analysis." *European Journal of Innovation Management* 7 (4): 303–13. http://dx.doi.org/10.1108/14601060410565056.

Warren, M. E. 2009. "Governance-Driven Democratization." *Critical Policy Studies* 3 (1): 3–13. http://dx.doi.org/10.1080/19460170903158040.

Wart, M. V. 2013. "Lessons from Leadership Theory and Contemporary Challenges of Leaders." *Public Administration Review* 73 (4): 553–65. http://dx.doi.org/10.1111/puar.12069.

Weber, E. P., and A. M. Khademian. 2008. "Wicked Problems, Knowledge Challenges and Collaborative Capacity Builders in Network Settings." *Public Administration Review* 68 (2): 334–49. http://dx.doi.org/10.1111/j.1540-6210.2007.00866.x.

Weber, M. 1922. *Economy and Society*. New York: Simon & Schuster.

Weber, S. 2003. *The Success of Open Source*. Cambridge MA: Harvard University Press.

Weick, K. E., and K. H. Roberts. 1993. "Collective Mind in Organizations: Heedful Interrelating on Flight Decks." *Administrative Science Quarterly* 38 (3): 357–81. http://dx.doi.org/10.2307/2393372.

Weingast, B. R., and M. J. Moran. 1983. "Bureaucratic Discretion or Congressional Control? Regulatory Policymaking by the Federal Trade Commission." *Journal of Political Economy* 91 (5): 765–800. http://dx.doi.org/10.1086/261181.

Weisberg, R. W. 2006. *Creativity: Understanding Innovation in Problem Solving, Science, Invention, and the Arts*. Hoboken: John Wiley.

Wenger, E. 1998. *Communities of Practice: Learning, Meaning, and Identity*. Cambridge: Cambridge University Press. http://dx.doi.org/10.1017/CBO9780511803932.

West, E., D. N. Barron, J. Dowsett, and J. N. Newton. 1999. "Hierarchies and Cliques in the Social Networks of Health Care Professionals: Implications for the Design of Dissemination Strategies." *Social Science & Medicine* 48 (5): 633–46. http://dx.doi.org/10.1016/S0277-9536(98)00361-X.

White, G. 2010. *Diffusion of ICT in Education and the Role of Collaboration: A Study of EdNA*. PhD diss., Curtin University, Perth.

Whitford, A. B. 2002. "Decentralization and Political Control of the Bureaucracy." *Journal of Theoretical Politics* 14 (2): 167–93. http://dx.doi.org/10.1177/095169280201400202.

Williams, P. 2002. "The Competent Boundary Spanner." *Public Administration* 80 (1): 103–24. http://dx.doi.org/10.1111/1467-9299.00296.

Wilson, W. 1887. "The Study of Administration." *Political Science Quarterly* 2 (2): 197–222. http://dx.doi.org/10.2307/2139277.

Wittgenstein, L. 1958. *Philosophical Investigations*. Oxford: Basil Blackwell.

Woodman, R. W., J. E. Sawyer, and R. W. Griffin. 1993. "Toward a Theory of Organizational Creativity." *Academy of Management Review* 18 (2): 293–321.

Young, I. M. 2000. *Inclusion and Democracy*. Oxford: Oxford University Press.

Zaltman, G., R. Duncan, and J. Holbek. 1973. *Innovations and Organizations*. New York: Wiley.

Zoghi, C., R. D. Mohr, and P. B. Meyer. 2010. "Workplace Organization and Innovation." *Canadian Journal of Economics. Revue Canadienne d'Economique* 43 (2): 622–39. http://dx.doi.org/10.1111/j.1540-5982.2010.01586.x.

Zornoza, C. C., M. B. Navarro, and M. S. Ciprés. 2007. "A Meta-analysis of Organizational Innovation." In *Contemporary Corporate Strategy: Global Perspectives*, edited by J. Saee, 61–75. New York: Routledge.

INDEX

Figures and tables are denoted by the letters f and t following the page number.

Index

ABOUT THE AUTHOR

JACOB TORFING, who holds a PhD from the University of Essex as well as the prestigious Danish *doctor scientiarum administrationis* degree, is a professor at Roskilde University and director of the Roskilde School of Governance. He is also a professor in the Faculty of Social Sciences at Nord University and has been a visiting researcher in the Department of Political Science at the University of California, Berkeley. He is the author, coauthor, or editor of twenty-two previous books including *Politics, Regulation, and the Modern Welfare State*, the coauthored *Interactive Governance: Advancing the Paradigm*, and the coedited book *Enhancing Public Innovation by Transforming Public Governance.*

www.ingramcontent.com/pod-product-compliance
Lightning Source LLC
Chambersburg PA
CBHW021109270326
41929CB00009B/790

* 9 7 8 1 6 2 6 1 6 3 6 0 7 *